D1461191

THE MARLBOROUGHS

JOHN AND SARAH CHURCHILL

1650–1744

Christopher Hibbert

VIKING

VIKING

Published by the Penguin Group
Penguin Books Ltd, 80 Strand, London WC2 0RL, England
Penguin Putnam Inc., 375 Hudson Street, New York, New York 10014, USA
Penguin Books Australia Ltd, Ringwood, Victoria, Australia
Penguin Books Canada Ltd, 10 Alcorn Avenue, Toronto, Ontario, Canada M4V 3B2
Penguin Books India (P) Ltd, 11 Community Centre,
Panchsheel Park, New Delhi – 110 017, India
Penguin Books (NZ) Ltd, Cnr Rosedale and Airborne Roads,
Albany, Auckland, New Zealand
Penguin Books (South Africa) (Pty) Ltd, 5 Watkins Street,
Denver Ext 4, Johannesburg 2094, South Africa

Penguin Books Ltd, Registered Offices: 80 Strand, London WC2 0RL, England
www.penguin.com

First published 2001
1

Set in 11.75/14.25 pt Monotype Bembo
Typeset by Rowland Phototypesetting Ltd, Bury St Edmunds, Suffolk
Printed in Great Britain by Clays Ltd, St Ives plc

A CIP catalogue record for this book is available from the British Library

ISBN 0–670–88677–7

For Bob and Brenda
with love

CONTENTS

CONTENTS

ACKNOWLEDGEMENTS

I wish to thank Her Majesty the Queen for gracious permission to make use of material in the Royal Archives and to reproduce paintings in the Royal Collection. I am much indebted to Oliver Everett, Assistant Keeper of the Royal Archives and the Queen's Librarian at Windsor for his help and advice, to His Grace the Duke of Marlborough and to the Rt Hon the Earl Spencer.

For their assistance I am also grateful to Mrs Marion Harding of the Department of Archives, National Army Museum, Chelsea; Mrs Linda Shaw, Assistant Keeper of the Department of Manuscripts and Special Collections, Hallward Library, Nottingham University; Ms M. Simms, Archivist, Oxfordshire Archives, County Hall, Oxford; Mrs Susan Laithwaite, Archivist, and Mrs A. M. Wells, Archivist, Devon Record Office, Exeter; Miss Rachel Watson, County Archivist, Northamptonshire Record Office, Northampton; Ms Zoë Lubowiecka, Library Officer, Hove Reference Library; Jeremy Taylor, Archivist, Berkshire Record Office, Reading; Mrs J. M. Jenkins, Assistant Keeper of Archives, Leicester and Rutland Record Office, Leicester; Mrs Claire Sawyer, Archivist, Bedfordshire and Luton Archives, Bedford; J. McIlwaine, Archivist, Hertfordshire Archives and Local Studies, Hertford; Mr Carter, Senior Research Archivist, Centre for Kentish Studies, Maidstone, and to the staffs of the British Library, the Bodleian Library, the London Library and the Ravenscroft Library, Henley-on-Thames.

For their help in a variety of other ways I want also to thank Richard Way, Diana Cook, Roger Katz, Robert Wyatt, the Hon Georgina Stonor, Bruce Hunter of David Higham Associates, Eleo Gordon of Penguin UK, Gráinne Kelly, who helped me choose the illustrations for the book, Claire Péligry, who edited it, and my wife, who has made the comprehensive index.

Finally I must say how grateful I am to Professor J. R. Jones, Emeritus Professor of History, University of East Anglia, for having read the book in typescript and for having given me much useful advice for its improvement.

LIST OF ILLUSTRATIONS

TITLE-PAGE: 'Malborouk', an early nineteenth-century illustration in a French broadsheet. (Bibliothèque Nationale de France/Fotomas)

ENDPAPERS: *The Great Court and North Front of Blenheim Palace*, early eighteenth-century engraving. (By kind permission of His Grace the Duke of Marlborough. Photo: © 2001 His Grace the Duke of Marlborough and Jarrold Publishing)

BLACK AND WHITE

COLOUR

AUTHOR'S NOTE

SPELLING In Marlborough's day the orthography of those who could spell at all was highly idiosyncratic, the Duke's especially so: 'sivell' for civil, for example, 'althofle' for although. The Duchess's spelling was little better, though she did not hesitate to criticize that of others. For ease of reading most of the letters and other documents here transcribed are given with the spelling corrected to conform with modern usage. Some, however, are printed uncorrected to give a flavour of the original.

PLACE NAMES Except in the case of small towns and villages, places have been given their present names: Trier, for example, for Trèves, Aachen for Aix-la-Chapelle.

DATES The Protestant English were slow in adopting the Gregorian Calendar introduced by Pope Gregory XIII in 1582, so English dates (Old Style) were behind those of continental Europe (New Style), ten days behind in the seventeenth century, eleven in the first half of the eighteenth. The dates in this book are given in Old Style when referring to events taking place in England and in New Style when referring to those taking place on the Continent.

MONEY According to figures compiled by the Bank of England, goods costing £74.59 in 1999 could have been bought for £1 between 1670 and 1710. That is to say, the thousand guineas which Colonel Parke received from Queen Anne for bringing her the news of the victory at Blenheim would today be worth about £75,000.

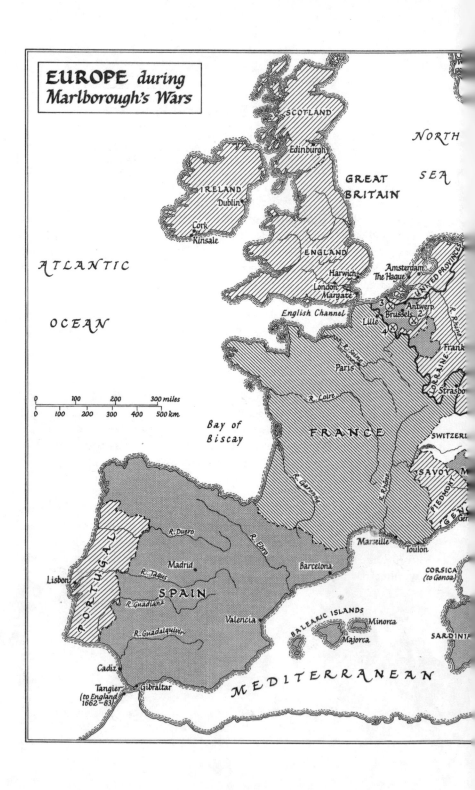

EUROPE *during*
Marlborough's Wars

NORTH

SEA

SCOTLAND

Edinburgh

GREAT
BRITAIN

IRELAND

Dublin

Amsterdam
The Hague

Cork
Kinsale

UNITED PROVINCES

ENGLAND

Harwich

3

Antwerp

London
Margate

Brussels 2

R. Rhine

Lille

ATLANTIC

English Channel

4

Frank

R. Seine

OCEAN

Paris

Strasbo

R. Loire

0   100   200   300 miles

0 100 200 300 400 500 km

Bay of
Biscay

FRANCE

SWITZERL

R. Garonne

SAVOY M

R. Duero

R. Rhône

PIEDMONT

Gen

R. Ebro

Marseille

Toulon

Ger

Madrid

Barcelona

CORSICA
(to Genoa)

R. Tagus

Lisbon

SPAIN

PORTUGAL

R. Guadiana

Valencia

BALEARIC ISLANDS

Minorca

Majorca

SARDINIA

R. Guadalquivir

Cadiz

Tangier
(to England
1662–83)

Gibraltar

MEDITERRANEAN

Christiania

Stockholm

SWEDEN

Baltic Sea

NMARK
Copenhagen

LITHUANIA

RUSSIA

PRUSSIA

BRANDENBURG
Berlin

R. Elbe

R. Vistula

Warsaw

POLAND

Prague

BAVARIA

Danube   Vienna

Munich

AUSTRIA

Buda   Pest

HUNGARY

R. Danube

BLACK
SEA

VENICE
Venice

R. Po

TUSCANY

OTTOMAN

PAPAL
STATES
Rome

Adriatic Sea

NAPLES

Naples

EMPIRE

THE TWO SICILIES

SICILY

SEA

WAV

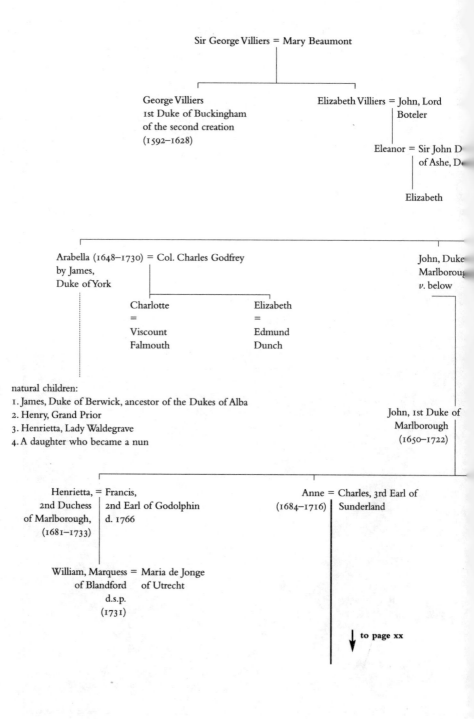

Sir George Villiers = Mary Beaumont

George Villiers
1st Duke of Buckingham
of the second creation
(1592–1628)

Elizabeth Villiers = John, Lord
Boteler

Eleanor = Sir John D
of Ashe, D

Elizabeth

Arabella (1648–1730) = Col. Charles Godfrey
by James,
Duke of York

Charlotte
=
Viscount
Falmouth

Elizabeth
=
Edmund
Dunch

John, Duke
Marlboroug
v. below

natural children:
1. James, Duke of Berwick, ancestor of the Dukes of Alba
2. Henry, Grand Prior
3. Henrietta, Lady Waldegrave
4. A daughter who became a nun

John, 1st Duke of
Marlborough
(1650–1722)

Henrietta, = Francis,
2nd Duchess   2nd Earl of Godolphin
of Marlborough,   d. 1766
(1681–1733)

Anne = Charles, 3rd Earl of
(1684–1716) | Sunderland

William, Marquess = Maria de Jonge
of Blandford   of Utrecht
d.s.p.
(1731)

to page xx

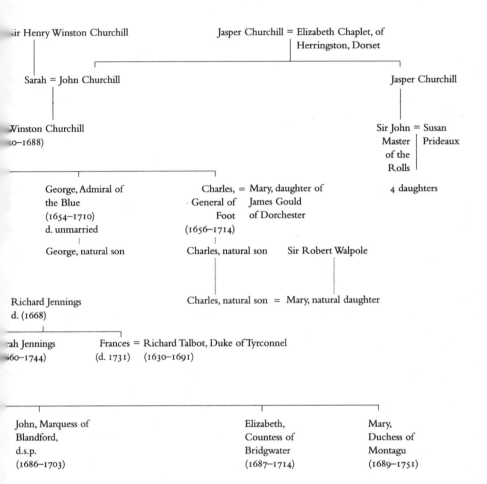

ir Henry Winston Churchill   Jasper Churchill = Elizabeth Chaplet, of
                                                      Herringston, Dorset

Sarah = John Churchill   Jasper Churchill

Winston Churchill   Sir John = Susan
;0–1688)   Master | Prideaux
                                                     of the |
                                                     Rolls |

George, Admiral of   Charles, = Mary, daughter of   4 daughters
the Blue   General of   James Gould
(1654–1710)   Foot   of Dorchester
d. unmarried   (1656–1714)

George, natural son   Charles, natural son   Sir Robert Walpole

Richard Jennings   Charles, natural son = Mary, natural daughter
d. (1668)

ah Jennings   Frances = Richard Talbot, Duke of Tyrconnel
60–1744)   (d. 1731)   (1630–1691)

John, Marquess of   Elizabeth,   Mary,
Blandford,   Countess of   Duchess of
d.s.p.   Bridgwater   Montagu
(1686–1703)   (1687–1714)   (1689–1751)

The Churchill Family

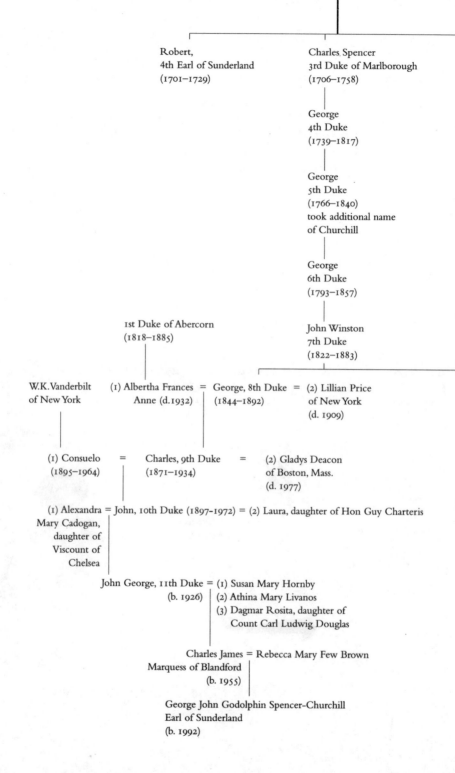

Robert,
4th Earl of Sunderland
(1701–1729)

Charles Spencer
3rd Duke of Marlborough
(1706–1758)

George
4th Duke
(1739–1817)

George
5th Duke
(1766–1840)
took additional name
of Churchill

George
6th Duke
(1793–1857)

1st Duke of Abercorn
(1818–1885)

John Winston
7th Duke
(1822–1883)

W.K. Vanderbilt
of New York

(1) Albertha Frances = George, 8th Duke = (2) Lillian Price
Anne (d. 1932)   (1844–1892)   of New York
                                          (d. 1909)

(1) Consuelo   =   Charles, 9th Duke   =   (2) Gladys Deacon
(1895–1964)   (1871–1934)   of Boston, Mass.
                                           (d. 1977)

(1) Alexandra = John, 10th Duke (1897–1972) = (2) Laura, daughter of Hon Guy Charteris
Mary Cadogan,
daughter of
Viscount of
Chelsea

John George, 11th Duke = (1) Susan Mary Hornby
(b. 1926)   (2) Athina Mary Livanos
            (3) Dagmar Rosita, daughter of
                 Count Carl Ludwig Douglas

Charles James = Rebecca Mary Few Brown
Marquess of Blandford
(b. 1955)

George John Godolphin Spencer-Churchill
Earl of Sunderland
(b. 1992)

John Spencer
(1708–1746)
from whom the
Earls of Spencer
descend

Anne
(d. 1769)
m. Viscount Bateman

Diana
(d. 1735)
m. Duke of Bedford

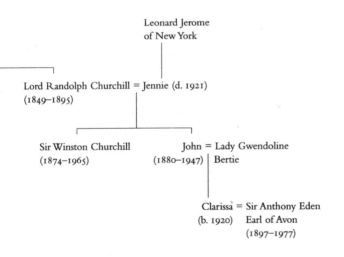

Leonard Jerome
of New York

Lord Randolph Churchill = Jennie (d. 1921)
(1849–1895)

Sir Winston Churchill
(1874–1965)

John = Lady Gwendoline
(1880–1947) | Bertie

Clarissa = Sir Anthony Eden
(b. 1920)   Earl of Avon
(1897–1977)

BOYHOOD

'. . . a hatred of poverty and dependence . . .'

One day towards the end of the nineteenth century, Field Marshal Lord Wolseley went down to the West Country to visit the spot where, as he put it, 'one of our greatest countrymen was born and passed his childhood'. The place was the small manor house of Ashe near the Devonshire village of Musbury, between Axminster and Lyme Regis. 'This untidy farmhouse,' so Wolseley thought, 'with its neglected gardens and weed-choked fish-ponds, round which the poor, badly clothed boy sported during his early years, seems to recall his memory more vividly than a visit to Blenheim Palace, or a walk over the famous position near the village of Höchstädt on the banks of the Danube. The place, the very air, seems charged with reminiscences of the great man who first drew breath here.'

More than two centuries before, during the Civil War, the place had belonged to Eleanor Drake, Sir John Drake's widow, who was proud to name the great Elizabethan sailor, Sir Francis Drake, among her husband's forebears. Unlike many of the gentry in that part of England, Lady Drake – the daughter of John, Lord Boteler, who had married the sister of George Villiers, first Duke of Buckingham – warmly supported the Parliamentarians against the Royalists in the war; and she had encouraged her tenants in the parishes adjoining Musbury to do the same. Accordingly she felt herself dangerously exposed to the anger of the Cavaliers and asked for a troop of Round-heads to protect her property from them. The soldiers were sent, but scarcely had they arrived than a Royalist force marched up to drive them off. The Cavaliers then burned down and demolished a large part of the house and 'stripped the good lady, who, almost naked and without shoe to her foot . . . fled to Lyme [Regis] for safety'.

Here the Parliamentarian commander, Colonel Robert Blake, a 'short, squat, ungainly figure', the eldest of the twelve sons of a Somerset merchant, was encouraging the garrison and local inhabitants to hold out against repeated attacks and continued to do so until the Royalists accepted the impossibility of taking the place and withdrew to Exeter 'with some loss of reputation for having lain so long before so vile and untenable a place' without taking it.

Lady Drake, who had been reduced to spinning and knitting stockings, 'got away and came to Parliament' in London, where, 'having been wholly ruined by the enemy', she was provided with a house belonging to a Royalist who was away fighting in the continuing war.

Eventually, after securing some compensation for her losses, she returned to Ashe, where her third daughter, Elizabeth, and Elizabeth's husband, Winston Churchill, joined her to live there upon her charity in a wing of the house which had not been destroyed in the fire.

Winston Churchill was the son of a successful lawyer, John Churchill, who had married into the aristocratic family of the Winstones of Standish in Gloucestershire. Impoverished by a crippling fine of nearly £4,500 imposed upon him for having fought on the losing side as a captain of Royalist cavalry, Winston chose as his motto, still borne by his descendants, *Fiel Pero Desdichado*, Faithful but Unfortunate. At Ashe he occupied himself, amid the ruins of the manor house, with the study of genealogy and a lengthy, learned and misconceived work, *Divi Britannici*, which was to be dedicated to the restored King Charles II, and in which Oliver Cromwell is described as a 'Devil' and his interregnum as 'an universal Darkness overspreading the State'.

While he was thus occupied, his wife, Elizabeth, gave birth to a succession of children, twelve in all, only five of whom survived their infancy. The eldest daughter, Arabella, was born in February 1649, a month after the execution of King Charles I, and the eldest son, John, was christened the following year on 26 May, the day of his birth.

Growing up as he did in the impoverished conditions at Ashe, in a family of differing sympathies and allegiances, the young John Churchill, so his father's namesake and his own biographer, Sir Winston Churchill, ventured to assert,

might well have aroused in his mind two prevailing impressions . . . first a hatred of poverty and dependence, and, secondly, the need of hiding thoughts and feelings from those to whom their expression would be repugnant . . . To have one set of opinions for one part of the family, and to use a different language for the other, may have been inculcated from John's earliest years. To win freedom from material subservence by the sure agency of money must have been planted in his heart's desire. To these was added a third, the importance of having friends and connexions on both sides of a public quarrel . . . Certainly the whole life of John Churchill bore the imprint of his youth. That impenetrable reserve under graceful and courteous manners; those unceasing contacts and correspondences with opponents; that iron parsimony and personal frugality, never relaxed in the blaze of fortune and abundance; that hatred of waste and improvidence in all their forms – all these could find their roots in the bleak years at Ashe.

Sir Winston further conjectured that John's father, with no estate to manage nor profession to pursue, and no money to travel, may well have taken a hand in the education of his children, supplementing the instruction given to them by a tutor described by an earlier biographer of John as 'a sequestred Clergyman who made it his first concern to instil sound Principles of Religion into him, that the Seeds of human Literature might take the deeper Root'.

Whether or not John Churchill was thus conscientiously instructed in literature and religious studies it is impossible now to say; but certainly his spelling remained defective for the rest of his life, far more idiosyncratic, indeed, than that of most of his more or less well-educated contemporaries, 'cotch' for coach, for example, 'some wher' for somewhere, 'on' for one, 'se' for see, 'siene' for seen.

It is also certain that, at some time after the Restoration of King Charles II in 1660, when he was thirteen or fourteen years old, John was enrolled as a scholar at St Paul's School, which had been founded in 1509 close to the cathedral by John Colet, the dean, to provide a free education for 153 boys, a number traditionally associated with the miracle of the draught of fishes. Here, according to the improbable recollection of an old clergyman, who said that John Churchill had been a fellow pupil of his at St Paul's and claimed to be 'well acquainted' with him, Master Churchill was frequently to be seen studying the Latin text of *Epitoma rei militaris, sive institutorum rei militaris* by the fourth-century Roman military expert, Flavius Vegetius Renatus. A more likely sidelight upon John Churchill's career at St Paul's was later provided by his wife, who stated that her husband had been 'whipt at St Paul's School for not reading his Book'. Certainly in later life he did not read much. Lord Chesterfield, who claimed to know him 'extremely well', described him as being 'eminently illiterate'. And it is, at least, an incontrovertible fact that upon leaving St Paul's at the age of about sixteen, he was appointed to a post at court as a page in the service of King Charles II's brother, the Duke of York.

By then, John's father had begun to receive rewards for his service as a cavalry officer in the recent war: he had been elected as Member of Parliament for Weymouth; he had been chosen as one of the original members of the Royal Society; in 1662 he had gone to Ireland as a member of the Court of Claims, taking his family with him to Dublin, where his son John had for a short time been a pupil at the Dublin Free Grammar School. In 1664 he had been knighted for his services, and, a few months later, appointed to a position in the royal household and allocated apartments in Whitehall Palace.

Soon afterwards his daughter Arabella was also offered an appointment at court as a maid-of-honour in the household of the King's sister-in-law, the Duchess of York.

The Duchess's husband, James, Duke of York, the master of Arabella's brother John, had few vices apart from an exasperating obstinacy; but his virtues were not attractive ones. He was provident but it was a providence close to parsimony; he was a firm friend but a 'heavy enemy'. Sincere but self-righteous, industrious but unimaginative, he bore himself with excessive hauteur.

Apart from a passion for hunting, the Duke had very few interests. Music appealed to him a little, but literature and painting scarcely at all. Like most egotists he had no humour. The principal objects of his life were to be the conversion of England to Roman Catholicism and the establishment of a monarchy similar to King Louis XIV's in France.

Described as 'a remorseless masochist', he was plagued by his unremitting desire for women; and so plain were most of those whom he took to bed that his brother, the King, observed that they must have been imposed upon him as a penance by his priests. Arabella Churchill, a tall, pale, thin girl of sixteen at the time of her appointment to the Duchess's household, was not as plain as most of these mistresses; but it was only to be expected that the Duke would sooner or later seduce her. It was commonly supposed that he had made up his mind to do so when he and the Duchess were on their way to enjoy a day's greyhound coursing near York. Arabella's horse bolted and she was thrown to the ground, her dress in disarray. The Duke galloped to her rescue and was enthralled by the sight of her exposed body. Over the next eight years or so she gave birth to four of his children, one of whom, James Fitzjames, created Duke of Berwick, was to become a marshal in the service of France. The younger son was created Duke of Albemarle; the elder daughter married Sir Henry Waldegrave, ancestor of the Earls Waldegrave; the younger became a nun.

2

LOVERS AT COURT

*'. . . I know the child is not mine, yet I will
acknowledge it for old times' sake.'*

John Churchill, at sixteen two years younger than his sister Arabella, seems to have enjoyed life at court, though well aware of the constraints, the need for complaisance, dissembling and deference which it imposed upon him. He had very little money to spend, but his surroundings were comfortable if not luxurious and the food served at the pages' table was of the best. His master, the Duke of York, who had been appointed Lord High Admiral upon his brother's accession to the throne, concerned himself as much with military matters as he did with naval, and was conscientious in his attendance upon the drills and parades of soldiers in the royal parks. John Churchill was with him on these occasions and, like him, displayed a lively interest in the troops' marching and counter-marching to the rhythm of fife and drum, their almost choreographic changes of front, the manner in which squares became columns, pikemen moving forwards to protect musketeers, horsemen charging headlong across the turf, a pistol in the left hand, a sabre or halberd in the right. It was not long before the boy set his heart upon becoming a soldier himself; and, with the Duke's encouragement, on 14 September 1667, soon after his seventeenth birthday, he obtained a commission as ensign in the King's Own Company in the 1st Guards, later to become the Grenadier Guards.

By then his charming manners and most handsome, almost femininely beautiful appearance had endeared him to the King's mistress, Barbara Villiers, the Earl of Castlemaine's wife, who was to be created Duchess of Cleveland in 1670 and who numbered, or was to number, among her numerous lovers, a rope-dancer whom she had met at Bartholomew Fair and the dramatist William Wycherley. She was Churchill's second cousin once removed and one of her most intimate friends was his mother's sister, Mrs Godfrey. Churchill was often to be found in this aunt's room, apparently eating sweets; and it was there that he and Lady Castlemaine met. Some time later they became lovers. He was twenty when they did so; she was twenty-nine.

Barbara Villiers was King Charles's 'first and longest mistress by whom he had five children', wrote Gilbert Burnet, Bishop of Salisbury.

She was a woman of great beauty, but most enormously vitious and ravenous; foolish but imperious, very uneasy to the King, and always carrying on intrigues with other men, while yet pretending she was jealous of him. His passion for her, and her strange behaviour towards him, did so disorder him that often he was not master of himself, nor capable of minding business.

She was, according to another observer of her times, 'the lewdest as well as the fairest of King Charles's concubines', an insatiably sexual woman, hot-tempered, extravagant and unpredictable.

Samuel Pepys was entranced by her, and it was the sight of her smocks and petticoats, 'laced with rich lace at the bottoms', hanging up to dry in the Privy Garden, which so excited his susceptible imagination that it did him 'good to look upon them'.

Gossip had it that George Villiers, Duke of Buckingham, who had quarrelled with his cousin Barbara, bribed a waiting-woman to keep him informed of the progress of her affair with Churchill, and that, having learned that he was likely to be in Barbara's apartments at a certain time, he contrived for the King to come there at that time also. One version of this story had it that, upon His Majesty's appearance, Churchill leapt out of bed and jumped out of the window. Another account suggested that Churchill concealed himself in a cupboard at the approach of the King, who, having failed to find him in the bed and supposing him to be hiding, asked for sweets and liqueurs which he knew to be stored there. Barbara said the key was lost. The King threatened to break the door down. She then opened the door and knelt submissively on one side of His Majesty while Churchill fell to his knees on the other. 'Go,' the King is said to have told him. 'You are a rascal, but I forgive you because you do it to get your bread.'

Whether or not either of these stories was based on fact, it was generally accepted that Churchill was the father of the Duchess of Cleveland's third daughter, born at Cleveland House, St James's, a fine house which, formerly known as Berkshire House, and since enlarged and much improved, had been given to her by the King. This child, sent to be educated with English nuns in Paris, was to become a prioress, having been the mistress of the Earl of Arran. 'You may tell [the Duchess of Cleveland],' the King is quoted as having said, 'that I know the child is not mine, yet I will acknowledge it for old times' sake.'

It was at about this time that Churchill came into possession of a large sum of money and, with that careful attention to the establishment of his fortune which was to characterize his later life, he prudently paid the rich Lord Halifax £4,500 for an annuity of £500. It was widely understood that the sum required for this transaction was given to him by the Duchess of Cleveland, who had acquired enormous sums of money, as well as jewels and property, from the King.

Although there is no contemporary record of his having done so, in 1668 John Churchill seems to have sailed for the North African outpost of Tangier, a vital Mediterranean base for naval operations against Algerian corsairs which had been acquired by England as part of the dowry of the small, dark, nervous Catherine of Braganza, daughter of King John IV of Portugal, King Charles II's Queen.* And, not long afterwards, Churchill apparently took part in a naval blockade of Algiers, headquarters of the Barbary pirates since the early sixteenth century.

---

* Tangier 'offered the hardest and most dangerous kind of military education: comparable to the North-West Frontier province of British India, it proved an incomparable training ground for those soldiers who survived service there . . . It gave Marlborough the lasting comradeship of young officers who for long retained the *esprit de corps* they acquired there' (Jones, *Marlborough*, 14).

Back in London by February 1671, after the valuable experience of these three years' service against the Moors, Churchill was reported to have fought a duel with a Mr Fenwick which 'ended with some wounds for Mr Churchill but no danger to life'; and in the summer of that year he fought another duel, again in the course of an unknown quarrel, with one Herbert who 'rann Churchill twice through the arme'. Then, at the end of May 1672, Ensign Churchill was with his company of the Guards aboard the Duke of York's flagship, the *Royal Prince*, in an engagement with a Dutch fleet off Southwold on the Suffolk coast; and it was in this sea battle, in which 200 men aboard the *Royal Prince* were killed or wounded – and the Duke of York was obliged to transfer his flag to the *St Michael* – that Churchill's brave and steady conduct earned him the promotion to a captaincy in the Lord High Admiral's Regiment over the heads of more senior officers and to the lasting resentment of some of them.

As a captain he was on the Continent again in 1673, serving with a small English force, the Royal English Regiment, which had been assembled under James, Duke of Monmouth, the natural son of Charles II by his Welsh mistress, Lucy Walter, to fight against the Dutch. He later played a courageous part in the siege of Maastricht, was at the Duke of Monmouth's side when the final assault was made, and was wounded and recommended by Monmouth on his return to Whitehall with the words, 'Here is the brave man who saved my life'.

In the following year John Churchill was in command of a regiment, and on 4 October he was in action with this regiment at Enzheim in Bavaria, where 'a great many officers' were killed in a savage and indecisive battle fought in these times of shifting alliances and enmities against the forces of the Austrian Emperor. 'I durst not brag of our victory,' he reported to the Duke of Monmouth, 'but it is certain they left the field as soon as we. We have three of their cannon and several of their colours and some prisoners.' As well as by Monmouth, Churchill's leadership in this engagement was praised in his dispatch by the French commander Henri de La Tour d'Auvergne, vicomte de Turenne, who referred to him as 'my handsome Englishman'.

Having received the thanks of King Louis XIV himself, Churchill returned home to London with his reputation still further enhanced. 'No one in this world,' wrote the French-born Marshal Turenne's nephew, Lord Duras, soon to be created Earl of Feversham, 'could possibly have done better than Mr Churchill has done.' By now he had a reputation not only for leadership and bravery but also, increasingly, for astonishingly good looks. His eyes were uncommonly large, his nose and lips 'beautifully formed'; his 'clear red and white complexion,' so a Dutch colleague was to say, 'could put the fair sex to shame', while his figure was 'as fine a one as you could see'. That fastidious judge, Lord Chesterfield, said that he 'possessed the Graces in the highest degree . . . His manner was irresistible [to] either man or woman.'

3

SARAH JENNINGS

*'Could you see my hart you would not be so
cruelle as to say I doe not love you . . .'*

At St James's Palace, where he was appointed the Duke of York's
Gentleman of the Bedchamber,★ John Churchill found that the
Duchess of Cleveland, preoccupied with the fortunes and futures of
her children, was a less predominant figure, while the King himself
was paying more attention to other mistresses. For his part John
Churchill was struck by a fresh arrival at court, Sarah Jennings.

There was an extremely improbable story going about St James's
that John Churchill finally contrived to disentangle himself from
the Duchess's toils by asking a young nobleman to have a bath in his
room when she was expected to visit him there. After his bath this lord
was to lie on a sofa with his face concealed. When the Duchess came
into the room she fell upon this inviting, almost naked body just as
Churchill himself appeared. Simulating rage at the Duchess's faith-
lessness, he declared that he would marry Sarah Jennings that very day.

Sarah Jennings's father was Richard Jennings (then spelled Jenyns),
Member of Parliament for St Albans, as his own father had been
before him. He came from an old Somerset family and held property
in that county and in Kent. For some time past, however, the
Jennings, a family very similar in social origins to the Churchills, had
been settled in Hertfordshire, and at the time of Sarah's birth in 1660,

★ He was also appointed Master of the Robes, an office he had purchased for a large
sum from the previous incumbent. It was common gossip at court that the money
required had been given to him by the Duchess of Cleveland, who had spent the
night with a rich and elderly philanderer in order to earn it.

her parents, who also owned a house at Sandridge, were living on the outskirts of St Albans.

After the death of her husband, when Sarah was eight years old, the widowed Mrs Jennings, daughter of Sir Gifford Thornhill, Baronet of Agney Court, Kent, came to court to occupy apartments in St James's Palace where, deeply in debt and with two daughters apart from Sarah to care for, she gained the reputation of being a formidable woman, something of a virago.

Some years later, when Sarah was thirteen years old, she was attached to the household of the Duchess of York, the Duke's second wife, as attendant upon the Duchess's stepdaughter, Princess Anne, the Duke's second daughter by his first marriage to Anne Hyde. Sarah was an attractive child; but, like her elder sister Frances and her mother, she was inclined to be mettlesome and haughty rather than chastened when rebuffed or criticized, and she had a very quick temper. She was also, and always remained, obstinate and highly indiscreet.

She and her mother were soon at daggers drawn. Indeed, according to a letter in the Rutland Papers, they were said to have had 'so great a falling out' that the daughter

complained to the Dutchesse that if her mother was not put out of St James's she would run away; so Sir Allen Apsley [Treasurer of the Duke of York's household] was sent to bid the mother to move, who answered 'with all my heart; she would never dispute the Duke and Dutchesse's commands, but with the grace of God she would take her daughter with her . . . Two of the maids have had great bellies at court. I shall not leave my child here to have a third' . . . So rather than part with her, the mother must stay, and all breaches are made up again.

Mrs Jennings did not stay long, however. Within a month Sarah was reported to have 'got the better' of her difficult mother, who was 'commanded to leave the Court . . . notwithstanding her petition, that she might have her girle with her, the girle saying "she is a mad woman".' She would, Sarah told a friend, 'provoke a sant'.*

---

* Relations between mother and daughter thereafter seem to have been rather strained, although Sarah apparently did what she could to repair them. In one letter to Mrs Jennings, Sarah asks to be forgiven for some unintentional slight that has upset her. The letter ends, 'The post is going and I can say no more but that I hope I shall

Sarah was about fifteen years old when Colonel Churchill returned to court from the Continent and appears to have been almost immediately captivated by her positive personality and beguiling looks, her bright, clear eyes and fine reddish gold hair springing, as though scattered by a gentle wind, from a smooth, high forehead in that kind of 'sweet disorder' which the poet Robert Herrick found so bewitching in his own loved one's dress.

Such notes and letters of Churchill's addressed to Miss Jennings which have survived contain protestations of an almost abject devotion and plaintive insecurity, wholly at variance with the forceful decisiveness and confidence he displayed as a soldier:

I beg you will let me see you as often as you can, which I am sure you ought to do if you care for my love, since every time I see you I still find new charms in you . . . On my faith I do not only now love you but do desire to do it as long as I live. If you can have time before you go to church, pray let me hear from you . . . When I am not with you the only joy I have is hearing from you . . . I have a thing to beg which I hope you will not be so barbarous as to deny me. It is that you will give me leave to do what I cannot help, which is to adore you as long as I live . . . On you depends the quiet of my soul . . . I take joy in nothing but yourself . . . Could you see my hart you would not be so cruelle as to say I doe not love you, for by all that is good I love you and only you . . . I never am truly happy but when I am with you . . . 'Tis you alone I love, so that if you are kind but one minute, that will make me happier than all the world can besides . . . Could you ever love me, I think the happiness would be so great that it would make me immortal . . . Oh, my soul, if we might be both happy, what inexpressible joy that would be . . . You are my life, my soul, my all that I hold dear in this world . . . I love you with all my hart and soul, and I am sure that as long as I live you shall have no just reason to believe the contrary.

Sarah did, however, often profess to believe the contrary. Her letters to Churchill frequently struck a quite different note from his

---

see you or hear from you very soon, and that I will ever be your most dutiful daughter whatever you are to me' (Blenheim MSS, quoted in W.S.C., i, 108–9).

Towards the end of her life, Mrs Jennings was fully reconciled with her daughter, who nursed her devotedly during her final illness and, in the opinion of her doctor, kept her alive longer than anyone would have expected (BL Add. MS 61415, fos. 51–81, quoted in Harris, *A Passion for Government*, 71).

to her: it is as though she was reluctant to trust him for fear that he might be trifling with her, or that, having caught him, it amused her to play with him. Her accusations that he did not really love her, that there were other women in his life, drew from him passionate protestations of his devotion: 'You say I pretend a passion for you when I have other things in my head. I cannot imagine what you mean by it, for I vow to God you do so entirely possess my thoughts that I think of nothing else in this world but your dear self.'

Sarah, however, was not to be convinced, or at least pretended not to be so; and when he hinted that, despite his urgent declarations of love, he did not consider his very limited means justified marriage, she became more warily dismissive than ever, readier to believe that the handsome rake merely wanted her as a mistress, as a replacement for the Duchess of Cleveland:

If it were true that you have that passion for me that you say that you have, you would find out some way to make yourself happy – it is in your power. Therefore press me no more to [see] you, since it is what I cannot in honour approve of . . . I find all you say is only to amuse me and make me think you have a passion for me, when in reality there is no such thing . . . As for seeing you I am resolved I never will in private, nor in public if I can help it . . .

The months passed; Sarah, increasingly temperamental and already harbouring ineradicable prejudices, was now seventeen. Her pretty, rather imperious sister, Frances, by this time married to Captain Sir George Hamilton, suggested that they go abroad together for a time. This proposition elicited a pathetic letter from Churchill: 'Your unkind, indifferent letter this morning confirms me of what I have been afraid of, which is that your sister can govern your passion as she pleases. My heart is ready to break. I wish 'twere over, for since you are grown so indifferent, death is the only thing that can ease me.'

Churchill's parents would have been pleased if their son's passion for this young woman, who was scarcely more than half John's age, had died much sooner. She was not in a position to do anything to further his career. It would be much better for his future prospects if he married an heiress. They would have liked him to propose to

Catherine Sedley, one of the Duke of York's mistresses. Admittedly she was extremely plain, tall and bony. She had once observed of herself and the Duke's other mistresses, 'What he saw in any of us I cannot tell. We were all plain, and if any of us had had wit, he would not have understood it.' Yet Catherine Sedley was not only an amusing and clever creature, she was also, and more importantly, the only daughter and heiress of the extremely rich Sir Charles Sedley.

Honoré de Courtin, the French ambassador, commented:

There was a small ball last Friday [7 December 1676] at the Duchess of York's where Lady Hamilton's sister who is uncommonly good-looking had far more wish to cry than to dance . . . [Churchill's] father urges him to marry one of his relations who is very rich and very ugly, and will not consent to his marriage with Miss Jennings. Churchill himself is also said to be not a little avaricious and I hear from the various ladies at court that he has pillaged the Duchess of Cleveland, and that she has given him more than the value of 100,000 livres. They make out that it is he who has quitted her and that she has taken herself off in chagrin to France to rearrange her affairs.

Sir Winston Churchill had good reason for wishing that his son should marry the rich Catherine Sedley rather than the relatively poor Sarah Jennings: he was himself in financial straits. Heavily in debt, with his property entailed, he appealed to his son to help him. Would John agree to surrender his inheritance so that the debts could be settled? John felt bound to consent.

At this juncture, so it seems, the Duchess of York came to the help of the attractive Colonel Churchill and the pretty Sarah Jennings. The exact nature of this help is unknown; nor is it known exactly when the marriage of Colonel Churchill and Sarah Jennings took place. But sometime in the winter of 1677–8, possibly in the Duchess of York's apartments, the Colonel and Miss Jennings were, indeed, married. They spent their honeymoon in the house of a relative of Sarah's, at Newsells Park, Royston, Hertfordshire.

Sarah was thankful to get away from court, having neither the patience nor the tact to be a courtier. 'I think anyone that has common sense or honesty,' she was to write, 'must needs bee very wary of everything that one meets with in courts . . . I confess that I was never pleased but when I was a child & after I had been maid of honour some time I wished myself out of the court as much as I desired to come into it before I knew what it was.'

GENTLEMAN OF THE
BEDCHAMBER

'I would not willingly have Churchill from me.'

Ever since his return from the Continent and his appointment as the Duke of York's Gentleman of the Bedchamber and Master of the Robes, Colonel Churchill had been occupied with his duties at St James's and on certain diplomatic missions of an unspecified nature in France. He had been considered for the command of the Royal English Regiment, which was still at that time fighting against the Dutch in the service of the French; and the Duke of Monmouth, Captain-General of the King's forces, recommended him to the French King for this appointment. Accordingly, Honoré de Courtin, the French ambassador, wrote to the marquis de Louvois, the Minister of War in Paris, to give him an account of Colonel Churchill's love affairs in London. Having read about these, Louvois decided that the man was probably too deeply embroiled with his women to give proper attention to his military duties. He would evidently give 'more satisfaction to a rich and faded mistress than to a monarch who did not want to have dishonourable and dishonoured carpet knights in his armies'. Even so, the command was offered to Churchill, who refused it. 'Mr Churchill,' Courtin reported, 'prefers to serve the very pretty sister of Madame Hamilton than to be lieutenant-colonel in Monmouth's regiment.'

In the early months of his marriage to this 'pretty sister', while waiting for some more agreeable appointment to be offered him, Churchill and Sarah lived with his parents at their house in Dorset or, when they were in London, at his bachelor lodgings at the west end of Jermyn Street, a fashionable area of London in process of development by that assiduous courtier of Charles II's mother, Henry Jermyn, Earl of St Albans, who had been granted the land by the King.

On 18 February 1678, however, Churchill was gazetted colonel of a new infantry regiment and the next month he was called to London from Dorset by the Duke of York, who, so Churchill wrote to his wife,

told me that the reason he sent for me was that he did believe that there would be occasion to send me to Holland and Flanders and that he would have me here . . . in Town . . . to be ready to go. By the French letters on Saturday, they expect we shall have peace or war; but whatever happens I believe I shall not be in danger this year.

Sarah remained behind in Dorset, an unwilling guest in the house of her mother-in-law, of whose behaviour she complained to her husband who replied, begging her to be patient for, as he said, 'She is my Mother and I hope at last she will be sensible that she is to blame in being peevish.' 'From the beginning of the world,' her daughter-in-law later decided, 'there has not been two women who were good mothers-in-law.'

Nor were relations between Sarah and her own mother much improved. Her husband lamented that when the two of them were together, there was likely to be much 'disorder and ell humer'.

John Churchill and his friend Sidney Godolphin, a most agreeable man from a similar West Country background, Tory Member of Parliament for Helston and a trusted courtier, were told to proceed to the Continent. They were to discuss with Spanish and Dutch representatives the necessary preparations for a proposed war against France – which, in fact, King Charles had no intention of waging – and to offer to Prince William of Orange 20,000 men and a proportionate number of guns.

Prince William, stadholder or chief magistrate of the United Provinces of the Netherlands for the past six years, was then twenty-seven years old, a few months younger than Churchill. The son of William II, Prince of Orange, and of Mary, the daughter of King Charles I of England, he had recently married his cousin Mary, daughter of Churchill's master, the Duke of York, by his first marriage to Anne Hyde.

The French had invaded his territories in 1672 and the terms of a peace settlement with King Louis XIV had still not been finally agreed when Churchill arrived in The Hague. His arrival was particularly welcome because William was relying on an English entry into the war to prevent the States-General concluding what he regarded was an unfavourable peace with France.

Prince William was not an attractive man. Distrustful, cold and autocratic in manner, by turns phlegmatic and irritable, he was so reserved that often at dinner he would eat the whole meal in silence. Reluctant to recognize his qualities as a brave soldier, his gifts as a statesman, his retentive memory and acute judgement of men in politics, or to sympathize with his high aims and ideals, the Englishmen who came into contact with him spoke of his lack of humour, his slow speech, awkward movements and pitted face, his constant cough and what Bishop Burnet called his 'very ungraceful manner of laughing, which he seldom did unless he thought he had outwitted somebody, which pleased him beyond measure'.

Colonel Churchill, however, got on well enough with him and evidently found him an interesting man to talk to about military matters, while Prince William, who was to indulge and extravagantly reward his young Dutch friends when he became King of England – surprising the duchesse d'Orléans by appearing to be in love with one of them, Arnold van Keppel, 'as with a woman', 'kissing his hands before all the court' – cannot have been insensitive to the charm of the handsome English colonel.

Churchill, generally recognized by now as a remarkable officer, respected by his fellow officers and trusted by his men, was not to remain a colonel for long. On his return to England he was promoted brigadier of foot, and in the summer he was writing to Sir Charles Lyttelton, governor of Harwich: 'We are very furious upon the war; so that I hope it will not be long before I have orders to come over.' A few weeks later he was on his way to the Continent again in command of a brigade of five battalions, two of them Guards. Before his departure, however, he assured his wife that he was not likely to be involved in any fighting since, despite Prince William's efforts, the peace negotiations would probably be concluded soon. 'I believe it will be about the beginning of October before I shall get back, which time will appear an age to me, since in all that time I shall not be made happy with the sight of you . . . So, dearest soul of my life, farewell. My duty to my Father and Mother and remember me to everybody else.' Sarah later endorsed this letter: 'To ease me when I might be frighted at his going into danger.'

When Churchill returned to England towards the end of the year, he found the country in turmoil. The claims of a renegade parson, Titus Oates, that there was a Popish plot to assassinate King Charles and establish the authority of the Pope in England had led to an outburst of anti-Catholic hysteria in London, during which several Catholics were executed for high treason. The Whigs seized the opportunity to demand that Parliament bring in an Act excluding the Catholic Duke of York from the throne and providing for the succession to pass to the Protestant Duke of Monmouth. Charles, however, refused to consider excluding his brother from the succession, and Parliament was dissolved after the second reading of an exclusion bill. But it was considered expedient to send the Duke of York out of the country for a time; so he sailed into temporary exile, first at The Hague, then at Brussels, taking his household with him.

Churchill, as a senior member of that household, was obliged to accompany him. Sarah and the Duke's second daughter, Princess Anne, and Sarah's sister Frances, by now a widow, were also of the party; and they were all still in Brussels that late summer of 1679 when King Charles fell ill in London. For fear that the Whigs might attempt to place the Duke of Monmouth on the throne in the event of the King's death, it was considered essential by his friends that the Duke of York should return to London. So Churchill was entrusted with the task of bringing him over.

According to an account by one of Lord Arran's correspondents, the Duke of York, wearing by way of disguise

a black perruque only and a plain stuff suit . . . rode post to Calais with Churchill, two other gentlemen of his household, and two footmen not in their livery. He then took ship and it was so bad a sail that though he had no ill wind he was nineteen hours at sea before he landed at Dover. He went immediately to the post house . . .

There Churchill, who tried to represent himself as 'the best man in the company', was immediately recognized by the postmaster, who also recognized the Duke, but, having regard to his disguise, said nothing. The next morning the party rode on to London, arriving in the evening at an inn at the Barbican, where, handing over their horses, they took a hackney coach to a lawyer's office in Lombard Street before proceeding to Windsor Castle, where the Duke

threw himself upon his knees, asking the King's pardon for his coming into England without his leave . . . And since that now he had that happiness to find His Majesty past all danger he was ready to return again that morning if it was His Majesty's pleasure . . . Upon this His Majesty cast his arms about him, kissed him and received him with all kindness imaginable and 'tis said by the standers-by that they both shed tears of joy at the interview.

Even so, the King thought it as well that his brother should not remain in England, where anti-Catholic feeling had made him so unpopular. So the Duke returned to Brussels; but, restless there, he sent Churchill back to England to obtain permission for him to 'go to London and thence by land to Scotland'. This he was allowed to do. The Duke's party accordingly once more set out for London, where Sarah Churchill, who was expecting a baby, remained in the lodgings in Jermyn Street while her husband accompanied the Duke to Edinburgh.

From there, while the Duke relentlessly, not to say ferociously, did all he could to suppress the anti-Catholic covenanters, Churchill addressed letters of fond concern to his wife:

You may guess by yourself how uneasy I have been since I left you, for nothing breathing ever loved another as well as I do you; and I do swear to you as long as I live I will never love another . . . Pray believe that I love nobody in the world but yourself . . . I do assure you that my thoughts are so fond of you that I cannot be happy when I am from you . . . None is so well loved as you are by me . . . You are dearer to me than ever . . . I swear to you were we not married I would beg you on my knees to be my wife

. . . I swear to you the first night in which I was blessed in having you in my arms was not more earnestly wished for by me than now I do to be again with you.

On a later occasion he proposed travelling a hundred miles for the pleasure of spending one night with her. She returned his affection and responded to his passion.

During this time in Edinburgh, Churchill was dispatched on various important missions for the Duke, which he performed so adroitly, with such patience, composure, persuasiveness, ingratiating friendliness, apparent sincerity and readiness to listen – with that mastery of 'deep dissimulation' upon which a Dutchman who knew him well was later to comment – that there was talk of him becoming British minister at The Hague – where Prince William declared that he would have warmly welcomed him – or even ambassador in Paris. This, however, remained mere talk, since the Duke of York, as he himself confessed, could not do without him. 'I would not willingly,' he said, 'have Churchill from me.' As though in compensation for the limits placed upon his ambition, Churchill's worth and diplomatic skills in the service of the Duke were recognized on 21 December 1682 by his being created Baron Churchill of Aymouth in the peerage of Scotland.

At the age of thirty-two he was acknowledged as a man of quite exceptional promise, Lord Chesterfield writing of him:

He gained whoever he had a mind to gain; and he had a mind to gain everybody, because he knew that everybody was more or less worth gaining . . . He studied the art of pleasing because he well knew the importance of it: he enjoyed it and used it more than ever man did . . . He had an inimitable sweetness and gentleness in his countenance, a tenderness in his manner of speaking, a graceful dignity in every motion, and an universal and minute attention to the least thing that could possibly please the least person . . . This was all art in him: art of which he well knew and enjoyed the advantages; for no man ever had more ambition, pride and avarice than he had.

Earlier that year of 1682, Churchill had almost lost his life when the frigate *Gloucester* ran aground on a shoal off the Norfolk coast as she was sailing for Scotland from London to bring the Duke of

York's household home. Buffeted into deep water, she foundered immediately. According to Marlborough's account, which he related to his wife, the Duke of York refused at first to get into the one long boat which the *Gloucester* carried. When at last he agreed to do so, the situation had become desperate. He handed his sword to Churchill to hold back the other passengers, who rushed forward to get into the boat with him and would, the Duke feared, swamp it. Less than fully laden, the boat, 'which might well have held fifty men', was pushed off, 'carrying the Duke, his dogs, his priest, Churchill and a few others. Some two hundred and fifty men were drowned as the *Gloucester* went down, the only survivor being my Lord Griffin who . . . threw himself out of a Window and saved himself by catching hold of a Hen Coop'.

5

PRINCESS ANNE

*'[The Princess] used to say she desired to
possess [me] wholly . . .'*

Having returned to England a few days before Christmas in 1682, Lord Churchill was established once more in the Duke of York's household at court. His finances had much improved. His income from annuities and other sources had now risen to some £800 a year and he had, in addition, his army pay, which was soon to be augmented by the money to be made as colonel of the King's Own Royal Regiment of Dragoons, an appointment which aroused some jealousy:

> Let's cut our meat with spoons
> The sense is as good
> As that Churchill should
> Be put to command the Dragoons.

Sarah also enjoyed a good income, having £300 a year – the pension of a former maid of honour – and soon to have an additional £400 a year as Groom of the Stole, as well as several large capital sums from selling places at court. So the Churchills were now able to live in some style both in Jermyn Street, where they kept no fewer than seven servants, whose liveries were embroidered with gold lace, and in St Albans at Holywell House,* which they now owned, having bought out Sarah's sister Frances's share.

The travel writer Celia Fiennes, who was to ride through St Albans in the 1690s, described it as 'a pretty large town taking all',

---

* Holywell House was demolished in 1827 and no trace of it remains.

though 'the great church' was 'much out of repaire . . . so worn away that it mourns for some charitable person to help repair it'. 'There are several good houses about the town,' she added, 'one of them, which [stands] by the bridge, on the river Ver belonging to the Churchills.'

Holywell House was remodelled and extended for them by William Talman, who was also employed by the Devonshires at Chatsworth. It stood in some twenty acres of grounds which were laid out under Churchill's personal supervision, a flower garden being created as well as a large orchard and a kitchen garden, where herbs and medicinal plants were grown as well as vegetables since Sarah was an enthusiastic and practised apothecary. There were also several ponds with water diverted from the river Ver, all well supplied with fish, and, behind the house, pasture for horses and a cow.

The Churchills were very happy here with their growing family of children (in their aunt Frances's words, 'all like little angils') and their 'easy and agreeable' friends, the company of whom, 'without ceremony', Sarah thought, was 'the best enjoyment that one can have in this life'. 'However ordinary [Holywell] may be,' she decided, 'I would not part with it for any house I have seen.'

Over the years her husband filled it with pictures and furniture, looking-glasses, tapestries, ornaments and china. In one letter of 1686, accompanying a hamper sent from The Hague, he wrote to Sarah:

I could not get a skipper to take in the hamper, because they say they dare not bring tea in. What I have sent is the best of the kind of everything. There is but little good tea and all cheaney [china] is very dear. I hope my lady will like the things. As for the chaney I have sent a full set for a desert for a large table . . . I have sent a few little things for fairings for the young ladies [their daughters].

He was also to send home trophies of war, and emblems of his military life, carved in stone, to be placed on the pediment.

Here, at Holywell House, the Churchills could live a far more domestic life than was possible in London; and here, too, their children could play and learn their early lessons.

Their first child, 'Hariote', born in October 1679, was mentioned

25

affectionately in letters from her father, who wrote in one of them that he hoped her red spots would be gone the next time he saw her and that her nose would be straight so that, as he said, 'I may fancy it be like the Mother, for as she has your coloured hair, so I would have her be like you in all things else.' This child died as a baby; but the next two children, Henrietta, born in July 1681, and Anne, born in February 1684, both survived and were to be followed by three other children, Elizabeth, Mary and John, who also survived their infancy. Their father took great pleasure in their company. 'You cannot imagine,' he once told his wife when she was away from home, 'how pleased I am with the children, for they having noe body but their maid, they are soe fond of me that when I am att home they will be always with me, kissing & huging me . . . Miss is polling me by the arme that she may writt to her dear mamma, soe I will say no more, only beg that you will love me always soe well as I love you & then we cannot but be happy.'

Their mother was to be a far more strict and demanding parent than their father, as their daughters' letters to her reveal. Henrietta once wrote to her mother:

I was the gladdest in the world to receive a letter from my dear Mama, little thinking upon my word it would bee such a one as I found it, and ever since I have read it I have allmost wished myself dead . . . Anything that I can do as long as I live I shall never think too much if my Dear Mama were but satisfied, which I can't but think she would easily bee if she did but remember she was once of my age herself.

Henrietta's younger sister, Mary, had occasion to write similar letters:

I can't help thinking my case very hard that you will give me over for so small a thing [as mislaying her clogs] & which is not my fault, for if I should buy a pair every day I should never have any, for the moment I take them off they are lost . . . I believe you could not be so angery with me for this but that you are angery for so many other things that if I should begin to speak of now I should never have don, so I will say no more but that since you have been so angery with me I have been so misarable that I have wish'd & pray'd for nothing so much as to dy that I might be no trouble to my dear mama & I hope much happier my self.

26

The girls' father was concerned that on occasions their mother was too severe with their daughters, too inclined to hold strictly to the view that 'children should be kept in their place, and ought never to be allowed, whatever might happen, to question authority'. 'Hetherto,' he wrote to their mother in one letter, characteristically and cautiously, almost apologetically, expressing his feelings in this matter, 'I really have not had time to write to my children, but when I do, bee assur'd that I shall let them know my heart & soul as to their living dutyfully & kindly with you, & let mee beg for my sake of my dear Soull that she will pass by little faults & consider they are very young . . .'

Much as the Churchills enjoyed their life together in the country, they were both soon to be drawn back to court again, for Princess Anne was married in the summer of 1683 and she offered an appointment in her household to Sarah, whom she had admired and been passionately fond of since she was a child of six and Sarah was ten.

Princess Anne was now eighteen years old. It was thought at one time that she might marry Prince George of Hanover, who was eventually to succeed her as King George I; but he, having come to England as a possible suitor, left without making any proposal, a slight for which Anne was never to forgive him. Before this she had conceived a most unsuitable affection for the Earl of Mulgrave, who was quickly sent packing to Tangier. It was then decided that she should marry Prince George of Denmark, brother of the Danish King Christian V; and, as a highly competent and trusted envoy, Lord Churchill was sent over to Denmark to bring Prince George back to England. Tall, fair-haired and asthmatic, he was rather fat though not unprepossessing and certainly good-natured. But he ate too much and drank too much; and when he spoke, which was not often, he did so in an atrocious accent. Charles II's derisive comment on him was to become well known: 'I've tried him drunk, and I've tried him sober, and there's nothing in him.' But Princess Anne undoubtedly became very fond of him, as he did of her. On asking her uncle, King Charles, how he might lose weight, Prince George received the answer: 'Walk with me, hunt with my brother and do justice to my niece.' And no one could deny that he faithfully followed the last part of this advice: during her life Anne was to become pregnant nearly twenty times. She miscarried frequently, however, and most of the babies that survived their birth died of hydrocephalus in their infancy, as did the eldest boy, who was to die soon after his eleventh birthday.

Princess Anne, a timid, reserved, short-sighted, taciturn young woman who had had no one else to love or be loved by in her girlhood, had always been fascinated by the pretty, amusing and strong-willed Sarah, so much cleverer, so much more self-confident and vivacious than herself. Years later Sarah herself wrote that the Princess's passion for her became 'too much to be hid', explaining:

[We] were shut up together for many hours daily. Every moment of Absence was accounted a sort of tedious, lifeless state. To see [me] was a constant joy; and to part with [me] for never so short a time, a constant Uneasiness . . . This worked even to the jealousy of a Lover. [The Princess] used to say she desired to possess [me] wholly, and could hardly bear that [I] should ever escape from this confinement into other Company . . . She grew uneasy to be treated by me with the form and ceremony due to rank, [so] one day she proposed to me, that whenever I should happen to be absent from her, we might in all our letters write ourselves by feigned names, such as would import nothing of distinction of rank between us. Morley and Freeman were the names her fancy hit upon, and she let me choose by which of them I would be called. My frank, open temper naturally led me to pitch upon Freeman, and so the Princess took the other, and from this time Mrs Morley and Mrs Freeman began to converse as equals, made so by affection and friendship.

Sarah's husband regarded this intimate friendship with high approval. If it continued harmoniously, it could not but be very profitable to them both in the future. He himself treated the Princess with respectful affection, assuming the role of a fond, protective brother. He grew to be genuinely attached to her. When others spoke ill of her, he was to protest that she was, on the contrary, 'a very good sort of woman', with a most pleasant speaking voice, 'though she had,' as Lord Dartmouth said of her, 'a bashfulness that made it very uneasy to herself to say much in public'.

★

At the beginning of February 1685 King Charles II lay slowly, very slowly, dying in his bedchamber in the Palace of Whitehall. The doctors had done their worst and he had received the Roman Catholic Communion. As he lingered on the brink of death, he apologized with characteristic politeness to those around him for keeping them waiting so long. He said goodbye to his tearful wife, Catherine, and to his brother and sister-in-law, the Duke and Duchess of York, who were both also in tears. His children came in one by one to receive his blessing. At six o'clock in the morning he asked for the curtains to be drawn so that he could watch the sun rise for the last time. He died at midday on the first Friday of the month.

6

MONMOUTH'S REBELLION

'I see plainly that I am to have the trouble,
and that the honor will be anothers.'

Appointed one of his Lords of the Bedchamber at a salary of £600 a
year by the Duke of York, now King James II, and soon to be created
a baron in the English peerage, Churchill was sent to convey the
news of the late King's death, and the accession of his brother, to
King Louis XIV. He was also instructed to endeavour to persuade
the French King to increase the subsidy which had been secretly paid
to Charles II. On his way to Paris, however, Churchill was informed
that Louis had offered James II an unsolicited present of half a million
livres, making it unseemly for the time being to ask for the larger
sum which King James had had in mind.

While Churchill was in France on this diplomatic mission, the
late King's bastard son, the handsome and charming Duke of
Monmouth, was in Brussels, urged by exiles and malcontents living
there, as well as by his mistress, the beautiful, ambitious Lady Wentworth, to press his claim to succeed his father as the rightful Protestant
King of England. He was encouraged to do so also by the Earl
of Argyll, who had fallen out with James II when he was Duke of
York, and by various Whigs who had fled abroad after conspiring
together to assassinate Charles II and the Duke of York as they
travelled from the Newmarket races to London past Rye House in
Hertfordshire.

It was decided that Argyll should sail to the Highlands of Scotland
to raise opposition there to King James while Monmouth invaded
England.

For over a fortnight the three ships of Monmouth's small invading force were tossed about in the Channel until, on 11 June 1685, they were able to land at Lyme and to disembark their queasy passengers together with such arms as they had been able to collect on the Continent, several of these bought with proceeds from the sale of Lady Wentworth's jewels. At Lyme the Duke marched from the quay to the Market Place, where a proclamation was read to the inhabitants, a copy of it being sent to London. This proclamation declared that Monmouth, or King Monmouth as his supporters were to call him, was 'now Head and Captain-General of the Protestant forces of this Kingdom', and, claiming that he had a 'legitimate and legal right to the Crown', maintained not only that the so-called King James II had instigated the Great Fire of London and murdered his brother, but also that Monmouth himself had been 'born in lawful wedlock'.

As hundreds of town and country people, though very few gentry, came forward to fight in support of Monmouth's claims, two customs officers instructed by the Mayor of Lyme galloped off to London to give their Member of Parliament the alarming news of the invasion. The Member was Sir Winston Churchill, formerly Member for Weymouth, who, immediately upon hearing of Monmouth's landing, set out to inform the King, accompanied by his son, John. Within hours Brigadier-General Lord Churchill was marching south towards the coast with eight troops of horse guards and dragoons and five companies of foot, covering an average of thirty miles a day and causing much resentment in the countryside through which he passed by seizing draught animals and farm wagons. He had hoped and expected to be given command of all the King's forces, and was disappointed when he learned that James II's friend, the French-born Lord Feversham, was to be commander-in-chief. 'I see plainly,' he wrote in disgruntlement to Lord Clarendon, the Lord Privy Seal and King James's brother-in-law, 'that I am to have the trouble, and that the honor will be anothers.'

In fact, Feversham gained little honour: his officers castigated him for his laziness and incompetence, maintaining that he thought only of eating and sleeping; that he was either in bed or tying his cravat when he should have been directing his forces; that the portrait of a simpleton, a 'frog' who could scarcely talk English – as he was to be depicted in the Duke of Buckingham's farce *The Battle of Sedgemoor* – was a fair enough portrait.

Churchill was careful not to join in this condemnation of Lord Feversham, much of it unjustified, and was rewarded by Feversham's gratitude and by his reporting of his subordinate's diligence to the King.

Lord Churchill certainly directed his troops with skill and fore-sight, demonstrating that enviable ability to be able to predict what steps his adversaries would take which was to characterize his later career, following the rebel army closely and confident, as he reported to the Duke of Somerset, also a Gentleman of the Bedchamber and soon to be appointed Colonel of the Queen's Dragoons, that he would be 'glad to meet' the Duke of Monmouth since his own men were in 'so good heart'. They were undoubtedly better disciplined and far better equipped than the rebels, some of whom were armed only with scythes fastened to broomsticks. But as Monmouth's forces moved about in the West Country, more and more men in this industrial region of England – where clothiers and miners had of late been enduring widespread hardship and unemployment – came to throw in their lot with his; while numerous militiamen took an early opportunity of deserting the King's side for that of 'King Monmouth'.

Gathering more men, many of them committed Nonconformists, with every day's march, Monmouth advanced from Axminster to Bridgwater, then to Glastonbury, Wells, Shepton Mallet and across the Mendip Hills towards Bristol, his numbers now increased to almost 10,000 men. Lord Feversham had entered Bristol before him, however; and, soon afterwards, Lord Churchill and his younger brother Charles, who had brought up a train of artillery from the Hampshire coast, both joined him at Bath.

Anxious to ensure that the King should entertain no doubts about his loyalty or of Feversham's good opinion of his services, Lord Churchill wrote a letter to Lord Clarendon, his spelling even more idiosyncratic than usual:

I doe ashure you, that you waire very Just to me in the opinion you had of me, for nobody living can have bene more obsarvant than I have been to my Lord feaversham, ever since I have bene with him, in soe much that he did tell me that he would writt to the King to lett him know how diligent I was, and I should be glade if you could know whether he has done me that Justice.

On 27 June there was a brisk skirmish south of Bath at Norton St Philip, where the rebels acquitted themselves well; but soon afterwards some 2,000 of their number wandered off. By 3 July Monmouth himself, chastened and despairing, was back at Bridgwater, and two days later, having been ordered to launch a night attack across the drained marshes of Sedgemoor, his ragged men, fighting bravely, were at last cut apart in the early morning light. Those who could still do so ran off, some of them, like Daniel Defoe, the twenty-five-year-old son of a Nonconformist tallow-chandler, escaping, many others hunted down and slaughtered wherever they could be found.

Lord Churchill, who had led his dragoons in a fierce charge against the ill-equipped rebels, took no part in this aftermath of slaughter; but even he, on 26 June, had halted his men and ordered the hanging of a prisoner, a feltmaker named Jarvis. Numerous other rebels were hanged in what became known as the 'Bloody Assizes', presided over by the Lord Chief Justice, Lord Jeffreys, who was said to have amassed a large sum of money by means of extortion from rebels or their friends. In addition to these executions for high treason, over 800 rebels, as well as young girls who had embroidered Monmouth's standards at Taunton, were given over to persons who enjoyed favour of court to be sold into slavery in the plantations of the West Indies, there to be treated, in Samuel Pepys's words, 'according to their deserts'. On his return from the assize at Bristol, Jeffreys, who had been described by Charles II as a man of 'no learning, no sense, no manners and more impudence than ten carted street-walkers', called at Windsor where King James, 'taking into his royal consideration the many eminent and faithful services' which he had rendered the Crown, promoted him to the post of Lord Chancellor.

Lord Churchill was well aware of the King's attitude to the rebels, on behalf of two of whom their sister, Hannah Hewling, came to beg mercy:

33

She was introduced for this purpose by Lord Churchill . . . While they waited in the antechamber for admittance, standing near the mantelpiece, Lord Churchill assured her of the most hearty wishes of success to her petition, 'But madam,' said he, 'I dare not flatter you with any such hopes, for that marble is as capable of feeling compassion as the King's heart.'

In this case it was shown to be true: both the brothers were hanged. And subsequently both the leaders of the rebellion were beheaded. The Earl of Argyll, his force reduced from 2,000 to 500 men, was taken to Edinburgh, where his head was struck off and placed upon a tall iron spike on the west end of the Tolbooth. The Duke of Monmouth, captured as he lay disguised as a farm labourer in a ditch, was taken to the Tower of London by an officer who had orders to stab him if any attempt was made to rescue him. He died at the hands of the clumsy executioner John Ketch, who, having failed to sever his head from his body after five blows of his axe, cut it off with a knife.

Henry Booth, second Lord Delamere, an extreme Whig who was said to have plotted to incite an uprising in the north of England, was spared. Accused of complicity in the rebellion, he was tried by his peers and in the presence of the King. As the junior peer there, Lord Churchill was asked for his verdict first. 'Not guilty,' he declared, 'upon my honour.' All the other peers, contrary to the advice given to them by Jeffreys, responded in the same way.

7

DESERTION

*'. . . I have been bred a Protestant, and intend
to live and die in that communion.'*

The new king, James II, now fifty-one years old, had the 'strange
notion', so Gilbert Burnet said of him, that no regard was 'to be had
to the pleasing of the people'. Certainly his practice of having Mass
celebrated in a wooden chapel borne on wheels and placed between
the cavalry and the infantry when he visited his soldiers' camps, and
his determination to have a large and disciplined army of some 40,000
men, including Roman Catholic officers, as a means, it was supposed,
of establishing an arbitrary power and himself as supreme ruler of a
Roman Catholic state on the model of Louis XIV's, aroused deep
suspicion in the country. So did his appointment of Roman Catholics
to important positions such as the command of the fleet, the gover-
norships not only of Dover and Hull, but also of Portsmouth, which
was bestowed upon the eighteen-year-old Duke of Berwick, his son
by Arabella Churchill, who had been educated in France in the care
of the Jesuits.

How far King James was prepared to go in realizing his ambition
was demonstrated in July 1687, when the Papal envoy was received
in state at Windsor Castle. 'The Duke of Somerset being in waiting
refused to attend in that ceremony,' according to Sir John Reresby,
Member of Parliament for the city of York, 'maintaining that the
recognition of Papal officials had been declared illegal at the
Reformation.' 'I am above the law,' the King told him. 'Your
Majesty is so,' Somerset replied, 'but I am not.' 'For this response
Somerset was refused coming to Court and lost all his places', while
'five of the six gentlemen of the Privy Chamber were put out of

their employment for the same cause'. Already the King – who had publicly attended the celebration of Mass at Windsor and had bought vestments and candlesticks as well as a new organ out of secret service money – had 'discharged the Dean of the Chappell and the Chaplaines from attending any more at that office', while the Anglican Clerk of the Closet had been replaced by the King's confessor, the influential Father Edward Petre, who was also appointed to the Privy Council together with four Catholic peers. Now James and his second wife, Mary, who was the daughter of Duke Alphonso IV of Modena, were, to the consternation of most of their subjects, prepared to 'parade the Papal Envoy', if not before the 'vast population of the capital', at least before the 'great multitudes that flocked' to Windsor to see an imposing procession of thirty-six coaches, each drawn by six horses led by the Knight Marshal's men, and a long train of running footmen.

Throughout these months in 1687 Lord Churchill remained at court, though little was heard of him: he was evidently being careful not to compromise himself. The few reports of his behaviour that came to public notice suggested that he was taking precautions, as a convinced Anglican, not to be seen as having the least sympathy for the King's religious actions. In the autumn he accompanied his royal master on a progress through the West Country during which, sometimes in the presence of Roman Catholic priests, the King touched some 5,000 people for the King's Evil, a scrofulous disease which, it was believed, could be cured by contact with royal hands, miraculously endowed with a healing power inherited from Edward the Confessor, the saintly Saxon king.

According to the anonymous author of *The Lives of the Two Illustrious Generals* (1713), who claimed to have been told of the conversation by Churchill himself, King James asked Churchill what people thought of his touching for the King's Evil in their churches. Churchill replied to the effect that they did not like the manner in which the ceremony was conducted since it persuaded them to suppose that it was 'paving the way for the introduction of Popery'. This reply evidently angered the King, to whom Churchill responded, 'What I spoke, sir, proceeded purely from my zeal for Your Majesty's service, which I prefer above all things next to that of God, and I humbly beseech Your Majesty to believe no subject in all your three Kingdoms would venture further than I would do to purchase your favour and good liking; but I have been bred a Protestant, and intend to live and die in that communion.'

It seems that he was true to his word, that he continued to carry out his duties in the King's service conscientiously and without complaint, standing behind his chair at meals, patient and enigmatic, riding with him in the hunting field, always ready to perform the duties and assignations of a Gentleman of the Bedchamber, but never acting against his Protestant conscience, declining, for instance, to support the King when it was proposed that the penal tests required of Roman Catholics should be repealed.

Gilbert Burnet, who said that Churchill was 'a very smooth man, made for a court and very fit for business if his own interests prevailed not too much over him', rather grudgingly conceded that he 'never set the King on violent measures, but, on the contrary, as oft as he spoke to him of his affairs (which was indeed but seldom) he gave him moderate counsels'.

Others of those in the King's service were prepared to abandon the faith in which they had been brought up in order to gain his favour or to retain their offices. The Earl of Salisbury did so; so did the Earl of Melfort; so did Archibald Campbell, tenth Earl and first Duke of Argyll, son of the Earl who had been executed in Edinburgh in 1685.

Had Churchill followed their example, he would not only have betrayed his conscience but affronted his wife and alienated his wife's friend, Princess Anne.

In accordance with the requirement of her uncle, King Charles II, Princess Anne, together with her sister, Princess Mary, had been brought up as a Protestant. Her tutor, by whom both pupils were much influenced and of whom they were very fond, was Henry Compton, Bishop of London, son of the Earl of Northampton and a former officer in the Horse Guards. As a firm opponent of Roman Catholicism, he was, upon the accession of King James, dismissed not only from the Privy Council but also as Dean of the Chapels Royal. He was later suspended from the exercise of all episcopal functions. He remained, however, a trusted friend and adviser of both Princess Mary after her marriage to Prince William of Orange and to Princess Anne, whose devotion to the Anglican Church was as deep and unwavering as Henry Compton's. She was comforted by the belief that her dear friend Sarah Churchill, 'Mrs Freeman', was also a convinced Protestant and that Lord Churchill was one too.

'I believe that he will always obey the King in all things that are consistent with his religion,' she told her sister Mary. 'Yet rather than change that, I daresay he will lose all his places and all that he has.' Churchill himself assured Prince William of Orange that this was, indeed, so: 'My places and the King's favour,' he wrote to him, 'I set at nought, in comparison of being true to my religion. In all things but this the King may command me.'

Princess Anne stood firm in resisting her father's continued attempts to convert her to Catholicism; and it was evidently with the Churchills' encouragement that she sought his permission to go to The Hague, ostensibly to see her sister, in reality to escape her father's influence.

The French ambassador in London, the well-informed Paul Barillon, reported to Versailles:

Princess Anne has strongly pressed the King to allow her to go [to The Hague] but he has bluntly refused . . . Once she was there she would have been prevented from coming back and the Protestant party would have been strengthened by the union of [herself and her sister Mary], the lawful heirs to the Crown, who could then make joint declarations against the whole Catholic movement. King James is suspicious that Churchill has been involved in proposing such a journey and that his wife, Princess Anne's favourite companion, has awakened her ambition.

Princess Anne herself wrote to her sister to tell her how grieved she was that their father had refused her permission to go to The Hague. She blamed the influence which was exercised over the King by that

very ill man [the devious Secretary of State] Lord Sunderland who is going on so fiercely for the interests of the Papists . . . Everybody knows how this man turned backwards and forwards in the late King's time . . . He is perpetually with the priests, and stirs up the King to do things faster than I believe he would of himself . . . I believe in a little while no Protestant will be able to live here . . . I had not your letter by Mr Dykevelt [Prince William's trusted Dutch envoy] till last week, but I have never ventured to speak to him . . . So I have asked Lord Churchill (who is one that I can trust, and I am sure is a very honest man and a good Protestant) to speak to Mr Dykevelt for me . . . for one dares not write anything by the post . . . Pray don't let anybody see this, nor don't speak of it . . . pray burn it.

Day by day, in the spring and early summer of 1688, the atmosphere at Princess Anne's house, the Cockpit, adjoining the Palace of Whitehall, grew more and more tense as emissaries came and went, people spoke in whispers and rumours were spread of conspiracies being formed to overthrow the King, who was said to be bringing large numbers of Irish troops into England and perhaps French troops too. There were rumours that Thomas Osborne, Earl of Danby, and the Whig leaders, Devonshire and Shrewsbury, were preparing to send a message to Holland inviting Prince William to come over to save the country from its Catholic monarch, whose wife, on 10 June, added a provocative challenge to his enemies by giving birth to a son whose right to the throne now took precedence over his daughters', but whose premature appearance in the world was widely supposed to have been the culmination of a plot: the child, so many were inclined to believe, was an impostor brought into the Queen's bed in a warming-pan.

Shortly before the appearance of this child, christened James Francis Edward in the presence of an assembly of persons mostly Catholic, the King had issued a Declaration of Indulgence relaxing the penal laws against Roman Catholics and, for good measure, Nonconformists, and requiring that the declaration should be read out in all the country's churches.

The Archbishop of Canterbury, William Sancroft, and six other bishops lodged a protest with the King, while few parsons were prepared to obey his order. James accordingly decreed that the recalcitrant bishops should all be put on trial for seditious libel and, in the meantime, he had them committed to the Tower of London. When they were brought out and taken downriver to court, immense crowds gathered to cheer them on their way.

On the evening of their acquittal, a party of men now ready for action met at Lord Shrewsbury's house to sign an invitation to Prince William to come over to England to take King James's place. As well as Shrewsbury himself, who, having put his signature to the document, mortgaged his estates for £40,000 and sailed to join Prince William in Holland, and Admiral Arthur Herbert, who, disguised as an ordinary seaman, also left for The Hague, the other signatories were Danby and Devonshire, Edward Russell, later Earl of Orford, Henry Sidney, later Earl of Romney, Lord Lumley, whose troop of horse had captured the Duke of Monmouth in 1685, and Bishop Compton. Devonshire immediately set about raising a regiment of cavalry from his tenants in Derbyshire; Danby left to raise men in the north; and Compton left London for Yorkshire with the excuse that he was going to visit his sisters.

Lord Churchill's signature did not appear on the invitation dispatched in cypher to Prince William; but on 4 August he wrote a letter to him and did so *en clair*:

Mr Sidney [Prince William's principal English contact at The Hague] will lett you know how I intend to behave my selfe. I think it is what I owe to God and my Country. My honor I take leave to put into your Royalle hiness hands, in which I think itt safe. If you think there is annything else that I ought to do you have but to command me and I shall pay an entier obedience to itt, being resolved to dye in that Religgion that it has pleased god to give you both the will and power to protect.

As it became clear that King James was being abandoned by so many of those who had formerly served him, his chief minister, the Earl of Sunderland, that recent convert to Catholicism, and Lord Jeffreys, his Lord Chancellor, both urged him to make concessions. But by the end of that summer it was already too late.

Towards the end of October, Prince William set sail for England beneath a flag embroidered with the words 'I will maintain the Protestant religion and the liberties of England'. His army, protected by sixty warships, contained Swedish, Danish and Prussian soldiers as well as Dutch, English, Scottish and Huguenots who had been expelled from France by the revocation of the Edict of Nantes, the charter of 1598 granting civil and religious liberties to Protestants. Stormy weather tossed the ships back on to the Dutch coast, a circumstance attributed by King James to the hand of God; and it was not until 5 November that Prince William was able to disembark his men in Torbay on the Devonshire coast. From there, taking with him a printing press, he marched to Exeter, while the King, suffering from a severe nosebleed on the way, brought his army to Salisbury.

In this army Lord Churchill was promoted to lieutenant-general; but, as in the Monmouth rebellion, the Frenchman Lord Feversham was commander-in-chief. Few of its officers were eager to fight, certainly Churchill was not; and several others were looking for an opportunity to go over to the enemy, following the example of Lord Cornbury, eldest son of Lord Clarendon, and cousin of Princess Anne, an officer in the Royal Dragoons, who had already deserted with some 200 of his men.

On 18 November, the day after her father set off from Windsor to join his army at Salisbury, Princess Anne wrote to her brother-in-law, Prince William, to tell him that she wished for his 'good success in this so just an undertaking'. Her husband, she added, would 'soon be with him' and she was sure he would 'do all the service' that lay in his power.

He went yesterday with the King towards Salisbury, intending to go from thence to you as soon as his friends thought it proper. I am not yet certain if I shall continue here [the Cockpit], or move into the City. That shall depend on the advice my friends will give me; but wherever I am, I shall be ready to show you how very much I am your humble servant.

Most of those who rode with the King for his army's camp at Salisbury had, like Prince George, decided to desert him when it seemed to them that the right time to do so had come. Among them was the King's nephew, the Duke of Grafton, second son of Charles II by Barbara Villiers, who commanded a regiment of Guards, and Lord Churchill, who, like Grafton, still protested that he would serve the King with the last drop of his blood. His descendant and biographer, Sir Winston Churchill, maintained that this undertaking was intended to refer only to 'defence of the King's person; not of his power, nor still less of his policy', and that

such equivocations were inevitable and common. They were the symptoms of violent times. A vast repudiation of allegiance united Englishmen of every rank and party. Those who, like Churchill, stood nearest the King until they quitted him had no other choice. But not often was treason less deceitfully veiled.

Churchill was reported to have been behaving lately quite without his usual diplomatic circumspection. He was said to have 'lolled out his tongue' at a review of the King's army in Hyde Park and to have been seen at Windsor in 'the greatest transports of joy imaginable' on hearing of Cornbury's desertion, even skipping along the castle gallery, hand in hand with his friend Sidney Godolphin. Listening to such stories, the King contemplated having Churchill arrested, while Lord Feversham positively urged his arrest. But

so many were involved, so near, so intimate, so long-trusted and proved so faithful, that the unhappy sovereign knew not where to begin, nor, if he began, where to stop. On all sides his narrow circle of Papists, Irish and Frenchmen encountered whisperings, averted eyes, even cold shoulders and hostile looks. The King hesitated, delayed, put the matter off until the morrow.

A council of war was held on the evening of 23 November. The King asked whether the army should advance towards the enemy or retreat. Grafton was for an advance, so was Churchill, no doubt calculating that an advance would bring him nearer to Prince William's camp. Feversham, however, was in favour of retreat. The King's army, some 25,000 men strong, was far larger than Prince William's; but it was shot through with uncertainty as to the justice of King James's cause and many of its officers were of very doubtful loyalty, a number of them urged to defection by Churchill himself.*

★ 'The central figure in the military conspiracy was John Churchill with his contacts in the army, the navy and the court, and with the solidly Protestant Princess Anne. By 4 August 1688 Churchill was definitely committed to the Orangist cause and he began to organize the Anglican Tory plotters at the court and in the army together with the small group of active Whigs and republicans' (Childs, *The Army, James II and the Glorious Revolution*, 148–9).

When the council was over, Churchill and Grafton, accompanied by some 400 officers and men, stole out of the King's camp and rode the fifty-odd miles to Crewkerne, a short distance from Prince William's camp at Axminster. Churchill left behind him a letter of apology, excuse and self-justification addressed to the King, from whose service he, and many other officers with whom he had been in contact, had decided to depart several months before.

My dutiful behaviour to Your Majesty in the worst of times . . . may not be sufficient to incline you to a charitable interpretation of my actions, yet I hope the great advantage I enjoy under Your Majesty, which I own I can never expect in any other change of government, may reasonably convince Your Majesty and the world that I am activated by a higher principle, when I offer that violence to my inclinations and interest as to desert Your Majesty at a time when your affairs seem to challenge the strictest obedience from all your subjects, much more from one who lies under the greatest personal obligation to Your Majesty. This, sir, could proceed from nothing but the inviolable dictates of my conscience, and a necessary concern for my religion . . . I will alway with the hazard of my life and fortune (so much Your Majesty's due) endeavour to preserve your royal person and lawful rights, with all the tender concerns and dutiful respect that becomes, sir, Your Majesty's most dutiful and most obliged subject and servant, Churchill.

A week or so later, in the George Inn at Salisbury, he put the matter more succinctly in conversation with Lord Clarendon. He would never have left King James, he said, 'but that he saw our religion and country were in danger of being destroyed'.*

* The Duchess of Marlborough was to state in her will that she was 'particularly anxious' that the authors whom she had commissioned to write her husband's biography should point out in their book that the Duke left James II 'with great regret' because he would do nothing to help 'settle popery' upon the nation (Reid, John and Sarah, Duke and Duchess of Marlborough, 1650–1744, 478).

8

THE FLIGHT OF THE KING

*'God help me! Even my children
have forsaken me.'*

The flight of Lord Churchill from the King's camp, and that of those officers whose defection he had organized, was followed by the flight of his wife and Princess Anne from the Cockpit. King James had sent orders for Lady Churchill's arrest, but the Princess had prevailed upon her stepmother, the Queen, to have the arrest delayed until the following morning; and in the night the two young women, accompanied by Lady Harding, a Lady of the Bedchamber, and a maid, fled from the house, the Princess, in Sarah Churchill's words, being ready 'to jump out of the window rather than face her father', and fearful of being shipped over to France. They hurried down a staircase which had been constructed a few weeks earlier to provide an escape route from the house in such an emergency as this, and met by arrangement Bishop Compton, who had recently returned to London, the Bishop's sturdy gardener and the Earl of Dorset, Compton's nephew, who offered his house, Copt Hall in Essex, as a temporary retreat. The fugitives then rushed to Charing Cross, the Princess losing one of her shoes in the mud which spattered the street, and made their way by carriage to the Bishop's official residence, London House, in Aldersgate Street. With an escort of forty horsemen, they rode to Epping Forest, and from there to Nottingham.

Here they were greeted by crowds of cheering people and by the Earl of Devonshire, who offered Bishop Compton 200 men to escort him back to Oxford. As a former army officer, Compton took command of this escort and, in full military uniform and bearing a naked sword, he marched south for Oxford and thence to London. Here Princess Anne's flight had by now been discovered by one of her bedchamber women, who, 'upon going into Her Highness's chamber to call her & receiving no answer to her call . . . opened [the bed curtains] and found the Princess gone & the bed cold, with all her yesterday's cloaths even to her stockings & shoes left behind'.

The Princess and Lady Churchill were entertained in Nottingham at a splendid banquet given for them by the Earl of Devonshire. One of the servitors at this meal was Colley Cibber, the future playwright, then an eighteen-year-old volunteer in the dragoons, who confessed that he could not take his eyes off Sarah Churchill:

If so clear an emanation of beauty, such a commanding aspect of grace, struck me into a regard that had something softer than the most profound respect in it, I cannot see why I may not without offence remember it; such beauty, like the sun, must sometimes lose its power to choose, and shine into equal warmth the peasant and the courtier.

The King had by now made his way back to London in despair. 'God help me!' he exclaimed. 'Even my children have forsaken me.' There was talk of a negotiated settlement with the Prince of Orange, who had, in fact, no wish to discuss a treaty, and was only too thankful that he would not now have to risk much of the support he enjoyed by fighting on English soil with a largely foreign army. Nor had King James any desire to endeavour to reach a compromise with his Protestant son-in-law: he would make sure that his wife and little son got away to France and then he would follow them.

He did so in the early hours of the morning of 11 December, throwing the Great Seal into the Thames on his way to the coast. Near the mouth of the river he managed to climb aboard a ship, but, discovered there, he was mistaken for a Jesuit endeavouring to escape to France. He was beaten, dragged back to land by his captors and held in the pound at Sheerness. Here the Earl of Ailesbury, one of his Gentlemen of the Bedchamber, found him and, impeded by his high jackboots, failed in his attempt to fall to his knees before him. But, by holding on to the table, he was later able to kneel to serve his royal master with a meagre meal. From time to time other members of the King's household appeared, followed by a troop of Life Guards.

Ailesbury succeeded in persuading the King to return with him to London. But he could not induce him to remain there; and, given further proofs of the impossibility of remaining in England, of which Prince William was now the indubitable master, the King felt compelled to ride back under escort to the Kentish coast and left England, never to return. Soon afterwards the French ambassador also left for the Continent, expelled from London on Prince William's orders.

On hearing of her father's flight, Princess Anne 'seemed not at all moved', according to her uncle Lord Clarendon, 'but called for cards and was as merry as she used to be . . . To emphasize their political sympathies she and her ladies dressed themselves in orange.'

Lord Churchill was careful not to commit himself when arguments now raged as to whether Prince William should be declared Regent or King, King in his own right or joint sovereign with his wife, or whether or not Mary should inherit her father's throne with Prince William as Consort. Prince William cut through these arguments by declaring that in no circumstances would he be 'his wife's gentleman-usher'.

When, however, it was at length agreed that Prince William and Princess Mary should be joint sovereigns, Lord Churchill supported this decision and suggested to his wife that she have a word with Princess Anne and prevail upon her to give her consent to this arrangement.

Well as Churchill and Prince William had got on when they had discussed military matters in Holland, there was a wariness in the Prince's nature which led him to entertain reservations about the man whose desertion of King James had so appreciably helped his own progress to the throne. When Lord Halifax had suggested to him that Churchill's influence would be useful in persuading Princess Anne to agree that she should surrender her right to succeed to the throne in the event of her sister Mary's death, Prince William snapped, 'Lord Churchill and Lady Churchill could not govern [me] nor [my] wife as they [do] the Prince and Princess of Denmark.'

However, Prince William could not but recognize Churchill's

qualities as a soldier and how much help he was likely to be able to offer in the mission which was ever in the forefront of his mind – the forthcoming war against France, a crusade upon which he had set his heart and the principal reason why he had sought the English throne, as a means of ensuring the country's support in the anti-French League of Augsburg of 1686.

Churchill was, accordingly, confirmed in his rank of lieutenant-general and was at the same time entrusted with the task of reconstructing the British army, a delegation of responsibility which irked the Graf von Schomberg, the German soldier of fortune who had been the Prince of Orange's second-in-command in the recent invasion and who was said to have commented contemptuously – and erroneously – upon Churchill's desertion that the man was the first lieutenant-general ever known to have 'deserted his colours'.

While bestowing honours and appointments on his Dutch friends, such as those of Groom of the Stole and First Gentleman of the Bedchamber on Hans Bentinck, later Earl of Portland, the Prince of Orange felt obliged also to honour Lord Churchill, who, when the Prince and his wife were crowned King William III and Queen Mary II in Westminster Abbey on 11 April 1689, was created an earl. He chose to be Earl of Marlborough, the title held by his grandmother's brother-in-law, James Ley, first Earl of Marlborough, a Lord Chief Justice and Lord High Treasurer whose grandson, the third Earl, had been killed at sea in 1665, and whose title had become extinct. The elevation of Lord Marlborough in the peerage provoked King James's friends and supporters to spread all manner of stories about the duplicitous man who, they said, had for personal gain so disgracefully betrayed his trust. It was alleged that he had had it in mind to capture James and hand him over to William, even that he intended to assassinate him. The charge of desertion of a master who had trusted him was, at least, never to be forgotten by many of his contemporaries, since Marlborough was not a man for whom excuses were readily found. He aroused affection in some intimate friends; but his sincerity was widely suspected, his success resented, his discretion condemned as secretiveness, his charm as spurious, his parsimony as avarice.

9

EARLY COMMANDS

*'. . . he displayed greater military capacity than do
most generals after a long series of wars.'*

Less than six months after the departure of James Stuart for the
Continent, England declared war on France. A powerful coalition
had been built up to oppose the ambitions of Louis XIV: Spaniards,
Dutch, Swedes, Prussians, North Germans and soldiers from the
Austrian Empire were all now in arms and on the march. The English
contingent, which had been entrusted to Lord Marlborough, were
in that part of the allied army commanded by the sixty-nine-year-old
Prince of Waldeck.

Waldeck was far from satisfied with his British troops, who were
notorious for looting whenever they had the opportunity to do so.
'The English,' so he said, 'suffer from sickness, slackness, wretched
clothing and the worst of shoes . . . Marlbrouck has much trouble
with them . . . But he is doing his best.' Indeed, having been well
drilled and disciplined and – as Marlborough was always to take
trouble to ensure – well fed and regularly paid, they acquitted
themselves well when, on 25 August 1689, they were led into action
against the French under Marshal d'Humières at the walled town of
Walcourt in the Spanish Netherlands. In the words of Waldeck's
reports they 'behaved themselves very well . . . and showed great
courage'. As for 'Monsieur Milord Marlbrouck', who had once again
displayed great bravery in leading a cavalry charge, 'despite his youth'
– he was thirty-nine – 'he displayed greater military capacity than do
most generals after a long series of wars . . . He is assuredly one of
the most gallant men I know.' Writing to congratulate Marlborough,
King William was generous in his praise:

8

I am happy that my troops behaved so well in the affair of Walcourt. It is to you that this advantage is principally owing. You will please accordingly accept my thanks and rest assured that your conduct will induce me to confer on you still further marks of my esteem and friendship on which you may always rely.

Soon after his return to England, Marlborough was appointed a member of a council of nine to advise Queen Mary while her husband left for Ireland, where her father, the former King James II, had been welcomed as a deliverer from the Protestant English and had established himself in Dublin in command of a Catholic army of some hundred thousand men supplied with French money and arms. On the banks of the river Boyne, north of Dublin, on 1 July 1690, King William forced King James's army to retreat and James himself to sail back to France.

A few weeks later Marlborough himself left for Ireland, where, against the advice of his fellow members of the council as well as of King William's Dutch advisers, he obtained permission from the King to attempt to seize the ports of Cork and Kinsale, through which the forces of King James's supporters, known as Jacobites, were supplied by France.

Marlborough hoped that in Ireland, if not yet on the Continent, he would be given an independent command. But in this he was again to be disappointed, for soon afterwards William appointed his Dutch friend, Godert de Ginkel, later to be created Earl of Athlone, commander-in-chief in Ireland, giving orders that Ginkel should send 5,000 men to serve under Marlborough at Cork. Marlborough asked for English troops, but instead Ginkel sent Dutchmen, Danes and French Huguenots under command of the Duke of Württemberg, who, because of his social rank, demanded to direct the whole operation.

Marlborough produced his commission signed by the Queen. The Duke lost his temper, but in the end agreed to a suggestion that the two generals should exercise the command at Cork on alternate days. On the morning of 1 October 1690, the assaulting forces plunged into the estuary at low tide and, as their guns bombarded a breach in the town wall, waded under heavy fire towards the counterscarp. With them, serving as a volunteer and struggling through water up to his armpits, was Charles II's son, the Duke of Grafton, who was mortally wounded by a musket ball that struck him in the chest and smashed two of his ribs. The Irish governor, despairing of being able to resist an assault, raised a white flag; Marlborough's troops entered the town, and 4,000 Irish soldiers surrendered.

At the end of the month, Kinsale, seventeen miles to the south, was also taken; and, leaving his younger brother, Charles Churchill, now a colonel in the 1st Foot, as governor there, Marlborough returned to England, having achieved all that he had undertaken to do. 'No officer living,' King William was reported to have said, 'who has seen so little service as my Lord Marlborough is so fit for great commands.'

Yet the King was still not disposed fully to trust Lord Marlborough, nor any of those men who had defected from King James. Nor was he ready to admit Marlborough to his intimate circle. When in attendance, Marlborough still stood attentively behind His Majesty's chair; but William never spoke to him, dismissing him before the meal was over. Indeed, the 'low Dutch bear', as he was known to the ladies, whom he all but ignored, still rarely spoke at mealtimes to anyone, even to such of those Dutch friends who were invited to sit with him, eating greedily, once annoying his sister-in-law, Princess Anne, by helping himself to an entire dish of new peas without offering her a single one. Only when he had finished eating and had left the room did he begin to talk and then most often, in the words of his handsome page and constant companion, Arnold Joost van Keppel, whom he created Earl of Albemarle, he 'talked enough over his bottle'.

He never spoke easily to Marlborough, whose qualities as a soldier he was prepared to recognize but whose career he was loath to advance, considering the man, as he told Lord Halifax, 'very assuming'. There was talk of Marlborough being raised to a dukedom, of his being created a Knight of the Garter. But nothing came of these rumours; and, while he felt he could not yet afford to maintain the style of a duke, Marlborough would have liked the Garter. He would also have liked to be appointed Master-General of the Ordnance, a lucrative position vacant since the death of Graf von Schomberg, who had been killed at the battle of the Boyne. But this appointment went to Henry Sidney, the Earl of Leicester's son, later Earl of Romney, a colonel in the Foot Guards who had been with the King at the Boyne but had little experience of military command, while Ginkel remained in command of the troops in Ireland, and the Prince of Waldeck, even though he had been decisively beaten by the French under the duc de Luxembourg at the battle of Fleurus in July 1690, was still in command of the army on the Continent.

Marlborough, however, was given the difficult and less responsible task of recruiting more soldiers in England, an employment made all the more difficult by what he described in a letter to the King as the interference and 'unreasonable way of proceeding' of the Lord President of the Council, Thomas Osborne, Earl of Danby, now Marquess of Carmarthen, who was 'very ignorant in what is fit for an officer, both as to recruits and everything else as to a soldier'.

Marlborough was also required to investigate the records and services of officers, confirming the commissions of those considered loyal to the new regime, and purging the army of the incompetent, the unreliable and the untrustworthy, a responsibility which was as well calculated to increase the growing number of the new Earl's enemies as it was, so Lord Ailesbury said, 'vastly' to increase Marlborough's fortune by means of the money to be earned from officers willing to pay for commissions and promotions, and by the exaction of douceurs and the acceptance of bribes.

Disappointed in not being appointed Master-General of the Ordnance, Marlborough was thankful to get away from England to the Continent to serve in that summer of 1691 in an army led by the King himself. It was, however, to be a short, frustrating campaign. The French, still commanded by Luxembourg, were in too strong a position before Mons to justify an attack; and so the two armies marched and countermarched opposite and beside each other in that almost choreographic manner which military convention then dictated, warfare being largely a matter of manoeuvre, and generals, before Marlborough questioned and derided the practice, being not so much intent upon bringing an enemy to decisive action as to perform movements in order to avoid it. Arguing vigorously for a standing army, Daniel Defoe wrote in 1697:

Now 'tis frequent to have armies of fifty thousand men of a side stand at bay within view of one another, and to spend a whole campaign in dodging, or as 'tis genteely call'd, observing one another, and then march off into winter-quarters . . . I grant that this way of making war spends generally more money and less blood than former wars did; but then it spins out wars to a greater length.

As well as a matter of manoeuvre, warfare was also one of sieges; and any enemy fighting France in the late seventeenth and early eighteenth centuries had to contend with a large number of strongly fortified towns, the defences of which had been constructed on lines designed by a military engineer of genius, Marshal Sébastien Le Prestre de Vauban, who revolutionized not only the science of defensive fortification but also the aggressive art of siege-craft.

Because of the difficulties now encountered in besieging fortresses, war was becoming an increasingly complex business. It was also becoming a more hazardous enterprise because of the growing efficiency of weapons, of the destructive power of cannon and mortars, and of muskets, no longer matchlock muskets, the fuses of which were quite likely to be extinguished by rain or strong wind, but flintlock muskets with a rate of fire almost twice that of the old matchlocks, and with an effective range of up to 100 yards. For combat at close quarters, a bayonet was fixed to the socket of the musket. This enabled the soldier to fire his weapon as well as stab and jab with it, which had not been possible in the days when the old plug bayonet had been fixed into the matchlock's muzzle.*

Recruiting able-bodied and reliable men who could be trained to use their weapons with skill, and to submit to harsh discipline for little material reward, was a perennial problem. Pay of eightpence a

---

* 'The "bayonet" (named after the putative place of invention, Bayonne) is mentioned by the French general de Puységur as having been first used in 1647, and it was first officially recognized in the French army in 1671. In the British service it was issued to the Tangier Regiment in 1663, to new dragoon regiments at home in 1672, and as a regular issue to grenadiers and fusiliers after 1678. The early "plug" bayonets (plugged into the musket muzzle) had the serious fault that once they were fixed, the musket could not be fired. After 1697 the socket bayonet permitted ease of fixing and unfixing and a firm and rigid lock on the musket. By 1705 the pike was obsolete' (Barnett, *Britain and Her Army, 1509–1970*, 128).

day subject to all manner of deductions was little inducement. Barracks were squalid, billets unwelcoming, householders and innkeepers hostile, punishments savage. A soldier rarely gained the respect that a sailor did.

As the Duke of Wellington said of the 'common soldiers' of a later generation, they were generally considered to be 'the scum of the earth'. 'None but the worst description of men' entered the service, the Duke maintained. 'People talk of their enlisting from their fine military feeling – all stuff – no such thing. Some of our men enlist from having got bastard children – some for minor offences – many more for drink. You can hardly believe such a set brought together.' They were 'constantly quitting their ranks in search of plunder'. It was 'really wonderful', Wellington added, that, considering the material upon which their officers had to work, they were turned into the 'fine fellows' they became.

To enlist men into the army of Marlborough's time, bounties had to be raised from £2 a head in 1703 to £5 a head in 1708; men with criminal records were increasingly drafted into the ranks, as were vagrants, debtors, the hungry unemployed and those gullible youths who were persuaded to join the colours by tricks practised and inducements offered by recruiting sergeants and officers like Sergeant Kite and Captain Plume in the 1706 play *The Recruiting Officer*, by the Irish dramatist George Farquhar. Himself an officer in Lord Orrery's regiment, Farquhar had been on recruiting service in Lichfield and Shrewsbury before being obliged to sell his commission when deeply in debt.

As with the ranks, among whom there was an essential leavening of responsible, brave and well-disciplined men, the officers, too, were of extremely variable quality. There were highly professional men among them, men dedicated to their profession and country; and there were God-fearing, even puritanical, men like Lieutenant-Colonel John Blackadder of the Cameronians.

Yet there were more than a few colonels who looked upon their regiments as a means of making a good profit from the sums they received for equipping them; there were junior officers who purchased commissions as investments to be sold and exchanged at a profit, and put in an appearance with their men as rarely as possible, leaving discipline, training and welfare in the hands of sergeants; and there were also those who, as one officer put it, 'instead of treating their men with GOOD NATURE, use them with CONTEMPT and CRUELTY; by which those gentlemen often meet their FATE in the day of battle from their own men'.

Growing weary of the manoeuvring and parade which characterized the campaign of 1691, King William withdrew from Hainaut by way of Fleurus, where the bones of the soldiers slain in the battle fought there in the summer before still lay unburied on the ground.

As far as Marlborough was concerned, there was scarcely an incident in this brief campaign worth recording, although one day he did suddenly wheel his troops about and lead a wholly successful attack upon the enemy rearguard, which was sent scampering off in all directions, leaving many dead or dying. The commander of the French cavalry in this short engagement was the vain, gasconading and highly talented thirty-eight-year-old Claude-Louis-Hector Villars. In the years to come he and Marlborough were repeatedly to face each other again.

Driven from Ireland, James, the 'King across the Water', lived on in exile with his friends and family at Saint-Germain-en-Laye near Paris. Hoping for French help in restoring him to his lost throne, he was encouraged by exaggerated reports of the extent of his support in England and of the numbers of those men of influence in London who were now regretting their betrayal of him, and their acceptance of the dour and unresponsive Dutchman who had taken his place. Among these men of influence, so James's friends claimed, was the Earl of Marlborough, with whom Jacobite agents were in touch.

It was undoubtedly the case that Marlborough was anxious to obtain the exiled King's pardon for deserting him in 1688, a pardon essential to the success of his future career in the not altogether unlikely event of James being restored to the throne. This and future contacts with the Jacobites and their agents were clearly designed to ensure that, whatever happened, he should not find himself a ruined man, having chosen the losing side.

King William was well aware of these contacts with the court at Saint-Germain and presumed that Marlborough's overtures were couched in such terms – ambivalent, ambiguous, always stopping short of direct undertakings – as to be seen more in the nature of insurance policies than as commitments.*

* In December, however, he went rather further than this, persuading Princess Anne to write a contrite letter to her father apologizing for her past conduct towards him, making her 'humble submission', and desiring 'to deserve and receive his pardon'.

'I have been very desirous of some safe opportunity to make you a sincere and humble offer of my duty and submission to you,' the Princess accordingly wrote, 'and to beg that you will be assured that I am both truly concerned for the misfortune of your condition and sensible, as I ought to be, of my own unhappiness. As to what you may think I have contributed to it, if wishes could recall what is past, I had long since redeemed my fault. I am sensible it would have been a great relief to me if I could have found the means to acquaint you earlier with my repentant thoughts, but I hope they may find the advantage of coming late, of being less suspected of insincerity than perhaps they would have been at any time before' (Brown (ed.), *The Letters and Diplomatic Instructions of Queen Anne*, 52).

10

DISGRACE

*'The Lord of Marboro . . . who being intirely advanced by
K James . . . Is now disgraced; and by none pittied . . .'*

Towards the end of October 1691, Lord Marlborough returned
from the Continent in King William's coach, which overturned on
Shooters Hill, throwing both him and the King as well as the King's
Dutch confidant, Hans Willem Bentinck, now Earl of Portland, into
the road. Marlborough, stunned by the crash, declared that his neck
was broken, an announcement which elicited from the King the dry
comment that if it were he would not be able to communicate the
fact.

Although his coach was greeted by cheering crowds when at last
it reached London, King William was by now gradually losing what
little popularity with the general public he had ever enjoyed. His use
of English troops and English money in his crusade against the
French, while endorsed by Parliament, which voted generous supplies for the prosecution of the war, was widely condemned, while
the favours and honours he bestowed upon his Dutch companions
aroused deep jealousy.*

Lord Marlborough, usually so discreet and calculating, so charming, even bland in manner, did not trouble to hide his dissatisfaction
with the slow progress of his career, the annoyance he endured when
foreigners of lesser talents were preferred to himself, when foreign
generals were placed in command of British troops. He spoke openly

---

* In 1691 only two out of the six lieutenant-generals in the army were English; so
were two out of five major-generals (Ogg, *England in the Reigns of James II and
William III*, 379).

of his discontent, of the resentment aroused by the King's predilection for Dutchmen, of the general unworthiness of those favoured, in particular that 'wooden fellow', the widely disliked, taciturn and graceless Earl of Portland. He condemned the expense of maintaining the King's Dutch guards, hinting that His Majesty's 'unpopular conduct' might lead to disaster, pronouncing, so Robert Harley, Member of Parliament for New Radnor, heard, that King William 'had not virtue enough to value high ends or courage to punish his enemies', making it clear – when it was suggested that he should accompany the King as a kind of military secretary on the following year's campaign in Flanders rather than as commander of the British troops – that he would rather stay at home.

He used his influence in Parliament, as well as in the army, to have the dissatisfaction aroused by the King's indulgence of foreigners brought forward as a national grievance; and, well aware of this, the King in turn began to speak openly of his distrust of Marlborough. One day at court, the Elector of Brandenburg's envoy in London overheard him remark that he had been treated 'so infamously by Marlborough that, had he not been a King, he would have felt it necessary' to challenge him to a duel.

More worrying to the King than Marlborough's antagonism to his foreign friends was the man's influence – and, even more so, the influence of Lady Churchill – over Princess Anne. Certainly, Princess Anne remained as close as ever to Lord Marlborough, whom she greatly admired, and to Lady Marlborough, whom she deeply loved. She also loved her dull, kindly husband, Prince George, and much resented the contemptuous manner in which the King treated him, reluctantly allowing him to accompany him when campaigning on the Continent but giving him little to do, and taking such scant notice of him when they were in England, so Lady Marlborough said, that Prince George might just as well have been a page of the backstairs. Admittedly the Prince had been rewarded for his having joined William at Sherborne within a few days of his landing in England by being created Earl of Kendal and Duke of Cumberland; but that had been the only recompense he received, and when in August 1691 he had made a vain request that Lord Marlborough should be honoured with the Order of the Garter for his services to the country, the Prince was able to remind the King that this was the only favour that he had ever asked of him.

That year, accepting the fact that the King would never allow him to enjoy any responsibility in the army, the Prince sought permission to go to sea as an ordinary seaman. The King made no reply to this request; and, taking silence for consent, the Prince, in Lady Marlborough's words, 'prepared his equipage and sent everything aboard'. But it afterwards appeared that the King, who was on the point of leaving for Flanders, 'had left orders with the Queen that she should neither suffer the Prince to go to sea nor yet forbid him to go, if she could so contrive matters as to make his staying at home his own choice'. Lady Marlborough, who was asked to persuade Prince George to say that he had changed his mind at the last minute about going to sea, flatly refused to do so.

Early the following January, after the King's return from the Continent, the Queen summoned Princess Anne to her presence and told her that her friend, Sarah Marlborough, must be dismissed from her service.

There had already been sharp and bitter disagreements over money between the Queen on the one hand, and her sister and Lady Marlborough on the other. 'The quarrel,' Robert Harley had reported in February 1691, 'is great between the Cockpit and Kensington.' Princess Anne, supported by Sarah, had considered that she should receive £70,000 a year for the maintenance of her household and that this sum should be granted by Parliament rather than by her sister and the King. Eventually a sum of £50,000, to be paid by a parliamentary grant, was agreed upon; but by then the Queen and the Princess, supported by the Churchills, were scarcely upon speaking terms. Then there was trouble over the posts of two pages in Princess Anne's household which were sold for £1,200. The Queen insisted that the persons intended to occupy these posts were unsuitable and must not be allowed to fill them. Sarah was furious when she was obliged to repay her £800 commission.

Relations between the Cockpit and the Palace, already bad, were much exacerbated when Princess Anne refused to obey the Queen's demand that her dear friend Sarah should be dismissed. Although she was enduring the difficulties of one of her numerous pregnancies, the Princess stood her ground until her sister, having lost her temper, told her to leave the room.

The next day Lord Marlborough waited upon the King as usual in his office as Gentleman of the Bedchamber, passing his shirt with the accustomed due ceremony to His Majesty, who accepted it, as usual, in silence. Later that morning, at eleven o'clock, the Earl of Nottingham, Secretary of State, called upon Lord Marlborough to hand him an order from the Queen dismissing him from court and depriving him of all his offices, military as well as civil. No reason was given for the dismissal, which for several days was almost the only topic of conversation at court, and the principal cause of which, so his wife said, was 'the Court's dislike that any Body should have so much Interest' with Princess Anne as she herself, 'who would not implicitly obey every Command of the King and Queen. The Disgrace of my Lord Marlborough was, therefore, designed as a Step towards removing me from about her.'

Although there were renewed rumours that Marlborough had become involved in a plot to remove the King and Queen from the throne and to have Princess Anne declared Queen in their place, these were not taken seriously. The general belief at the time was that the King had told Nottingham that Marlborough had to be disgraced for fomenting discord in the army and being in highly compromising correspondence with the exiled King James at Saint-Germain, or, possibly, that Marlborough had let slip some secret military intelligence, which had by some means reached the French. Only three men had been let into this secret by the King, one of them Marlborough, who was asked if he had told anyone about it. 'Upon my honour, Sire,' replied Marlborough, 'I told it to nobody but my wife.' The King said, 'I did not tell it to mine.'

It was thought that Lady Marlborough had told her sister, Frances, whose second husband, the Duke of Tyrconnel, had recently died. The widowed Duchess was then living in France and the secret, so it was said, had thus got to Saint-Germain and thence to Paris and Versailles.

A rather more likely explanation, at least in some respects, was given in a report to Vienna by the Austrian envoy in London:

As Marlborough did not become Quartermaster-General after the taking of Kinsale, he first attempted to stir up the English people against the Government by complaints that all the higher army commands were reserved for foreigners . . . Secondly, he had publicly accused the King of ingratitude . . . Thirdly, Marlborough had tried, by means of his wife, who is the principal lady-in-waiting to the Princess of Denmark, to cause discord between the Queen and the Princess. Finally, what is more important, despite the fact that he had betrayed King James, he had endeavoured to seek that monarch's forgiveness.*

In his diary, John Evelyn expressed a commonly shared view of Marlborough's disgrace:

The Lord of Marboro, L: Gen: of K Williams Army in England, Gent of Bedchamber, etc. dismissed from all his Charges Military and other; and given to divers others: for his excessive taking bribes and Covetousenesse and Extortion upon all occasions from his inferior officers: Note this was the Lord who being intirely advanced by K James, the merit of his father being the prostitution of his Daughter (this Lords sister) to that King: Is now disgraced; and by none pittied, being also the first who betrayed and forsooke his Master K: James, who advanced him from the son of Sir Wi[nston] Churchill.

While Marlborough himself made no recorded comment on his dismissal, his political associates, Lord Godolphin, the Lord Treasurer, and Lord Shrewsbury, Secretary of State, as well as Admiral Edward Russell, made it known that they sympathized with him and deprecated the King's ingratitude for past services.

Princess Anne was much upset, believing that her own quarrel with her sister, and her refusal to dismiss Lady Marlborough from her service, were responsible for the disgrace of the man who had always been kind to her. She stayed away from court for three weeks; but then she returned and, to her sister's profound annoyance, she took Lady Marlborough with her, a provocation which drew from

---

* The suspicions that Marlborough had been at least partly responsible for turning Princess Anne against her sister, and that he had serious Jacobite connections, were, indeed, contributory reasons for his disgrace, but the most serious misdemeanour in King William's eyes was his 'role in alienating the British officer corps from the Dutch and German generals' (Childs, *The British Army of William III, 1698–1702*, 63).

Queen Mary a long and angry letter, in which she declared that she 'had all the reason imaginable' to look upon her sister's bringing into her presence the wife of the man whom the King had so rightly punished as 'the strangest thing that ever was done'. The letter continued:

I tell you plainly Lady Marlborough must not continue with you in the circumstances [in which] her Lord is . . . I will end this with once more desiring you to consider the matter impartially and take time for it. I do not desire an answer presently [immediately], because I would not have you give a rash one. I shall come to your drawing-room tomorrow.

'I must fully own,' the Princess replied, 'that as I think that this proceeding can be for no other intent than to give me a very sensible mortification, so there is no misery that I cannot readily resolve to suffer rather than the thoughts of parting [with Lady Marlborough].'

As a response to this letter, the Lord Chamberlain was required to order the removal of Lady Marlborough from the Cockpit; and, by way of response to this command, Princess Anne asked the Duke of Somerset if she might move into Syon House for an indefinite period, and there, by now heavily pregnant, she took her entire household.

Having vainly asked the Duke of Somerset to remove her from Syon House, the King ordered the withdrawal of her guards and of the ceremonies formerly accorded to her as a Princess of England. Her friends were instructed not to visit her; and, when she left Syon House for Bath, the Lord Mayor of that city was told not to accompany her when she went to church.

Upon her return to Syon House, after the death of her baby, the Princess received a visit from her sister, who repeated her order that Lady Marlborough should be dismissed. She refused then and she refused later, begging her friend not to think of attempting to mend her relationship with the King and Queen by leaving her. 'Dear Mrs Freeman,' she wrote in one letter, 'I hope in Christ that you will never think more of leaving me for . . . nothing but death could ever make me part with you. For if it be possible, I am every day more and more yours.'

A CHARGE OF HIGH TREASON

'Yes, I must confess I had a paper in my pocket which I designed to put somewhere in the house.'

At a meeting of the King's Council, at the beginning of May 1692, discussion centred upon the report of 'a villainous conspiracy'. A man named Robert Young claimed that a compromising document in the form of a bond of association was to be found concealed in the house of Thomas Sprat, the witty, learned Bishop of Rochester and Fellow of the Royal Society. This document bound its signatories to work for the restoration of James II, to 'furnish him with a considerable sum of money for the support of his army', and to 'sieze upon the person of King William'.

As well as by Sprat, it was alleged to be signed by the Earl of Salisbury, Lord Cornbury, the former Archbishop of Canterbury, William Sancroft, and Lord Marlborough. What was not known at that time was that Robert Young, a bigamist and cheat who had passed himself off as a parson and was then held in Newgate Prison, was a forger of such consummate skill that Marlborough, when shown his forgeries, could scarcely tell the man's handwriting from his own. Having carefully transcribed the false signatures at the foot of the document, Young persuaded an accomplice, Stephen Blackhead, to gain entry to Bishop Sprat's house at Bromley under the pretence of delivering a letter from an imaginary doctor of divinity. Claiming to have great reverence for the entourage of a bishop, Blackhead persuaded the butler to show him his master's study, where he had intended placing the forged document among the papers on his desk; but, having failed to do this, he concealed it in a flowerpot he found in a disused parlour.

An initial search of the Bishop's house failed to recover the document; but these were alarming times: papers recently found on a captured ship revealed that an invasion force of 20,000 French soldiers and Irishmen were assembling around Cherbourg; and Admiral Russell, in command of the English fleet, was known to have been in touch with the Jacobites, as was Marlborough. Not knowing whom to trust and fearful of an invasion while so many British troops were out of the country, King William's Council acted hastily: three of its members, Devonshire, Bradford and Montagu, declined to sign the warrant on the flimsy evidence so far produced; but Marlborough was nevertheless arrested on a charge of high treason on 5 May 1692 and escorted to the Tower of London.*

The days passed and he remained in custody, while his wife was abandoned by nervous friends who had in the past 'lived in the family like near relations' but were now too frightened to visit her; and she herself, so a Dutch intelligence agent reported, could not appear in the street without being jeered at by the mob.

Marlborough was, at least, gratified to hear that the English navy had won a notable victory in the deep bay of La Hogue, ruining the enemy fleet in operations which lasted for six days and from which the French navy was not to recover until Marlborough's days as a soldier were over. He was also comforted by visits from Sarah, who had left Syon House for London, where she received further affectionate letters from Princess Anne beseeching her again not to leave her:

* There are several references in the Finch MSS in the Leicestershire and Rutland Record Office to the suspected Jacobite tendencies of Lord Marlborough (referred to by one of the Earl of Nottingham's correspondents as 'Lord Plausible'). In an affidavit endorsed by Nottingham in 1692, Richard Kingston, a former chaplain in ordinary to Charles II who became a political pamphleteer, deposed: 'Richard Kingston clerke maketh oath that being in company with the Earle of Marlborough a little after his lordship's releasment out of the Tower, his lordship in the hearing of this deponent uttered these words viz: that King William at his first coming into England promised to redress the grievances of the late reign, but being made a King he exercised a more arbitrary and tyrannical power than King James did; and therefore his government could not last long; for it was not to be endured any longer, but every good man ought to lay his helping hand to put an end to it. Ric. Kingston' (HMC report on Finch MSS, iv, 9 Nov. 1692).

Let me beg once more, for God's sake, that you would never mention parting more, no nor so much to think of it; and if you should ever leave me, be assured it would break your faithful Mrs Morley's heart . . . There is no misery I cannot readily resolve to suffer, rather than the thought of parting from you. And I do swear I would rather be torn to pieces than alter this my resolution . . . I swear I would live on bread & water between four walls, with dear Mrs Freeman without repining; for as long as you continue kind, nothing can ever be a real mortification to your faithful Mrs Morley, who wishes she may never enjoy a moment's happiness, in this world or the next, if ever she proves false to you . . . My dear Mrs Freeman was in so dismal a way when she went from hence, that I cannot forbear asking how she does, and if she has any hopes yet of Lord Marlborough's being soon at liberty. For God's sake have a care of your dear self, and give as little way to melancholy as you can.

By the time this last letter was written Lord Marlborough was, indeed, close to liberty.

Robert Young had dispatched his accomplice, Blackhead, back to Bromley to retrieve the forged paper from the flowerpot and had sent it on to the Secretary of State, Lord Sidney. A meeting of the Council was accordingly convened and Blackhead and Young were summoned to appear before it on 11 June. Questioned by the Earl of Nottingham, Blackhead gave hesitant and equivocal answers; but in the end, under Nottingham's persistent examination, he confessed to what he had done at Young's request. Bishop Sprat wrote a detailed account of the inquisition:

NOTTINGHAM: But what made you, when you were at Bromley, so earnestly desire of the Bishop's butler and his other servants that you might see the rooms in the house, especially his study?

BLACKHEAD: No, I do not remember that I desired to see the study. The house I might out of curiosity.

NOTTINGHAM: But here are some of the Bishop's servants without, who are ready to swear, that you pressed very often to get a sight of his study . . .

BLACKHEAD: I cannot deny that I did desire to see the Bishop's study . . .

NOTTINGHAM: What reason had you to be so importunate to see that or any of the other rooms? Had you any paper about you that you designed to drop or leave in any part of the Bishop's house?

Here Blackhead stopped as very loth to out with it; till divers of the lords urged him to tell the truth. At last he went on, though with much hesitancy.

BLACKHEAD: Yes, I must confess I had a paper in my pocket which I designed to put somewhere in the house.

NOTTINGHAM: What did you do with it?

BLACKHEAD: I did leave it in the parlour next the kitchen.

NOTTINGHAM: In what part of the parlour?

BLACKHEAD: In the flowerpot in the chimney.

NOTTINGHAM: Blackhead, what paper was it you left in the Bishop's chimney?

BLACKHEAD: It was the association.

NOTTINGHAM: Was it this paper here (*showing the association that lay upon the table*)?

BLACKHEAD: Yes, it was.

NOTTINGHAM: How came you by it? And who advised you to lodge it there?

BLACKHEAD: I had it from Mr Young and he advised me to leave it in the Bishop's house, as I did.

NOTTINGHAM: Did Young direct you to put it in the flowerpot in the parlour?

BLACKHEAD: Yes he did, and I put it there accordingly . . .

Young, who behaved throughout with 'a daring, unconcerned confidence', vehemently denied having given Blackhead such instructions; but no one believed him and the Earl of Danby observed, 'Young, you are the strangest creature that ever I heard of. Dost thou think we could imagine that the Bishop of Rochester would combine with this thy confederate to have an association written with his own hand to it and then laid it in his own house in a flowerpot there? which, if it had been found must have endangered his life; and we see it was the most remarkable good fortune to him that almost ever happened to any man, that it was not found there.'

Four days after this examination, Young having been returned to Newgate, Lord Marlborough brought his case before the court of the King's Bench on a writ of Habeas Corpus. He was successful in his plea; and, with Halifax and Shrewsbury acting as sureties, he was released on bail.

His return to his wife at Berkeley House, Piccadilly, where Princess

Anne was now living, was not, however, a very cheerful one. Three weeks before his younger son, Charles, had died shortly before his second birthday, not long after the death of a baby boy who lived but a very short time; his wife's continuing quarrel with her mistress's sister had temporarily soured his own relations with the Queen; and he was disturbed to hear that Robert Young, now back in Newgate, and intent upon revenge, had been found to be plotting with another accomplice to bring further charges against both him and Bishop Sprat.*

From abroad came dismal news: at Steenkirk on 3 August 1692, King William's army – the British contingent of which, formerly commanded by Marlborough, had by then been entrusted to a Dutch officer, the arrogant and less than competent Count of Solms-Braunfels – was badly mauled and forced to retreat. Less than a year later at Landen, in a bloody battle against the French, commanded by the duc de Luxembourg, King William lost a further 20,000 men.

When Sarah Churchill heard of these appalling losses, she could not but feel profoundly grateful that her husband was not serving in the King's army. Living 'very much at St Albans in these months,' she wrote, 'we had frequent news of Generals killed in the Wars, & I own as publick-spirited as I am, at this time I had rather have had the King of France Master of England, than have had [my husband] hazarded in Battles when so many Generals were killed . . . In this retired way we lived a great while.'

In June 1694 the allied forces suffered another repulse. For several months King William and his Council had been planning an attack on Brest, the French port in the Bay of Biscay. The enemy had soon got wind of the attack; and the defences of the place had been improved and greatly strengthened by Marshal Vauban, while the garrison had been reinforced by several thousands of both cavalry and coastguards.

---

* Young was prosecuted for perjury and sentenced to a further term of imprisonment in the King's Bench Prison, from which he escaped in 1698 to set himself up as a coiner. Tried at the Old Bailey for this offence, he was hanged at Tyburn on 19 April 1700, having confessed his forgeries in the 'Flowerpot Plot' of 1692.

The British naval forces were to be commanded by Admiral Russell, the army by General Thomas Tollemache, who was, after Marlborough, considered the most talented general in King William's service, and who had made himself a respected figure in the army by strongly supporting Marlborough's criticisms of the employment of so many foreign officers.

The attack took place in the first week in June 1694. The British ships and troops immediately came under extremely heavy fire from the French batteries; but Tollemache was determined to press ahead with the dangerous enterprise, declaring that the die was now cast and they could not in honour retreat. So, on the morning of 8 June, he led his troops ashore, only to be driven back across the sands by greatly superior forces. Most of Tollemache's men were killed or captured; he himself received a wound from which he was soon to die.

'I own to you,' King William wrote from Flanders to the Secretary of State, the Duke of Shrewsbury, on learning of this fiasco, 'that I did not suppose they would have made the attempt without having well reconnoitred the situation of the enemy . . . since they were well apprised of our intended attack.'

In writing of this defeat in his *History of England*, Lord Macaulay – who lost no opportunity of denigrating Marlborough and his motives – recorded that a letter implicated him in the disaster. This letter, the original of which does not survive, evidently by Marlborough and written in French, informed the enemy of the impending attack and assured him that 'no consideration ever could prevent the writer from informing him of all that he believed could be for his service'. 'Therefore,' the letter continued, 'you may make your own use of this intelligence which you may rely upon as exactly true.'* Ignoring the fact that the French had known of the projected attack long before Marlborough was supposed to have told King James about it, and pursuing Marlborough with what J. W. Croker,

---

* It has been contended that this letter may have been a forgery. It was discovered among the Nairne Papers which were published by Sir James Macpherson, the eighteenth-century antiquary, the authenticity of whose translations of the third-century Ossianic poems was challenged by Samuel Johnson and dismissed by him in the celebrated contention that 'a man might write such stuff for ever if he would *abandon* his mind to it' (Boswell, *Life of Johnson*, 1207).

the politician and essayist, described as 'more than the ferocity and much less than the sagacity of a bloodhound', Macaulay wrote:

It may be confidently affirmed that to serve the banished family was not his object, and that to ingratiate himself with the banished family was only his secondary object. His primary object was to force himself into the service of the existing Government, and to gain possession of those important and lucrative places from which he had been dismissed more than two years before. He knew that the country and Parliament would not patiently bear to see the English army commanded by foreign generals. Two Englishmen only had shown themselves fit for high military posts, himself and Talmash [Thomas Tollemache]. If Talmash were defeated and disgraced, William would scarcely have a choice. In fact, as soon as it was known that the expedition had failed, and that Talmash was no more, the general cry was that the King ought to receive into his favour the accomplished captain who had done such good service at Walcourt, at Cork and at Kinsale.

Marlborough undeniably wished to remain on as good terms as was possible with the banished family and had, indeed, seen David Floyd, James II's Groom of the Bedchamber, when that envoy visited London in March 1694, as had Shrewsbury, Godolphin and Russell. But Floyd had found Marlborough, though polite as always, bland, uncommunicative and unforthcoming. And, while it was also true that Marlborough was anxious to regain his lost position in the army and the country, to suggest that he had betrayed King William's plans to Saint-Germain as a means of ridding himself of a well-liked and talented professional rival was to cast him in as murky a light as Macaulay could well conceive. Yet it is not difficult to suppose that the letter was, indeed, written to ingratiate Marlborough with Saint-Germain in the knowledge that the proposed attack on Brest was known and expected there. Certainly he had already written to the exiled King James to seek approval of his acceptance of reinstatement in his former commands if this were to be offered him.*

* Commenting upon the Brest debacle, Professor Jones has written: 'At the very least it was improper for Marlborough to give additional credibility to reports of the attack ... to confirm earlier reports that a combined fleet and small army were preparing to attack Brest and [to give] details of the force, the name of the military commander, and the date at which it would sail' (Jones, *Marlborough*, 51). And John Childs has gone further in his criticism: 'Those attempting to exonerate their hero

Tollemache's death did undoubtedly lead to demands for Marlborough's reinstatement in the army. Writing on the subject of the
failure of the assault upon Brest, Shrewsbury told King William in
Flanders on 22 June, 'It is impossible to forget what has here become
a very general discourse, the probability and conveniency of Your
Majesty receiving my Lord Marlborough into your favour. He has
been with me since this news to offer his services, with all the
expression of duty and fidelity imaginable.' King William, however,
remained unmoved by such pleas, replying, 'I do not think it for the
good of my service to entrust him with the command of my troops.'

Six months after this letter was written, on 28 December 1694,
the death of Queen Mary from smallpox exacerbated King William's
dislike and distrust of the man who remained so close to the sister
with whom his wife had quarrelled, a man of whom Mary herself
had said that he could 'never deserve either trust or esteem'.

Indeed, Queen Mary's death had a profound effect upon the King,
who had treated her with a harshness which she appeared never to
resent or even to regret, contenting herself, as Horace Walpole
sardonically observed, 'with praying to God that her husband might
be a great hero since he did not choose to be a fond husband'. Pious
and charitable, modest and retiring, she had been left to occupy
herself with gardening and music and the collection of porcelain,
while he, keeping his mistress, Elizabeth Villiers, out of sight, chose
to spend his leisure hours with those Dutch friends who were
suspected of being something more than friends.

Yet during her illness he had been 'in an agony that amazed us
all,' Bishop Burnet wrote, 'fainting often and breaking out into most
violent lamentations. When she died his spirits sunk so low that there
was great reason to apprehend that he was following her . . . He

---

[Marlborough] have not had an easy task . . . [They maintain that he] had only
contacted St Germain after he already knew that Louis had received identical
information from another source . . . By this line of argument, Marlborough was not
technically a traitor but merely an extremely astute politician who took advantage of
a unique occasion to keep his image shining brightly before the exiled king . . . This
is an exceptionally flimsy defence . . . The honour of a soldier is entirely absent . . .
It seems more likely that Marlborough spilled the beans about Brest in order to effect
the downfall of his rival' (Childs, *The British Army of William III, 1698–1702*, 224–6).

turned himself much to the meditations of religion and secret prayer.'
His mistress, who, so Swift said, squinted 'like a dragon', he married
off to an army officer and he kept his wife's wedding ring and a lock
of her hair next to his heart. He began to drink heavily, usually alone,
and his voice, already weakened by his asthma, became fainter than
ever. His body shrank to a pitiful thinness, while his legs swelled to
an immense size.

He and his sister-in-law, Princess Anne, remained on the worst
of terms. He was persuaded by Lord Sunderland and Lord Somers,
the Lord Keeper, to pretend to a formal reconciliation. He received
her with due and public ceremony at Kensington; and she, accompanied by Sarah, left Berkeley House for apartments in St James's
Palace. Yet relations between the King and his sister-in-law continued to be cool, not to say frigid; and consequently Lady Marlborough was not well received at the King's court while her husband
was still cold-shouldered there.

Princess Anne was urged to write to the King congratulating him
upon a rare military success when Namur was besieged and retaken
in September 1695. Against Lady Marlborough's advice, she did
write such a letter; and, receiving no acknowledgement of it, she
sent a copy, which, like the original, was not answered.

Meanwhile, the death of Queen Mary led the Jacobites to hope
that William would not survive for long as King without her; and
plots were hatched to take advantage of the uncertain times. King
James's son, the Duke of Berwick, came to England in disguise with
instructions to see the known supporters of his father's cause and to
develop a concerted plan of action with the conspirators.

At length it was agreed that a party of forty men should waylay
the King at Turnham Green as he returned from hunting. But two
of these men divulged the plan to Bentinck, and so the King did not
go out that day. Several conspirators were arrested, and Parliament,
in a sudden access of sympathy for the King, suspended the Habeas
Corpus Act and resolved that the succession should be ensured in
obedience to the Declaration of Rights which had secured William
and Mary the throne. Some of the Jacobite conspirators were then
executed, to general satisfaction.

★

At this time another conspirator, one who endeavoured to implicate Lord Marlborough in another Jacobite plot, was arrested. This was Sir John Fenwick, son of Sir William Fenwick of Wallington Castle, Northumberland, and son-in-law of the Earl of Carlisle. He had succeeded his father as Member of Parliament for Northumberland, had reached the rank of major-general, made no secret of his Jacobite sympathies and had been briefly committed to the Tower for fomenting disturbances soon after William and Mary's succession to the throne. A noisy frequenter of what became known as Jacobite Lane in London, he had been involved in the summer of 1692 in a Jacobite riot in Drury Lane.

Tolerated for long, Fenwick was arrested in 1696 and immediately undertook, in exchange for a free pardon, to reveal all that he knew of the Jacobite conspiracies in which he was involved. In his confession, designed to make political capital for the Jacobite cause, he alleged that Russell, Godolphin and Shrewsbury, as well as Marlborough, were all involved in treasonable correspondence with Saint-Germain and that King James was relying on Marlborough to bring over the army to his cause whenever the exiled monarch should choose to land in England. Fenwick then went on to maintain that Marlborough was 'the greatest of criminals where he had the greatest obligations' and that he had written to King James to say that he hoped he might have his pardon for deserting him if he performed an 'extraordinary service . . . and a little after he did a considerable piece of service'. This was presumably a reference to his letter about the proposed attack on Brest.

When shown this confession and its accusations against his ministers and their friends, the King – who already knew that they had been in touch with 'the King across the Water' and who also knew of the allegation that Marlborough had divulged to James the planned attack on Brest – wrote from Holland to say that his confidence in his ministers was undiminished.

This, however, was not enough for the House of Commons. They ordered Fenwick to appear before the bar of the House to answer questions about his confession. He was accordingly brought into the chamber, where he refused to add anything to what he had already divulged and remained silent when, at Marlborough's instigation, his brother-in-law, Arabella's husband, Colonel Godfrey, asked him to state fully and without equivocation the basis of his allegations. He declined to do so, and was accordingly sent back to prison, while the House carried, without a division, a motion that his confession was false and scandalous.

The House then set about the business of bringing Fenwick to face death under an Act of Attainder. Marlborough's younger brother, George, a naval officer and Tory Member for St Albans, was vehement in condemnation of the accused. 'Damn him,' he declared one day in the lobby. 'Thrust a bullet down his throat. Dead men tell no tales.' Lord Marlborough himself, however, maintained his usual suavity, while Shrewsbury was deeply distressed by the whole affair, retiring to the country, giving it out that a fall in the hunting field had made it impossible for him to conduct public business and trying in vain to persuade the King to allow him to resign; and while Godolphin, in Macaulay's words, 'uneasy, but wary, reserved and self-possessed, prepared himself to stand on the defensive' but eventually felt obliged to resign as Treasurer; and while Russell 'went into a towering passion, and breathed nothing but vengeance against the villainous informer', Marlborough 'behaved himself in a manner singularly characteristic', preserving 'a serenity, mild, majestic, and slightly contemptuous'.

He was, however, described by a contemporary as being 'very hearty in this matter', speaking firmly in support of the Bill of Attainder in the House of Lords and voting for it in the divisions. The Bill was finally carried in the Commons by 189 votes to 156 and in the Lords by 68 to 61. Fenwick was beheaded on Tower Hill on 28 January 1697 and buried that same day in the church of St Martin-in-the-Fields. He died, so Burnet said, 'very composed, in a much better temper than was to be expected, for his life had been very irregular'. And, widely as his behaviour was condemned and much as people shared King William's indignation at the 'fellow's effrontery', there was also criticism of the hasty manner in which his fate had been decided and the use of the process of attainder to decide it. 'I do not find many concerned for his person,' commented George Smalridge, the future Bishop of Bristol. 'The course of his life has been such ... that he has few friends; but the method of punishing him being out of the common road, and such as has not been often used, and, when it has, been condemned by those who have judged coolly, is what some are startled at.'

POLITESSE AND PARSIMONY

'. . . he never spent a shilling beyond
what his income was . . .'

When commenting upon Marlborough's 'irresistibly engaging and graceful manner', Lord Chesterfield maintained that it was by this charm

that he was enabled during all the war [of the Spanish Succession] to connect the various and jarring Powers of the Grand Alliance, and to carry them on to the main object of the war, notwithstanding their private and separate views, jealousies and wrongheadedness . . . He was always cool, and nobody ever observed the least variation in his countenance; he could refuse more easily than others could grant; and those who went from him the most dissatisfied as to the substance of their business, were yet charmed by his manner, and, as it were, comforted by it.

He never, throughout the whole course of the war, lost sight of what he took to be essential for its successful conduct, the preservation of the alliance formed for its prosecution.

Thomas Bruce, the Jacobite Earl of Ailesbury, who did not like him, provided a briefer, more critical and, indeed, unjust assessment – 'timorous in council and cunning in politics, obliging words but no performances' – while John Evelyn, who disapproved of him also, was equally succinct: 'He is indeed a very handsome proper well spoken, and affable person and supplys his want of acquired knowledge by keeping good Company: In the meane time Ambition and love of riches has no End.'

As for his appearance, he was even more good-looking now in early middle age than he had been as a young man. His 'handsome

1. John Churchill in his thirties: a portrait attributed to John Riley. The star of the Order of the Garter, which Churchill was awarded in 1707, was added later.

2. Sir Winston Churchill, John
Churchill's father: a portrait by
J.M. Wright.

3. Barbara Villiers, Lady Castlemaine,
later Duchess of Cleveland
(1641–1709), mistress of both King
Charles II and John Churchill: a
portrait by Sir Peter Lely.

4. A view of Westminster and Whitehall (*below and opposite*), c. 1675, by
Hendrick Danckerts.

5. James and Anne, Duke and Duchess of York, portrayed by Sir Peter Lely in 1668–70. The two children, Lady Mary (*left*) and Lady Anne, were added by Benedetto Gennari in 1680. Windsor Castle is seen in the background.

6. John Churchill:
a portrait, possibly
by Johann Baptist
Closterman,
painted c. 1687.

7. Holywell House, Sarah's father's house on the outskirts of St Albans, which later became the Marlboroughs'.

8. A detail of Hendrick Danckerts's drawing of Whitehall, showing the Cockpit opposite the Palace, where Princess Anne had her household.

9. Sarah Churchill, the Duchess of Marlborough, reading a letter in an orangery: a portrait by Sir Godfrey Kneller.

10. John and Sarah Churchill, Duke and Duchess of Marlborough, by Enoch Seeman.

11. Princess Anne and
her son, William, Duke
of Gloucester, who
died in 1700, about six
years after this portrait
was painted by the
studio of Sir Godfrey
Kneller.

Sidney Lord Godolphin.
Lord High Treasurer of England.

12. Marlborough's
friend and colleague
Sidney Godolphin, first
Earl of Godolphin:
a portrait after Sir
Godfrey Kneller, 1705.

13. Robert Harley, first Earl of Oxford: a portrait by Sir Godfrey Kneller, 1714.

14. Charles Talbot, twelfth Earl and only Duke of Shrewsbury: a portrait after Sir Godfrey Kneller, 1685.

15. The coronation of King William III and Queen Mary II in 1689: an engraving of a painting from the German school.

and delicate countenance' engaged 'every one in his favour at first sight', wrote the Dutch deputy, Sicco van Goslinga.

He is about the middle height, and has the best figure in the world; his features are without fault, fine, sparkling [greyish green] eyes and good teeth . . . In short, apart from his legs, which are too thin, he is one of the handsomest men ever seen. His mind is clear and subtle, his judgement sound, his insight both quick and deep. He has a consummate knowledge of men . . . He expresses himself well, and even his very bad French is agreeable. His voice is harmonious [although others described it as being rather too high-pitched] and as a speaker in his own language he is reckoned one of the best. His address is most courteous.

It had to be admitted though, that, while they were light in the scale when 'weighed against the rare gifts of this truly great man', his character had its defects: he was, said Goslinga, 'a profound dissembler, all the more dangerously so, since his words and manner [give] the impression of frankness itself'. Goslinga added:

His ambition knows no bounds. Although he has courage – and of this there is no question, whatever may be said by those who envy or hate him – he lacks that firmness of soul which makes the true Hero . . . Sometimes [Goslinga's comments become increasingly unjust] on the eve of an action, he is irresolute. He will not face difficulties, and occasionally lets reverses cast him down: of this I could give more than one instance as an eye-witness . . . An avarice which I can only call sordid, guides his entire conduct.

While it was agreed that he was, on occasions, generous where large sums were involved, it had to be conceded that he was often extremely mean in petty ways. Numerous stories were told of his notorious parsimony in this respect, many of them apocryphal. It was related, for instance, that, upon receiving a letter from him, Prince Eugène of Savoy, being unable to make out the handwriting, passed it on to another officer. Finding it just as difficult, this officer commented that it was particularly hard to decipher because Marlborough did not dot his i's. The Prince laconically observed, 'That saves ink.'

Then there was the occasion when Marlborough was playing cards with Lord Bath and General Pulteney. When it was time to go home, Marlborough, who had lost money, asked Pulteney to lend him sixpence to pay for the hire of a sedan chair. Pulteney did so; and, when Marlborough had gone, Lord Bath said to him, 'I would venture any sum now that he goes home on foot. Do pray follow him out.' Sure enough, going out after him Pulteney saw him walking back to his lodgings. And then there was the tale of the officer who brought a message to his tent at night when he was asleep. Was the message written or verbal? he asked. When told it was verbal, Marlborough said, 'Put out the lantern, then.'

On another occasion, when his gaiters were so shrunken by rain that they had to be cut off, he gave careful instructions to the orderly to make sure that he cut them at the seams so that they could be resewn.

He tipped other men's servants with evident reluctance, yet he was most indulgent towards his own, allowing them a latitude which astonished those who observed it. 'For his natural good temper,' Lord Ailesbury wrote in his memoirs, 'he never had his equal. He could not chide a servant and was the worst served possible; and in command he could not give a harsh word, no not to the meanest sergeant, or soldier.'

His servants were, indeed, treated with remarkable laxity: one of his commissaries told the story of how he and Marlborough were caught one day in a rainstorm. They called for their cloaks. The commissary's was produced immediately. Marlborough waited patiently for his until, the rain increasing torrentially, he called out to his servant, who was fumbling about with the straps and buckles, to ask what he was about. 'You must stay,' the man replied impatiently, 'even if it rains cats and dogs, until I can get at it.' Another of Marlborough's servants, a dishonest man named Will Lovegrove, made off with much of the contents of his master's cellar, including '17 dossen of old Sack', '14 quarts of Usqubath [whisky]' and '117 bottles of Tokay'. A list of these was endorsed in his wife's hand: 'This Will Lovegrove cheated him & . . . most of his servants were of the same sort.'

While not yet as rich as some jealous contemporaries alleged him to be, Marlborough was already a wealthy man, having, among other astute investments, done extremely well out of holdings in the

Hudson's Bay Company and in speculations in the stock of the recently founded Bank of England.

Yet, determined though he was to extract as much as he possibly could from the offices he held, from commissions on bread contracts and on the pay of mercenaries, he does not appear to have taken more than custom or the law allowed; and this was at a time when peculation was common, when paymaster-generals habitually made fortunes, and when his brother George, the unpopular and taciturn admiral of the blue, and their younger brother, Charles, promoted lieutenant-general in 1694, and for many years Member of Parliament for Weymouth and Melcombe, were both sent to the Tower for financial offences.

'From the very beginning of his life,' Marlborough's wife averred, 'he never spent a shilling beyond what his income was . . . [He] never had any vanity, and . . . was without the least affectation . . . and, while handsome as an angel, [he was] ever so carelessly drest.' Others said of him that he had no more than three coats, one of which he wore only on important state occasions. After his death, his wife wrote:

Living so many years with great employments he left a great estate: which was no wonder since he . . . never threw any money away. And money was for many years at six per cent. He had a great deal of compassion in his nature, and to those that he had been long acquainted with he gave money out of his pocket . . . tho' they were not of his opinion. I am living witness of this . . . for I was directed by him to pay some pensions when he was abroad, and have letters that prove the truth of it from the persons.

Whether at home or abroad, on campaign or on holiday, he chose to live simply, 'his inclination', as Sarah said, 'lying that way'. Nor did he entertain friends or colleagues with any lavishness, as was the common practice of so many other men of high social rank and generals of armies. Yet he was not above celebrating special occasions and, according to Samuel Johnson's friend, William Seward,

while no epicure himself [he] had, in common with Louis XIV, a pleasure in seeing others eat, and when he was particularly pleased he exercised this pleasure, though it cost him something. Lord Cadogan used to say that he remembered seeing the Duke completely out of humour one day, a thing very unusual with him, and much agitated. In the evening, however, a messenger arrived who brought him some news which he liked. He immediately ordered the messenger to be placed in a situation where no one could speak to him, and ordered his coach to be opened, and some cantines to be taken out, containing hams and other good things, and spread before some of the principal officers, he looking on and tasting nothing.

13

GOVERNOR, FATHER AND
DIPLOMATIST

*'A finer work of art had never been
shown at The Hague.'*

After the Peace of Ryswick, which was signed by plenipotentiaries of France, England, the Netherlands, Spain and the Holy Roman Empire on 20 September 1697, by which King Louis XIV surrendered most of the territorial gains which he had made in the war and recognized William III as King of England, relations between William and the Earl of Marlborough began to improve. The King still did not altogether trust Marlborough, finding him, as so many others did, unfathomable; but he seemed, in spite of himself, to be beguiled by his captivating charm and he could not but recognize his intelligence and worth and the regard they both shared for the army, which was summarily dismembered after the war – all foreigners, including the Dutch guards, being dismissed and what regiments of cavalry still remained being employed as military police to track down and bring to the gallows or the whipping block those of their former comrades in arms who had drifted into crime.

Indeed, so changed was the King's attitude towards Marlborough, who had been allowed to appear again at court after Queen Mary's death, that when Princess Anne's son, the Duke of Gloucester, was old enough to be taken from the care of women into that of a governor, Marlborough was chosen for the appointment.

The Duke of Gloucester was now nine years old. A promising though delicate boy, he had suffered in his earlier childhood from what was diagnosed as water on the brain and had had to be carried from room to room by servants. He had developed a passion for playing with toy soldiers and cannon; and, when it seemed that he had recovered from his early illness, he was allowed to have boys of his own age to play with him, including Lord Marlborough's surviving son, John. With these boys, in the words of one of his attendants, 'every night the little Duke had the ceremony of beating up the Tatta-ta-too, and the Word, and the Patrole, as in garrison; which latter was sometimes an excellent piece of diversion'.

The post of governor to this child had first been offered to the Duke of Shrewsbury, who was still living in retirement in the country; but he refused it. There was then talk that the appointment would go to Princess Anne's uncle, the Earl of Rochester; but the Earl of Sunderland recommended Marlborough as Shrewsbury had done and as the King's Dutch friend, Arnold Joost van Keppel, Earl of Albemarle, also did. Albemarle's recommendation was decisive. Had the King's other Dutch intimate, the Earl of Portland, been in England, he might well have strongly advised against Lord Marlborough being chosen, disliking the man and always ready to disagree with his rival for the King's affection and regard. But Portland was serving in Paris as England's ambassador there. So, in the summer of 1698, Marlborough was summoned to the presence of the King who told him, with unaccustomed grace, that he was to be entrusted with the education of the boy at a salary of at least £2,000 a year. The Prince, the King added, was to be brought up to look upon the governor himself as a model, and then 'he would not lack accomplishments'. A few days later the appointment was announced in the *Gazette*:

His Majesty has been pleased to appoint the Right Honourable the Earl of Marlborough to be Governor of His Highness the Duke of Gloucester, as a mark of the good opinion His Majesty has of his lordship's zeal for his service and his qualifications for the employment of so great a trust.

As confirmation of this good opinion, Lord Marlborough was restored to membership of the Privy Council and to his military rank, while his son, John, although only twelve years old, was appointed Master of the Horse at a salary of £500 a year.★ At the same time Gilbert Burnet, the Bishop of Salisbury, accepted the post of preceptor, having made it a condition that, in the summer, the Prince should live at Windsor, which was in his diocese, and that he should have ten weeks' leave each year.

Another appointment to the Prince's household was to have profound consequences for the Marlboroughs. This was of a poor relation of Sarah's, the daughter of one of the twenty-two children of her grandfather, Sir John Jennings. Having so many offspring, Sir John had been unable to provide adequately for them all and had been hard put to it to give this daughter a modest dowry of £500 on her marriage to a merchant named Hill, who subsequently fell on hard times after making some unwise investments. The Hills had four children and the elder daughter, Abigail, was recommended by her cousin, Sarah Marlborough, for a minor post at court. She was a rather plain woman with a big red nose, a feature which was to be eagerly seized upon by lampoonists. Lord Dartmouth, who did not like her, described her as being 'exceeding mean and vulgar in her manners, of a very unequal temper, childish, exceptious and passionate'. A less prejudiced observer might well have remarked upon her quiet demeanour and her discretion, qualities not to be found in Lady Marlborough. Lady Marlborough herself felt sorry for her, a sentiment she was profoundly to regret.

At this time, however, it was Sarah Marlborough's evident fondness for Abigail Hill which disturbed Princess Anne, who wrote to her:

I hope Mrs Freeman has no thoughts of going to the Opera with Mrs Hill and will have a care of engaging too much in her company; for, if you give way to that, it is a thing that will insensibly grow upon you. Therefore give me leave once more to beg for your own sake, as well as poor Mrs Morley's, that you would have as little to do with that enchantress as 'tis possible.

Three months or so before Lord Marlborough's appointment as the Duke of Gloucester's governor, his eldest daughter, the

---

★ As a lieutenant-general Marlborough was entitled to £4 a week. Generals of the horse and foot received £6 and major-generals £2, while colonels had 12 shillings. The pay of a private in a foot regiment was 8d. a day. A general, therefore, earned 180 times as much as a private.

eighteen-year-old Henrietta, had made a marriage which much pleased her parents, who had proposed it.★ They could have hoped for a richer man as a son-in-law than Francis Godolphin, but he was a charming young man and Henrietta was much in love with him. Moreover, his father, the widowed Earl of Godolphin, had been Marlborough's close friend for many years and in Sarah's opinion, written in her Bible at his death, was 'the best man that ever lived'. He often stayed with them at Holywell House, whence he wrote to his sister soon after the birth of his first grandchild, 'All here are very well at present and Willigo begins to make a noise which he is pleased with himself because he takes it for speaking, but it's a language not much understood in the world hitherto.'

Lord Godolphin, at fifty-three five years older than Marlborough, son of Sir Francis Godolphin of an old Cornish family, had been a page in the household of Charles II, then Groom of the Bedchamber and Master of the Robes. For a short time he had been an army officer before entering the House of Commons and becoming a Commissioner of the Treasury, then Secretary of State and Lord Treasurer. A competent official, pleasant in manner, he was appointed Chamberlain to Queen Mary of Modena on the accession of James II, and was said to have entertained a romantic attachment to her. His appearance, disfigured by smallpox, was by no means inspiring and physiognomists, so Jonathan Swift said, 'would hardly discover by consulting [his] aspect that his predominant passions were love and play, that he could sometimes scratch out a song in praise of his mistress with a pencil and a card or that he had tears at his command like a woman, to be used either in an intrigue of gallantry or politics'.

He was said to have lost large sums on the race course; and this, together with his unusual honesty in financial matters, was responsible for his relative poverty at a time when other statesmen

---

★ The Duchess saw to it that all their daughters married well and married young, Anne and Mary at seventeen and Elizabeth at fifteen. 'It must be admitted that none of them did otherwise than rejoice at their swift escape from their mother's thraldom' (Reid, *John and Sarah, Duke and Duchess of Marlborough, 1650–1744*, 419).

succeeded in accumulating tens of thousands of pounds and bequeathed fortunes to their heirs. He himself was to leave but a meagre
£14,000, and was certainly unable to contribute much to his son's
finances on his marriage to Henrietta Churchill. Her father, however,
provided her with a dowry of £5,000, to which Princess Anne gave
a further £5,000 and would have given a sum twice that amount
which Marlborough would have accepted had not Sarah thought it
as well to have the additional £5,000 reserved for their second
daughter, Anne.

Anne, an entrancing girl, was her father's favourite, and described
by one of the Duke of Gloucester's attendants as 'as sweet a creature
as ever was seen'. She, too, married well. Her husband, Lord Spencer,
an uncompromising Whig of republican inclinations and bookish
tastes, was the son and heir of the Earl of Sunderland. His mother,
the extremely rich and beautiful daughter of the Earl of Bristol, was
a close friend of Lady Marlborough, whose intimacy with her aroused
a jealousy which Princess Anne found it impossible to hide.

Lady Marlborough seems to have warmly approved of the match
between her friend's son and her own delightful daughter; but her
husband was not disposed initially to consent to it, not only on
political but also on personal grounds. Lord Spencer was ten years
older than Lady Anne Churchill and had been married before to
Lady Arabella Cavendish, daughter of the Duke of Newcastle, who
had soon afterwards died. He had the reputation of being so blunt
and assertively arrogant a man as to be an intimidating husband as
well as a coarse one: during a debate in the House of Commons he
had shocked his father by declaring that he hoped to live 'to piss
upon the House of Lords'.

Marlborough did not believe that he would make his daughter
happy. Sarah, however, did all she could to persuade him otherwise,
even though she had to admit that Spencer had 'no more genteelness
than a Porter'; and his father, a man as smooth as the son was rough,
undertook to see that his heir would be 'governed in everything
public and private by him'. So Marlborough reluctantly gave his
consent; and it was agreed that Lord Spencer should marry Lady
Anne, to whose dowry Princess Anne gave £5,000 as she had done
to that of her sister, Lady Henrietta.

83

At both these weddings, as she readily admitted, the bride's mother, 'could not hold from dropping tears', an emotion displayed throughout her life when watching the marriage of 'any child or friend'.

With daughters married or about to be married so well, his son a playmate of the son of the heir to the throne, and his wife an intimate friend of that heir, Lord Marlborough's future as a courtier and politician, if not yet as a soldier, seemed bright and assured as the century drew to a close.

In the summer of 1698, when the King, increasingly inclined to favour him – and to admit him to his circle of intimate friends – left on one of his frequent visits to Holland, Marlborough was appointed one of the nine Lords Justice who were to act as a council of regency in His Majesty's absence. His views on Europe and on Louis XIV, on the dangers of headlong disarmament and disbandment of the army, and on the wild mutual antagonism of extreme Whigs and Tories were much in tune with King William's. Yet Marlborough was careful to keep a certain distance from the court, not to become too closely identified with any political faction, while cultivating friendships among both Whigs and Tories in the House of Commons as well as in the House of Lords. Additionally his friendship with Princess Anne remained as intimate as ever.

There was talk of his being appointed a minister. In February 1699 James Vernon, a Privy Councillor, told the Duke of Shrewsbury that he had heard from Sir John Forbes of an exchange being negotiated: 'that Lord Marlborough should be [Lord] Chamberlain and you Governor . . . I observe Lord Marlborough is frequently with the King and therefore I hope they are well together.'

They might have been better together had there not at this time been trouble over landed estates in Ireland, which, confiscated from rebels, had been forfeited to the Crown and had been handed over by the King to friends of his, mostly foreigners, including his mistress, Elizabeth Villiers, an *intrigante* who much disliked the Marlboroughs and acquired estates extending to some 90,000 acres.

The House of Commons firmly demanded the reclamation of these estates for the nation; and the King's ministers, unwilling to clash with the Commons on such an issue, declined to support the King; and so the lands were taken back from those to whom he had given them.

Lord Marlborough, although disapproving of the King's grants, endeavoured, as so often he did, to stand aloof from the controversial business, and consequently annoyed the King by not speaking in his support, at the same time displeasing both ministers and Commons by declining to show more openly where his sympathies lay. 'The feelings of the King,' commented Archdeacon William Coxe, the historian and author of *Memoirs of John, Duke of Marlborough*, 'were too much wounded to regard with indulgence anyone who had favoured the obnoxious [Bill for the resumption of the estates in Ireland]; while the victorious party stigmatized all who had not fully entered into their measures, as enemies to the country'.

Marlborough himself wrote to the Duke of Shrewsbury: 'The King's coldness to me still [in May 1700] continues, so that I should have been glad to have had your friendly advice; for to have friends and acquaintances unreasonably jealous, and the King at the same time angry, is what I know not how to bear; nor do I know how to behave myself.'

Within a year, however, Lord Marlborough was in favour once more with the King; and on 31 May 1701 he was appointed commander-in-chief of the British forces in Holland. Moreover, at the end of the following month, he was nominated ambassador extraordinary to the United Provinces. Three days later he was aboard the royal yacht sailing for The Hague with the King.

His orders entailed a grave and wide-ranging responsibility: he was, first of all, to endeavour to preserve the temporary, uneasy peace; but, if war seemed inevitable, he was to organize a Grand Alliance against France, making treaties with Holland and the Empire and with Prussia, Denmark, Sweden and as many of the German states as could be induced to join the alliance. At the same time he was to settle with these allies the numbers of soldiers and sailors they were to bring into the war with France; and, as commander-in-chief, to supervise the organization of these troops and their supplies and armaments.* To assist him with these military matters, he was to have the help of William Cadogan, an Irishman, the son of a Dublin lawyer and grandson of the governor of Trim, an officer in the Inniskilling Dragoons, who, as a boy cornet, had fought in the battle of the Boyne and had attracted Marlborough's notice at the capture of Cork and Kinsale. He was by now no more than twenty-six, but Marlborough had no hesitation in appointing him his quartermaster-general. He was to be of exceptional value to Marlborough, who was to employ him not only as quartermaster but as chief of staff and director of intelligence.

Also of inestimable value to Marlborough was Adam de Cardonnel, the son of a French Protestant, who had had wide experience of army administration as chief clerk in the war office. He had been acting as Marlborough's military secretary on and off for several years and was to remain with him, an implicitly trusted member of his staff, for the whole of the rest of his master's military career, not only taking down his dictation and copying his letters with the many accessary amendments to Marlborough's faulty grammar and idiosyncratic spelling, but drafting letters himself.

At The Hague, Lord Marlborough and his staff lived at the Mauritshuis, a fine house overlooking the waters of the Hof Vijver which had been lent to them by the National Assembly (the States-General); and here he held meetings with the representatives of the various countries which, it was hoped, could be persuaded to join the Grand Alliance against France.

He was a born diplomatist. 'The statesmen of Europe were received at the top of the staircase by a glorious living portrait of a Milord,' G. M. Trevelyan wrote in the first volume of his *England under Queen Anne*. 'A finer work of art had never been shown at The Hague . . . [He was] every inch a soldier and a courtier; said indeed to be fifty years of age but in the prime of manly beauty . . . talking charmingly in bad French; seeming to understand and sympathise with everyone.'

---

* Although their population was less than half that of the British, the Dutch consistently raised far more men than any of their allies – over 100,000 in the years 1695–7 (Childs, *The British Army of William III*, 127).

He spent much time discussing the formation of the various treaties with King William's adviser, Anthonie Heinsius, the chief executive or Grand Pensionary of Holland, the dominant of the seven United Provinces, who made reports to King William at Loo.

Suave and tactful, disarming and persuasive, Marlborough conducted these negotiations with great skill, rarely showing any emotion and never, it seems, breaking out in real or simulated anger, as he for once did when he heard that the Dukes of Bolton and Newcastle and some other peers were plotting to bring the Elector of Hanover over to England and to place him on the throne instead of Princess Anne. 'By God,' Marlborough exclaimed on that occasion, 'by God, if ever they attempt it, we would walk over their bellies.'

14

THE QUEEN AND HER MINISTERS

'I know my own heart to be entirely English.'

While preparing for war and, accompanied by King William, inspecting army camps and garrisons, Marlborough was still also working for peace, having long conversations at The Hague with the French minister in residence there and negotiating with the Spanish minister, but making little headway with either. When the French minister was ordered back to Paris, he wrote to Sarah to tell her that she 'must defer' the 'kind thoughts' she had entertained of going over to Holland to be with him until he knew 'a little more certainly' what France would 'think to do'.

A fortnight or so later, he learned that the French marshal François de Neufville, duc de Villeroi, had left for Italy and supposing, therefore, that operations in northern Europe would be postponed at least for that season, and that Britain and the Dutch Republic would not declare war until early 1702, Marlborough told Sarah she might now come over to Holland. During her visit, he signed on his country's behalf treaties with Holland and the Empire, which were soon followed by pacts entered into with representatives of those other states with whom he had been in patient though frustrating, and – to use his own word – 'tormenting' negotiations.

Much had been left to his own discretion: the treaty with Sweden being signed without reference to London, because he knew that King William would support him and that it was vitally necessary to prevent French diplomacy freeing King Charles XII from his war with Russia and diverting him into war against the Empire.

Soon after agreement had been reached as to the number of

soldiers the various states should bring into the field – Holland 100,000; the Hapsburg Empire 82,000; the British 40,000 – King James, who had spent hours on end in his declining years praying on his knees, died in his chapel at Saint-Germain on 16 September 1701. Immediately upon hearing of his death, Louis XIV proclaimed James's son, the nineteen-year-old Prince James Francis Edward, King of England, Scotland and Ireland. This impertinent contradiction of the terms of the 1697 Peace of Ryswick, which had acknowledged William III as King of England, aroused more anger in England than even the attempt of the dead King to regain his throne had done. Whigs and Tories alike condemned the effrontery; Jacobites who played the part of heralds in the streets, proclaiming the accession to the throne of King James III, were pelted with rotten eggs; the French ambassador was told to leave St James's; the English ambassador was recalled from Paris; the people as a whole were now provoked to accept another war.

A few months after the death of James Stuart, King William's horse, Sorel, which had once belonged to Sir John Fenwick, stumbled on a molehill as he was riding in the park at Hampton Court. The King only broke a collarbone, but, although no more than fifty-two, he had aged much of late and had been failing in health for some time. At the beginning of March, Lord Albemarle came to give him a satisfactory report of Marlborough's proceedings at The Hague; but the King received it apathetically and later said, '*Je tire vers ma fin.*' He died the next day, 19 March 1702, leaving Marlborough to finish the work he had himself so doggedly undertaken.

While endeavouring to bring together the various strands of the alliance being formed to challenge King Louis XIV, Marlborough was also doing what he could to ensure that there would be a strong administration with parliamentary approval to support the war at home. In this undertaking he had the full backing of the new Queen, like himself a Tory, if a far more decided one. The husband of her beloved friend Sarah, he remained a trusted and much admired adviser with whom she shared a strong dislike of factions in politics and a warm desire for national unity. Sarah, however, was as committed a Whig as ever and watched with concern as the Tories, little better than Jacobites in her opinion, pressing for a limited war at sea rather than a continental campaign, filled almost all the seats in the Privy Council.

Queen Anne's first appearances before the Privy Council and the Houses of Parliament were both highly successful. She was no more a naturally imposing figure than she was a clever one; but, having studied a portrait of Elizabeth I and done her best to overcome her natural shyness – though still in the disarming habit of blushing frequently – she presented herself before her councillors, and both Lords and Commons, magnificently clothed in red velvet lined with ermine and trimmed with gold braid. She wore a crown and the ribbon of the Order of the Garter. 'I know my own heart to be entirely English,' she declared in her clear and pleasant voice. 'You shall always find me a strict and religious observer of my word.'

She let it be known how gratefully she would depend upon the man who had been so kind and good a governor to her late lamented son, the Duke of Gloucester, who had died of hydrocephalus in 1700, shortly after his eleventh birthday had been hopefully celebrated with an exciting party and a magnificent display of fireworks.

Lord Marlborough, the Queen was anxious to emphasize, had shown great skill as a soldier and diplomatist on the Continent and in Ireland. But his gifts had not been sufficiently valued or exploited by her predecessor. Nor had those of her husband, her decent, dense, boring and placid husband whom she wished to create King Consort, an elevation against which Marlborough strongly advised her and which would necessarily have brought her into conflict with Parliament. She gave way on this point; but she insisted upon appointing the Prince Generalissimo of her armed forces and Lord High Admiral. At the same time, Marlborough, as well as Captain-General of the British land forces, was to hold the office he had long desired of Master-General of the Ordnance, which carried with it, among other duties, responsibility for the equipment and barracks of the army as well as fortifications. Marlborough was also to be a Knight of the Garter, an honour which the Queen had vainly sought for him in the time of her brother-in-law, who had always been reluctant to bestow it upon him.

As well as honouring her friend Marlborough, the Queen was

anxious, now that she was in a position to do so, to bestow favours also on his wife, 'Mrs Freeman', who was made Groom of the Stole, Mistress of the Robes and Keeper of the Privy Purse, with emoluments of £5,600 a year. Her two married daughters were appointed Ladies of the Bedchamber at £1,000 a year each, and Sarah herself given the services of a page, 'the handsomest Boy' she had ever seen, who was to attend her when she went about the town. She was also offered the much disliked Dutch Earl of Portland's place as Ranger of Windsor Park. On 19 May 1702, soon after her accession to the throne, the Queen wrote to her:

Mentioning this worthy person [the Earl of Portland] puts me in mind to ask dear Mrs Freeman a question which I would have done some time ago; and that is, if you would have the [Ranger's] Lodge for your life . . . and anything that is of so much satisfaction as this poor place seems to be to you, I would give dear Mrs Freeman for all her days, which, I pray God, may be as many and as truly happy as His world can make you.*

In making her appointments and dismissing those of whom she disapproved, the Queen displayed both her prejudices and her sense of loyalty. If a simple woman, she was also a courageous and constant one, unimaginative and obstinate but affectionate, generous and passionately patriotic, as devoted to her country as she was to the Church of England – or at least to those clergymen and bishops in its community who were as High Church as she was herself – and devoted also to Marlborough, who, returning her affection, knew so well how to please her, how to treat her, how to exploit his closeness to her for the furtherance of his own ambitions. It was soon to be calculated that the joint income of the Marlboroughs was over £64,000 a year, that is to say over £4 million a year in modern terms.

Soon after Princess Anne became Queen, Lord Marlborough had to part once again from his wife on setting out upon another mission

---

* Sarah was delighted to be given the Ranger's Lodge, a handsome and commodious house, then known as Byfield House and later as Cumberland Lodge, to the south of the castle. When the court was not in residence at Windsor, it was, she said, 'of all the Places that ever I was in, the most agreeable to me' (Hudson, *Cumberland Lodge*, 60).

to the Continent. He did so with a sense of foreboding, for he did not know when, if ever, he would see her again. 'It is impossible to express with what a heavy heart I parted with you when I was by the water's side,' he wrote to her as soon as he could.

I could have given my life to come back, though I knew my own weakness so much that I durst not, for I know I should have exposed myself to the company. I did for a great while, with a perspective glass, look upon the cliffs, in hopes I might have had one sight of you. We are now out of sight of Margate, and I have neither soul nor spirits, but I do at this time suffer so much that nothing but being with you can recompense it . . . I pray to God to make you and yours happy; and if I could contribute anything to it with the utmost hazard of my life, I should be glad to do it.

Just as Marlborough's influence in England was much enhanced by his friendship with the Queen, so it was in Holland by his friendship with the Grand Pensionary, Anthonie Heinsius, the most powerful member of the States-General, a rather lonely bachelor from a patrician family of Delft, whose determination to resist the power of France had been hardened by his own treatment at Versailles, where, as the Dutch envoy there, his forceful championship of Dutch interests had caused so much annoyance that he had been threatened with incarceration in the Bastille by the determined and ruthless, marquis de Louvois, Louis XIV's Secretary of State for War and the highly successful and unscrupulous reorganizer of the Sun King's army.

Conscientious, austere and given to bouts of deep depression, Heinsius was on occasions found in tears at his desk in his small house in The Hague, where Marlborough would visit him and be touched by the man's gentle manners and modesty, his patience, his clear, resourceful mind and ardent patriotism.

There was, however, a problem: the English queen had set her heart upon her husband being placed in command of both the Dutch and English armies in the forthcoming campaign. He had never, she insisted, been given an opportunity to show his true worth. Naturally the Dutch did not agree with her. King William had not been a great general but he was a man of will, intelligence and tenacity. Even if Prince George was advised by more capable and experienced generals in a council of war, the very thought of being commanded by a

Danish prince, of whom no one except his wife spoke highly, was intolerable to the Dutch, who had capable commanders of their own, among them Opdam, Overkirk, Slangenberg and, most notably, Godert de Ginkel, the Earl of Athlone. For the moment, and as a holding measure, the States-General of the Republic appointed the Prince of Nassau-Saarbrück to the supreme command of their army as *veldtmarschal*.

Marlborough assured Godolphin that he had done all he could to 'incline these people to have the honour of having [Prince George] to command their army as well as the English'. Other names had been mentioned, among them the King of Prussia, the Elector of Hanover, the Duke of Celle and the Archduke Charles. But Marlborough, with the intention of pleasing the Queen, said that he considered Prince George was the only man who could 'unite the forty thousand [troops] paid by England'. Nothing, however, had been settled about the future command when it was secretly agreed by the allies that war should be declared upon France at the beginning of May 1702.

It was now essential to have a ministry in England capable of giving full support to the prosecution of that war. So far as Marlborough was concerned, although a mild Tory himself, he did not much mind what the political complexion of the government was so long as the war was energetically supported;★ and if its principal ministries were to be held by Tories, it would be as well that lesser ones should be held by Whigs. The Queen was persuaded to agree with him.

She was at this time a highly popular figure in the country. Johann Phillipp von Hoffman, the Austrian minister in London, reported to Vienna after Her Majesty had declared she would give 'to the public service' £100,000 of the income the House of Commons had voted to allow her: 'Since Queen Elizabeth there has been no instance of such graciousness . . . The Queen has completely won the hearts of her subjects.'

★ 'I hope I shall always continue in the houmor I am now in which is to be governed by neither party,' Marlborough told his wife, 'but to doe what I think is best for England, by which I know I shall disoblige both partys' (Snyder (ed.), *The Marlborough –Godolphin Correspondence*, i, 240).

With her approval, and with the discreet and reticent help of her friend Lord Marlborough, the Whigs, who had filled so many important offices in King William's time, began to be replaced, though the Tory Earl of Jersey, described as 'making a very good Figure in his Person, being tall, well-shaped, handsome and dresses clean' and as having 'gone through all the great Offices of the Kingdom with a very ordinary Understanding', retained his place as Lord Chamberlain of the Royal Household, in which the elderly grumpy and arrogant Sir Edward Seymour, a former Speaker of the House of Commons and a man of much influence with Tory gentlemen in the West Country, was appointed Comptroller.

The Earl of Macclesfield, a man whose loyalty to the Crown was suspect, was dismissed from office. So was the Marquess of Wharton, King William's Comptroller of the Household, whose private life was notorious for its licentiousness.

The Earl of Rochester, the Queen's ingratiating uncle, a heavy drinker said to 'swear like a trooper', whose attachment to the Church of England was as strong as that of his niece, was retained as Lord Lieutenant of Ireland, a post from which he had been on the point of dismissal by King William. The tall, thin Earl of Nottingham, a staunch Tory, known as 'Don Dismal' because of his dark complexion and lugubrious manner, who had been out of office on the King's death, was appointed Secretary of State for the Southern Department and the lawyer Sir Charles Hedges, also a Tory and a friend of Lord Rochester, became Secretary of State for the Northern Department, much to the annoyance of the Whig Lady Marlborough, who said of him, 'He has no capacity, no quality nor interest, nor ever could have been in that post but everybody knows my Lord Rochester cares for nothing so much as a man that he thinks will depend upon him.'

The Marquess of Normanby, with whom the Queen had had a flirtation in years gone by, was appointed Lord Privy Seal and soon afterwards created a duke, royal favours which caused some disquiet because he was known to have been on terms of intimate friendship with the French ambassador, the comte de Tallard. Count Wratislaw, the Emperor's ambassador, gave voice to this anxiety in one of his reports, in which he reported a conversation he had had with Lord

Marlborough regarding the possibility of secret intelligence about the forthcoming war being divulged to the enemy. 'I am aware of his bad qualities, and anxious about the results,' Marlborough was quoted to have said; 'but it is not in my power to intervene in everything. Anyway, the Lord Privy Seal has nothing to do with foreign affairs.'

While Marlborough had, indeed, had no say in the appointment of Normanby as Lord Privy Seal, he did press for the position of Lord Treasurer, the virtual head of the Cabinet, being given to Sidney Godolphin, his close friend and his daughter's father-in-law, who was also very much *persona grata* to the Queen, to whom he had always behaved with kindness and sympathy. She bestowed upon him one of those familiar names which were a token of her affection and regard, 'Mr Montgomery'.

Godolphin expressed reluctance to return to such high office: he would rather play cards or go to the races at Newmarket. He was getting on for sixty, readily disheartened and, having lost his wife, John Evelyn's friend Margaret, years before, anxious to lead a quiet life, undisturbed by the bossy interference of Lady Marlborough, who took it upon herself to tell him what to do when her husband was not there to do so himself.

In the end, however, Lord Marlborough's persuasiveness was decisive, and Godolphin again became Lord Treasurer, a position which he held for the next eight years.

Marlborough was not, however, so successful with the Duke of Shrewsbury, whom, as a leading Whig, he would have liked to have in the Government to lend it a more national appearance. But Shrewsbury, had gone to live in Italy, where he was to marry the daughter of the marchese Palleotti and he could not be persuaded to return, declaring that he could not understand how any man who had the bare necessities of life in England could bear to be 'concerned with business of state'. 'Had I a son,' he declared, 'I would sooner bind him a cobbler than a courtier, and a hangman than a statesman.'

Marlborough and Godolphin were, however, much gratified that they were to have the support of Robert Harley in the House of Commons, where, in October 1702, he was for the third time elected Speaker.

On the afternoon of 4 May that year, a procession of heralds and guards, accompanied by the King-of-Arms, had marched down St James's and, by way of the Strand and Charing Cross, to the City, to announce that war had been declared against France.

15

RIVAL ARMIES

'. . . he was not unmindful to provide money and order Regular
payments for everything that was brought into the camp . . .'

In October 1700 in his palace in Madrid, the puny, deformed
and dim-witted King Carlos II, who, in the words of the English
ambassador, 'looked like a ghost and moved like a clockwork image',
had lain slowly dying, his sufferings much exacerbated by his doctors,
who vainly dosed him with pearls dissolved in milk, painted essence
of cantharides on to his feet and placed the entrails of freshly killed
animals on his chest and stomach.

Since he had no children and no designated heir, the future of his
domains had long been a matter of contention and debate. These
realms were immense. They included over half the Italian peninsula,
Mexico and most of Central and South America, the Philippines,
the Canaries, much of the West Indies and the whole of the Spanish
Netherlands, comprising most of what is now Belgium and Luxembourg. And there was widespread fear in Europe that they might
pass into the hands of King Louis XIV of France, whose mother was
the eldest daughter of the Spanish King Philip III and whose wife
was the daughter of Philip IV, whose only other surviving child was
married to the Emperor.

In England and Holland it was unthinkable that the territories of
the French monarchy should be so vastly increased in this way, that
so large a share of the world's trade should fall into French hands,
that control of the Spanish Netherlands, the barrier between the
Dutch United Provinces and their potential enemies, be seized by
the already overweening power of France.

In Vienna the Austrian Hapsburgs were equally concerned that

97

the immense territories of the Spanish Hapsburgs should not become French possessions. The Austrian Emperor, Leopold I, had trouble enough already with rebels in Hungary and with his enemies in the Ottoman Empire. Besides, he himself could put forward a strong claim to the Spanish throne, since King Philip III of Spain was his grandfather and his first wife was a daughter of Philip IV. The Emperor's grandson from that marriage, Prince Joseph Ferdinand of Bavaria, could also stake a claim to the Spanish throne.

Indeed, King Louis XIV and King William III had already come to an agreement that Prince Joseph Ferdinand should be advanced as their agreed candidate upon Carlos II's expected death. But the Bavarian Prince had died before the Spanish King, and William and Louis had been obliged to confer together again. By the Second Partition Treaty of 1700, it had been agreed that upon King Carlos's demise the Emperor Leopold's second son, the Archduke Charles, should become King of Spain and ruler of the Spanish Netherlands and of Spain's empire in the west, while King Louis XIV's heir, the Dauphin, should be compensated with Sardinia, Naples and the long-disputed territory of Lorraine.

All this was settled without regard to 'the Sufferer' in Madrid, who, having developed enteric fever, been gripped by a fearful flux, passed 'almost 250 motions in nineteen days' and become stone deaf, died in the early morning of 1 November 1700. He left a will by which he bequeathed his domains to France in the person of King Louis's grandson, Philip, duc d'Anjou, and, failing him, to another grandson, the duc de Berry, with the proviso in both cases that the inheritance should include his realms in their entirety 'without allowing the least dismemberment or diminution of the monarchy founded with such glory by [his] ancestors'.

Despite the provisions of the Second Partition Treaty, which had not been agreed by the Emperor, King Louis accepted the will and, in February 1701, he asserted the right of the duc d'Anjou to succeed to the Spanish throne and thus, in time, combine France and Spain in a family-based alliance intolerable to the rest of Europe. As though to give notice that he was prepared to enforce the provisions of King Carlos's will, King Louis's army took possession of the Spanish Netherlands, imprisoning the garrisons in the Dutch-occupied barrier fortresses. These garrisons would be held captive, Louis declared, until the Dutch States-General formally recognized his grandson, the duc d'Anjou, as King Philip V of Spain. The loss of the fortresses deprived the Dutch Republic of the security upon which its very existence depended. With its defence policies destroyed at a stroke, it could not begin military operations in 1701, as the Emperor did in northern Italy, but the War of the Spanish Succession was now made inevitable.

France, with a population of about twenty million, four times that of England, was already the most powerful state in Europe; and Louis XIV, who had assumed power at the age of twenty-two in 1661, was by far the most powerful monarch. Ever since 1643, when the duc d'Enghien had decisively beaten the Spanish army of Philip IV at Rocroi, King Louis's army, reformed by two energetic and far-sighted war ministers, Michel Le Tellier and his son, the marquis de Louvois, had been more than a match for the combination of other armies brought against it.

Commanded by such gifted and highly successful marshals as the duc de Vendôme and the duc de Luxembourg, it was composed largely of French-born soldiers but contained also mercenaries, many of them Swiss or Irish Roman Catholics, known as the 'Wild Geese'.

It was constantly growing in numbers and was, in fact, to double in size within twenty-five years, its fire power and strict obedience to orders represented by such fine newly formed regiments as the *Fusiliers du Roi*, later the *Artillerie Royale*, and the *Régiment du Roi*, the first commander of which was Colonel Jean Martinet, the man whose name was to become synonymous with rigid discipline.

The army's strength was reinforced by a large militia raised in towns and villages throughout France and subjected to a discipline far stricter than that imposed upon militias in other European countries.

The structure of the English army was less formal than that of the French. Regiments were known by the names of their colonels and changed their names when a new colonel took them over. As with many civil offices, commissions were bought and sold, frequently going for exceptionally large sums, so that although a list of officers considered worthy of promotion was kept for reference by the

Secretary-at-War, certain regiments of both infantry and cavalry often passed into the hands of rich men not always suitable to command them. A colonelcy in the 1st Foot Guards could cost over £5,000.

Having bought the regiment, a colonel had not only to provide the men with their uniforms, equipment and pay, but also to provide for men who had been wounded and for the widows of men who had been killed. The pay for a cavalry trooper was 2s.6d. a day; for a dragoon, that is to say a mounted infantryman, 1s.6d.; and for a foot soldier 8d. What was known as 'subsistence money' was paid at the rate of 2s., 1s.2d. and 6d., out of which the men had to pay for their accommodation, for fodder for their horses and for their food. Rations and quarters were provided only when men were serving in the field.

Modest as these remunerations were, they were subject to certain stoppages, such as payment to the surgeon or contributions to the Chelsea Hospital, or were frequently withheld or reduced on various pretexts, so that the soldier was often an object of pity or contempt, usually ill-housed and often ill-fed, subject not only to fraud but also to savage punishments.

Strokes of the lash, administered to the victim's bare back, were the usual punishment. But others were common enough, among them the strappado, a peculiarly painful punishment in which the soldier's hands were tied behind his back and secured to a pulley; he was then hoisted from the ground and let down halfway with an agonizing jolt.

Enlistment was, therefore, by no means always voluntary. Recruiting parties, led by drummers and commanded by recruiting officers, entered village taverns to press the King's shillings into the hands of men who were either too drunk to resist them, or tempted and seduced by the uniform and promises of the recruiting sergeant, a master of persuasion in the disapproving opinion of the pious Captain John Blackadder of Ferguson's Regiment, who described a characteristic example as a 'rakish fellow' who could 'ramble and rove, and drink and tell stories, and wheedle and insinuate'. Many another recruit was willing enough to suppose that life as a soldier would be better than life with no work at all, and certainly better than the years in prison or incarceration in the workhouse from which enlistment saved many. Empowered by Recruiting Acts passed with the intention of enlisting men with 'No Lawful Calling or Imployment', recruiting parties marched criminals and debtors off to barracks or billets; then, briefly trained and provided with a uniform, they were put aboard battered troopships for what might well prove to be as dangerous a sea passage as that endured by Lieutenant Pope of Schomberg's Horse:

After having met with a violent storm in which we had our sails blown away, and sprung a leak, which kept us to the exercise of continual pumping, one of our guns broke loose, and had like to have overset the ship . . . With the loss of eighteen horses of the regiment, we arrived, having run more dangers than a man need do in several campaigns.

Since the most energetic recruitment drives rarely succeeded in raising the required numbers of men, resort, as in the French army, was had to the employment of foreign contingents hired *en masse*, usually from the states of Germany, so that it had become common enough for British generals to find themselves in command of armies in which a large proportion of their soldiers were foreign troops of sometimes doubtful reliability.

With very few exceptions, infantry regiments in the English army comprised a single battalion of some 700 men. In the absence of its colonel, who might well hold an appointment on the general staff, it was usually commanded by a lieutenant-colonel with a major as his second-in-command and a captain as adjutant. There were thirteen companies in a battalion, each commanded by a captain, assisted by a lieutenant and an ensign. Every regiment was also supposed to have a quartermaster, a chaplain and a surgeon, assisted by a surgeon's mate. Cavalry regiments also had a kettledrummer, who, according to one authority, was 'required to be a man of courage, preferring to perish in the fight than allow himself and his drum to be captured'. He should also have 'a pleasing motion of the arm [and] an accurate ear'.

Cavalry regiments were smaller than infantry regiments, consisting of about 450 men divided into nine troops of some fifty men, each troop being commanded by a captain, with a lieutenant and a cornet. Dragoon regiments, originally mounted infantry, had come to be regarded as cavalry regiments when on active service and as infantry when in garrison. They were armed with handguns or fusils as well as swords, the cavalryman having a pistol in addition to his sword.

Pistols, however, on Marlborough's orders, were to be used only in exceptional circumstances and never in action: no more than three rounds were issued to each man. The cavalryman was, therefore, expected to charge the enemy as a shock trooper, wielding his sword rather than firing his pistol, and trusting that the counter-blows and thrusts of the enemy would be deflected by his steel cuirass, which, reintroduced on Marlborough's orders to withstand the French cavalry's pistol-fire, now had no back, since this, he considered, should be unnecessary.

Swords were also carried by infantry soldiers as well as their officers, who were additionally armed with pistols. The pike, a sharp metal-tipped pole commonly seven-foot long, became obsolete at the beginning of the eighteenth century; but the halberd was still held by sergeants as a kind of badge of office, while spontoons, a species of half-pike, continued to be carried by officers.

Men on the march were weighed down by a heavy load of equipment as well as by their weapons and ammunition. Cartridge boxes were slung over their shoulders; greatcoats, blankets or cloaks were rolled up on their backs; they carried cooking pots in addition to knapsacks and, on occasions, mills for grinding corn and fascines for filling in the trenches that formed part of a fortress's defence works.

They were very rarely to be ill-fed when under the care of Marlborough, who always kept a careful watch upon the supply system of his armies, employing the most resourceful and reliable contractors, entering into detailed contracts with them, and taking the greatest trouble to ensure that supplies of ammunition as well as food arrived when and where they had been ordered. Furthermore, wrote one of his staff officers,

to make things yet more easy both to the Armies and the Countries marched through, he was not unmindful to provide money and order Regular payments for everything that was brought into the camp; a thing hitherto unknown . . . and to prevent any failure herein he order'd the Treasurer of the Army to be always in cash to answer Bills, and daily to have a Month's subsistence before hand.

16

FROM THE HAGUE TO LIÈGE

'I shall soon rid you of these troublesome neighbours.'

When Lord Marlborough returned to The Hague, three weeks after the declaration of war against France in May 1702, the question of who was to command the allied armies had still not been decided. Indeed, the King of Prussia, Frederick I, was on his way to the city to advance his own claim in person, while the Earl of Athlone and other Dutch generals were also making it clear that they, too, were ready to accept the command. Heinsius and his colleagues had decided that, with a large French army so close at hand, the matter must be decided without further delay. So, at last, as the only general who could command the respect of them all, Marlborough was given command of the British, Dutch and hired German forces of the Grand Alliance at a salary of £10,000 a year. The command was, however, a limited one: as captain-general he was to be accompanied by two Dutch deputies, Baron van Heyd and Mynheer Geldermalsen, a former ambassador in London, without whose agreement the enemy were not to be engaged in battle.

Marlborough was only too well aware of the problems inherent in this limited command. 'The station I am now in,' he replied to a letter from Godolphin congratulating him on his appointment, 'would have been a great deal more agreeable to me if it could have been had without dispute and a little less trouble. But,' he added on a more optimistic note, 'patience will overcome all things.'

To Sarah on 17 July he complained of the hot weather, which he hoped at least would be ripening the fruit at St Albans; he complained also of the amount of paperwork he had to get through, of his having

103

to be, when not on horseback, 'answering letters all day long', letters not only concerning 'the business of the army' but also in answer to correspondence 'from The Hague, and all other places where Her Majesty has any Ministers'. 'So, if it were not for my zeal for her service,' he told her, 'I should certainly desert, for you know of all things I do not love writing . . . No ambition can make me amends for being from you . . . When you are [at St Albans] pray think how happy I should be walking alone with you.' 'I doe assure you,' he later wrote, 'that your letters are so welcome to mee that if thay shou'd come in the time I was expecting the enemy to charge me, I cou'd not forbear reading them.'

The next few weeks were deeply frustrating. The Dutch generals and deputies – naturally alarmed by the threat of invasion by so powerful an enemy and the dangers to which their fortresses and towns would consequently be exposed – seemed content merely to protect their frontier from incursions by the French, whereas Marlborough was hoping to defeat the enemy in some decisive battle. One day he took a group of his allies to see for themselves the camp of the French troops which were commanded by the duc de Boufflers, a skilful marshal who had been in King Louis XIV's army for over forty years. 'There,' he said, throwing out his arm towards the enemy's tents in an unwontedly dramatic gesture. 'I shall soon rid you of these troublesome neighbours.' He was not, however, allowed to do so. When at Little Bruegel, on the night of 1 August, he proposed a full-scale attack the next day, the Dutch deputies at first agreed; then, learning that more French troops, commanded by Marshal le comte de Tallard, were on the march to support Boufflers, they changed their minds and withheld their permission for an attack.

Marlborough was obliged to defer to their reluctance, but asked them to ride out with him to see the opportunity they had missed. He took them to rising ground where they could look down upon Boufflers's entire large army marching across their front, its flank dangerously exposed to assault. That night the French reached Zon-hoven and, believing that what the deputies had seen in the morning would convince them that Boufflers would still be exposed to an attack as his troops straggled across the heath the following day,

Marlborough again asked for their agreement to an assault upon them. Again they were reluctant to give their consent.

King James II's son, the Duke of Berwick, who was serving as a lieutenant-general in Boufflers's army, commented in his *Memoirs* that

it was very fortunate for us [that the deputies of the States-General] would not consent to an attack either upon the heath or on our camp at Zonhoven . . . for we were posted in such a manner that we should have been beaten without being able to stir, our left being very high, and our right sunk into a cul-de-sac between two rivulets.

Later on that month another opportunity to fall upon the French army presented itself. Again Marlborough proposed an attack and again Baron van Heyd and Geldermalsen demurred: better, they said, to wait to see what happened the next day. 'Tomorrow,' Marlborough said, 'Monsieur de Boufflers will be gone.' He was.

Two days later Marlborough reported to Godolphin:

I believe we should have had a very easy victory . . . However, I have thought it much [better] for her Majesty's service to take no notice of it, as you see by my letter to the States-General. But . . . I am in so ill houmer that I will not trouble you, nor dare I trust myself to write more.

But, if he did not trust himself to write more to Godolphin, he did feel compelled to write to Boufflers, unable to bear the thought that he and the Duke of Berwick would consider him so incapable or timorous a general as to refrain from attacks when good opportunities offered themselves. Accordingly, he sent a messenger with a letter to both the Marshal and the Duke explaining that it was not by his decision that no attack had been launched.

By the end of August Marlborough had moved to Asche, where, with some 45,000 men, he was carefully watching Boufflers's army to ensure that it did not move north to attempt the relief of Venlo, the strongest of the fortresses on the Meuse river north of Maastricht, the French garrison of which was being besieged by a large force commanded by the Prince of Nassau-Saarbrück. The siege works at Venlo were progressing slowly under the direction of the ploddingly methodical, elderly and ailing Dutch engineer Baron Menno van Cohorn, who, so Adam de Cardonnel said, would not begin work on the defences of a fortress until he had 'everything ready to a tittle'. So slowly did the works at Venlo progress, indeed, that Marlborough was induced to complain to Heinsius that the army was in danger of losing 'all the frute of this campagne'. The 'demands of stores made by Mr de Cohorn [gave him] the spleen'. 'The troupes has been before Venlo thes eight days,' he continued in another letter, 'and they now talke of opening the trenches two days hence. If this be zele, God preserve mee from being so served as you are my friend.'

He also gave vent to his frustration in letters to his friend Godolphin: 'It is not to be imagined the backwardness and sloth of thes pepell, even for that which is for their own good.'

The works at Venlo were still not prepared to Cohorn's satisfaction when an assault was nevertheless made on Fort St Michael, a strong outwork of the fortress, by a brigade comprising the Royal Regiment of Ireland, later the 18th Royal Irish, and two English battalions commanded by Lord Cutts, who was, in Jonathan Swift's opinion, as 'brave and brainless as the sword he wears . . . the vainest old fool alive'.

Robert Parker, a captain in the Irish regiment, described his men as rushing forward 'like madmen without fear or wit' and succeeding in their assault 'to the greatest astonishment of the whole army', as well as of the men themselves when they 'came to reflect upon what [they] had done'. 'However,' Parker added, 'had not several accidents occurred in the affair, hardly a man of us would have escaped being either killed, drowned [in the deep moat] or captured.'

In the end, however, 'success crowned the event', wrote Brigadier-General Richard Kane, at that time a gentleman volunteer in the Royal Irish, taking up Parker's story; and this 'got the Lord Cutts great applause of which he boasted all his life after, though neither he nor any of the noblemen stirred one foot till we were masters of [the outwork] except the young [8th] Earl of Huntingdon, who stole out of the trenches and kept up with the foremost'.

The subsequent fall of the main fortress, which surrendered four days after the capture of Fort St Michael, was followed by the capture from the French of two other important fortresses on the Meuse, Stevensweert and Roermond; and with these in allied hands and Liège, south of Maastricht, threatened, Marlborough once more proposed a battle to scatter or destroy the French army still in the field. But, once again, he was refused permission by the Dutch, who were quite content with what had already been achieved that season. So Marlborough marched his men past the French army towards Liège, which, after a fierce bombardment and the opening up of a satisfactory breach, was commanded to capitulate on 22 October. The governor refused to surrender. So a general assault was ordered and the troops, led by the British contingent, charged through the breach into the citadel, giving 'no quarter for some time', according to Captain Parker, 'so that the greater part of the garrison was cut to pieces'. A few days later the garrison of the Chartreuse fort showed their readiness to surrender by covering their ramparts with flags; and, granted 'honourable terms', the enemy troops marched out without weapons, 'with their hands in their pockets, and every man was to go where he pleased, by which means the officers carried few of them home'. Parker continued:

Thus ended the Lord Marlborough's first campaign, which established his character among the Allies, and gave great satisfaction in particular to the States-General, for not only the Field-Deputies, but even the Earl of Athlone who at first disputed the command with him [and was spoken of in private by him with what Geldermalsen described as 'great scorn'] and all their general officers gave an extraordinary character of him.

Yet Marlborough was not satisfied. The Dutch were quite content that Venlo, Stevensweert, Roermond and Liège had all been taken and that the course of the Meuse and the Lower Rhine were now in allied hands. But Marlborough was concerned that, for all his urging, no attempt had been made to get to grips with the French army and to fight it in the field. The war could not be won by marching and countermarching, taking forts and losing too many men in doing so – some 500 men had been killed or wounded in the storming of the citadel of Liège alone. Sooner or later a battle would have to be fought.

★

A few days after the capture of the Chartreuse fort at Liège, Marl-borough, with one of his clerks, Stephen Gell, and the two Dutch deputies boarded a boat to be towed down the Meuse towards The Hague. After passing Venlo their cavalry escort was forced by the lie of the land to leave the river bank and, while they were thus unprotected, a raiding party of French troops led by an Irishman named Farewell, who had deserted the Dutch service for the French, suddenly loomed out of the darkness of the night, pulled the boat to the bank by its tow-rope, fired a volley of shots as a warning and jumped aboard. The two Dutch deputies produced the safe-conducts commonly issued by commanders on one side in a war to important persons on the other who were travelling in a non-military capacity, and, in this case, signed by the duc de Bourgogne, the French King's grandson and nominal commander of his army. Marlborough had not troubled to obtain one, trusting to the escort to drive off any marauding French troops they might encounter on their journey.

While the deputies' passes were being examined in the light of a lantern in the cabin, Marlborough was aware of a piece of paper being passed into his hand by his clerk. It was a pass made out in the name of Marlborough's brother Lieutenant-General Charles Churchill, who, having been relieved of his post as governor of Kinsale, was now serving in Marlborough's army. The pass, which Stephen Gell had fortuitously produced from among his master's papers, was out of date, and much argument ensued as to its validity, bribes presumably having changed hands before this was accepted. By his own account Marlborough was 'kept in the power of the French party nine hours'; 'thank God they did not know', he added, the true identity of their prisoner. Taken for his brother, he was allowed to proceed on his way, having been deprived of his money and plate and of the services of the party's cook, as well as those of the men of the cavalry escort who had by now appeared on the river bank and been promptly taken prisoner.*

---

* It was afterwards suggested that Farewell had been bribed to let his captive go, 'this being one of the occasions when milord Marlborough did not exercise his usual thrift'. Certainly Farewell soon afterwards returned to the Dutch service, was granted a free pardon for his desertion and promoted to a captaincy. Stephen Gell was

Rumours that Marlborough had been taken prisoner with his brother and was still held by the French reached The Hague before he arrived there himself. These misleading reports also reached Venlo and Nijmegen, with the additional misinformation that the Captain-General had been taken to the nearby fortified town of Geldern, which was still in French hands. The allied officers who had been appointed governors of Venlo and Nijmegen accordingly set out with their entire garrisons for Geldern, as did troops sent there by the States-General, who also dispatched couriers to Vienna with an urgent request that the duc de Villeroi, who had been taken prisoner by the Austrians, should be kept in confinement in case the French would agree to his being exchanged for Lord Marlborough.

While the French governor of Geldern, as the supposed captor of Lord Marlborough, was attempting to appease the angry would-be saviours at his gates by offering up the Englishman's cook and his plate, Marlborough himself arrived at The Hague to the jubilation of the cheering crowds that filled the city's streets. 'My room is full at this time,' he told Godolphin a day or two later,

I being [all the more] welcome to them by an accident I had of being taken by a French party. Till they saw mee they thought mee a prisoner in France, so that I was not ashore one minut, before I had great crowds of the Common pepell, some endeavouring to take mee by the hands, and all cryeing out welcome. But that which moved mee most was, to see a great many of both sexes crye for joye. I have been extremely obliged by the kind reception I have met with: for from five in the afternoon till after ten at night, there was a perpetual firing in the streets, which is their way of rejoicing.

---

rewarded by Marlborough with a pension of £50 a year for life and found employment in the Exchange of Prisoners Office. Marlborough seems to have rather
regretted being so generous to Gell. Some time after granting him this reward, he
told Sarah, evidently rather grudgingly, that the man had been costing '50l. a year
ever since' (Coxe, *Memoirs of John, Duke of Marlborough, with His Original Correspondence* (1820), i, 99).

17

THE DEATH OF THE HEIR

*'For God's sake, if there be any hope of
recovery let me know it.'*

While Marlborough was still at The Hague, his wife received
an unexpected letter from Queen Anne, who wrote to her to say
that it troubled her 'poor unfortunate, faithful Morley to think
that [there was] so little in her power to show how truly sensible'
she was of all Lord Marlborough's kindness, 'especially at a time
when he [deserved] all that a Rich Crown could give'. The letter
continued:

But since there is nothing else at this time, I hope that you will give me
leave as soon as he comes home to make him a Duke. I know my dear Mrs
Freeman does not care for anything of that kind nor am I satisfied with it,
because it does not enough express the value I have for Mr Freeman, nor
ever can how passionately I am yours, my dear Mrs Freeman.

When she received this letter, so Sarah said, she let it drop from
her hand and she was 'for some minutes like one that had received
the news of a death of one of her dear friends'. Ever since the Queen's
offer had been expected, Sarah had hoped it would not be made,
because of the jealousy it was bound to arouse in people envious
enough already. Besides, a dukedom might well prove a burden
which her husband's present circumstances could not well support.
At present she had only one son, but there might well be more, and
in 'the next generation a great many'.

When, therefore, she wrote to tell her husband of the Queen's
offer, she advised him to decline it. He was, however, not inclined
to do so himself, provided a sufficient income was provided for him

to maintain himself and his family in the state and style a duke was expected to do, and replied:

You know I am very ill at compliments, but I have a heart full of gratitude; therefore pray say all you can to the Queen for her extraordinary goodness to me . . . I do agree with you that we ought not to wish for a greater title till we have a better estate.

He consulted Heinsius about the Queen's offer, and in a long letter to Sarah he told her that the Grand Pensionary was convinced that he ought to accept the title, which would place him in a more authoritative position when dealing with subordinates in the allied army, so many of whom were of princely status. Besides, Heinsius did not doubt that the Queen would be generous when it came to increasing Marlborough's already enormous income. He assured his friend that, whatever was done at this time for his fortune, it would, 'like the title, be quite without envy since all the people were pleased with what [he] had done'. All in all, therefore, Marlborough, while assuring his wife that he had 'a mind to do nothing but as it may be easy' to her, decided that it was 'his duty to accept the Queen's gracious offer'.

Three days after this letter to Sarah was written, a new Parliament met in London and dutifully congratulated the Queen on the satisfactory outcome of the recent fighting, the Commons including in their declaration a derogatory reference to King William, calculated by the Tories to annoy the Whigs: 'The vigorous support of Your Majesty's Allies, and the wonderful progress of Your Majesty's arms under the conduct of the Earl of Marlborough, have signally retrieved the ancient honour and glory of the English nation.'

The Members of both Houses, accompanying the Queen and Lady Marlborough, made their progress to St Paul's Cathedral through cheering crowds on 12 November 1702; and a fortnight later Marlborough himself landed at Margate and drove quietly to London, anxious to avoid the limelight, being well aware that jealousy was being aroused by the exceptional favours which the Queen was bestowing upon him.

Having, at the beginning of December, publicly expressed her intention of making him a duke, the Queen then announced that she wished to grant him £5,000 a year from the revenues of the Post Office for the support of this title during her lifetime.

This raised protests from Members of Parliament, who had argued in the past against such national revenues being handed over to individuals and had strongly condemned the lavish awards granted to King William's Dutch favourites. The protests became more heated than ever when the Queen further proposed, as Marlborough had requested, that Parliament should find means for settling the grant permanently upon the Duke and his heirs. Rather than be involved in such angry controversy, Marlborough asked the Queen to forgo her second message to Parliament on his behalf, 'since it might embarrass her affairs and be of ill consequence to the public'. The Queen reluctantly did forgo her message, whereupon the House of Commons recorded their 'inexpressible grief' at having felt it necessary to protest against being asked to approve of such an alienation of the revenues of the Crown, which had already been 'so much reduced by the exorbitant grants of the last reign'.

Having withdrawn her request for a permanent grant to Marlborough's family, the Queen wrote to Sarah:

I cannot be satisfied with myself without doing something towards making up what has been so maliciously hindered in the Parliament, and therefore I desire that dear Mrs Freeman and Mr Freeman would be so kind as to accept of two thousand a year out of the privy purse, besides the grant of the five. This can draw no envy, for nobody need know it. Not that I disown what I give to people that deserve it . . . You may keep it a secret or not as you please. I beg my dear Mrs Freeman would never any way give me an answer to this; only comply with the desires of your poor unfortunate friend Morley, that loves you most tenderly, and is with the sincerest passion imaginable yours.

Although Marlborough was, according to Cardonnel, 'a little chagrined' by the refusal of the House of Commons to allow him and his descendants to have the £5,000 a year from the Post Office in perpetuity, he and his wife decided for the moment not to accept the additional £2,000 a year which the Queen had offered them, wary of arousing more jealousy and provoking more accusations of greed than had already been directed against them.

'After [th]e excesse of honors conferred by the Queen on the E. of Marborow,' John Evelyn wrote in his diary on 30 December 1702,

to make him a . . . Duke for the success of but one Campagne, [that] he should desire 5000 pounds a yeare out of the Post-office to be settled on him was by the parliament thought a bold and unadvised request, who had besides his owne considerable Estate, above 30000 pounds per Ann in places and Employments, with 50000 pounds at Interest . . . This . . . love of riches . . . was taken notice of and displeased those who had him til now in great esteeme.

Marlborough and his wife were in agreement over their rejection of the £2,000 a year offered by the Queen, but they were soon to find themselves in opposite camps over a proposed Occasional Conformity Bill, which was designed to prevent Nonconformists from receiving communion occasionally in the Anglican Church simply in order to qualify themselves for civil or military appointments. Believing this to be a blatant attempt by the Tories and the Church to persecute freethinkers and to undermine the strength of the Whigs, Sarah, as a most vehement Whig, was passionately opposed to the Bill and was furious when she learned that her husband and Sidney Godolphin both intended voting for it.

All rancour was, however, forgotten when the Marlboroughs learned that their son, John, who, since his father's elevation in the peerage, bore the courtesy title of Marquess of Blandford, had fallen dangerously ill.

Blandford was then sixteen years old. He had already left Eton and was an undergraduate at Cambridge in the care of Dr Francis Hare, an Old Etonian and an alumnus of King's College, who, after serving as chaplain-general of the army in Flanders, was to become Bishop of Chichester. He was a learned man and a prolific author, 'of a sharp and piercing wit', so it was said of him, 'of great judgement and understanding in worldly matters . . . but of a sour and crabbed disposition . . . haughty, hotheaded, injudicious and unpopular'. Yet Blandford seems to have progressed satisfactorily under his supervision, and, in the words of his father's biographer,

Archdeacon William Coxe, the boy 'set an example of affability, regularity and steadiness above his years'. His father proposed taking him on his staff when next he served abroad, but his mother considered him too young and so it was decided that he should stay another year at Cambridge, where Dr Hare could continue to keep his stern eye upon him and where he could spend a few days' holiday now and then at Lord Godolphin's house nearby at Newmarket.

He was staying there in the autumn of 1702, 'the best natured and most agreeable creature' in his host's opinion, when there was an outbreak of smallpox in the town. However, Godolphin thought that there was no danger of Blandford contracting it since, 'going into no house' but his, the boy would surely 'bee more defended from it by ayr and riding . . . than possibly he could bee anywhere else'. But no sooner had Blandford returned to Cambridge than he fell ill with all the symptoms of a particularly severe strain of the disease. His mother rushed to his side; so did the royal physicians, sent by the Queen, who told Sarah she was 'truly afflicted for the melancholy account of poor dear Lord Blandford'. 'I pray God grant he may do well,' she added. 'And give me leave once more to beg you for Christ Jesus' sake to have a care of your dear precious self.'

The boy's father also wrote to Sarah:

I am so troubled at the sad condition this poor child seems to be in that I know not what to do. I pray God to give you some comfort in this great affliction. If you think anything under heaven can be done, pray let me know it. Or if you think my coming can be of least use let me know it. I beg I may hear as soon as possible, for I have no thought but what is at Cambridge. Medicines are sent by the doctors. I shall be impatient to the last degree till I hear from you.

That night the anxious father wrote another letter:

I was in hopes I should have heard again before this time for I hope the doctors were with you early this morning . . . If we must be so unhappy as to lose this poor child I pray God to enable us both to behave ourselves with that resignation which we ought to do. If this uneasiness which I now be under should last long, I think I could not live. For God's sake, if there be any hope of recovery let me know it.

Soon after this letter was written, all hope that the boy would recover was lost, and Marlborough received the summons to Cambridge which he had been dreading. His son died that day, 20 February 1703. The parents left within hours for St Albans to be alone in their grief.

Grieving for the loss of a beloved son, his only surviving son, the heir who was to have carried on the ducal dynasty in the years to come, Marlborough sat down to make a new will before leaving once more for the Continent. He provided for his fortune to pass to his wife to be held in trust for their eldest daughter's husband, Francis Godolphin, to whom he wished the dukedom to pass.

'I've lost what is so dear to me,' he said gloomily to the exiled Jacobite Lord Ailesbury upon his return to The Hague. 'It is fit for me to retire and not toil and labour for I know not who: my daughters are all married.'

The death of the boy was constantly in his mind. One day, upon encountering 'a very great procession', he 'thought how pleas'd' the boy would have 'been with such a sight'. 'The thought added very much to my uneasyness,' he told Godolphin. 'Since itt has pleased God to take him, I doe wish from my soull I cou'd think of him less.'

So did the boy's mother, who was so grieved by his death – a 'strock of fortune' compared to which only the death of her husband would have been 'more grievous' to her – that it was said that her brain was 'near touched'. She was seen by the boys of Westminster School 'pacing in the cloisters of the Abbey in deep mourning, mingling with the vagrants who came there for shelter'.

In Holland again Marlborough rode energetically about day after day, as though anxious to overcome his grief, reviewing troops, inspecting fortresses, holding meetings with Heinsius and Dutch generals. While thus engaged, he was elated to hear from Sarah that she was pregnant again, and he began to hope and pray for another heir. But then came a second letter from her to say that she was mistaken: she was not with child after all. A letter also arrived from Godolphin warning him that his wife was not at all well.

It was thus with a heavy heart that Marlborough turned his mind to the consideration of plans for operations which would not only hold back the French army, under the duc de Villeroi in the Spanish Netherlands, but also contain the enemy forces in Germany, now strengthened by their Bavarian allies under the Elector Maximilian II Emmanuel, who had chosen to come into the war on the side of Louis XIV in the hope that his dynasty, the Wittelsbachs, might thereby supplant the Hapsburgs on the imperial throne.

The Dutch, however, fought shy of the Duke's ideas and, their minds concentrated upon fortresses, they suggested a siege of Bonn. Marlborough gave way to them and, in the middle of May 1703, he was able to write to Sarah to tell her that, after a bombardment from over 1,000 mortars and cannon, Bonn was stormed and taken. The garrison, he wrote, 'are to march out on Friday, but I shall not stay to see them, being resolved to be with the army on the Meuse from whence you shall be sure to hear from him who loves you with all his soul. My humble duty to the Queen.' To this he added a postscript with an eye, as always, to petty saving: 'I hope she will excuse me for not putting her to the expense of an express to bring the news of Bonn being taken.'

Having gone back to the Meuse from Bonn, Marlborough turned his mind to what, in correspondence with the States-General, he termed with unaccustomed hyperbole, his 'Great Design'. This involved the taking of Antwerp by means of an assault upon the so-called Lines of Brabant, a system of well-manned and strongly defended fortifications, palisades and inundations designed by Marshal Vauban, stretching from Antwerp to the Meuse near Namur.

Marlborough's plan was a highly complicated one, dependent upon deceiving Villeroi, who nevertheless was not deceived, and the close cooperation of two Dutch generals, a disputatious Baron van Cohorn, who went off on a pillaging expedition, and the unpredictable General Opdam, who, in Marlborough's opinion, was 'very capable' of being defeated and, indeed, was so. The 'Great Design', therefore, ended in disaster; and the Dutch once more turned their attention to fortresses and sieges.

The Duke reported to Lord Godolphin that 'no ambition of [his] own inclined [him] to wish a battle, but with the blessing of God [he thought] it would be of far greater advantage to the common cause than the taking of twenty towns'. He said as much to Anthonie Heinsius, to whom he vented his despair and annoyance in a letter dated 21 July: 'It is impossible the warr can goe on att this rate . . . It is in my opinion impossible to avoyde in length of time some great misfortune . . . I own to you that I have the spleen to a very great degree.'

18

THE PHANTOM AFFAIR

'. . . it can never go out of my mind
the opinion you must have of me . . .'

In England, meanwhile, more voices began to be raised in denigration of the royally indulged Duke of Marlborough, whose name, in Whig circles, was dragged into general attacks on the recent unsatisfactory conduct of the war. Nor were the Tories, already hotly arguing over conflicting attitudes towards the Occasional Conformity Bill, prepared to give him their united support, many of them condemning his campaigns in the Low Countries and vociferously advocating the so-called 'Blue Water' strategy of concentration on naval and colonial operations. 'The very ladies,' commented Jonathan Swift, 'are split asunder into High Church and Low and, out of zeal for religion, have hardly time to say their prayers.' 'Even the dogs in the street' were, he added, 'much more contumelious and quarrelsome than usual'.

For Marlborough that summer of 1703 was as frustrating as the spring had been. The Dutch remained as determined as ever to prevent the Captain-General from fighting the battle which he believed his local superiority in numbers over the French could allow him to win. He was obliged to content himself with the siege and surrender of Huy, which would 'make very little noise in the world', and the subsequent taking of Limburg, another 'small gain' which, nevertheless, highly gratified the Dutch. The names of both Huy and Limburg, with that of Bonn, were placed upon a medal which was struck to commemorate their capture, and which bore a likeness of Queen Anne on one side and one of Marlborough on the other, together with the inscription: VICTORIOUS WITHOUT SLAUGHTER.

All plans for another attack on the Lines of Brabant were, however, frustrated; and a letter proposing an operation to break through them, signed by Marlborough and by twelve allied generals, English, Danish and German, pressing for such an attack, had no effect. The Duke wrote to Heinsius:

I am sure you will observe all thay [the Dutch generals] say is to incline us to act defensively, which I take to be destruction . . . I do call God to witness that . . . we could have forced the Lines with the loss of very few men . . . The discord in our camp will encourage the enemy . . . If I might have millions given mee to serve another year and be obliged to doe nothing by the *unanimous consent* of the Generals, I would rather dye.

As it was, the 'unreasonable opposition' of the generals so heated his blood that he was 'almost mad with the headache'. If only he had had an unfettered command, he was 'veryly persuaded that with the blessing of God [he] would have had a glorious campagne' since he had had many occasions to make 'use of the bravarie of the troupes'.

Despite his frustration and disappointment at having nothing more worthwhile to celebrate than the capture of a fortress or two from the French, who were still in possession of ten times as many, Marlborough preserved his accustomed urbanity and polite deference when engaging with the Dutch – politicians and generals alike – in endless discussions. But in letters to Godolphin, as in some of those to Heinsius, he spoke of his unhappiness. 'I really am so weary of the business of this world . . . I hope this is my last year of serving . . . I am not very fond of staying with an Army that is not to do more than eat forage.'

His normally good health began to deteriorate still further. Excessively dejected, suffering from what he called 'spleen', as well as from agonizing headaches and sleeplessness, he was thankful when the time came for his return to England and his family.

Upon his return, Marlborough found the country's dissatisfaction with the progress of the war more widespread than he had imagined it to be. The Whigs, who had previously lent their support to him and Godolphin despite political differences, had now turned against them, accounting them both guilty of failing to provide gains commensurate with the funds which they had generously voted in Parliament for the prosecution of the war, and accusing Marlborough of incompetence in his direction of operations. The High Tories, too, and the Earl of Nottingham, the Secretary of State, in particular, added their condemnations to those of their political opponents, and joined with them in accusing Marlborough of what one of them described as feathering his nest in salaries and perquisites not only from English and Dutch funds, but also from other allies whose troops were serving in his army. So virulent, indeed, did these accusations become that both Godolphin and Marlborough, always highly sensitive to criticism, let it be known that they, as well as the Duchess of Marlborough, considered withdrawing to that quiet, private life which Godolphin so often thought of enjoying by the stables at Newmarket, and of which Marlborough so often wrote to his wife, imagining them in retirement together in their house beside the orchards and fishponds in St Albans.

The Queen, endeavouring to put such ideas from their minds, wrote to the Duchess from Windsor:

The thoughts that both Mrs Freeman and Mr Freeman seem to have of retiring gives me no small uneasiness and therefore I must say something on that subject. It is no wonder that people in your posts should be weary of the world, who are so continually worried with all the hurry and impertinences of it; but give me leave to say you should a little consider your faithful friends and poor country, which must be ruined if ever you should put your melancholy thoughts in execution. As for your poor unfortunate Morley, she could not bear it; for if you should forsake me, I could have nothing more to do with the world, but make another abdication, for what is a crown when the support of it is gone. I never will forsake your dear self, Mr Freeman, nor Mr Montgomery, but always be your constant faithful servant; and we four must never part . . .

If ever Marlborough had seriously intended retirement at this time, he soon abandoned the idea; and when it was proposed to him that he should consider serving under Prince George, the Elector of Hanover, should this heir to the English crown be appointed commander-in-chief, he readily agreed to do so, well aware, no doubt, that the Dutch would never agree to this change of command.

★

While Marlborough's future was in the balance in the spring of 1704, he and Sarah had the first serious quarrel of their married life. Sarah was at this time forty-three years old, still grieving for the loss of her son, living through her menopause and saddened by the thought that she could no longer bear another son.

She had been led to believe that her husband was having an affair. Marlborough thought that the informant was their son-in-law, Charles Spencer, who had become Earl of Sunderland on his father's death two years before. The new Lord Sunderland, as a dedicated Whig, had recently protested against a Bill which settled upon the Queen's husband, Prince George, a most generous annuity of £100,000 a year and contained a clause exempting the Prince from a provision in the Act of Succession designed to exclude 'strangers, though naturalized' from English offices and peerages should a Hanoverian prince become king, an exemption which implied that the peerages created by King William would lapse on the death of Queen Anne.

Sarah Churchill had been furious when the tiresome young Lord Sunderland objected to this Bill. She had been doing all she could to reconcile the Tory Queen to the Whigs; and now this dreadful man was undoing all the headway she had made in persuading the Queen that the Whigs were really just as loyal to the monarchy as the Tories were. Her passionate nature revolted against her son-in-law, who was clearly going to prove difficult and obstructive. He, in turn, returned her dislike, and was naturally suspected of telling tales about her husband, who, from his soul, cursed 'that hour in which [he gave his] poor dear child to a man who [had made him of all mankind] the most unhappiest [of beings]'.

Marlborough vehemently denied the charge of adultery. In the summer of the year before, he had been much concerned by reports of his wife's poor health. That August, he had written to her:

I have received yours of the 23rd which has given mee, as you may easily beleive, a good deal of trouble. I beg you will be so kind and just to me, as to beleive the truth of my heart, that my greatest concern is for that of your own health. It was a great pleasure to me when I thought we should be blessed with more children. But as all my happyness centers in living quietly with you, I do conjure you, by all the kindness I have for you, which is as much as ever man had for woman, that you will take the best advice you can for your health, and then follow exactly what shall be proscribed you, and I do hope you will be so good as to let me have an exact account of it, and what the physicians' opinions are . . . Think as little as is possible of worldly business, and be very regular in your diet . . . Your health is much dearer to me than my own . . . I shall have no rest till I hear from you again. For God's sake let me know exactly how you are . . . It is impossible for me to express what I feel, having [had a letter from] my Lord Treasurer to say that he thought that you were very far from being well.

To Godolphin himself he had expressed his great anxiety:

For God's sake let me have a particular account; and if she does not go to the Bath with the Queen, I hope her Majesty and yourself will prevail with her to enter into such a course of physic as she shall be advised to, or that the Queen will take her to the Bath with her: for I am very sure to leave her alone will not be good for her health . . . [If it would do her any good], with the Queen's leave I would immediately come over, notwithstanding that I am very sensible how the world would censure me . . . I have no ambition or other thought left, but of serving the Queen to the utmost of my power, and ending my days quietly with Lady Marl.

He knew how deeply distressed she had been by the death of their son and heir – indeed, a friend of Abigail Harley's, Lady Pye, was not alone in thinking that it had affected her mind as well as her physical health. The Duke had tried to comfort her:

You and I have great reason to bless God for all we have, so that we must not repine at His taking our poor child from us, but bless and praise Him for what His goodness leaves us; and I do beseech Him, with all my heart and soul that He would comfort and strengthen both you and me, not only to bear this, but any other correction that He shall think fit to lay on us.

It was all the more distressing for him on his return to England in the spring of 1704, and after a short but perfectly happy time at Holywell, to find Sarah so suddenly furious with him, accusing him of being unfaithful to her, even of hating her. In an undated and scarcely coherent letter sent in April 1704, he wrote to her:

After your kind way of living with me since we last came from St Albans which made me think I should always be happy, I did little except to have had anybody put you in so ill a humour as to make me so miserable as I am at this time. As for your suspicion of me as to this woman, that will vanish, but it can never go out of my mind the opinion you must have of me, after my solemn protesting and swearing that it did not gain any belief with you. This thought has made me take no rest this night, and for ever makes me unhappy. I know not what to say more but do assure you in the presence of God this is the truth of my soul . . . I do call God to witness, and he may be merciful to me the last day, that when I came home this last time I loved you so tenderly that I proposed all the happiness imaginable in living quietly with you the remaining part of my life. I do to my great grief see that you have fixed in your so very ill opinion of me that I must never more think of being happy.

In another letter, he persisted:

When I do swear to you as I do that I love you, it is not dissembling. I can't forbear repeating what I said yesterday, which is that I never sent to her in my life. May I and all that is dear to me be curs'd if I ever sent to her, or had anything to do with her, or ever endeavoured to have.

At the same time he wrote to Godolphin explaining why he could not go to see him for a day or two. 'You know the tender concern I have for Lady Marl.; so that I need not tell you how unhappy her unkindness makes me, but I am not fit for any company.' His misery and anxiety made him physically ill as well as depressed. He suffered from more than usually painful headaches and from indigestion, as a cure for which he took liquorice and rhubarb, without effect.

On 8 April he left London for the coast at Harwich. Sarah came to see him set sail. But, in painful contrast to her demeanour on his departure two years before, there was no affection in her farewell. Angry still and as miserable as he was himself, she handed him a paper listing her grievances and renewed accusations, and protesting about some clauses in the new will which he had made after his son's death.

Accompanied by his brother, Lieutenant-General Charles Churchill, Count Wratislaw and various members of his staff, including Cardonnel, Marlborough landed in Holland on 21 April 1704. He found Heinsius in poor health and the other members of the States-General with whom he spoke dejected and apprehensive. They, in turn, found him quite unlike the agreeable, accommodating man they had grown to know. At a meeting in Heinsius's house, having already caused consternation by informing them that he would in future take it upon himself to engage the enemy in battle if and when it seemed to him opportune to do so, he now told them that it had been agreed in London that he was to march with his British troops, and the other troops in British pay, to Koblenz, at the junction of the Rhine and the Moselle. He produced an Order in Council signed by the Queen authorizing him to carry out whatever plans he proposed in sending 'a speedy succour to His Imperial Majesty and the Empire'.

'I am very [conscious of the knowledge] that I take a great deal upon me,' he told Godolphin. 'But should I act otherwise, the Empire would be undone and consequently the [alliance].'

What he did not tell the Dutch deputies was that he had already decided to strike at the French well to the east of the Moselle: he was intent upon a march of dramatic daring as far as the Danube in order to prevent the French from gaining entire control of southern Germany, and to aid and rescue the Hapsburg Empire, threatened as it was by enemies closing in upon it in both Germany and Italy and endangering Vienna itself.

Marlborough was much encouraged in his planning of this audacious stroke by receiving a letter from Sarah which, from the tone of his response, seems to have been, if not loving and forgiving, at least conciliatory:

You are so good to take notice that I might not like something you had written in the paper you gave me at Harwich. I do own to you that I have had more melancholy thoughts and spleen at what you said in that paper than I am able to express but was resolved never to have mentioned it more to you after the answer I gave to it, which I hope is come into your hands.

A few days later, however, he received another letter which put his mind quite at rest and elicited a most grateful and affectionate reply. It was a 'dear letter', he wrote, 'so very kind' that he 'would in return lose a thousand lives to make [her] happy'. On receipt of it he took the paper she had given him at Harwich out of his strongbox and burned it. He would read and reread this most recent and loving letter often; it would be found among his papers at his death; it had made him so happy, so 'transported him', that he loved her 'better than ever' he did before. Having begged her to continue to love him as she did now, for then no harm could come to him, he ended his long letter:

You have by this kindness preserved my quiet, and I believe my life; for until I had this letter I have been very indifferent of what should become of myself. I have pressed this business of carrying an army into Germany in order to leave a good name behind me . . . I shall now add that of having a long life that I may be happy with you.

He entreated her to go on writing to him regularly: her letters were a comfort to his 'very being'.

He told her something of his plans and of his intended and successful deception of the French command, careful not to divulge too much, just as he was intent upon keeping his true intentions hidden from the Dutch and the Tories and all but a very few discreet friends such as Godolphin and Heinsius.

I reckon to leave this place [The Hague] upon Monday [5 May] and I intend to lie one night at my Lord Albemarle's, so that [on 10 May] I shall dine with the Army on the Meuse and continue there 2 or 3 days, and afterwards join those troops that are designed for the Moselle. But I shall not continue [thereabouts] for long, for I intend to go higher up into Germany, which I am forced as yet to keep here a secret, for fear [the Dutch] would be apprehensive of letting their troops go so far.

Nothing could have made me take so much upon myself in this matter, but that I see the French must overrun the Empire if we do not help them at this time. I am very sensible that if we have not success I shall be found fault with . . . [but] if we have good success the Empire [will have to] own that [we] have saved them . . . *Whatever happens to me* I beg you will believe that my heart is entirely yours and that I have no thoughts, but what is for the good of my country.

Remember me kindly to my dear Children.

19

THE MARCH TO THE DANUBE

'Surely never was such a march carried on
with more order and regularity . . .'

Having made his peace with Sarah, Marlborough was in good humour as his coach rumbled along on the rough roads that led to the Meuse, believing, as he put it, that the troops he led were 'very good' and would do whatever he would have them do. 'Before you receive this,' he wrote in a letter addressed to Sarah from Kühlseggen on 21 May, 'I believe you will hear that the French have sent a great number of their troops towards Germany, and I am assured that the Marshal de Villeroy will march with them. Let them send them what they will. I have great hopes God will bless this undertaking. I am heart and soul yours.'

Marlborough did not, however, underestimate the difficulties which his army of 40,000 men – later to number some 60,000 when joined at Koblenz by Prussian and Hanoverian contingents – would have to face on their long march of over 250 miles around France's eastern frontier and into southern Germany. The going would be hard, the rivers difficult to cross by the long lines of marching soldiers, the rumbling, rattling carts and cannon and the jingling cavalry. Forage and fodder for well over 20,000 draught animals and horses would have to be found, apart from the rations for the men, for whom bread ovens, each requiring a cartload of 500 bricks, would have to be set up, and cobblers would have to be employed in the mending of shoes. Almost 2,000 wagons would be needed as well as prompt supplies of money for the mercenaries.

Well aware of the risks he was taking, Marlborough fully realized that to fail in his endeavour would be to fail catastrophically: failure, as he told Count Wratislaw, would mean the end of his military career.

In the early morning of 20 May 1704, the camp around the little village of Bedburg, twenty miles from the Rhine at Cologne, was struck and the army marched off confidently to the rhythms of tapping drums. Three days later at Bonn, however, Marlborough received from Frankfurt 'the ill news of the French having joined [their ally], the Elector of Bavaria, at Villingen with 26,000 men'. 'I hope they are mistaken,' he reported to Godolphin, 'or we shall pass our time ill; for it is most certain that the Maréchal de Villeroy is marching with the best of the troops from Flanders. So that if the Dutch do not consent to the strengthening of the troops I have, we shall be overpowered by numbers.'

On 27 May the head of the long column of allied troops reached the confluence of the Rhine and the Moselle at Koblenz, a hundred miles from the Dutch border. And here, surrounded by the vineyards of Germany, Marlborough wrote to Godolphin: 'I doe with all my heart wish you and Lady Marl some Moselle that I have this day tasted, for I never drank any like it, but I do not know how to send it.'

In his account of the march, Captain Robert Parker reported:

Now when we expected to march up the Moselle, to our surprise we passed that river over a stone bridge, and the Rhine over two bridges of boats, and proceeded on our march through the country of Hesse Cassel, where we were joined by the Hereditary Prince with the troops of that country; which made our army 40,000 fighting men complete.

We frequently marched three, sometimes four days, successively, and halted a day. We generally began our march about three in the morning, proceeded about four or four and a half leagues [about twelve or a little over thirteen miles] a day, and reached our [camping site] about nine. As we marched through the countries of our Allies, commissaries were appointed to furnish us with all manner of necessaries for man and horse. These were brought to [the camping site] before we arrived, and the soldiers had nothing to do but to pitch their tents, boil their kettles, and lie down to rest. Surely never was such a march carried on with more order and regularity, and with less fatigue both to man and horse.*

All this was organized by a small but highly competent staff which numbered scarcely more than forty-five officers, quartermasters and clerks, most notably William Cadogan, Marlborough's trusted Irish quartermaster-general, Adam de Cardonnel, and Henry Davenant, the English agent at Frankfurt. These men and their staffs ensured that Marlborough's orders were carried out to the letter and that the camps continued to be supplied with the provisions and other necessities regularly carried into them in those sturdy well-made wagons which almost two centuries later were still known as 'Marlbroucks'.

Marlborough himself gave the greatest attention to the well-being of the men under his command, always concerned to ensure that they were well fed and, so far as was possible, regularly paid, doing all he could to guarantee the ready cooperation of the local population by not living off the country, taking the trouble to visit outposts as often as he could, worrying that the 'poor men' would suffer when the rain poured down, maintaining a perfect calm in the face of difficulties and obstruction, and giving no indication that for days on end he was plagued by fearful headaches.

Welcomed by the people of the Rhine valley, who were gratified by Marlborough paying for what the army consumed and not trying to live off the land as the French were, the troops were showered

---

* A French army on the march, by contrast, was far readier to live off the country. The comte de Mérode-Westerloo, a Flemish officer serving in the French army, described an incident which occurred at this time during its march through the Black Forest: 'I found a great brass alpen horn [in a building at Rozberg]. Try as I might I couldn't get a sound out of it. Eventually everybody had a go, and at last one of them with stronger lungs than mine got the thing to work. So well did he trumpet that a moment later we heard the lowing of cattle all around in the woods, and out they came, trotting from the trees towards the fort, obeying our horn. The soldiers regarded this as manna from heaven, and in no time at all the camp resembled a slaughterhouse. However, this droll incident had one unfortunate repercussion; it encouraged the troops to scatter into the woods and hills – we could do nothing to stop them – and a few regrettable incidents resulted. The enraged peasantry eventually killed several thousand of our men before the army was clear of the Black Forest' (Chandler (ed.), *Robert Parker and Comte de Mérode-Westerloo*, 160).

with bouquets of flowers thrown at them by smiling girls, some of whom, as one of their officers rather superciliously put it, were 'much handsomer than we expected to find in this country'.* On towards Mainz the soldiers marched, across the river Main and the Neckar, through Gross Heppach and Gross Süssen towards Ulm, past castles perched high above the rocky banks of rivers, through villages and by cattle-sheds, across vineyards and by cornfields, down muddy tracks and rutted roads.

Having been greeted by the Elector of Trèves (now Trier) Marlborough dined with him in the castle above the river at Ehrenbreitsein on 26 May and by 2 June he was at Weinheim, where he wrote to Sarah:

I take it extreme kindly that you persist in desiring to come to me, but I am sure when you consider that three days hence will be a month that the troops have been in a continual march to get hither, and we shall be a

---

* In later campaigns local inhabitants were to be less welcoming and Marlborough had occasion to issue stern prohibitions against plundering. One such was, for instance, to be issued at Terbanck in June 1708: 'Whereas greate Disorders have been committed by soldiers marauding and plundering the country contrary to good Discipline and the rules of warr which if not timely prevented for the futur may reduce the troops to greate necessity for want of provisions being brought in from the country and it being both our intentions and for advantage of the troops to protect all the inhabitants in the full and perfect Enjoyment of their estates goods and effects we do hereby strictly forbid all the officers and soldiers of the army to offer the Least Injury to the Inhabitants but that on the contrary they do give them all necessary aid and assisstance . . . Moreover such soldiers as shall be found plundering or doing the least Damage or violance to the said inhabitants . . . shall be immediately punished with Death . . . And for the Better preventing all marauding we do further declare that any Regiment or Corps to which any soldiers may belong that shall be found transgressing these our orders Be obliged to make imediate Satisfaction for whatever Loss or damage they may have sustained . . . And to the end none may protest Ignorance we do hereby direct that these our orders may be imediately read and published at the head of each Squadrone and Battallione of the army and that printed Copys be Distributed to the several Troops and Companys – Given at the Camp at Terbanck the eleventh of June new style 1708, John Duke and Earle of Marlborough prince of the Holy Empire, marquis of Blandford Baron Churchill of Aymouth and Sandridge, one of her majestys most Honorable privy Council, Knight of the most noble order of the Garter, master Generall of the ordinance, Collonel of the first Regiment of ffoot Guards, and Captaine General of her majesty's Land fforces' (National Army Museum Archives, ref. 6309/9/3).

fortnight longer before we shall be able to get to the Danube, so that you could hardly get to me and back again to Holland, before it would be time to return to England. Besides, my dear soul, how could I be at any ease? For if we should not have good success, I could not put you to any place where you would be safe.

I am now in a house of the Elector Palatine, that has a prospect over the finest country that is possible to be seen. I see out of my chamber window the Rhine and the Neckar and his two principal towns of Mannheim and Heidelberg; but would be much better pleased with the prospect of St Albans, which is not very famous for seeing far.

A week later he was at Mundelsheim, and here a staff officer came to inform him that Prince Eugène of Savoy, the general commanding the forces of the Austrian Emperor, had arrived in the town with Count Wratislaw and would be with him in time for dinner.

20

PRINCE EUGÈNE

'I do not know of anyone who has more understanding,
experience, industry and zeal for the Emperor's service . . .'

Prince Eugène of Savoy was born on 18 October 1663 in the Hôtel
Soissons, a fine house in Paris converted from a nunnery by Catherine
de' Medici. He was the fifth and youngest son of the comte de
Soissons, a scion of the house of Savoy-Carignan whose ancestors
were Dukes of Savoy and whose members later became Kings of
Sardinia and eventually of a united Italy.

His mother, Olympia, was of less exalted stock. She and her sisters
had been brought to Paris from a relatively humble home in Rome
by her uncle, Cardinal Mazarin, the Italian-born first minister of
France during the boyhood of King Louis XIV. Not long after her
arrival in Paris, Olympia had married the kindly, indulgent Prince
of Savoy-Carignan, who could be relied upon to be often away from
Paris with his regiment or in the hunting field, leaving her free to
accept the post of Superintendent of the Queen's Household and to
become a promiscuous, lively and ambitious presence at the court
of the King. Suspected of having poisoned her husband, who died
suddenly in 1673, she thought it as well to leave France, to which
she never returned.

Her youngest son, Eugène, ten years old at the time of his mother's
flight from Paris to Brussels, was left in the care of his grandmother,
Princess of Carignan. He had been indulged by his mother, left much
to his own devices and, according to at least one observer, had been
allowed to 'run around like a street-urchin'. This same observer,
Liselotte, duchesse d'Orléans, who admittedly was not an impartial
witness, added that his companions at this time were extrovertly

131

effeminate and that he himself 'played the part of a woman amongst the young people'.

He was not a prepossessing boy. Small and puny, he had been destined for the Church and, at the King's suggestion, he had been tonsured and required to wear a soutane. He was 'always dirty', the duchesse d'Orléans said, and had straight and lanky hair. His upper lip was so short that his two large front teeth were always visible, a misfortune which imposed upon his features a look of disturbing vacancy.

As though in revolt against this unfortunate appearance and the feckless life he had led when his domineering and awesome mother was still in Paris, he began, after her departure, to lead a more purposeful life. He took vigorous exercise in an effort to become stronger and more athletic; he refused to entertain any longer a career in the Church; he began seriously to study mathematics, the science of fortifications and the history of war; he conceived an ambition to join the army; and, having left his grandmother's house for lodgings in Paris, he prevailed upon a friend, prince de Conti, who was Louis XIV's son-in-law, to approach the King on his behalf and to inform His Majesty of this aspiration.

The King was not sympathetic: he had settled in his mind that the frail-looking boy, to whom he referred disparagingly as '*le petit Abbé*', should become a priest, and he sent Conti away. Eugène was dissatisfied and angry but no less determined to become a soldier. One of his brothers had recently been killed fighting against the Turks in the service of the Holy Roman Emperor, Leopold I. Eugène, too, decided to go to Austria and offer his services to the Emperor, who listened to his request far more sympathetically than the Bourbon King of France had done. His application was gratefully accepted and Eugène was sent immediately to serve in the army commanded by the duc de Lorraine, the Emperor's brother-in-law, who had received orders to relieve Vienna, which was now being besieged by a Turkish army 200,000 strong, twenty times as numerous as the city's garrison. In the subsequent fighting, Eugène so distinguished himself that the duc de Lorraine, in offering his congratulations, gave him a pair of golden spurs, while the Emperor undertook to nominate him to the command of a regiment.

In this command Eugène gained further distinction and in 1685 his services were such that, at the age of twenty-two, he was promoted major-general and already recognized as being a most remarkable soldier. Before he was thirty years old, the Emperor promoted him field marshal and he was appointed Supreme Allied Commander in Italy.

Yet, admired by the men whom he led with such infectious élan, he was not much liked by most of his fellow officers in the Imperial army, many of whom were jealous of his success and of the favours shown and land given to him by the Emperor, enabling him to add to his ever-increasing fortune and to commission architects to build him palaces in Hungary and Vienna.

With this passion for building and for the acquisition of works of art and books went a certain indeterminate sexuality. It was noted that when on leave in Venice during the carnival, while other officers enjoyed the favours of the city's celebrated courtesans, Eugène preferred to take solitary walks and to look round the famous Arsenale.

Didactic, tactless and outspoken, he had never hesitated to criticize the behaviour and inactivity of his fellow officers. Nor did he shrink from questioning those rules of warfare which most of his contemporaries considered inviolable if not sacrosanct. Like Marlborough, he contended that campaigns should not be limited to those seasons of the year to which they were then generally confined; nor should they concentrate on attacking and defending fortresses. The conduct of war should not be a kind of formalized parade ruled by accepted practices and rituals but a contest of movement and surprise; and those who disagreed with him about this were fools.

Eugène did have his admirers and supporters in high places, however; and when it became necessary to appoint a commander of the Imperial armies to face a new threat from the Turks, the president of the Imperial War Council informed the Emperor that he did 'not know of anyone who [had] more understanding, experience, industry and zeal for the Emperor's service or who [held] the love of the soldiers in a higher degree' than Prince Eugène.

The appointment of Eugène to this command was fully justified: on 11 September 1697 at Zenta, under his skilful and bold direction,

20,000 Turkish soldiers were killed on the field of battle and a further 10,000 were drowned in the river Theiss. Very few prisoners were taken.

This remarkable victory was followed by others over the French and their allies in Italy; and Prince Eugène, so the Emperor was informed, came to be revered by the English as one of their own heroes.

21

THE STORMING OF
THE SCHELLENBERG

'I verily believe that it would have been quite impossible
to find a more terrible representation of hell itself than was
shown in the savagery of both sides on this occasion.'

The Duke of Marlborough and Prince Eugène of Savoy got on well together from the beginning. It was apparent that there was an understanding and rapport between them as soon as they met at Marlborough's headquarters at Mundelsheim on 10 June 1704. Marlborough's cook served an unusually splendid dinner, after which the two men discussed the war for several hours, being completely agreed as to its conduct and to the need of a victorious battle to give essential heart to the Grand Alliance by reducing French military predominance and shattering their reputation for invincibility. 'Prince Eugen,' Marlborough told Sarah, 'has in his conversation a great deal of my Lord Shrewsbury [in Swift's opinion 'the finest gentleman we have'] with the advantage of seeming franker. He has been very free with me.'

Prince Eugène returned the compliment, writing in a letter to the Emperor of the 'incomparable ability' of the Duke. Later he drew the following 'true picture' of Marlborough: 'Here is a man of high quality, courageous, extremely well-disposed, and with a keen desire to achieve something of consequence; with all these qualities he understands thoroughly that one cannot become a general in a day, and he is diffident about himself.'

On the morning after their first meeting, Prince Eugène inspected Marlborough's cavalry escort and observed, 'I never saw better horses, better uniforms, finer belts and accoutrements; but money, which you don't want in England, will buy clothes and fine horses, but it can't buy that lively air I see in every one of these troopers' faces.'

'Sir,' replied Marlborough, returning the compliment, 'that must be attributed to their heartiness for the public cause and the particular pleasure and satisfaction they have in seeing your Highness.'

'My Lord Marlborough,' an Englishman at the Hanoverian court wrote to a friend on 25 June, 'has joined the troops under Prince Lewis of Baden [the Margrave of Baden], not far from Ulm, and the success of this affair will either gain him a great reputation, and very much shelter from his enemies (which are not few) or be his ruin.'

Marlborough himself was well aware of this and only too conscious of the fact that the next stage of his campaign, which was to attack the fortress known as the Schellenberg outside Donauwörth – and thus gain a valuable bridgehead on the Danube, a magazine for his army and a gateway into Bavaria – was an enterprise that would inevitably entail great slaughter. He did not altogether trust the Margrave; and certainly considered his proposals for advancing towards Donauwörth impractical, if not downright absurd. Nor were the Margrave and those at home whom Marlborough described in a letter to Sarah as likely 'to be glad of' his 'not having success in this undertaking' his only causes of worry and concern. By 29 June the Danish cavalry he had been promised had still not joined him and, as he told Sarah, he did not feel 'able to act against the Elector of Bavaria' as he would wish.

Two days later, however, he began to make detailed plans, involving what was to become a common ingredient of his tactics, an assault on a certain sector of the enemy lines, accepting necessarily heavy casualties, in order to deceive his opponents as to the place where he intended to launch his principal attack.

One hundred and thirty men from each of his battalions were chosen to form a special assaulting force 6,000 strong, and these were to be reinforced by three battalions of Imperial grenadiers supplied by the Margrave, and eighty volunteers led by Lord Mordaunt to form a forlorn hope, or storming party.

At about eight o'clock in the morning of 2 July at Donauwörth, where work was rapidly progressing on the improvement of the defences, the Bavarian commander, Marshal d'Arco, a spy-glass to his eye, was surveying the shrub and woodland to the west of the fort beyond the winding waters of the Wernitz stream when he caught sight of horsemen, followed by infantry, approaching at a distance of about five miles. These troops were followed by what appeared to be quartermasters, who could be seen marking out with flags the lines along which the tents of the various regiments were presumably to be pitched. D'Arco naturally supposed from this that the approaching army would remain in camp that day, resting after a long march, and launch their attack the following morning. He and his staff accordingly rode down into the town at about midday for a meal.

That afternoon, however, there came reports from the outworks that the allied troops were advancing beyond the ground being marked out as though for a camp and were placing planks to serve as bridges across the Wernitz. More and more troops appeared from the woods as the men from the Bavarian outposts fell back towards the fort, setting fire to the isolated buildings on their way and joining their comrades, some 14,000 in number, behind the still uncompleted defences of the Schellenberg.

An assault had, indeed, been ordered for that evening, despite the tiring march the men had already endured, Marlborough's decision to launch it having been finally settled by a report which had been brought to him by Prince Eugène's adjutant-general, Baron Moltenburg, to the effect that the French marshals, Villeroi and Tallard, were both advancing to support and reinforce the Elector's army.

At about a quarter past six, therefore, the men of the assaulting party, commanded by the Dutch lieutenant-general van Goor, and led by the forlorn hope under Lord Mordaunt, went forward up the hill followed by men of the 1st Guards and of Ingoldby's, Orkney's and Meredith's Regiments. Under a storm of musket fire and cannon shot, they advanced with measured tread, shouting 'God save the Queen', their muskets shouldered, holding bundles of brushwood with which to fill up the ditch beneath the breastworks. Men fell on all sides; General van Goor was one of the first to die; the 1st Guards lost half their men and most of their officers.

Marlborough had felt obliged to accept such slaughter: by re-morselessly attacking here, he hoped, if he could not break

137

through, to draw so many of the enemy away from other parts of the defences that a secondary, successful attack upon them might be mounted.

Soon it seemed that this main attack would, indeed, be unsuccessful. One of d'Arco's French officers, Colonel Jean Martin de La Colonie, described the scene:

The enemy broke into the charge, and rushed at full speed, shouting at the top of their voices, to throw themselves into our entrenchments. The rapidity of their movements, together with their loud yells, were truly alarming . . .

The English infantry led this attack with the greatest intrepidity, right up to our parapet, but there they were opposed with a courage at least equal to their own. Rage, fury and desperation were manifested by both sides, with the more obstinacy as the assailants and assailed were perhaps the bravest soldiers in the world. The little parapet which separated the two forces became the scene of the bloodiest struggle that could be conceived . . .

During this first attack . . . we were all fighting hand to hand, hurling the assailants back as they clutched at the parapet; men were tearing at the muzzles of guns and the bayonets which pierced their entrails; crushing under their feet their own wounded comrades, and even gouging out their opponents' eyes with their nails, when the grip was so close that neither could make use of their weapons. I verily believe that it would have been quite impossible to find a more terrible representation of hell itself than was shown in the savagery of both sides on this occasion.

At last the enemy . . . were obliged to relax their hold and they fell back for shelter to the dip of the slope, where we could not harm them. A sudden calm now reigned amongst us, our people were recovering their breath, and seemed more determined even than they were before the conflict. The ground around our parapet was covered with dead and dying . . . but our whole attention was fixed on the enemy and [their] movements. We noticed that the tops of [their] standards still showed at about the same place as that from which they had made their charge in the first instance, leaving little doubt that they were re-forming before returning to the assault.

Marlborough had, indeed, already ordered a second assault. This was to be led by Lieutenant-General Count Styrum, who soon fell mortally wounded like many another officer before the assailants

16. Marlborough: a portrait attributed to John Riley, c. 1680.

17. Soldiers being drilled on Horse Guards Parade: detail from a painting by Hendrick Danckerts.

18. *The East Front of Cumberland Lodge*, c. 1754, by Thomas Sandby. The house, then known as Byfield House, was granted to the Duchess of Marlborough as Ranger of Windsor Park.

19. Sarah Jennings, first Duchess of Marlborough: an oil sketch by Sir
Godfrey Kneller, c. 1690–95.

20. Queen Anne in the House of Lords, by Peter Tillemans, c. 1708–14

21. Queen Anne in
her robes of state,
by Sir Godfrey
Kneller,
1702–4.

22. Abigail Hill, Lady
Masham: a portrait
by an unknown
artist, formerly
attributed to Sir
Godfrey
Kneller
c. 1700.

23. The Marlborough family, by Johann Baptist Closterman. On the Duke's right are Elizabeth, Mary, the Duchess, Henrietta, Anne and John. According to George Vertue, the painter had 'so many

differences with the Duchess that the Duke said, "It has given me
more trouble to reconcile my wife and you than to fight a battle."
Hence, no doubt, the Duchess's rather grumpy expression.

24. An allegorical representation of Queen Anne offering the royal manor of Woodstock to Marlborough, by Sir Godfrey Kneller.

were again forced back to the relative safety of the ditch. By this time the Margrave had begun his own attack further down the line of defences, while Marlborough, who was himself in the ditch, also ordered an attack by eight of his reserve battalions on another sector of the line where a feint assault had discovered the defences to be almost entirely unmanned. Marlborough also gave orders for yet another assault at that point where the dead and dying already lay so thick upon the ground. This third assault – in which Lord John Hay's regiment of dragoons were dismounted and ordered to attack with the infantry – was not pressed home with the verve and urgency of the two previous attempts upon the fortress. But the attack of the Margrave's German troops on the less well defended breastworks to Marlborough's right proved successful and, as the Margrave himself was wounded and his horse was shot, his men in overwhelming numbers, having thrown their bundles of brushwood into the ditch, 'forced their way into the entrenchments' and, in the words of the official German report, 'after prolonged hand-to-hand fighting, they were able to maintain themselves in good order'.

Then, at about half past seven, Colonel de La Colonie 'noticed all at once' what he called 'an extraordinary movement on the part of the enemy infantry, who were rising up and ceasing fire'. His account continued:

I glanced around on all sides to see what had caused this behaviour, and then became aware of several lines of infantry in greyish-white uniforms on our left flank. From their dress and bearing, I verily believed that reinforcements had arrived for us, and anybody else would have believed the same . . . So I shouted to my men that they were Frenchmen and friends . . .

Having, however, made a closer inspection, I discovered bunches of straw and leaves attached to their standards, badges the enemy are in the custom of wearing on the occasion of battle, and at that very moment I was struck by a ball in the right lower jaw which wounded and stupefied me.

No sooner had the Margrave's troops gained control of the entrenchments to the right than Marlborough's men on their left also managed at last to scramble over the breastworks in their front; and, as dusk began to settle over the cornfields, the remnants of

Marshal d'Arco's battalions could be seen running from the Schellen-berg towards the river, where a bridge of boats had been shattered by the long line of carts of a rumbling wagon-train. Re-forming his infantry, Marlborough sent his cavalry off in pursuit; and they, Prussian squadrons as well as English, including Hay's dragoons by now remounted, spared none, slashing at the backs of the fleeing enemy, littering the fields with the wounded and the corpses of the dead, and driving those who managed to escape their sabres into the river.

Colonel de La Colonie was also in the river, swimming as fast as he could out of range in the fast current. Previously encumbered by what he described as his 'richly embroidered uniform' and his long, tight boots, he had been helped to drag these off by the wife of a Bavarian soldier, who had also been fleeing from the merciless horsemen; and the colonel was thus enabled, with the help of a sergeant, to clamber up the bank. He was one of only some 5,000 men out of about 14,000 engaged who managed to rejoin the Elector's army.

Marlborough's losses were also painfully heavy, particularly among the English troops engaged, some 1,500 being killed or wounded, many of them officers, some of high rank. Five lieutenant-generals had been wounded, a further six had been killed. Four major-generals and twenty-eight brigadiers, colonels and lieutenant-colonels also lay dead or were being treated for wounds by surgeons in the makeshift hospitals in and around Nördlingen, north of Donauwörth on the road to Nuremberg.

In Donauwörth itself, which the enemy had not had time to set on fire in their headlong flight, large amounts of provisions and stores fell into the allies' hands. But neither these, nor the establishment of a bridgehead on the Danube, were held in certain quarters to justify the great loss of life entailed. The Dutch indicated their disapproval by striking a medal inscribed, 'The enemy defeated and put to flight and their camp plundered at Schellenberg near Donauwörth 1704'. It featured a relief of the Margrave but not of Marlborough.

In Hanover, the old Electress Sophia, granddaughter of King James I and mother of the future George I, wrote to her friend, the polymath Gottfried Leibniz:

The Elector [of Hanover] is saddened by the loss of so many brave subjects in consequence of the mistakes made by the great general Marlborough. He says that the Margrave of Baden did very much better, and that without him there would have been complete failure, as on the other wing proper measures had not been taken.

Such sentiments were also being expressed in The Hague, where the States-General had resented the way in which they had been manoeuvred into agreeing to their soldiers being taken so far away from home. In London similar objections had been made to hostilities being conducted in a theatre so very many miles from England's shores. After it became known how many lives had been lost at the Schellenberg, these cavils seemed to Marlborough's critics only too well justified.

22

BAVARIA LAID WASTE

'As a result of the ravaging . . . there
will be little of Bavaria left.'

Marlborough was further and widely attacked when, after the capture of Donauwörth, he put into execution his threatened plan of laying Bavaria waste, burning its villages and their grain in an attempt to force the Elector to return to his allegiance to the Grand Alliance. Neither Prince Eugène nor the Margrave, nor yet the Emperor, approved of this policy. Indeed, the Margrave protested that he would not make war 'like a hussar' but only like 'an experienced general'; while distaste for the whole enterprise was expressed by Marlborough's own staff. 'We have made no progress since our success at the Schellenberg,' Adam de Cardonnel told the poet Matthew Prior, 'except that it be in burning and destroying the Elector's country . . . Our last march was all in fire and smoke . . . I wish to God it were all over that I might get safe out of this country.' Marlborough, however, insisting upon the necessity of the devastation as practised by the French in the Palatinate in 1689, went so far as to order the Imperial cavalry to play their part in the work of burning and destruction. 'As a result of the ravaging, the fires and the forced contributions,' the Margrave wrote to the Emperor, 'there will be little of Bavaria left.'

Marlborough himself confessed that he was loath to continue the spoliation, even though it was proving successful, not only in denying supplies to the enemy but also in obliging the Elector to employ a considerable part of his army to protect his own properties, his houses, estates and salt-mines, which might otherwise have been destroyed.

Marlborough's letters to Sarah reveal his distaste for a policy which he deemed necessary and which was no doubt at least partly responsible for the renewed and violent headaches he suffered at this time, as so often at times of anxiety and distress.*

We sent this morning [30 July] 3,000 horse to his [the Elector's] chief city of Munich with orders to burn and destroy all the chief cities about it. This is so contrary to my nature that nothing but absolute necessity could have obliged me to consent to it, for these poor people suffer from their master's ambition. There having been no war in this country for about sixty years, these towns and villages are so clean that you would be pleased with them . . .

You will I hope believe that my nature suffers when I see so many fine places burnt, and that must be burnt . . . I shall never be easy and happy till I am quietly with you, my dearest soul, whom I love above my own life.

There was also, as he explained to Godolphin, a disadvantage to this policy of devastation which affected his own army: 'We are doing all the mischief we can to this country . . . and as we advance we burn and destroy; but if this should not make [the Elector] come to a treaty, I am afraid it may at last do ourselves hurt for want of what we destroy.'

The Elector prevaricated, alarmed by the threats of further destruction and tempted by all manner of inducements to return to the Grand Alliance. The Emperor's representative in Bavaria, Count Wratislaw, promised him that, if he did return to his previous loyalties, his country would be increased in size to include Pfalz-Neuburg and Burgau. Moreover, a large sum of money would be given to him for the rebuilding and restoration of the places which had been burned or demolished.

The Elector still hesitated: the French, too, were making threats and promises. Marshal Ferdinand Marsin, their army's commander in Bavaria, warned him that if he went, as he had agreed, to the monastery in Fürstenfeld to meet Count Wratislaw and discuss with

---

* Marlborough himself was well aware of the likely psychosomatic cause of these 'violent headaches'. 'I own to you,' he once wrote to Sarah, 'that my sickness comes from fretting' (Coxe, *Memoirs of John, Duke of Marlborough, with His Original Correspondence* (1820), i, 279).

him the terms upon which he would change sides, the French would immediately march out of Bavaria, having burned all the baggage of the Elector's army before they left.

But then, while Wratislaw was actually waiting to receive the Elector at the monastery of Fürstenfeld, there came news that a large French army, commanded by Marshal Tallard, was marching through the Black Forest towards Villingen to support the Elector against the allies. The Elector decided, therefore, not to go to Fürstenfeld.

It seemed to Prince Eugène that Marlborough and the English army had lost their impetus since their hard-fought success at Donauwörth. After resisting for a week, the garrison of the small fortified town of Rain had agreed to undemanding terms; and Marlborough had gone on to occupy Neuburg, some twelve miles upstream from the Danube crossing at Donauwörth, while the Rain garrison were permitted to rejoin the army at Augsburg. Since then, the siege train promised by the Emperor having not yet arrived and both Munich and Ulm consequently remaining untaken, operations had come to a virtual standstill. Prince Eugène was, therefore, becoming increasingly disillusioned with his allies and concerned by the unsatisfactory relationship between Marlborough and the Margrave. 'Up to now everything has gone well enough between them,' he told the Duke of Savoy; 'but I fear greatly that this will not last. And, to tell the truth, since the Donauwörth action I cannot admire their performances.' 'Since that action,' he added,

nothing has been done, although the enemy so far has let them have all the time they wanted . . . They have amused themselves with the siege of Rain and burning a few villages instead of, according to my ideas, which I have put before them plainly enough, marching straight upon the enemy. If unable to attack them . . . take up a position, encamp half an hour from them, and by their being so superior in cavalry in an open country, cut their communications . . . Stop their foraging and oblige them to quit Augsburg. Then would be the time to exploit the retreat and pursue the enemy so closely that they would not be able to avoid a battle. It was even in their power to prevent the junction with Tallard who is already near Villingen . . . To put things plainly, your Royal Highness, I don't like this slowness on our side. The enemy will have time to form magazines of food and forage, and all our operations will become the harder . . . The Duke is more than a little hesitating in his decisions.

Marshal Tallard, a scholar and an urbane diplomatist rather than a soldier, had not wanted to serve in Bavaria. But his King had required it and so he had come. He found the garrison at Villingen far more resolute in the town's defence than he had expected and, when Prince Eugène appeared with a large force a few miles away at Rothweil, he raised the siege and withdrew to Ulm. From there he moved to Augsburg, where, on 6 August, the Bavarian army joined him. Three days later the combined force was on the move towards the Danube at Lauingen.

The next day Marlborough received a letter from Prince Eugène, who was then some fifteen miles further up the Danube at Münster:

The enemy have marched. It is almost certain that the whole army is crossing the Danube at Lauingen . . . The plain of Dillingen is crowded with troops . . . With eighteen battalions I dare not risk staying here the night . . . I am therefore marching the infantry and part of the cavalry to a camp I have marked out before Donauwörth . . . Everything, milord, depends upon speed and upon your setting out immediately to join me tomorrow. If not I fear it will be too late . . .

I have just heard that the whole enemy army has crossed. Thus there is not a moment to lose.

Two days later, when the Margrave had been encouraged to march off to lay siege to Ingolstadt, thus ensuring that he took no part in the coming battle, Marlborough had joined forces with Prince Eugène near Münster, where, riding a mile or so south together to climb the tower of the parish church of Tapfheim, they could clearly see, some five miles distant, the enemy camp behind the sluggish waters of the river Nebel between Oberglau and the village of Blindheim, which the English were to know as Blenheim.

23

THE BATTLE OF BLENHEIM

*'. . . I can't end my letter without being so vain as to tell my
dearest soul that within the memory of man there has been no
victory so great as this . . .'*

The French position between Oberglau and Blenheim was a strong
one, so strong indeed that one of Marlborough's most experienced
generals, Lord Orkney, said later that had the decision rested with
him, he would not have decided to attack it.

In Marshal Tallard's camp it was generally supposed that the allies
would not stay to fight, but in one of those movements favoured in
contemporary warfare would quietly slip away the next morning
towards Nördlingen, a misconception fostered by some allied spies
who had been ordered to put themselves in the way of being captured
as prisoners of war by French cavalry scouts.

It came, therefore, as all the greater a shock when, at about six
o'clock the next morning, 13 August 1704, the comte de Mérode-
Westerloo was suddenly woken up by his head groom in his camp bed
in the barn where he had spent the night. The previous evening he had
enjoyed a convivial meeting and 'a good hot plate of soup' in Blenheim
with some other officers. 'I was never in better form,' he wrote, 'and
after wining and dining well, we all dispersed to our quarters [where]
I don't believe I ever slept more soundly than on that night.' The
groom shook him awake and flung open the barn door, through
which on the plain, bright in the morning sun, their standards and
colours easily counted, were numerous squadrons of enemy cavalry.
'I rubbed my eyes in disbelief,' Westerloo recorded in his memoirs,

and then coolly remarked, that the enemy must at least give me time to
take my morning cup of chocolate. Whilst I was hurriedly drinking this

and getting dressed, my horses were saddled and harnessed. As my lodging was the nearest in the village to the enemy, I ordered my servants to pack my kit with all speed . . . [Then] jumping on my horse I rode off accompanied by two aides-de-camp and taking with me my thirteen spare chargers.★

There was not a single soul stirring as I clattered out of the village. Nothing at all might have been happening. The same sight met my gaze when I reached the camp – everyone still snug in their tents – though the enemy . . . were already pushing back our pickets. But nobody seemed at all worried by it. I could see the enemy advancing ever closer in nine great columns, filling the whole plain from the Danube to the woods on the horizon . . . I still had received no instructions.

Soon afterwards all was frantic movement in the French camp as bugles were blown and trumpets blared. 'We saw all their camp in a motion,' recalled a sergeant in Hamilton's Regiment, 'their Generals and their Aids de Camp galloping to and fro to put all things in order.'

The allied army of rather more than 55,000 men, less than 10,000 of them British, the rest mostly Austrians, Prussians, Danes, Hanoverians, Hessians and Dutch, had started their march at three o'clock on a dark and misty morning, following tracks clearly marked for their guidance. Prince Eugène commanded on the right flank, Marlborough on the left. About five and a half hours later they came within range of the French cannon, which opened up on them; and, as the allied field batteries replied, the din was so deafening that the Margrave, forty miles away outside Ingolstadt, could hear the roar of the guns distinctly, while the bitter smell of gunsmoke pervaded the slowly darkening air.

★ All of these were killed or otherwise lost in the ensuing battle. Thereafter he was to lose many more 'through the ravages of the so-called "German Sickness" which', so he said, 'put all our cavalrymen on their feet. The disease started in my stable the day of the battle . . . [Thereafter] one or two fell sick every day, dying forty-eight hours later. Thus between Blenheim and Brussels I lost ninety-seven horses . . . I was fortunate to keep my two dozen mules which carried my most vital possessions . . . But I lost my carts, all my field furniture, chairs, tables, beds, utensils, field ovens, the lot' (Chandler (ed.), *Robert Parker and Comte de Mérode-Westerloo*, 181).

Soon after these guns began their cannonade, Marshals Marsin and Tallard and the Elector met in Blenheim to discuss the disposition of their 60,000 men, as the allied army drew ever closer. At ten o'clock Lord Cutts's column, on the far left of the allied line, having driven the enemy from two water mills on the Nebel, marched across the marshy ground beyond them to within less than 200 yards of Blenheim village. Here they came under devastating fire from the French batteries, while, to their right, Marlborough's working parties, under an equally heavy cannonade, struggled to repair a stone bridge across the Nebel. At the same time efforts were made to construct wooden bridges over the stream and to build causeways across the marsh with bundles of faggots and brushwood, as the heavy shot thudded and splashed into and over the mud, tearing gaps in the rows of infantry and dismounted cavalrymen, who sat or lay amid the stubble of the cornfields, waiting for the crossing places to be completed so that their advance could continue.

Still under fire from the heavy guns of the French, to which no reply could be made until the allied artillery came up – and which cost the loss of almost 2,000 of their comrades – the men ate their midday meal and listened to their chaplains going hurriedly through the form of morning service,* then to the bands playing martial airs and the constant tapping of kettledrums.

Marlborough, who himself had said his prayers and received the Sacrament from the chaplain-general, Francis Hare, shared the danger of his men. Conspicuous in his red coat, riding a white horse and wearing the ribbon of the Order of the Garter, he rode up and down the lines. Appearing unmoved when a roundshot struck the ground at his horse's feet, sending up a spray of damp earth, he effectively disguised his concern that Prince Eugène had not yet

---

* Marlborough, who had no high opinion of most of his chaplains, had recently issued an order admonishing them for 'neglecting to attend to their duty': 'I do hereby Direct that no Chaplain of any Regiment do presume to be absent from his Duty . . . upon pain of his having another Chaplain immediately Commission'd in his Room, and do further require the Chaplain Generall to give me immediate notice of any Chaplains that shall be absent from their Regiments and to recommend at the same time fitting persons to Supply their Places' (National Army Museum Archives, Acc. No.: 7405-25).

appeared on the scene, though it was now almost midday. He sent William Cadogan to find out what had happened to him. Cadogan, galloping back with the news that the Prince was almost ready, was soon followed by an aide-de-camp who rode up to say that His Highness would 'give the signal for attack at half-past twelve'. Immediately, Marlborough, springing onto the horse from which he had recently dismounted, said to the officers who had gathered round him, 'To your posts, gentlemen.' A short time later, Lord Cutts on the far left of the allied front led his men across the now completed bridges and causeways towards Blenheim – to which Marlborough intended to draw French reinforcements so as to weaken the enemy's capacity to mount a counter-attack when his own major attack went in at the centre – while General Charles Churchill's infantry, to their right beyond the narrow Donauwörth and Hochstadt road, marched with a steady step for the crossings over the Nebel, making for the centre of Marshal Tallard's position.

Leading the way, General Rowe's brigade of five battalions of foot, still marching in regular order and intimidating silence, with bayonets fixed, approached the palisades and defensive works which the enemy had hastily erected in front of their position.* Rowe ordered them not to open fire until he was seen to hit the paling of the fences with the flat of his sword. The French had already opened a devastating fire themselves when he did so; but his men marched on, kicking and tearing at the palisades to get at the enemy, and 'according to command', in the words of Private John Marshall Deane of the 1st Regiment of Foot Guards, 'fought our way into the village wch. was all of a fire, and our men fought in and through the fire and pursued [the enemy] through it, until many on both sides were burned to death'.

Rowe was mortally wounded and both the staff officers who tried to carry him away were killed. So were many of his men, while the

---

* 'About 3 a clock in the afternoon,' Private Deane recorded in his journal, 'our English on the left was ordered by my Lord Duke to attacque a village full of French called Blenheim wch. village they had fortifyed and made soe vastly strong and barrackaded so fast with trees, plants, coffers, chests, wagons, carts and palisades that it was almost a impossibility to think wch way to gett into it' (Deane, *A Journal of Marlborough's Campaigns during the War of the Spanish Succession, 1704–1711*, 12).

survivors were beaten back by a charge of French gendarmerie who charged out of Blenheim village, dispersed the men of Rowe's Regiment and seized the regiment's colours before being driven back themselves by squadrons of Hessian cavalry. In a second assault, scores more reinforcements were called up by the French commander until there were over 10,000 men crammed within the streets, gardens and whitewashed houses of the village, scarcely able to move amid the crush of bodies.

Outside the village almost 2,000 dead and wounded now lay upon the ground over which Lord Cutts was preparing to lead a third attack when a message came from Marlborough ordering him to withdraw his men out of range of the enemy muskets and then to advance each company separately to fire upon the French before once again retreating out of range.

There was fierce fighting, too, on the right of the allied line around the village of Oberglau, where the French commander, the marquis de Blainville, sent out nine battalions, including the Irish brigade in the French service, the 'Wild Geese', against ten battalions of allied troops under the Prince of Holstein–Beck, which were advancing to storm the village. Threatened at the same time by Marshal Marsin's cavalry, Holstein–Beck sent a message asking for support to the commander of the Imperial cuirassiers, a regiment in Prince Eugène's army. Major-General Fugger, commander of the cuirassiers, replied that he could not act without Prince Eugène's orders. The Prince of Holstein–Beck's two leading battalions were consequently overwhelmed by Blainville's men; Holstein–Beck was mortally wounded; and the French threatened to drive a wedge between Marlborough's and Eugène's armies.

Marlborough decided he must now intervene personally. Riding across one of the causeways spanning the Nebel, he took command of three Hanoverian battalions from Holstein–Beck's reserve, called up a battery of Colonel Blood's artillery, sent a message to Prince Eugène asking for help from Fugger's Imperial cuirassiers, and advanced upon Oberglau, forcing the 'Wild Geese' into retreat.

Although Prince Eugène was himself in difficulties, he did not hesitate to grant his friend's request. The cuirassiers appeared on the scene, charged Marsin's cavalry and sent them hurtling off in disorder.

Marlborough then continued his advance upon Oberglau with his three Hanoverian battalions, supported by other troops previously commanded by the Prince of Holstein-Beck, and pushed the enemy back towards the village.

It was now about three o'clock. Not long before, Francis Hare had thought that the allies 'had lost the day'. So, too, had Marshal Tallard. Indeed, while the allies had succeeded in getting across the Nebel stream and marsh and had made some further advances since, Blenheim had still not been taken; nor had Oberglau.

After having been on the move since early morning, the troops in the allied army were now tired out; a lull, punctuated by the cries and groans of the wounded, the swish of the occasional cannon ball and the chink of the cavalry's accoutrements, had settled over the battlefield.

The Duke of Marlborough, however, appeared to be full of confidence, and not without reason. At the beginning of the battle his numbers had been considerably less than those of the French and he had lost far more men than they; but since then his numbers had been gradually increasing as more and more battalions of infantry and squadrons of cavalry, not previously engaged, had come up and were being marshalled in strength – horsemen in front, infantry behind, supported by field batteries – along the whole two-mile front between Blenheim and Oberglau.

When Prince Eugène was ready to move, he led the Imperial cavalry forward as the Prince of Anhalt-Dessau advanced with the Prussian foot at a steady pace. The musketry of these advancing troops, accompanied by the thunder of a battery of Colonel Blood's guns firing grapeshot, was returned by the French, who stood their ground bravely, forming squares to resist the onslaught of the enemy cavalry. One of the allied officers lost his nerve and began to ride off the field with the remnants of a shattered squadron of horse. He was stopped by Marlborough, who said to him, 'Mr —, you are labouring under a misapprehension. The enemy lies that way. You have nothing to do but face him and the day is your own.'*

---

* It seems that Prince Eugène dealt with deserters in a more summary fashion. 'In a spasm of temper he is said to have shot two fugitives from the fighting . . . and then went forward to the most exposed of his troops' (Henderson, *Prince Eugen of Savoy*, 110).

Soon after this, Marlborough was satisfied that the enemy were no longer able to resist a determined assault. So, giving order to the trumpeters to sound the charge, he allowed the cavalry to break into a trot as they bore down on the French, sword in hand, their faces blackened and streaked by powder and sweat. By now the French had suffered enough: they broke ranks and fled, racing towards the river, in which many of them were to be drowned, Marlborough and his exhilarated cavalry charging after them. 'Hordes of the enemy were pushing round our flanks,' Mérode-Westerloo recorded,

and soon we found ourselves faced by numerous enemy squadrons on no less than three sides – and we were borne back on top of one another. So tight was the press that my horse was carried along some three hundred paces without putting hoof to ground, right to the edge of a deep ravine [near Sonderheim]. Down we plunged a good twenty feet into a swampy meadow. My horse stumbled and fell. A moment later several men and horses fell on top of me as the remains of my cavalry swept by, all intermingled with the hotly pursuing foe. I spent several minutes trapped beneath my horse.

Marshal Tallard, the Order of Saint-Esprit conspicuous on his uniform, was taken prisoner with several members of his staff and marched off to be presented to the Duke of Marlborough, who politely offered him the use of his coach, in which he was driven away past Blenheim. Here there was a flare-up in the fighting between General Charles Churchill's battalions, which had been given the task of securing his brother's flanks, and the French infantry remaining in the village. To prevent them breaking out of Blenheim, Lord Cutts's infantry were sent in to engage the enemy in hand-to-hand fighting. Witnessing this, Marshal Tallard persuaded one of the officers who formed his escort to take a message to the Duke asking him to allow the 'poor fellows' cooped up in Blenheim to retreat with the rest of the army. In return he would order them to lay down their arms. Marlborough, who was now making arrangements for a final cavalry charge upon Marshal Marsin's troops on the French left flank, coldly replied, 'Inform Monsieur de Tallard that in the position in which he now is, he has no command.'

Having broken off the pursuit of Marshal Marsin, Marlborough wrote a message to Sarah in his childish handwriting on the back of a tavern bill given to him by one of his staff:

> August 13 *1704*
>
> I have not time to say more but do beg you will give my Duty to the Queen, and let her know her Army has had a Glorious Victory. Mon.^{sr} Tallard and two other generals are in my Coach and I am following the rest. The bearer my aid.de.camp Coll Parke will give Her and [*sic*] account of what has pass'd. I shall doe it in a day or two by a nother more att large.★

The next day Marlborough sent Sarah a more detailed account:

> Before the battle was quite done yesterday I wrote to my dearest soul to let her know that I was well, and that God had blessed her majesty's arms with as great a victory, as has ever been known . . . In short, the army of M. de Tallard, which is that which I fought with, is quite ruined; that of the Elector of Bavaria and the marshal de Marsin, which Prince Eugen fought against, I am afraid has not had much loss . . . As soon as the Elector knew that monsieur de Tallard was like to be beaten he marched off . . . I am so very much out of order with having been seventeen hours on horseback yesterday, and not having been able to sleep above three hours last night, that I can write to none of my friends. However, I am so pleased with this action that I can't end my letter without being so vain as to tell my dearest soul that within the memory of man there has been no victory so great as this . . .

Four days later in a letter informing her that for the past few days he had 'been so very much out of order' that he had 'been obliged . . . to be let blood', he added:

> This day the whole army has returned their thanks to Almighty God for the late success, and I have done it with all my heart; for never victory was

---

★ Daniel Parke was not serving as an officer in the British army but held a colonelcy in the Virginia militia. He seems to have been on the point of leaving Marlborough's camp when he was instructed to take this letter to England. Not long after his arrival he was appointed governor of the Leeward Islands, having been warned by the Secretary of State, Lord Sunderland, that the post would require the 'utmost discretion, temper and humanity'. Displaying none of these qualities, his high-handed behaviour provoked a riot in 1710 in Antigua, where he was dragged out of Government House and murdered (Bill Laws, *Distinction, Death and Disgrace*, Institute of Jamaica, 1976: Royal Archives). The widow of Parke's grandson, Daniel Parke Custis, married George Washington in 1759.

so complete . . . My dearest life, if we could have another day as Wednesday last, I should then hope we might have such a peace as that I might enjoy the remaining part of my life with you.

The allies had lost some 13,000 men killed or wounded; but, by the end of the day, the French and Bavarians had lost far more: as many as 30,000 casualties, about 11,000 taken prisoner and no less than 6,000 men who had deserted their colours.★

The carcasses of thousands of horses littered the field, polluting the air. Soldiers were forbidden to touch them for fear of infection. The human dead lay where they had fallen, stripped of their uniforms, awaiting the burial parties.

Sergeant John Millner listed with pride the booty taken. So did Captain Robert Parker, who provided a similar inventory: 117 cannon and mortars, 239 colours and standards, '17 pair of kettle drums, 3,600 tents, 15 pontoons, 34 coaches, 24 barrels of silver, and 30 laden mules, with all the plate and baggage of the officers'. It was, commented one of Marlborough's officers, Richard Kane, 'the first fate Blow that Lewis XIV had received during his whole Reign'.

The prisoners, so the chaplain-general wrote, were

divided and disarmed and ordered to the adjacent villages in the rear of our Army, guarded by several squadrons of Horse Dragoons . . . I was commanded to take a list of the French generals and other officers . . . and [on entering a room containing at least sixty or seventy officers] I found some blaming the conduct of their own Generals, others walking with their arms folded, others lamenting their hard fortune and complaining of want of refreshment . . . But their chief concern was for their King, abundance of them muttering and plainly saying, 'Oh, que dira le Roy.'

★ The French command acknowledged these heavy losses. In a letter to the Hon Alexander Stanhope, English envoy at The Hague, dated 28 August, Marlborough wrote: 'I am very much obliged to you for your kind felicitations upon Our late Victory which indeed appears every Day greater then other [sic]. We have intercepted severall Letters going to Paris by which the Enemy own their loss to exceed fforty Thousand men killd, taken prisoners and by the great Desertion in their fflight towards the Black Forest. It is such a Blow that I hope the Enemy will not be able to recover in many Years . . . We are marching toward the Rhine by Three different Routs. Hoping God Almighty may have yet further Blessings for Us in store before the end of the Campagne' (Stanhope Papers, U1590 027/1).

The Duke, Francis Hare continued, was solicitous for the welfare of these captured officers. 'Whereas Prince Eugen was harsh,' wrote the French chronicler the duc de Saint-Simon, 'the Duke of Marlborough treated them all, even the humblest, with the utmost attention, consideration and politeness, and with a modesty perhaps more distinguished than his victory.'

The marquis de Silly, one of the generals taken prisoner, was allowed two months' parole and a safe-conduct through Germany so that he could go home to see his family, while Silly's friend, Marshal Tallard, whom Marlborough had known well when the marshal was serving as French ambassador in London, was permitted to send one of his officers to Versailles with his account of the battle to Louis XIV. Treating him with particular sympathy because the marshal's son had been killed in the battle and the marshal himself had not yet recovered from his wound, Marlborough saw to it that an escort was sent to restore his coach to him.

'I am very sorry,' the Duke said to him, 'that such a cruel misfortune should have fallen upon a soldier for whom I have had the highest regard.'

'And I congratulate you,' the marshal replied, 'on defeating the best soldiers in the world.'

'Your Lordship, I presume, excepts those who had the honour to beat them.'*

* Tallard was taken to Nottingham, where his captivity was not a close one. The garden of his house there was laid out for him by Queen Anne's gardener, Henry Wise, and Wise's colleague, George London, who described it in their *The Retir'd Gard'ner*, published by Jacob Tonson in 1706. Tallard was, at one time, credited with introducing celery, a Mediterranean vegetable eaten in France since the beginning of the seventeenth century, to the people of Nottingham.

24

HOMECOMING

'I long extremely to be with you and the children, so that you
may be sure I shall lose no time when the wind is fair.'

Colonel Parke was eight days on road and sea before arriving on 21
August in London with Marlborough's letter to his wife. The Duchess immediately sent Parke with the letter to Windsor, where, so it
is said, he found the Queen either in the bay-window of the castle's
Long Gallery, or on the castle terrace, playing checkers with her
husband. Having read the letter, the Queen apparently told Parke as
he knelt before her that he had given her more pleasure than she had
ever enjoyed in her life. She asked the colonel to say what he would
like to have as a reward for bringing such splendid news. Five
thousand guineas, it had been suggested, would be appropriate in
such circumstances, but Parke, with becoming modesty and appropriate flattery, asked for a miniature of Her Majesty instead. Accordingly she presented him with one set in diamonds, adding to it a
reward of 1,000 guineas. She then wrote to the Duchess:

I have had the happiness of receiving my dear Mr Freemans [letter] by Coll
Parke with the good news of this glorious victory, which, next to God
Almighty, is wholly owing to dear Mr Freeman, whose safety I congratulate
you with all my soul. May the same Providence that has hitherto preserved,
still watch over, and send him well home to you.

The next day, she sent a letter to Marlborough himself:

You will very easily believe that the good news Colonel Parke brought me
yesterday was very welcome, but not more, I do assure you, than hearing
you were well after so glorious a victory. [It] will not only humble our
enemyes abroad but contribute very much to the putting a Stop to the ill

designs of those at home. I will not give you any account of what passes here, knowing you have it from other hands, but end this with my sincere wishes that God Almighty will continue His protection over you, and send you safe home to the joy of your friends.

As soon as the great victory became known to the general public, London and provincial cities all over the country erupted in the most joyful celebrations. Church bells rang and cannon boomed. Copies of the Duke of Marlborough's pencilled note to the Duchess were printed and distributed in their thousands; crowds poured into the streets; bonfires were lit.

Loyal, honest Englishmen repaired in crowds to the coffee-houses and you might see satisfaction in every face. Bohee tea, coffee, chocolate, ratafia and Nants Brandy were insipid liquors. Away they adjourned to the tavern. Every bumper was crowned with the Queen's or the Duke of Marlborough's health and the loyal citizens emptied the cellars so fast I think two-thirds were foxed [drunk] next morning. Never were such illuminations, ringing of bells, such demonstrations of joy since the laying of London stone.

On the Continent there were joyful celebrations, too. There was general agreement, as Henry Davenant, the English financial agent in Frankfurt put it, that Marlborough had 'beyond all dispute saved the Empire'.*

After the strain and anxiety of the long march and the battle, and the pitiable sights of the mangled dead and the thousands of wounded whose plight the few surgeons in the allied army could do so little to alleviate, Marlborough was feeling physically and emotionally exhausted, and in no mood to respond to his wife's persistent urgings

---

* The dismay in Paris was evidently short-lived. 'We were not accustomed to defeat,' the duc de Saint-Simon wrote. 'All [the King's] anger fell upon . . . a few individuals, the innocent as well as the guilty . . . Amidst this general woe the revels and rejoicings over the birth of the Duc de Bretagne [the King's grandson] continued unabated. The city of Paris gave a fête with a display of fireworks on the river . . . There was lavish spending on eating and drinking . . . The King did not long remain in the shadow of the defeat of Blenheim' (*Memoirs of the Duc de Saint-Simon*, ed. and trans. Lucy Norton, i).

to have more concern for the political imbroglios in which she so passionately involved herself. His only wish, he said in frustration, was to 'leave a good name behind [him] in country's that have hardly any blessing but that of not knowing the detested names of Wigg and Torry'. Four days after the battle his troops were drawn up at Steinheim for a service of thanksgiving and on that day he wrote to Godolphin: 'Ever sence the battaile I have been so employ'd about our wounded men and the prisoners, that I have not one hour's quiet, which has so disorder'd mee that were I in London I shou'd be in my bed in a hie feavour.'

'I am suffer'd to have so little time to my self,' he continued a few days later,

that I have a continual feavour on my spirits, which makes me very weak, but when I go from hence I am resolv'd to keep in my coach til I come to the Rhine . . . Nothing but my zeal for her Majesty's service cou'd have enabl'd me to have gone thorow the fatigues I have had . . . I am too sure when I shall have the happyness of seeing you [again] you will find me ten years older.

He wrote to Sarah in the same vein,

My dearest life, if we cou'd have another such day as Wensday last, I shou'd then hope we might have such a Peace that I might injoye the remaining part of my life with you . . . For thousands of reasons I wish myself with you. Besides I think if I were with you quietly at the Lodge, I should have more health, for I am at this time so very lean, that it is extreame uneasy to mee, so that your care must nurse me this winter . . . What you say of St Albans [that he should retire there for good when he came home so as to recover his strength] is what from my Soull I wish, that there or somewhere else we might end our days in quietness together; and if I considered only my self, I agree with you, I can never quit the world in a better time, but I have too many obligation to the Queen to take any resolution, but such as Her Service must be first consider'd.

Before returning home, Marlborough was obliged to visit the courts of Prussia and Hanover in an attempt to gain more German troops for the next campaign, which, it was hoped, might bring the war to a successful conclusion in 1705. Tired out after almost three months of marches and sieges which had brought his army back to the Rhine, he set out for Berlin in discontented mood. 'I think to begin my journey on Friday or Saturday next,' he wrote to Godolphin on 10 November 1704 from Weissemburg. 'I own that my heart aches at the thought of it, since I shall be forced to go about eight hundred miles before I get to The Hague, in the very worst time of the year; and that, which is worse of all, with very little hopes of succeeding.'

The journey down the rough and muddy German roads in his rattling coach was quite as unpleasant as he had feared. 'The ways have been so bad,' he told Sarah upon his arrival in Berlin, 'I have been oblig'd to be every day 14 or 15 hours on the road, which makes my side very sore; but three or four days I shall stay here will make me able to go on.'

He was, however, obliged to stay three days longer than he had intended before being able to obtain an undertaking for the raising and pay of 8,000 men. He then set off for Hanover, taking with him the best wishes of the people of Berlin – who had treated him with great courtesy and respect – and presents from the Prussian King, including 'a hat with a diamond button and loop and a diamond hatband, valued at between twenty and thirty thousand crowns', and 'two fine saddle horses with rich furniture'.

Welcomed with as much enthusiasm in Hanover as he had been in Berlin, he was greeted with exceptional warmth by the old Electress, whom he set out most successfully to charm. In the words of the German historian Onno Klopp:

He showed towards the Electress a deference which surpassed all the customary forms of the German Courts. He refused to sit down in her presence even at a ball. The Electress invited him to take part in a game [of cards] so as to force him to sit down . . . In accordance with the English court custom, he knelt and kissed her hand.

There were rumours that the Duke had in mind to have his youngest daughter, Lady Mary, married to the Electress's grandson, the future King George II of England, and there was no doubt that, had dynastic considerations been laid aside, she would have welcomed the Duke's daughter into her family. Before she had met him, she had always referred to him somewhat dismissively and had blamed him for the large numbers of Hanoverian soldiers killed in the storming of the Schellenberg; but now she decided that she had 'never become acquainted with a man' who knew 'how to move so easily, so freely and so courteously'. 'He is,' she concluded, 'as skilled as a courtier as he is a brave general.' She gave him, as a parting present, a valuable piece of tapestry, while her son, Prince Georg Ludwig, the future George I of England, presented him with a jewel valued at 20,000 thalers.

On 2 December, Marlborough wrote to Sarah from Hanover:

I have met with more kindness and respect everywhere than I could have imagined. I shall go from hence on Thursday, so that on this day se'nnight I hope to write from the Hague, where I will make as little stay as the business will allow of . . . We have the news here that Landau and Trarbach are taken, so that thanks be to God, this campaign is ended, to the greatest advantage for the allies that has been for a great while. I long extremely to be with you and the children, so that you may be sure I shall lose no time when the wind is fair.

Although there had been much adverse comment about his taking Dutch troops so far away from their homeland, where so many were now buried, he was greeted with as much ceremony and respect at The Hague as he had been in Berlin and Hanover. The Grand Pensionary, Anthonie Heinsius, and seven deputies welcomed him with due ceremony; and, in the name of the republic, expressed their warmest thanks for all that he had achieved, presenting him with a golden basin and ewer to add to the other valuable presents he had already received. With all these safely packed in his baggage, he sailed from Rotterdam in the middle of December and arrived home at Greenwich in time for Christmas after an absence of eight months.

The Duke had brought with him not only Marshal Tallard but sixteen captured generals and nineteen other senior officers. He had also brought all the standards and colours captured by his troops at Blenheim, including those taken by the Dutch, to the great annoyance of the States-General, who reprimanded the Dutch general Count Hompesch for handing them over. All these trophies were taken to the Tower of London, to be stored there until the time came for them to be paraded through the streets in the splendid celebrations already planned.

Having paid his duty to the Queen, Marlborough then went to Parliament to receive the thanks of the House of Lords, rendered in sonorous tones and lengthy sentences by Lord Cowper:

Your Grace has not overcome young, unskilful Generals, raw and undisciplined troops; but . . . has conquered the French and Bavarian armies; armies that were fully instructed in all the arts of war; select veteran troops, flushed with former victories, and commanded by Generals of great experience and bravery . . .

The Empire is therefore freed from a dangerous Enemy . . .

This most honourable House is highly sensible of the great and signal services Your Grace has done Her Majesty, this campaign, and of the immortal honour you have done the English Nation; and have commanded me to give you their thanks for the same.

The Duke's reply was far more succinct:

I must beg on this occasion, to do right to all the officers and soldiers I had the honour to command. Next to the blessing of God, the good success of this campaign is owing to their extraordinary courage. I am very sure it will be a great satisfaction, as well as encouragement, to the whole Army, to find their services so favourably accepted.

After Christmas that year, the captured trophies were paraded through the streets, from the Tower to Westminster Hall, by cavalry and foot guards, to the acclamations of the crowds and the roar of cannon in the parks. Three days later the Lord Mayor and aldermen gave a banquet for the Duke and the Queen's ministers in Goldsmiths' Hall.

John Evelyn, who met 'the Victorious Duke of Marlborou' at the Lord Treasurer's on 9 February, was struck by his modesty and charm:

He took me by the hand with extraordinary familiarity and Civility, as formerly he was used to doe without any alteration of his good nature. He had a most rich George [the jewel of the Order of the Garter] in a sardonix set with Diamond of an inestimable Value; for the rest very plaine: I had not seene him in 2 yeares and believed he had forgotten me.

Satisfactory as were the celebrations held for the victory at Blenheim, it was widely proposed that some more permanent recognition of the Duke's triumph should be made. One proposal was that an area of London should be cleared for the building of a square bearing his name, and that a suitably imposing house should be erected in this square, which would also contain statues both of the Duke and of the Queen he had so bravely served.

This, however, did not meet with much approval, even among the Duke's most faithful supporters and friends. Godolphin wrote to Harley:

I am not fond of the proposal of two statues, one for the Queen and th' other for the Duke of Marlborough. What merit soever a subject may have, I am doubtful that may set him upon too near an equality with one upon the throne. My own opinion inclines most to an anniversary thanks-giving by Act of Parliament for so entire a victory, as the most public, the most decent, and the most permanent record of it to posterity.

Unable to decide upon a suitable memorial, ministers and Parliament concurred in approaching the Queen, who proposed that the grant of £5,000 a year, which she had already made to the Duke for his lifetime from the Civil List, should be made permanent by Parliament and that she should convey the royal park and manor of Woodstock in Oxfordshire, extending to several thousand acres worth about £6,000 a year, to the Duke and his heirs. It was further proposed that the Commons should grant a sum for the construction of a fine house within the grounds of Woodstock Manor as an appropriate commemoration of his great victory at Blenheim, after which it should be named. As a symbolic quitrent for the estate, it was agreed that on the anniversary of the battle, and for ever more on that day, a silk standard emblazoned with three gilded fleurs-de-lys on a field argent, a facsimile of the standard of the French royal household troops, the Corps du Roi, should be presented to the monarch at Windsor.

The architect chosen for the design of Blenheim Castle, as the building was at first known, was Sir John Vanbrugh.

25

JOHN VANBRUGH

'. . . almost as great a genius as ever lived . . .'

John Vanbrugh was born in London in the parish of St Nicholas Acons in January 1664. He was a poor, sickly-looking child, too weak to be taken to church and just as likely to die as his mother's first two babies had already done. So the rector of the parish was called to the house to christen him there.

His father, Giles, was the son of a Dutchman, Gillis van Brugg, a merchant from Ghent, a man of distinguished lineage who had come over to England after the Duke of Alba had been sent to the Netherlands to punish the Calvinist rebels there. Received into the Church of England, van Brugg had prospered in his adopted country and, having married an English girl, had died a respected member of his community. His son, John's father, also did well for himself. He married the daughter of Sir Dudley Carleton, nephew and heir of Viscount Dorchester, British ambassador at The Hague; and, having left London for Chester, he established himself in a good way of business there as a sugar-baker and became the father of nineteen children.

It seems that such boys as survived, including John, were sent to King's School, Chester, a respected establishment founded in 1541. Certainly, at the age of seventeen, John was working in London in the wines and brandies trade. His employer, a cousin, soon became bankrupt; and between 1683 and 1685 Vanbrugh was employed in India for the East India Company. Upon his return to Chester, he obtained a commission in an infantry regiment, from which, however, he resigned not long afterwards.

He was then heard of in France, where, possibly on an espionage mission, he was arrested for not having a passport and, held as a possible exchange for a French prisoner in English hands, he was incarcerated in the prison at Vincennes and subsequently in the Bastille, where he seems to have passed the time in sketching out comedies for the theatre, an occupation for which he found he had a natural facility. Released after eighteen months, he returned to England, where he was promoted captain of marines with a salary of £180 a year.

Captain Vanbrugh was by then thirty-one years old, a handsome, amusing, charming young man, moving easily in the fashionable world of London, which formed the background of the plays he was to write. His first success was *The Relapse, or Virtue in Danger*, which was, he said, 'got, conceived and born in six weeks' and was greeted with an enthusiasm not in the least dampened by the appearance on stage of the quarrelsome and dissolute George Powell, who fell, hopelessly drunk, upon one of the outraged actresses. The triumph of *The Relapse* was followed by *Aesop*, also performed at the Theatre Royal, Drury Lane. Then came *The Provok'd Wife* at the New Theatre in Little Lincoln's Inn Fields, with the great Thomas Betterton as Sir John Brute. This was an even more successful production which confirmed Vanbrugh's reputation as a writer of brilliant comedies and which was to induce Charles James Fox to describe its author, with understandable hyperbole, as 'almost as great a genius as ever lived'. Vanbrugh was soon to display his genius in a quite different form of art.

There was in London at this time an influential club of gentlemen, mostly Whigs, founded by the bookseller Jacob Tonson, and named the Kit-Cat Club, after the pastry cook Christopher Katt, at whose house the club first met and whose mutton pies its members relished. Among these members, then and later, were Joseph Addison, Richard Steele, William Congreve and Sir Godfrey Kneller, who painted their portraits – less than half-length and still known as kit-cats – which hung in the club's dining room, the ceiling of which was too low for it to contain portraits of larger size. Apart from writers, artists and poets such as the now-forgotten Samuel Garth, said to be the fattest man in London, who once defeated the almost equally fat Duke of Grafton in a race of 300 yards down the Mall, several noblemen belonged to the club, including the notorious duellist Lord Mohun, and the Earl of Carbery, a former governor of Jamaica, who was said to have increased his large fortune by selling his servants and the tenants from his Welsh estates as slaves on West Indian plantations. Less disreputable members of the Kit-Cat Club were the Earls of Scarborough, Halifax and Carlisle, Lord Cobham and the Dukes of Manchester and Marlborough, all of whom were to employ their fellow member John Vanbrugh as architect.*

It is unclear where Vanbrugh acquired his skill as an architect. It has been suggested that he studied books of architecture while he was in France, and certainly he had ample time to do so during his months in the Bastille, where in his by no means harsh confinement he had access to a library. He also had an opportunity to study the architecture of the subcontinent when he was in India. But all that is known for sure is that when he was commissioned to design a palatial house in Yorkshire for a fellow member of the Kit-Cat Club, Charles Howard, the young, rich and cultivated third Earl of Carlisle, Vanbrugh's name was unknown as an architect and his skill at realizing his plans – which he sketched with the same easy facility with which he wrote his plays – had never yet been put fully to the test. It had been expected that Carlisle would choose Sir Christopher Wren, the greatest architect of his time, whose works had graced so many of London's parishes since the Great Fire of 1660, or William Talman, the King's Comptroller of Works, who had worked at Chatsworth for the first Duke of Devonshire and who had designed Uppark for Lord Tankerville and Stanstead Park in Sussex for the Earl of Scarborough.

But Vanbrugh would at least have the assistance of Nicholas Hawksmoor, a Nottinghamshire yeoman farmer's son who had worked in Wren's office since he was eighteen years old, a fine draughtsman who could furnish such practical and technical knowledge as Vanbrugh lacked. So pleased was Lord Carlisle with the

* 'Marlborough's appearances [at the Kit-Cat Club] were few; but his absences were in the cause of history' (Whistler, *Sir John Vanbrugh*, 86).

work which Vanbrugh, with Hawksmoor's assistance, completed for him at Castle Howard that, as First Lord of the Treasury and responsible for appointments to the Board of Works, he displaced Talman as Comptroller and appointed Vanbrugh in his place with a salary of 8s.8d. a day. Later, although Vanbrugh had very little knowledge of heraldry and had, indeed, mocked the subject in one of his plays, Lord Carlisle caused much offence at the College of Arms by appointing him Clarenceux King-of-Arms, the second most important office in the college, an appointment which, according to the college's historian, was greatly resented as a

slight put upon [the other heralds and pursuivants] in having a total stranger made king-at-arms; the more, because . . . Vanbrugh was totally ignorant of the profession of heraldry and genealogy, which he took every occasion to ridicule. Lord Carlisle was very reprehensible in sacrificing the duty he owed to private attachment.*

Just as it had been supposed that Wren, the King's Surveyor, would be appointed architect at Castle Howard, so it was believed that he would be asked to draw up plans for the grand house to be built at Woodstock for the Duke of Marlborough. Indeed, if the choice had been left to her, the Duchess would certainly have chosen Wren, whom, although he was by then nearly eighty years old, she later did appoint as her own architect for the building of her London residence, Marlborough House, on land at the western end of Pall Mall which was leased to her by the Crown.

'I have no great opinion of this project,' the Duke was to write of Marlborough House, 'for I am very confident that in time you will be sensible that [it] will cost you double the money of the first estimate.' He was, however, as usual, prepared to indulge his wife, wishing her 'all happiness and speed' with her new house in London, while begging her not to be hindered from 'pressing forward the building at Blenheim'. 'I am so desirous of living at Woodstock,' he reminded her, 'that I should not much care to do anything but what is necessary anywhere else . . . I am confident you will find 'twill

---

* Vanbrugh sold his office as Clarenceux King-of-Arms to Knox Ward in 1725 for £2,500 (Downes, *Sir John Vanbrugh: A Biography*, 241).

cost you much more money than the thing is worth . . . But I would have you follow your own inclinations in it.' He thought 'nothing too much for the making [her] easy'.

Having got her way, as she had, of course, expected to do, the Duchess, employing over 100 bricklayers and masons on the site, called up craftsmen from Blenheim as well as the gardener Henry Wise, while the Duke arranged for the money to be made available for her and wrote to ask for the measurements of the walls so that tapestries could be made for the rooms.*

Marlborough House cost some £50,000, which was £20,000 more than the sum provisionally allocated for it by the Duchess, who borrowed £22,000 from the privy purse accounts without troubling to inform the Queen. For this large additional expenditure she blamed Sir Christopher, who, 'from his age', had evidently been 'imposed upon by the workmen and had paid prices for all things which were much too high for ready money and sure pay'. Even so, the cost of Marlborough House was 'not really as extravagant' as it seemed, she insisted, since it was the 'strongest and best house that ever was built'.†

Marlborough, left by the Queen to make his own choice of architect for his great house at Woodstock, 'cast his eye upon the Board of Works', in Vanbrugh's own words, 'and there (for reasons best

* One of these rooms, the central saloon, and the staircase are now lined with a series of historical paintings of Marlborough's battles by Louis Laguerre. Gentileschi's *Arts and Sciences*, painted in 1636 for the Queen's House at Greenwich, was removed from there with the permission of Queen Anne and placed on the saloon ceiling.

† The house remained in the possession of the Marlborough family until 1817, when it reverted to the Crown, a third storey having been added by Sir William Chambers in the 1770s. It was subsequently occupied by Prince Leopold of Saxe-Coburg-Saalfeld, then by the Dowager Queen Adelaide and subsequently Edward, Prince of Wales, for whom Sir James Pennethorne removed Chambers's attic storey, replacing it by two of his own. Until his father's death in 1910, King George V lived here as Prince of Wales. It then became the home of his mother, the widowed Queen Alexandra. Upon the death of King George V, his widow, Queen Mary, moved here and died in the house in 1953. In 1959 it was donated to the Government for use as a Commonwealth Centre (*The London Encyclopaedia*, ed. B. Weinreb and C. Hibbert (1983), 498–9).

known to himself) not inclining to engage Sir Christopher Wren, he fix'd upon the next officer to him'. The choice caused much surprise, despite the admiration aroused by Vanbrugh's design for Castle Howard – a model of which he showed to the Duke – and the friendship likely to exist between two members of the close-knit Kit-Cat Club. 'I suppose, my Lord,' Lord Ailesbury was to observe to the Duke sardonically, 'you made choice of him because he is a profound Whig', almost adding the words which were, so he confessed, at his 'tongue's end', 'You ought as well to have made Sir Christopher Wren Poet Laureate.'

Marlborough, however, knew what he was about. Although he had seen no active service, Vanbrugh had been a soldier; and, in the words of his biographer, Laurence Whistler,

just as he loved to write metaphors of storming castles and defending breaches, so did he love to build bastions and towers, trophies and stone bombs . . . He became obsessed with the fortified air, the martial grandeur. 'The Bastille' was the name of his own house [which he built for himself at Greenwich] and it cannot be stressed too much that he was always a builder of *castles*. It seems as if, in some way haunted by the memory of imprisonment, he was ever trying to escape from those phantom walls by building them in a happier context.

He and Marlborough, who had also been imprisoned once and was to be so again, went down together to Woodstock with a shared idea of the grandly magnificent appearance of the future edifice. Like Kimbolton, which Vanbrugh designed for the Duke of Manchester, it was to have 'something of the castle air', was, in fact, to be not so much a 'private Habitation' for the Churchill family as a monument, 'as emphatic as an oath', to military glory, to the memory of the Duke of Marlborough, of his benefactress, Queen Anne, and of the armies the Duke had commanded. 'It ought in short,' Vanbrugh said, 'to be considered as both a Royal and national monument with the appropriate qualities viz. Beauty, magnificence, duration.' He was to concede that it was, indeed, a monument rather than a dwelling. 'One may,' he said, 'find a great deal of pleasure in building a palace for another when one should find very little in living in it oneself.'

The parkland in the Oxfordshire countryside, through which sluggishly meandered the Glyme stream and its tributaries in their marshy beds, was not an ideal site. But it could be made so, while the existing manor house was a picturesque ruin which, in Vanbrugh's romantic opinion, would, when viewed from the windows of the great house, make 'one of the Most Agreeable Objects that the best of Landskip Painters could invent'. This crumbling ruin had a legendary history to match its appearance. It was here that King Henry I, son of the Conqueror, had kept his menagerie and here that Henry II installed his mistress, Rosamund Clifford, keeping her hidden from the Queen's jealousy in a secret chamber within a maze. It was here that the Black Prince, eldest son of Edward III, was born. It was here also, in the summer of 1554, that Princess Elizabeth was kept imprisoned, suspected of being involved in a plot against her half-sister Queen Mary, and here that she scratched with a diamond on a window-pane:

> Much suspected, by me
> Nothing proved can be,
> Quoth Elizabeth, prisoner

It was here, too, that Cromwell's soldiers roamed about smashing everything they could reach.

Moved by these stories, Vanbrugh gave orders for the habitable part of the house to be repaired to prevent it falling down and to make the rest a 'little decent' for his own use when working on his plans for the great house. As for the two ancient causeways that crossed the marshy ground, these, he decided, should be replaced by a magnificent bridge spanning a fine expanse of ornamental water.

The Duke listened to his architect's extravagant schemes with noncommittal reserve. Although fully sharing Vanbrugh's vision of an English Versailles, a grand and permanent memorial to his own and his army's achievements and a stately palace for his descendants, he was wary of committing himself personally to any great, unnecessary expense.

The financial arrangements made for the building of his palace, which was eventually, with its courts, to cover seven acres, were not very satisfactory. The Treasury was authorized to supply the Duke with unspecified sums of money to hand over to Henry Joynes, an intelligent young draughtsman and future architect who had been appointed comptroller of the works at Woodstock. Joynes, in turn, was to pay the craftsmen and workmen for their labours on the 'large Fabrick' while it was under construction. But no specific sums were mentioned, and the whole future of the works depended upon the Queen remaining upon the throne and the administration of government remaining in the hands of men who approved of the Duke of Marlborough being honoured in the way she had prescribed. Only too well aware of this, the Duke – whose name was mentioned four times in the building warrant, the Queen's not once – scrupulously avoided signing any bills, lest his signature should be assumed as constituting his personal responsibility for the authorization of highly expensive work, which Wren, called in for an independent estimate, calculated would cost £100,000, over twice the sum Marlborough had been led to expect. Both Godolphin and Sarah were appalled by this huge sum and she appealed to him to try to make her husband see sense. Marlborough conceded that, if it were considered 'not a proper time for the Queen to make such an expence', it would be 'no great uneasiness to [him] if it were lett alone'. Nevertheless, he instructed Vanbrugh 'to press ahead with his plans as fast as possible'.*

From the very start the Duchess, who, as she said, mortally hated 'all Grandeur and Architecture', disapproved of the whole venture, 'Vanbrugh's madness', 'that wild unmerciful house'. 'At the beginning of those works,' she was to write, 'I never had spoake to him [Vanbrugh], but as soon as I knew him & saw the Maddnesse of the whole Design I opposed it all that was possible for me to doe.' She could not, however, curb the Duke's enthusiasm; and on 18 June 1705, in the presence of Vanbrugh and Hawksmoor, a huge polished

---

* 'Marlborough is often represented as over-submissive to his masterful wife, and was himself fond of remarking that he could never refuse her anything,' Sarah Marlborough's biographer has written. 'Yet nothing demonstrates the limitations of her influence with him in some matters more clearly than the continued slow rise of his baroque palace in the Oxfordshire countryside, in spite of all she could do or say to hinder it' (Harris, *A Passion for Government*, 120).

foundation stone, eight feet square, was lowered into the earth beneath the site of what was to become the Bow Window Room at the eastern end of the palace. It was inscribed with the words: 'In memory of the Battel of Blenheim June 18, 1705, Anna Regina.' The antiquary William Upcott recorded:

There were several sorts of musick, three morris dances; one of young fellows, one of maidens, and one of old beldames. There were about a hundred buckets, bowls and pans, filled with wine, punch, cakes, and ale. From my lord's house all went to the Town Hall where plenty of sack, claret, cakes etc, were prepared for the gentry and better sort; and under the Cross eight barrels of ale, with abundance of cakes, were placed for the common people.

Before long 'near fifteen hundred' men were at work on the foundations, digging manure into the ground which was to be laid out as parterres, creating a ha-ha to keep animals out of the gardens. Under the direction of Henry Wise, hundreds of trees were brought from his nursery gardens at Brompton in osier baskets to be planted in the grounds, together with thousands upon thousands of bulbs and shrubs and scores of fruit trees, including nearly 700 peach, pear, cherry and apple trees.

Soon the vast site became a jumble of sand and gravel, lime and lead, marble, slates, bricks, timber and cartloads of stone brought to Woodstock from Lord Rochester's quarry at Cornbury, Sir John Wheate's at Glympton and from no fewer than twenty-one other quarries.

26

THE LINES OF BRABANT

'The kindness of the troops has transported me.'

Marlborough returned to The Hague in the second week of April 1705, having endured a fearful crossing during which his ship went aground on the sandbanks off the Dutch coast and he spent hours in a tossing open boat before reaching dry land. 'I have been so very sick at sea,' he told Sarah, 'that my blood is as hote as if I were in a feavour which makes my head eake extreamly, so that I beg you will make my excuse to Ld Treasurer, for I can write to nobody but my dear soull, whom I love above my life. I am just now going to bed, although I know I cannot sleep.'

His hopes of another successful campaign were soon to be disappointed. At first it was but petty irritations of which he had cause to complain: he had not yet received the drawings Vanbrugh had promised him; he could 'get no Tee fit to be drunk'; the painting of the battle of Blenheim for which he had paid fifty pounds was not worth ten. But then there were more serious causes for vexation. The Dutch generals, and in particular General Slangenberg, who was most reluctant to serve under him, were in a surly mood, jealous of his success. The Margrave of Baden, still troubled by the wound in his foot – which he had made worse by treating it with Schlangenbad water – and preoccupied with the building of a new palace at Rastadt, was still smarting with resentment at having been encouraged to go off to besiege Ingolstadt and thus deprived of the glory of Blenheim. Like Slangenberg, he was strongly disinclined to serve under the extravagantly admired Englishman. He protested that his foot was too painful for him to attend a meeting which had been arranged to take place at Kreuznach, obliging Marlborough to travel at the rate of sixty miles a day to Rastadt, where, on the first afternoon after his arrival, the Margrave's foot did not prevent him from proudly conducting his visitor on a tour of the palace gardens, then in elaborate construction.

Earlier that month the Emperor Leopold had died and his eldest son and successor, Joseph I, who spoke highly of the Duke of Marlborough's talents, urged the Margrave to cooperate more closely and willingly with him than the Margrave himself was disposed to do.

The Margrave grudgingly agreed to consult the Duke about their future combined operations; but he warned him that he would be quite unable to bring nearly as many men into the field against the French as Marlborough had hoped he would. Nor were the forces which the Empire could contribute to the allied campaign as strong as the Duke had been led to expect: many regiments were operating in Italy under the command of Prince Eugène, while many others were tied down in Hungary, where rebels were in the second of their eight-year uprising against Hapsburg domination. In a covering letter to Godolphin, sending him a field state of the available Imperial forces, Marlborough wrote: 'You see what a miserable thing a German army is.' 'I am like a sick body that turns from one side of the bed to another,' he had already complained to Sarah. He was longing to get away to his own army, where he hoped 'to find more quiet'; but God only knew what ease he might have when he got there. He was sure of only one thing: he never could be happy until he was once more with his 'dearest soul'.

When he arrived at Trier on the Moselle on 26 May, after an exhausting six days on the road, he found conditions quite as bad as he had feared they might be. The store-houses there were half empty; an incompetent or corrupt commissary employed by the Dutch to keep them properly supplied had deserted to the enemy, and the whole surrounding valley had already been stripped of forage by the French.

Despite these misfortunes and the failure of the German troops to arrive, Marlborough decided to advance against the enemy in the hope that his relatively small army would induce Marshal Villars to attack him and that he would be victorious in the ensuing battle, as he had been at Blenheim. In a letter to Godolphin written on 2 June 1705, he explained:

What I have always believed proves true, that the Germans would not be able to act till the middle of June; for till that time I shall have neither the Imperialists nor the Prussians with me. However, forage is so very scarce here that I shall be obliged in five days to march, so that if Marshal Villars has power to venture a battle, he may have it. Though I [still lack] one third of the troops that [were] to compose this army, I depend so much upon the goodness of these I have here that, with the blessing of God, I do not doubt of good success.

So at two o'clock the next morning, his English and Dutch troops advanced against the French, whose outposts before Sierck withdrew in haste into their well-fortified positions. Assuming that the English general would not dare to assault them, Marshal Villars held his ground and waited, confident that Marlborough, finding no means of existing in a countryside bereft of all supplies, would soon be obliged to withdraw. And, tireless as were his efforts to provide his men with bread, Marlborough was, indeed, compelled to retreat. He was satisfied that he was right to do so when, having lost 'a great many men' through desertion, his quartermaster-general, whom he had sent to the Margrave's camp to find out what had happened to the reinforcements promised him, returned with a depressing report: the Margrave had retired to a spa to take the waters for the sake of his painful foot and had been succeeded by a general evidently in no great hurry to reinforce Marlborough, even though the French army had been reinforced by troops under the command of Marshal Marsin.

So vexed that he made himself ill, and, as he put it, 'weary of [his] life', Marlborough was now begged for help by the Dutch, whose outnumbered troops were threatened by Villeroi on the Meuse. So, during the night of 17 June, in the pouring rain, the Duke withdrew his men, having concluded a friendly correspondence with Villars, to whom he sent 'a quantity of English liqueurs, Palm wine and cider', at the same time informing him that his English opponent was 'in despair, because the Margrave [had] broken his word and that it was the Margrave, and the Margrave only, who was responsible for the breaking up of all our plans'. For, although his own conduct of this brief campaign was open to much criticism, Marlborough wanted there to be no doubt in Versailles, as there must be no doubt in London, that it was his so-called allies' dilatoriness and incompetence that had obliged him to withdraw his army to Trier. Had he been reinforced and supplied as he had been promised, the result, he inferred, would have been likely to be very different.

There was worse yet to come. Having crossed the Moselle and made north through the wild, mountainous region of the Eifel, Marlborough learned that the commander of the allied garrison in Trier, Count d' Aubach, had abandoned it at the first sign of French activity in the area, burning the stores and equipment which had been collected there. There was no possibility now of Marlborough's returning to the Moselle.

Frustrated in his attempts to bring Marshal Villars to battle, Marlborough now turned his attention to the Lines of Brabant, sixty miles of earthworks and other defences which extended from the sea at Antwerp to the Meuse near Namur. Behind these lines were ninety-two battalions of infantry and 160 squadrons of cavalry commanded by Marshal de Villeroi, an enemy force slightly larger than Marlborough's own. At a council of war with the Dutch generals he proposed a plan for breaking through them. Nearly all the generals were opposed to this plan, most insistently Marlborough's old rival and critic, General Slangenberg. But one of them, Hendrick Overkirk, an elderly *veldtmarschal*, brave and imaginative, for whom Marlborough had much respect, differed from the rest. So the Duke decided to take this officer into his confidence and reveal to him the details of his proposed attack upon the Lines, which were, for the moment, to be kept hidden from the other Dutch generals, who, he knew, would disapprove of them as constituting too risky an undertaking. And so he confided in Overkirk his clever, complicated plans, involving feints and bluffs, marches and counter-marches, by which he hoped to deceive – and, indeed, succeeded in deceiving – both Villeroi and the Dutch generals as to his real intentions.

The execution of these movements was faultless; and on the night of 17/18 July, having passed Landen, where the skeletons of soldiers killed in the savage battle fought here in the summer of 1693 still lay thick and grisly upon the ground, Marlborough's leading columns, followed by Overkirk's force, which had been suddenly wheeled about, succeeded in crossing the stream, known as the Little Geet, that flowed beneath the fortications of the Lines at Elixhem. Scrambling up the bank, they broke through the formidable but less strongly garrisoned breastworks and ramparts in this sector of the Lines before the French and Bavarians could march up to prevent them. More and more allied troops followed them until, by five o'clock the next morning, Marlborough had succeeded in getting over 6,000 of his men through the enemy's entrenchments.

Marlborough himself rode through at about seven o'clock and, cheered loudly by officers as well as his men, he led a cavalry charge against a squadron of black-armoured Bavarian cuirassiers, who, appearing too late to contest the allied breakthrough, were hurtled back and driven into flight. More enemy cavalry appeared and these, too, were charged and dispersed, Marlborough once again riding with his cheering men. Lord Orkney, the commander of the leading cavalry, wrote:

My Lord Marlborough in person was everywhere and escaped very narrowly; for a squadron which he was at the head of, gave ground a little, though soon came up again; and a fellow came to him and thought to have sabred him to the ground, and struck at him [with such force that], missing his stroke, he fell off his horse.

About an hour later, almost the whole of Marlborough's army was within the French defences and, by ten o'clock, Overkirk's men, having by then marched almost thirty miles since the operation began, were within them too. 'It is impossible to say too much good of the troops that were with me, for never men fought better,' Marlborough reported to his wife.

Having marched all night, and taken a good deal of pains this day, my blood is so hot that I can hardly hold my pen; so that you will, my dearest life, excuse me if I say no more, but that I would not let you know my design of attacking the lines by the last post, fearing it might give you uneasiness; and now, my dearest soul, my heart is so full of joy for this good success, that should I write more I should say a great many follies.

'The kindness of the troops has transported me,' he added two days later, on 20 July, as the demolition of the Lines began. '[They] made me very kind expressions, even in the heat of the action, which I own to you gives me great pleasure, and makes me resolve to endure everything for their sakes.'

In answer to her plea that he should not take such risks as he did, he wrote reassuringly:

I never venture myself but when I think the service of my Queen and country requires it. I am now at an age when I find no heat in my blood that gives me temptation to expose myself out of vanity; but as I would [want to] deserve and keep the kindness of this army I must let them see that when I expose them I would not except myself.

There were those among his critics who now complained that the Duke spent far too much time writing such letters when he should have been following up his success, taking the advice of General Slangenberg, who, annoyed that the Englishman had succeeded where he had predicted failure, told him grumpily, 'This is nothing. We should march on Louvain or Parc.'

Colonel Cranstoun of the Cameronians was also critical of the Duke's conduct, of his taking so much

pleasure in writing letters, with accounts of [his] success, to the Emperor, the Queen, the States and others and [of] signing warrants for safeguards of which above two hundred were writ and signed [in a single] afternoon . . . This correspondence took up so much of his time that the Duke forgot to pursue the advantages which were certainly in [his] hands.

In his report to Godolphin, written on 18 July, Marlborough spoke of his intention of marching the next day towards Louvain 'to see what Monsieur de Villeroy will do', characteristically adding a suggestion – no doubt prompted by shocked thoughts of the thousand guineas impulsively offered by the Queen to Colonel Parke after Blenheim – that £500 would be quite enough reward for Colonel Durel, the messenger sent on this occasion.

Having read the Duke's report of his success in breaking through the Lines of Brabant, now being demolished, Robert Harley, an increasingly important member of the administration, wrote a fulsome letter of congratulation:

You have, my Lord, exceeded our very hopes and expectations, and no person could have done it but yourself . . . I took the liberty to say to the Queen . . . that no subjects in the world have such a prince, and no prince in the world has such a subject as your grace . . . Your friends and servants here cannot be without concern upon your grace's account when we hear *how much you expose* that precious life of yours *upon all occasions* . . . I hope your Lordship's unwearied care and unparalleled merit will in due time procure a lasting and sure peace for Europe, with repose and eternal renown to your grace.

Welcome as such praise usually was – if not from Harley, whom he could not abide – Marlborough was too concerned at this time fully to appreciate it, deeply worried as he was by the difficulties of his relationship with the Dutch and the problems presented by his still limited command, the 'private animositys' of senior officers and the endless carping of the tiresome Slangenberg, who seemed 'better pleased when anything [went] ill' than by success.

'It is absolutely necessary that power bee lodged with the general as may enable him to act as he thinks proper,' the Duke told Heinsius, adding that he was quite ready to resign if it was considered that anyone else could exercise that command better than himself. In the meantime he would continue to act without showing any resentment, bearing in mind that to act otherwise would not only antagonize the Dutch but also encourage the enemy and that, were he to exercise the authority granted to him by the States-General to give orders to the Dutch when his army was united with theirs, he might both risk the refusal of the Dutch generals to obey these orders and seriously damage Anglo-Dutch relations, upon the harmony of which so much depended. He even brought himself to speak politely to General Slangenberg, whom he assured with astonishing insincerity, 'I am happy to have under my command an officer of your courage and skill.'

27

A GRAND TOUR

'. . . his manners are as obliging and polished
as his actions are glorious and admirable.'

Determined to do all he could to bring the enemy to battle before
the campaign of 1705 ended, Marlborough saw his opportunity in
the wooded land south of Brussels by the waters of the river Yssche,
where he believed that he had manoeuvred them into a position in
which he could, outnumbering them, defeat them. 'Gentlemen,' he
said to the Dutch field deputies, 'I congratulate you on the prospect
of a glorious victory.' The deputies demurred: they must seek the
opinion of their generals first. Marlborough could not but agree to
this; and when these officers had been assembled he addressed them
in words overheard by the chaplain-general: 'Gentlemen, I have
reconnoitred the ground, and made dispositions for an attack. I am
convinced that conscientiously, and as men of honour, we cannot
now retire without an action. Should we neglect this opportunity,
we must be responsible before God and man. You see the confusion
which pervades the ranks of the enemy, and their embarrassment at
our manoeuvres.'

General Slangenberg, 'that beast', immediately and predictably
gave it as his opinion that Marlborough's proposals were impracticable, that they would end in 'murder and massacre', while the other
generals turned away to discuss the matter with the field deputies
and, after considering it and making their own careful reconnaissance,
decided, as Marlborough explained in a letter to Sarah, that 'they
could not consent to our engaging'. 'I do assure you,' he continued,
'that our army were at least one third stronger than theirs. We are

now returning; for we cannot stay longer than the bread we have brought with us will give us leave.'

'This last action of the Dutch generals has given us great mortification,' the Duke told Godolphin. 'I beg you will give my duty to the Queen, and assure her that had I had the same power I had last year I should have had a greater victory than that at Blenheim.' To Heinsius he wrote: 'I do before God declare to you that I am persuaded that if Slanenbourg [*sic*] had not been in the army, at this day we might have prescribed to France what peace we might have pleased.' And to the States-General he reported: 'I am sure that the Deputies will explain to Your Mightinesses the reason [which decided them against sanctioning an attack] and at the same time that they will do justice to M. Overkirk in stating that he shared my feelings that the occasion was too good to throw away. I submitted, however, although with much regret.'

He told Sarah that it was impossible for him to express how much he longed for the end of the campaign and for the opportunity of going home again. Both the Queen and Prince Eugène endeavoured to comfort him. The Prince wrote:

It is extremely cruel that opinions so weak and discordant should have obstructed the progress of your operations, when you had every reason to expect so glorious a result. You will never be able to perform anything considerable with your army unless you have absolute power . . . I am quite as anxious as you are to be united with you once again in command.

The Queen wrote to say how extremely sorry she was to hear he was 'so very much in the spleen'. She was only too well aware of 'the disagreeable things' he had 'met with this summer'; and these were 'a very just cause of it'. But, for the good of the country and the sake of his friends, she hoped he would be able 'to banish his melancholy thoughts'.

The Dutch general Count Oxenstiern endeavoured to cheer him up by inviting him over to his headquarters from the convent outside the gates of Tirlemont where he was then staying before going to take a course of spa waters, which he did not expect to do him 'much good'. A fellow guest was the Jacobite Lord Ailesbury, who was still living in exile in Holland. The Duke 'embraced me much', Ailesbury recorded in his *Memoirs*, 'and made me many protestations. At dinner sitting by me, he would constantly take me by the hand, but politickly (of which he was a great master) putting his hand under the napkin.'

That night a 'vast supper' was given for Ailesbury by Lord Orkney, who had distinguished himself during the assault on the Lines of Brabant. While the hautboys of the Foot Guards were playing their 'best airs', 'who should come in but my Lord Marlborough', who had not been invited to the meal as he did not usually have any supper. 'My Lord Orkney,' he said, pointing to Ailesbury, 'do not take it ill, if I come here for the sake of this Lord.' 'He was perfectly merry,' Ailesbury reported,

and, for him, ate much and drank heartily, and we all found the effects of the excellent wine, and I never saw more mirth. The next day he asked me where I dined. I told him . . . at Count Oxenstiern's. 'I shall not be so happy,' he said, 'for I am condemned to dine with base company, and shall have as base a dinner.' The three State Deputies of the Army had invited him and they were three sad fellows and great pedants.

The next day, at Landen, Lord Ailesbury encountered the Duke again in the house of the handsome and companionable Lord Albemarle. Marlborough was on the point of leaving when he remembered that he had not shown Ailesbury the plans which had been drawn up 'for his house and gardens at Woodstock'. 'In pointing out the apartments for him and his lady, etc,' Ailesbury continued,

he laid his finger on one and told me, 'That is for you when you come and see me there' . . . I asked him who was his Architect (although I knew the man that was), he answered Sir Jo. Vann Brugg . . . I understand but little or nothing of this matter but enough to affirm (by the plan I saw) that the house is like one mass of stone, without taste or relish.

Before going home to see Sarah and his children, his friends and Vanbrugh, as he so much wanted to do, Marlborough was required to undertake a journey of some 2,000 miles around Europe in order to strengthen the loosening ties which bound together the Grand Alliance, to confer with the bankers of Frankfurt, and to exercise his charm upon the Elector Palatine, the Margrave of Baden, the Austrian Emperor and the Electress and her son in Hanover.

Starting out on 26 October 1705, he made first for Düsseldorf and on the 29th of the month he was entertained by the Elector Palatine in a marquee erected by the roadside. Having settled his business with the Elector, who agreed to contribute another 3,000 troops to the armies of the alliance, he drove on to Frankfurt, where he was greeted by a salute of cannon fire and by the Margrave, to whom he spoke with his accustomed sauvity as though there had been no disagreements between them in the past and giving no hint that in Vienna he was to endeavour to have the tiresome fellow removed from his command.

In Vienna he stayed at the British embassy as a guest of the ambassador, George Stepney, an indifferent poet and gifted linguist who had caused such offence in Vienna by his sympathetic attitude to the cause of the Hungarian insurgents that Prince Eugène had asked for his recall. Marlborough, however, had the utmost confidence in him and persuaded Prince Eugène to withdraw his demand. Nevertheless, giving no hint to Stepney that it was his intention to do so, he 'privately engaged to remove [him] from the Embassy' and have him transferred to The Hague.

The day after his arrival in Vienna, Marlborough suffered from a particularly painful attack of gout and was obliged to conduct his official business in the bedroom at the embassy, where his own 'field bed' had been set up for him. Despite his illness, his visit to Vienna was a success. He was able to promise a loan of a quarter of a million pounds for the upkeep of Prince Eugène's army and to establish a friendly rapport with the Emperor Joseph I.

The Emperor, much taken with the Duke, was anxious to redeem a promise made to him by his father, Leopold I, who had offered to create the Duke a Prince of the Holy Roman Empire. Having secured Queen Anne's permission to accept the honour, and having overcome his wife's scruples, the Duke made it clear, in an interview with the Emperor's representative Count Wratislaw, that he would decline the honour unless it was bestowed upon him with the usual grant of lands and a seat in the Diet of the Empire. Eventually, after a lengthy correspondence, it was settled that the Duke should be created Prince of Mindelheim, a principality which produced the equivalent of £1,500 a year. This, however, was swallowed up by an Imperial tax imposed in wartime of some £6,000, while the cost of installation would entail a further sum of not less than £12,000. These sums naturally disconcerted the parsimonious Duke, who insisted that he could not afford more than £4,500 for his installation and that he did not consider that the war tax should apply to him. After much argument and discussion, and after the exchange of many more letters, this was at last agreed. The King of Prussia proposed that the princely title should descend to the Duke's heirs; but the princes of the Empire, unsurprisingly, would not agree to this. The Emperor Joseph's successor, his younger brother Charles VI, however, later overruled this decision; and the Dukes of Marlborough are Princes of Mindelheim to this day.

From Vienna, towards the end of November, Marlborough set out for Berlin and the court of King Frederick I of Prussia, who, like the Emperor Joseph, was captivated by the insinuating charm of the Duke, who assured him of the Queen of England's friendship and respect. The King, in turn, promised to raise the Prussian contingents serving alongside the English and Austrians to their full strength.

Taking with him a valuable jewelled sword presented to him by King Frederick, Marlborough now set out for Hanover, where he had to undertake the delicate task of smoothing feathers ruffled by the English Parliament's Bill requiring the Electress Sophia and her Protestant descendants to enter into union with the Church of England before any of them could ascend the throne. This mission the Duke performed with his accustomed grace, skill and flattery, so much so that not only was he presented with a coach and six horses to take him on his journey in place of the carriage in which he had arrived, but his wife received a fine tapestry from the Electress under cover of a letter thanking Sarah for the present of a portrait of Queen Anne:

I think that after all the kindness you have had the goodness to show me you will be pleased with my acquainting you with the joy we felt at having had my Lord Duke here in person, and in finding that his manners are as obliging and polished as his actions are glorious and admirable.

By the middle of December, the Duke was back in The Hague; but contrary winds kept him in Holland for Christmas and he did not get home until the beginning of the new year 1706.

The Duke remained in England for three months. It was a far more contented time than the recent past in Holland: both Houses of Parliament warmly congratulated him on the successes of his last campaign, and little objection was made to the voting of generous supplies for the next.

Marlborough had already given much thought to the form this campaign might take. He considered marching into Italy to cooperate with Prince Eugène; he contemplated an invasion of France from the Bay of Biscay in the area around La Rochelle. This 'descent' (his strangely idiosyncratic spelling had it as 'decent') was to be carried out by battalions of Huguenot refugees supported by British troops – and an invasion force was actually assembled at Portsmouth and the Isle of Wight for this purpose. But these and other projects had to be abandoned when Marshal Vendôme defeated General Raventlau, commander of the Imperial forces, at Calcinato during Prince Eugène's absence in Vienna, and the duc de Villars attacked the Margrave in Germany and pushed his army back across the Rhine.

So Marlborough was obliged to turn his thoughts once more to the Flanders front and to operations with the Dutch. The idea depressed him. The States-General, admittedly, were more cooperative than they had been in the past. Provided the Duke remained in Flanders to command the Dutch forces, they were prepared to send another 10,000 men to reinforce Prince Eugène, who had lost that number, taken prisoner or through desertion, in the rout that had followed Raventlau's defeat at Calcinato. They were also willing for him in certain circumstances to act without the interference of field deputies, that severe limitation in his command which had so much hampered him in the past. One of the three newly appointed deputies, however, was likely to be troublesome. This was Sicco van Goslinga, an untiringly energetic man who had the highest opinion of his own often hare-brained military plans and was to prove a positive encumbrance because of his frantic excitability on the battlefield. But the other two deputies, Ferdinand van Collen and Baron de Renswoude, were not expected to give Marlborough any trouble: nor did they.

Yet the Duke was depressed by being 'in a condition of doing nothing at all' that would 'make a noise'. 'I shall make the whole campagne in this Country,' he wrote to his 'dear Soull', Sarah, on 4 May, 'and consequently not such a one as will please mee. But as I infinitely vallu Your estime . . . let me say for my self that there is some merit in doing what is good for the publick, than in prefering ons private Interest.' 'Pray lett mr [Samuel] Travers [the agent at Woodstock] know that I shall be glad to hear sometime from him how the Building goes on,' he added in one of those regular references in his letters to the grand house gradually taking shape and never far from his thoughts. 'For the Gardening and Plantations I am at ease, being very sure that mr Wise will bee diligent.'

When he reached his headquarters, Marlborough's gloom deepened. He had been told he would 'find the army in a condition to march'. But neither the artillery horses nor the bread-wagons had yet come up and he could not move without them. 'God knows I go with a heavy heart,' he told Godolphin; 'for I have no prospect of doing anything considerable, unless the French would do what I am very confident they will not', that was to say 'march out of their lines'. In his opinion, so he told Anthonie Heinsius, there was 'nothing more certain' than that the French would 'remain on the defensive in Flanders and Germany in this campaign in order to be the better able to act offensively elsewhere'.

The French King, however, was urgently pressing Marshal Villeroi to do what Marlborough believed they would not do, that is to say move out of their lines. According to the duc de Saint-Simon, Villeroi, a brave man from a noble family, the son of a marshal who had been Louis XIV's governor, was wounded by the King's reiterated admonitions. He had the feeling that the King doubted his courage since he considered it necessary to spur him so hard. He resolved to put all at stake to satisfy him and to prove he did not deserve such harsh aspersions.

So it was that on 18 May, Marlborough's spies reported that the

French were stirring in their camp beyond the Dyle between Wavre and Louvain. The next day this report was confirmed: they had now crossed the river and almost reached Tirlemont. Immediately Marlborough sent orders to the officer commanding his Danish troops to bring his cavalry 'by a double march' to join him 'at the earliest moment' and to have his infantry follow them 'with all the speed possible without exhaustion'. 'I hope they may be with us on Saturday,' the Duke wrote to Robert Harley, 'and then I design to advance towards the enemy, to oblige them to retire, or with the blessing of God to bring them to a battle.'

28

THE BATTLE OF RAMILLIES

'[He] exposed his person like the meanest soldier.'

In dense fog, at three o'clock on the dark morning of 23 May 1706, Marlborough's army, over 60,000 strong, Danes, Swiss, Dutch and British, marched towards the enemy on a front extending over four miles. Eight hours later they were crossing the ruins of the Lines of Brabant, which had by now been almost entirely demolished. The French army marched towards them across the wide plain at Ramillies on an equally broad front, presenting, as one of their officers said, 'a magnificent spectacle', the whole force being seen 'in such fine array that it would be impossible to view a finer sight'. Another officer riding beside him remarked that 'France had surpassed herself in the quality of these troops'. He believed that the allies had 'no chance whatever of breaking them in the coming conflict. If defeated now, we could never again hope to withstand them.' Marlborough himself later described Villeroi's army as 'the best he had ever seen'.

At about one o'clock the French artillery opened fire; and soon afterwards the allied guns, heavier and more numerous than the enemy's, replied, covering the wide expanse of open upland with clouds of smoke.

The first significant engagement took place on the extreme left of the British line, around two small, strongly defended villages, Taviers and Francqnée, which protected the French right flank. Cannon were dragged up to fire at close range upon the houses in these villages, crumbling and shattering their walls. Four battalions of Dutch infantry then rushed forward to occupy what remained of the buildings, driving out the defenders and later repelling a force of French dragoons and Swiss infantry sent to retake them. As the enemy fell back from Taviers and Francqnée, squadrons of Danish cavalry thundered down upon them and sent them hurtling away.

As they retreated from Taviers, they collided with Colonel de La Colonie's Bavarian brigade, which had been sent to retake the village. La Colonie's musicians had been playing their hautboys to encourage his men but, 'startled by the booming of guns', the band had already 'disappeared like a flash'. Now his infantry were swept away by their companions-in-arms who, as the colonel recorded, 'came tumbling down upon my battalions in full flight, just as I was re-forming them' after their difficult crossing of the marshy ground by the banks of the Mehaigne river. His account continued:

The runaways threw themselves amongst my men, and carried them off with them, and I was never more surprised in my life to find myself left standing alone with a few officers and the colours. I was immediately filled with rage and grief; I cried out in German and French like one possessed; I shouted every epithet I could think of . . . I seized a colonel's colour, planted it by me, and by the loudness of my cries I at last attracted the attention of some few of them. The officers who had stood by me rushed after the fugitives, also shouting and pointing out the colonel's colour which I still kept in my hands and at last they checked the stampede.

Marlborough himself was also in difficulties. He had come down with his staff from the high ground between Ramillies and Offus, where he had watched the steady advance of the masses of Dutch and British infantry, and, having reached the lower ground, where he 'exposed his person', as one of his officers said, 'like the meanest soldier', he entered the ferocious cavalry battle now being fought in the space, some mile and a half in extent, between Taviers and Ramillies. Almost 25,000 horsemen were engaged in this mêlée, which Marlborough was confident would end in the allies' favour. 'I have,' he had said earlier, somewhat exaggerating his preponderance in cavalry, 'five horses to two.'

Twice he led charges himself; and, in his scarlet coat, immediately recognizable amid the blue and grey of the Dutch uniforms, he became a target for French fire. After the second charge, he pulled his horse round and galloped away, jumping across a ditch and failing to clear it. His horse fell and, in the words of Colonel Cranstoun of the Cameronians:

some ran over him. Major-General Murray, seeing him fall, marched up in all haste with two Swiss battalions to save him . . . The Duke, when he got to his feet again, saw Major-General Murray coming up and ran directly to get into his battalions. In the meantime Mr Molesworth [Captain Robert, later first Viscount Molesworth] quitted his horse and got the Duke mounted again, and the French were so hot in the pursuit that some of them before they could stop their horses ran in upon the Swiss bayonets and were killed, but the body of them, seeing the two enemy battalions, shore off to the right and retired.

Having gained some sort of security behind General Murray's battalions and having been joined, one by one, by his scattered staff officers, Marlborough was now able to resume his direction of the battle. One of these staff officers, Colonel Bedingfield, came up with one of the Duke's spare chargers, which he decided to mount instead of Molesworth's horse. As he was throwing his leg across the saddle, a cannon ball flew across the horse's back, hit Bedingfield who was holding the stirrup and took his head clean off.*

The battle was now reaching its climax. On the right Orkney's battalions, having crossed the marshy ground by the river Geet, were entering the village of Autréglise under as heavy a fire from musketry and cannon as their commander had ever before endured. At this point, however, a message was brought to him by one of the Duke's aides-de-camp, ordering him to retire. Supposing that he had been told to do so because of the difficulties encountered – but by then overcome – in crossing the marsh, Orkney persisted in his attack, unaware that it was intended by Marlborough as a feint, a fact concealed from him so that it would be pressed home with vigour and thus mislead the enemy into supposing it was a serious attempt. Message after message came to Orkney by a relay of aides-de-camp

---

* As soon as she heard of this, Sarah Marlborough arranged for Bedingfield's widow to receive a pension from the privy purse of £100 a year (Harris, *A Passion for Government*, 123).

and equerries; but still he persisted until General Cadogan galloped up to tell him that his attack was a feint and that the Duke had gone to the left of the allied line and taken the cavalry of the right wing with him. There was accordingly no cavalry to support Orkney's advance. So, with the utmost reluctance, he obeyed the order and, as he put it, 'much vexed', took his men back across the marsh to the higher ground on the other side of the river. From here, while the first line of his battalions held this ground, the second line received orders to march to the support of the main attack.

Marshal Villeroi was still expecting the principal assault to be pushed home on his left when he learned that his troops on the right had been dispersed and his flank turned. He attempted to form a new front; but it was too late. By six o'clock Marlborough and Overkirk had re-formed their cavalry; and, by now far outnumbering the enemy, these horsemen began to move forward in menacing and orderly array.

By the time the light of the early evening began to fade, the French were in headlong retreat. 'We had not got forty yards,' an Irish officer in the French army recorded, 'when the words *sauve qui peut* went through the great part, if not the whole army, and put all to confusion. Then might be seen whole brigades running in disorder.'

The French lost some 10,000 men killed or wounded. Many of those who had survived the battle threw down their arms in their anxiety to escape the swords of the pursuing cavalry. But thousands were cut down without mercy. Five thousand more were taken prisoner together with numerous cannon, colours and trophies.

It was, commented Villars, 'the most shameful, humiliating and disastrous of routs'; while Marlborough congratulated himself in a letter to Godolphin on the likelihood of his victory being 'of greater advantage than that of Blenheim; for we have the whole summer before us . . . I think we may make such a campaign as may give the queen the glory of making an honourable and a safe peace.'

To his wife he wrote:

I did not tel my dearest soull in my last the designe I had of ingaging the enemie if possible to a battaile, fearing the concern she has for me might

190

make her uneasy, but I can now give her the satisfaction of letting her know that on Sunday last we fought, and that God Almighty has been pleased to give us a victorie . . . Pray believe me when I assure you that I love you more than I can expresse.

29

COLLAPSE IN BELGIUM

*'I am so persuaded that this campaign will give us a good peace
that I beg of you to do all you can that the house at Woodstock
may be carried up as much as possible . . .'*

By midnight on 23 May 1706, having been on horseback for almost
twenty hours, Marlborough was twelve miles away from the scene of
his triumph, exhausted and bruised by the fall from his horse and by
the men subsequently scrambling over him. Hoping to snatch a few
hours' sleep before daylight, he asked for his cloak to be spread on the
ground; then, catching sight of the difficult field deputy, Sicco van
Goslinga, and considering how well it would be to have his goodwill
in the future, he asked him if he would care to share the cloak with him.

The next day the allied army continued the pursuit of the shattered
forces of the enemy, whose commander, Marshal Villeroi, wrote to
King Louis to say that the only happy day he foresaw in his life in
future was that of his death. He declined to resign the command,
however, and was dismissed. He was succeeded by Marshal le duc
de Vendôme, who had commanded the French army in the bloody
battle of Luzzara in Italy and had had the distinction of defeating
Prince Eugène's army at Calcinato.

Marlborough's brother Charles having entered Brussels that morning, the Duke himself took formal possession of it on the evening of
28 June to the acclamation of the people, who lined the streets to
watch the great general pass by.* After Brussels, a succession of other

---

* It is believed that it was on this occasion that the city of Brussels presented
Marlborough with the five tapestry panels depicting the *Art of War* by Lambert de
Hondt, woven by Jerome Le Clerk and Jasper van der Borcht. Three of these,
Campement, *Rencontre* and *Attaque*, are in Blenheim Palace in the Bow Window
Room, the other two *Pillage* panels are in the Third State Room. Another set of ten

towns fell into his hands: Ghent, Bruges, then Antwerp – where he was accompanied in a torchlit procession to a reception at the Bishop's palace by a parade of civic dignitaries – then Ostend, where, after a brief siege and storm, two French men-of-war and ninety cannon were taken; and, wherever he went, people spoke of his courtesy and tolerance, his kindness to prisoners of war and to the wounded. No one could guess that, for days after the battle, so he had told his wife, he had slept so unquietly that he could not get rid of one of his agonizing and persistent headaches and was quite unable yet to experience the pleasure he had hoped to 'enjoy at [having won] this great victory'. He had ended his letter:

I bless God that He has been pleased to make me the instrument of doing so much service to the Queen, England, and all Europe, for it is most certain that we have destroyed the greatest part of the best troops of France . . . I am so persuaded that this campaign will give us a good peace that I beg of you to do all you can that the house at Woodstock may be carried up as much as possible.

'My dearest soul,' he did not forget to conclude, expressing the hope so very often affirmed in his letters to her, 'I have now that great pleasure of thinking that I may have the happiness of ending my days in quiet with you.'

Numerous other letters flowed from his pen or from that of Adam de Cardonnel on his behalf or at his dictation. He wrote to all the allied sovereigns, to the Emperor, the Margrave, the King of Prussia, to Prince Eugène, Godolphin and the Queen, who replied to assure him that 'the Blessing of God [was] sertinly with [him]'.

Marlborough continued to advance, threatening the French frontier. Following the capture of Ghent, Bruges and Antwerp, Dendermonde on the Scheldt was also taken, then, on 4 October, Ath on the Dender. As Marlborough said, 'So many towns have submitted

---

large panels hang in the three main state rooms and in an inner room adjoining the apartments of the Duke and Duchess. They depict Donauwörth, Blenheim, the Lines of Brabant, Oudenarde, Wynendael, the surrender of Lille, Malplaquet and, three of them, Bouchain. They are the work of the Brussels weaver Judocus de Vos (Wace, *The Marlborough Tapestries at Blenheim Palace*, 43–89).

since the battle, that it really looks more like a dream than truth.'
The Queen wrote to him:

The great Glorious Success wch God Almighty has bin pleased to Bless
you wth, & his preservation of your person, one can never thank him
enough for & next to him all things are owing to you; it is impossible for
me ever to Say soe much as I aught in return of your great & faithful
Services to me, but I will endeavour by all ye actions of my life to Shew
you how truly Sensible I am of them.

But by now the Dutch believed that quite enough, if not almost
too much, had been done. Satisfied as they were with what had been
achieved, they could not but regret that it had been won at so great
a cost to themselves. The victory at Ramillies, they contented with
some justification, had been won largely by their own endeavours.
After all, their losses were higher than those of the English and Danes
combined. 'It is publicly said at The Hague,' Marlborough wrote to
Godolphin, 'that France is reduced to what it ought to be, and that
if the war should be carried further, it would serve only to make
England greater than it ought to be. In short, I am afraid our best
Allies are very fond of peace.'

Nor did the Dutch take it kindly when it was proposed by the
Emperor that the Duke of Marlborough should be appointed viceroy
of the newly acquired provinces in Belgium, with an income of
£60,000 a year. Naturally the Duke was tempted by this proposal,
which, in addition to promising so large an increase in his already
enormous income, would most probably have entailed his being
awarded that most coveted decoration, the Order of the Golden
Fleece, founded in 1429. But he realized that he could not accept
the offer without the agreement of the States-General and, as he
supposed might well be the case, they objected strongly, particularly
so as the offer had been made to him before they had been told of
it. His friend Jacob Hop, the Dutch Treasurer, happened to be at
his headquarters when the Emperor's letter reached him. He showed
it to Hop, who raised objections immediately: the States-General
would contend that the Emperor was obviously proposing the Duke
as viceroy only to deprive the Dutch of the ability to exploit the
wealth of these Belgic provinces. And so they did contend, main-

taining that the Emperor had no right to arrange for the future government of Belgium without the prior agreement of the States-General.

In England the Queen and her ministers were perfectly agreeable to the Duke's accepting the Emperor's offer. But, as Marlborough told Godolphin, Anthonie Heinsius, Jacob Hop and the deputies, without exception, maintained that his acceptance of it would 'create a great jealousy which might prejudice the common cause'. Heinsius was particularly disturbed, and so concerned was Marlborough that he might lose the Grand Pensionary's friendship and confidence that he thought it as well to write to assure him that he would take

no step in this matter but what shall be by the advice of the States. For I prefer infinetly their friendship before any particular interest to myself; for I thank God and the Queen I have no need or desire of being richer, but have a very great ambition of doing everything that can be for the Publick good.

So, much disappointed by having to do so and forfeiting the large addition to his fortune, he declined the Emperor's offer and sent a letter to the Queen informing her of his decision. 'I hope Her Majesty will approve,' he then wrote to Godolphin. 'I beg you to be so just and kind to me as to assure her that, though the appointments of this Government are three-score thousand pounds a year, I shall with pleasure excuse myself since I am convinced it is for her service.'

After the surrender of Ostend, Marlborough's army, reinforced by Prussians, Hanoverians and troops from the Palatinate, advanced to Courtrai and prepared to attack the fortresses of Ypres, Tournai and Menin.

Menin, the defences of which had been skilfully designed by Marshal Vauban, was invested first on 4 August; and on the evening of the 18th the place was stormed by Prussian troops, commanded by General Scholtz, and by a British force led by Lord Orkney, 8,000 men in all. The garrison stubbornly resisted in the fierce fighting which followed; and, by the time a white flag had been raised on the breach, the allies had lost 2,500 men. But yet another fortress had been taken and the duc de Vendôme admitted in a letter to Chamillart, the French war minister, that he was surrounded by 'sadness and frustration'. 'I will do my best to reanimate our people,' he promised, 'but it will not be an easy task, if indeed I can manage it, for every one is ready to doff his hat when one mentions the name of Marlborough . . . Let me tell you candidly that the job is much harder than I expected.'

Warned by Prince Eugène that Vendôme was 'ever ready to challenge' an enemy, that 'nothing whatever can shake him', and that he was 'beloved by the common soldiers', Marlborough himself was soon not only to respect the marshal's ability but also to be given evidence of his chivalry when the Duke's friend and quartermaster-general, William Cadogan, was reported as having been taken prisoner or killed. This report gave him 'a great deal of uneasiness', he told Sarah, 'for he loved me and I could rely on him. I am now sending a trumpet to the Governor of Tournai to know if he be alive . . . I have ordered the trumpet to return this night, for I shall not be quiet till I know his fate.'

There were, in fact, no grounds for Marlborough's anxiety, since, being informed of his adversary's affection for Cadogan, Vendôme immediately ordered his release, while Marlborough in return and by way of thanks released a Savoyard general who had been captured at Ramillies.

While the Duke had been turning his attention to the capture of Ath, news arrived of Prince Eugène's victory over the duc d'Orléans and Marshal Narsin at Turin, where the fate of Italy was decided and where Eugène received yet another of the thirteen wounds he suffered in battle.

Within hours of his victory, the Prince wrote to Marlborough to give him the news of it and to thank him for the troops he had sent to him. 'It is impossible to express the joy it has given me,' the Duke told Sarah; 'for, I do not only esteem, but I really love that Prince. This glorious action must bring France so low that if our friends can be persuaded to carry on the war one year longer with vigour, we could not fail, with the blessing of God, to have such peace as would give us quiet in our days.'

In a letter to Heinsius, the Duke, intending to lead him to persuade the Dutch public to persist with another year's campaign, wrote, 'I am assured that the French take more to hart their misfortunes in Italie, then [than] they did that of Ramillie.'

Encouraged though he was by Prince Eugène's victory at Turin, the Duke was feeling depressed and out of sorts that October of 1706. 'If it were not for my duty to the Queen, and friendship to the Lord Treasurer, I should beg that somebody else might execute my office,' he told Sarah not long after his fifty-sixth birthday. 'The weight is too great for me, and I find a decay in my memory. Whatever may be told you of my looks, the greatest part of my hair is grey.'

Much of his worry was caused by the urgent desire of his close friend, Lord Godolphin, to resign. He had worn out his health in the service of the Crown as Lord Treasurer and wished to spend 'the small remainder of his days in liberty and quiet'.

When the Duke heard of Godolphin's intention, he strongly, almost vehemently, urged him to reconsider it:

I am positively of the opinion that should you quit the service of the Queen, you would not only disturb the affairs of England, but also the liberties of Europe. I conjure you not to have a thought of quitting till we have obtained a good peace . . . I think both you and I are in conscience bound to undergo all the dangers and troubles that is possible to bring this war to a happy end . . . Without flattery, as England is divided, there is nobody that can execute your place but yourself.

The Queen added her pleas to those of Marlborough: 'I cannot bear the thought of parting with you,' she told Godolphin; 'and I hope that after what the Duke of Marlborough has said to you, you will not think of it again . . . Let his words plead for her who will be lost and undone if you pursue this cruel intention.'

Eventually Godolphin was persuaded to stay in office; but he was soon complaining once more that the 'life of a slave in the galleys' would be as a paradise in comparison with his.

30

THE KING OF SWEDEN

*'. . . I wish I could serve some campaigns
under so great a general as your Majesty . . .'*

When Marlborough returned to England towards the end of 1706, he was still feeling low in spirits and looking forward to 'a retired life'. In October he had written to Sarah:

I hope you will order it so that after I have been some days in London we may go to the lodge [at Windsor] and be quiet, for I am quite weary of the world; and since I am afraid there is a necessity of my serving [abroad] as long as this war lasts, let me have a little more quiet in England than I have been used to have, and then I shall be better able to go through what I must endure.

It was impossible, of course, that his return to England should go unrecognized; and before he and Sarah could retire together to Windsor or St Albans there were certain ceremonies and receptions to attend in London. Not all of these were disagreeable to him. Both Houses of Parliament greeted him with acclamations and made no difficulty about granting his request that, now that his heir was dead, his title might descend through the female line, nor about extending the settlement of the pension of £5,000 a year granted to him in 1702 to his heirs, female as well as male, in perpetuity, so that there 'should never lack one of his name' to bear testimony to what was described as his 'glorious deeds'.

With cannon thundering in the parks, he was driven in a procession of carriages and horsemen past cheering crowds to the City, where, in the Guildhall, the standards captured at Ramillies were hung around the walls. In the still uncompleted St Paul's, choir and congregation joined together in hymns of praise; and the City of

London offered him their warmest congratulations at a splendid banquet in Vintners' Hall.

On his return to the Continent at the beginning of 1707, Marlborough became deeply involved in plans for that year's campaigns. But, before agreement on these could be reached, there was a delicate diplomatic mission to undertake.

For some time now, there had been worrying speculation about the intentions of Charles XII, King of Sweden, who had suddenly appeared on the European stage like an unpredictable deus ex machina. He had come to the throne at the age of fifteen and within ten years had won a succession of remarkable victories over the Danes, over the Russians at Narva, and over the Poles and Saxons at Klissow in 1702. In 1704 he had dethroned King Augustus II of Poland in favour of his ally, Stanislaw Leszczyński.

There was accordingly much anxiety as to what the remarkable young man would do next. As a self-proclaimed champion of Protestantism, he was known to dislike France and the French King, the enemy of the Huguenots; he also hated the Russians and had quarrelled with the Empire. He was now in Saxony, where the presence of 'the Sweeds', as Marlborough spelled their name, would 'create a great degree of trouble'. In April the Duke went to King Charles's headquarters in the Castle of Altranstädt, near Leipzig, to 'endeavour to penetrate his designs', to discover, despite his dislike of the French, whether or not he was likely to succumb to King Louis XIV's overtures to enter the war on their side, and what his intentions were with regard to Austria.

On arriving at Altranstädt, Marlborough asked to see the King's chief minister, Count Karl Piper. Intending to put the Englishman in his place, Piper sent word that he was too busy to see him for the moment. So, when Marlborough saw the impertinent man half an hour after the time fixed for his appointment, he got down from his coach and, without removing his hat, walked past the minister as though he had not seen him. He walked on to the grass beside the drive 'as if', so his biographer Thomas Lediard said, 'to make water'. After standing on the grass for some time, he turned around and, approaching the embarrassed Count Piper, greeted him with due courtesy.

He was then taken in to see the King, to whom he handed an effusive letter from Queen Anne, in which she had written of her regret that her sex prevented her crossing the sea 'to visit a prince admired by the whole universe'. 'I am in this particular more happy than the Queen,' the Duke said in his most excessively flattering manner; 'and I wish I could serve some campaigns under so great a general as your Majesty that I might learn what I yet want to know of the art of war.'

In his *Histoire de Charles XII*, Voltaire suggested that the King must have considered this compliment as fulsome as, indeed, it was. Voltaire also wrote that the King thought that, despite his red uniform with its ribbon and glittering star of the Order of the Garter, his visitor did not present a very soldierly appearance.

He knew, however, that both at Blenheim and Ramillies the Duke had displayed a rash bravery by charging with his men, and he asked him why he had thought it necessary to expose himself in such a way. Marlborough replied that if he had not done so, his men would not have respected him. The King, who as a boy had been noted for his reckless intrepidity, agreed that to gain the respect of his soldiers was a necessary task for a general.

Although the King was a gifted linguist, able readily to translate Swedish and German literature into Latin, he did not speak French well and spoke English scarcely at all, so the British envoy to Sweden, the Rev. John Robinson, a former chaplain to the embassy and future Bishop of London, was summoned to act as interpreter.

The Duke thought it as well to steer clear of controversial political and diplomatic matters in his subsequent conversation with the King, confining himself mostly to military affairs; but he did gain the impression that King Charles was not a threat to western Europe and that he had a 'natural aversion to France'. Having spoken to Sarah about the matter after her husband's death, Voltaire wrote:

Marlborough mentioned the Tsar to him and observed that the King's eyes always kindled at the name . . . He noticed, also, a map of Russia lying on the table. He needed no more to convince him that the real design and sole ambition of the King of Sweden was to dethrone the Tsar as he had done the King of Poland.

The next day Marlborough, dating his letter from the King of Sweden's headquarters, wrote a brief report to Godolphin:

I got to this place last night so early as to have one hours Conversation with Comte Pyper, and this morning a little after ten I waited on his Ma^ty. He kept me with him til his hour of dining which was at twelf . . . [After dinner] he took me again into his Chamber wher wee Continued for above an hour, and then his kettledroms called him to prayers. Mr Robinson was with me all the time.

It was Robinson who 'was utilised to administer the bribes' to Count Piper and other Swedish ministers. Marlborough, who had made arrangements for large sums to be made available for this purpose, did not think it necessary to pay such excessive amounts: there was no need, he protested, to spend money to deflect King Charles from operations in western Europe which he clearly did not, in any case, intend to undertake. However, Robinson wrote to Robert Harley, the Secretary of State responsible for such matters: 'By his Grace's orders I have acquainted Count Piper, M. Hermeline and Cederheim that Her Majesty will give yearly pensions to the first £1,500 and to each of the others £500 . . . and that the first payment should be made without delay.'

Marlborough rejoined the army near Brussels on 21 May. A few weeks before, a fierce battle had been fought outside the walled town of Almanza, south of Valencia, in Spain. A force of French and Spanish troops, commanded by the English Jacobite the Duke of Berwick, had defeated an allied force of British, Dutch, Huguenot and Portuguese soldiers commanded by the French Huguenot Henri de Massue de Ruvigny, who had been created Earl of Galway in 1697. 'This ill success in Spain,' Marlborough wrote, 'has flung everything backwards, so that the best resolution we can take is to let the French see that we are resolved to keep on the war, so that we can have a good peace.'

For his own part, he took his army a few miles south of Brussels beyond Hal as though to threaten the duc de Vendôme, whose forces, slightly superior in numbers to those of the allies, were encamped north of Mons. Marlborough got as far as Soignies, where his intelligence officers informed him that the enemy were also moving forward. So, much to the indignation of the Dutch deputy Sicco van Goslinga – who claimed to have galloped up to the Duke to protest at the ignominy face to face – Marlborough decided upon a withdrawal beyond Brussels. As the allied troops withdrew, news reached their commander that Marshal Villars had captured the formidable defensive works of the Lines of Stollhofen on the Upper Rhine, which, extending from the mountain barrier of the Black Forest to the river north of Strasbourg, had been designed to prevent the invasion of Germany.

These Lines had been the pride of Prince Louis, Margrave of Baden, whose fine palace and gardens at Rastadt lay just to the north-east of them. He had ensured that they were as secure as earthworks, bastions, redans, parapets, ramparts and ravelins could make them. But Prince Louis had at last succumbed to the blood poisoning spreading from his foot and had been succeeded in command by Charles Ernest, Margrave of Bayreuth.

The Lines, starved of troops, had been easily overrun by Marshal Villars, who, on the morrow of a ball at Strasbourg as splendid as that which the Duchess of Richmond was to give at Brussels on the eve of Waterloo, had thrown his army at their astonished and unsuspecting defenders. Before nightfall, Marshal Villars was comfortably installed in the late Prince Louis's palace at Rastadt.

For long Marlborough had been considering, although with reserve, the possibility of opening up a new theatre of operations in France – if not in western France on the coast of the Bay of Biscay, then in the south at Toulon in the Gulf of Lyon, the French navy's principal Mediterranean base and dockyard. Also warmly advocating such an enterprise was the brave and enterprising Admiral Sir Cloudesley Shovell, who pressed for an attack on Toulon, from which, when taken, a British fleet might sail to dominate the Mediterranean.

Prince Eugène, never an enthusiast for naval operations, of which he had no experience, was not an eager participant in the allied plans; but he did undertake to march with 35,000 men from northern Italy down to the Mediterranean and then, by the narrow, winding coastal road, past the poor fishing villages of what was to become renowned as the Côte d'Azur, through Nice and Cannes and across the Var towards Toulon, while Admiral Shovell's ships sailed close to shore beside him. The going was necessarily slow, and by the time the combined forces had reached the defences of Toulon, the French commander there, Marshal Tessé, had been reinforced by several thousand men.

The admiral pressed for an immediate assault, but Prince Eugène, as John Chetwynd, English minister at the court of the Duke of Savoy, told Marlborough, had 'little hope of our succeeding'. 'I know he never had a liking for this project,' Chetwynd added, 'but I thought when he was here he would have acted with his usual vigour. How this will end God knows, but I have yet reason to fear it will not be to our satisfaction.'

Nor was it. The French King, as anxious to retain Toulon as the allies were to seize it, ordered reinforcements to defend it from all over Europe until Prince Eugène was fully convinced of the impossibility of taking it. He complained to Count Wratislaw that his colleagues were 'all enraged' with him because of his reluctance to attack and that the Duke of Savoy, 'seeing the great difficulties, not to say impossibilities', threw all the responsibility on him so as not to 'disgust England and Holland'. The admirals, so Eugène wrote to the Emperor, 'do not understand the land service; they refuse to listen to facts, adhering obstinately to their opinion that everything must be staked on the siege of Toulon. Yet the obvious impossibility of this is clearly before their eyes.'

By the middle of August the admirals were forced to recognize this themselves. Days of bombardment from ships' cannon and successive attacks by ground troops upon the defences had failed to enforce surrender. On the night of 21 August, as the buildings of the port lay smoking behind them, the allied army marched away in the darkness towards the Savoyard frontier.

'I have been uneasy in my head ever since I left off the Spa water,' Marlborough had written to Godolphin some days before the allied retreat; 'but if the siege of Toulon goes prosperously, I shall be cured of all diseases except old age.'

While waiting to receive the good news which meant so much to him, he had been having a most trying time in Germany. Marshal Villars, having left men to demolish the Lines of Stollhofen, had pushed forward rapidly from Rastadt to Stuttgart, driving the incompetent Margrave of Bayreuth back towards Nördlingen. Marlborough begged Count Wratislaw, 'in the name of God', to get rid of the Margrave and appoint in his place a general who could stop the rot. He was convinced, as he told Robert Harley, that 'if they had a good general in Germany' they could bring together enough troops to 'oblige the French to retire over the Rhine', particularly so as the threat to Toulon had drawn more and more French troops to the Mediterranean. Moreover, he was confident that Villars had, at the most, 16,000 men under his command, apart from the militia, 'on which he would never dare depend'.

As for his own army, he was still constrained by the Dutch field deputies, who would, as he said, 'not venture' unless they had an advantage, which, he was quite sure, 'they would not be given'. When he had learned from his spies that Marshal Vendôme had received orders from Paris to send no fewer than thirteen of his battalions and six squadrons to the southern front to save Toulon, he had appealed for permission to make a threatening movement against Vendôme's communications which would send him hurrying back to save them. But Vendôme, ordered to avoid any engagement in his weakened state, had managed to evade him; and as the French escaped towards Ath, sloshing as fast as they could through roads thick with the mud churned in the persistent summer rain, messengers were approaching the allied headquarters with the news that Prince Eugène and Admiral Shovell had withdrawn from Toulon.

31

CRISIS AT COURT

'. . . I went on to reproach her with her ingratitude and
her secret management of the Queen.'

Preoccupied as he was that summer with military and diplomatic
problems, the Duke often found his mind wandering to thoughts
of home, to Sarah, to St Albans and to Woodstock. 'It is true what
you say of Woodstock,' he had written to Sarah at the end of
May,

that it is very much at my heart, especially when we are in prosperity, for
then my whole thoughts are of retiring to that place. But if everything does
not go to our own desire, we must not set our hearts too much upon [it],
for I see very plainly that whilst I live, if there be troubles, I must have my
share of them. This day makes your humble servant fifty-seven. On all
accounts I would wish myself younger; but for none so much as that I
might have it more in my power to make myself more agreeable to you,
whom I love with all my soul.

Three weeks later, complaining of the heat at his headquarters at
Meldert, he had expressed the hope that it was hot and sunny also at
Woodstock so that the orchard there was prospering well.

The orchard at Woodstock was, however, of trivial concern when
compared with what he had heard at this time of a growing crisis at
court in London.

The Queen and Sarah were no longer on those terms of affectionate friendship which they had enjoyed in the past. No longer did
Sarah receive those devotedly loving letters which her mistress had
formerly sent to her, begging her 'for Christ Jesus sake never to think
of being any where but with me as long as I am above ground',

assuring her that 'you will never find in all ye search of love a hart like your poor unfortunate faithfull Morlys', and telling her that she had kissed her 'deare kind letter a hundred times' and that she could never express how much she longed to see her. Sarah had grown weary not only of such passionate, reiterated, effusive pleas and assurances, but also of the petty ceremonious formalities and claustrophobic atmosphere of life at court, which was governed by rules of the most tedious etiquette. 'There was a drawing-room today at Court,' wrote Jonathan Swift,

but so few company that the Queen sent for us into her bedchamber, where we made our bows, and stood about twenty of us round the room while she looked at us round with a fan in her mouth and once a minute she said about three words to some who were nearest to her; and then she was told dinner was ready, and went out.

The Queen noticed at once if anyone present was improperly dressed and would express her disapproval of any man who appeared before her in the wrong sort of wig. Once one of her ministers came to her in a tie-wig instead of a full-bottomed one, and although she had sent for him in the greatest haste, she was thoroughly disconcerted. 'I suppose,' she said crossly, 'that the next time his lordship appears at court he will come in his nightcap.'

With regard to her own dress she was particularly careful and, despite the dullness of the result and her negligence when she was feeling ill, she spent a great deal of time each day at her toilet, an operation performed with all due ceremony.

The Duchess had no patience with this ceremony, nor now with the Queen herself, whose company she found increasingly irksome. 'Her conversation,' she wrote, 'was chiefly upon fashions and rules of precedence, or observations upon the weather, or some such poor topics without any variety of entertainment.' She had, admittedly, an extraordinarily retentive memory, 'but chose to retain in it very little besides ceremonies and customs of courts and such like insignificant trifles'. The woman, the Duchess complained, was often unwell, sometimes petulant and frequently very boring and, in a favourite dismissive word, 'rediculous'. The Queen, for her part, had grown weary of the Duchess's political harangues, her increasingly sharp and haughty manner, the way in which she would flounce out of the room after some difference of opinion with the words, 'Lord, Madam, it must be so'.

Their differences were now exacerbated by the growing influence over the susceptible Queen of Sarah's poor relation, Abigail Hill, who had been promoted from her minor position at court to the post of bedchamber woman.

The Queen found her most agreeable and comforting, a pleasant, commiserating companion, playing the harpsichord with skill and reading aloud with feeling. She was also an attentive nurse when she was ill, as well as a sympathetic presence when the intrigues and complications of the political world had proved too much for Her Majesty to bear. Unlike the Duchess of Marlborough, Abigail Hill did not distress the Queen by denigration of the Tories and commendation of the Whigs. On the contrary, when she spoke on political matters, which she did far less frequently than the Duchess, her discreet remarks were such as to please the Queen rather than exasperate her and, while Abigail was not on the best of terms with Lord Godolphin, whom Her Majesty too had found rather tiresome of late, she enjoyed a most friendly relationship with Robert Harley, Secretary of State, to whom she was distantly related, a moderate Tory, devious, shrewd and unscrupulous, a political manager of exceptional skill, though by no means an orator.

Sarah was exasperated by the influence that Harley's confidante, this plain, red-nosed, ingratiating young woman, Abigail Hill, whom she had done so much to help, exercised over the Queen, who seemed, indeed, to be in love with her. 'She came often to see the Queen when the Prince was asleep,' so Sarah said; and one day she 'unlocked the door in a loud, familiar manner', and 'tripped across the room with a gay air' until, catching sight of the Duchess, 'she immediately stopped short and acting a part like a player, dropped a low curtsey . . . and in a faint, low voice cried "Did Your Majesty ring?"'

The Duchess made no secret of her jealousy and chagrin. She declined to attend court functions; she wrote cross and haughty letters; she accused Abigail Hill of prejudicing her mistress against her former friends, of interference and malicious gossip. The Queen commented that she believed others who had been in Hill's station 'in former times' had been 'tattling and very impertinent'. For Sarah, the most gross and hurtful insult was the discovery that Abigail Hill had secretly married Samuel Masham, Groom of the Bedchamber to Prince George – a 'good-natured, insignificant man, always making low bows to everybody and ready to skip to open a door' – and that the Queen had been present at the ceremony without the Duchess knowing anything about it. The fact that Abigail had not told her of the marriage might perhaps, the Duchess confessed, be attributed to 'Bashfulness and want of Breeding', but that the Queen had also concealed it from her was unforgivable, and she did not hesitate to 'expostulate with her upon the Point'. She asked her why she had not been informed and the Queen, 'in a sort of passion', replied that she had told Abigail to do so 'a hundred times'.

Thereafter Sarah rarely spoke of the Queen without remarking upon some fault in Abigail's character or unworthiness in her behaviour. As for Abigail Masham, towards the end of 1707, 'it was thought proper,' the Duchess wrote,

that she should write to me and desire I would see her, to which I consented . . . When she came I began to tell her that it was very plain the Queen was much changed towards me, and that I could not attribute this to anything but her secret management . . . To this she gravely answered that she was sure the Queen, who had loved me extremely, would always be very kind to me. It was some minutes before I could recover from the surprise with which so extraordinary an answer struck me. To see a woman, whom I had raised out of the dust, put on such a superior air, and to hear her assure me, by way of consolation, that the Queen would always be very kind to me! At length I went on to reproach her with her ingratitude and her secret management of the Queen.

When Marlborough arrived home, at the end of November 1707, he became unwillingly embroiled in this quarrel and in other disputes both political and familial. Yet no one who attended his morning levees would have supposed there were worrying problems on his mind. Greeting those who called upon him with his customary composure and bland charm, he behaved in an inimitably engaging manner 'calculated to offend no one', in the words of the Genoese envoy in London. 'Every morning he has in his antechamber gentlemen of the first quality, including ambassadors and ministers of foreign princes; he dresses, even shaves and puts on his shirt in public.'

Yet there was much to worry him. Shortly before his arrival in England, Admiral Sir Cloudesley Shovell, on returning from his bombardment and destruction of the French warships at Toulon, had been thrown ashore when his flagship broke up in a tempestuous sea on the rocks of the Scilly Isles. Still living, though unconscious, he was approached by a woman who killed him before pulling an emerald ring from his finger.

Another admiral, Marlborough's youngest brother, George Churchill, who governed the navy as Marlborough governed the army, was at the same time under fierce attack for all manner of faults in the naval service as well as for financial peccadilloes. 'Your disasters at sea have been so many, a man scarce knows where to begin,' declared Lord Haversham, a former Lord of the Admiralty, in the House of Lords. 'Your ships have been taken by your enemies, as the Dutch take your herrings by the shoals upon your own coasts; nay your royal navy itself has not escaped. These are pregnant misfortunes and big with innumerable mischiefs.' An emphatic and outspoken Tory, overbearing and widely disliked, though supported by the Queen and her husband, Admiral Churchill survived in office, denying, with some convincing arguments, the charges of incompetence levelled against him, but failing to clear himself of accusations of financial irregularity. Certainly it seemed unlikely that the great fortune which he had acquired was solely attributable to the traditional perquisites of his office, many and lavish as these were. Certainly, too, the accusations which Admiral Churchill had to face caused people to murmur to each other that acquisitiveness was not limited to one particular member of his family.

Nor was the admiral's brother, the Duke, left unscathed in Parliament. In the House of Lords, the arrogant High Tory Earl of Rochester criticized his conduct of the last campaign since Ramillies, stinging the Duke into an uncharacteristic angry response. He had, he said, not lost a moment in going after Marshal Vendôme once it was possible for him to do so. But the man could not be 'brought to fight'. It was not possible 'to promise victories every day'.

Then Marlborough's friend, Godolphin, was in trouble. He had been approached by the members of the so-called 'Junto', a group of leading Whigs, who had told him that one of their members must be appointed Secretary of State and proposed as their candidate Marlborough's son-in-law and dedicated Whig, Lord Sunderland, whom the Queen much disliked. Urged by Godolphin to accept the necessity of making concessions to the Whigs, so that there should be at least one of 'that party in a position of trust to help carry on the business of the war', the Queen replied:

I am of the opinion making a party man Secretary of State when there are so many of their friends in employment of all kinds already is throwing myself into the hands of a party, which is a thing I have been desirous to avoid, and what I have heard the D[uke] of Marl[borough] and you say I must never do. Maybe some may think I would be willing to be in the hands of the Tories, but whatever people may say of me, I do assure you I am not inclined nor ever will to employ any of those violent persons that have behaved themselves so ill towards me. All I desire is my liberty in encouraging and employing all those that concur faithfully in my service, whether they are called Whigs or Tories, not to be tied to one or the other; for if I should be so unfortunate as to fall into the hands of either, I shall look upon myself, though I have the name of Queen, to be in reality but their slave; which as it will be my personal ruin, so it be the destroying of all Government, for instead of putting an end to faction, it will lay a lasting foundation for it.

Strongly disinclined to do more for men she disliked and distrusted, she resented Lord Godolphin's efforts to change her mind. Even more so did she resent those propositions so relentlessly, so tiresomely and tirelessly, so imperiously and tactlessly and, on occasions, so insultingly, in person and by letter, pressed upon her by the Duchess of Marlborough.

The Duke was greatly distressed by all this unpleasantness and bickering. He told Godolphin how 'uneasy' it made him feel to hear of his strained relationship with the Queen; and he wrote to his wife to say how upset he was to receive letters from her upbraiding him for not taking a firmer line with Her Majesty, couching his complaint in those cautious, careful tones in which he so often wrote to her when a far stricter hand was called for.

To the Queen he wrote as firmly as he thought appropriate.

The truth is that the heads of one party [the High Tories] have declared against you and your government as far as it is possible without going into open rebellion. Now, should your Majesty disoblige the others, how is it possible to obtain near five millions for carrying on the war with vigour, without which all is undone?

At last the Queen was persuaded she must give way; and having reluctantly agreed to accept the prominent Whig Lord Cowper as Lord Chancellor, she consented to the appointment of Sunderland as Secretary of State for the Southern Department. The Whigs had had their way, but the Queen was much displeased, and sought comfort in the company of Abigail Masham and Robert Harley.

Sarah, predictably, much disliked Harley, whom she called 'the Sorcerer'. In her opinion he was

a cunning and a dark man of too small abilities to do much good but with all the qualities requisite to do mischief & to bring on the ruin & destruction of a nation. This mischievous darkness of his soul was written in his countenance & plainly legible in a very odd look, disagreeable to everybody at first sight, which being joined with a constant awkward motion or other agitation of his head & body betrayed a turbulent dishonesty within, even in the midst of all those familiar, jocular, bowing, smiling airs which he always affected.

His manner of speaking, she added, made him sound more like a dervish than a man who had been Speaker of the House of Commons.

Harley was undoubtedly a devious man, known as 'Robin the Trickster'. But the Queen listened gratefully to his advice. Like him, she disagreed with the policy practised by Marlborough and Godolphin of giving way to pressure by the Whig Junto. She, like Harley, was concerned that, unless a stand were made against the Whigs, they would demand more and more offices in the administration and she would become a prisoner of a party.

Marlborough's growing dislike and distrust of Harley brought him into direct confrontation with the Queen, who was at her most persistent, obstinate and tearful in Harley's defence. Marlborough, more forceful than was wont to be with Her Majesty, declared that he would never again sit in Council with the man. The Queen made no comment. The Duke said he would resign rather than have anything more to do with him. The Queen, suppressing her tears, replied that he might just as well 'draw his dagger and stab her there and then as do such a thing'.

Marlborough repeated in writing his determination not to 'serve any longer with that man'. 'And I beseech your Majesty,' he added, 'to look upon me, from this moment, as forced out of your service as long as you see fit to continue him in it.'

On 9 February 1708, in a terse audience, she accepted the resignation of both Godolphin and Marlborough, letting Godolphin go without regret, but making a last, unavailing effort to persuade the Duke not to abandon her.

At a subsequent Council meeting attended by the Queen on the day of Marlborough's resignation, when Harley rose to open the proceedings he was not immediately interrupted but the shuffling of feet and suppressed murmurs clearly showed that he did not have his fellow Councillors' full attention. Then, as Harley paused in his speech, up stood the Duke of Somerset, the Queen's Master of the Horse and, in Marlborough's opinion, a worthless man unsuited to any higher appointment.* 'I do not see,' Somerset observed, 'how we can deliberate when the commander-in-chief and the Lord Treasurer are both absent.'

---

* Such dismissive characterizations as this are common enough in his correspondence with Godolphin; and, as the editor of these letters has written, 'the suspicion and resentment that many of his contemporaries held for him were not unjustified when one has an opportunity to read his frank comments about them' (Snyder (ed.), *The Marlborough–Godolphin Correspondence*, i, xxiv).

The Dukes of Newcastle and Somerset and the Earl of Rochester all came in for censure. Lord Raby, the ambassador to Prussia, was 'a very medling, worthless, insignificant creatur'; Alexander Stanhope, the English envoy at The Hague, ought to be posted somewhere else since his 'being apt to believe mallicious things that are writ from England, and his easy temper of receiving and countenancing every disaffected Englishman does a very great deal of hurt here'. The Earl of Halifax was not fit to be in the Cabinet and had 'the same ill qualitys of vanity and pride' as the Earl of Orford. As for Lord Wharton, it would be 'scandelous to put trust in him', while Robert Harley was 'the worst of men'.

Harley sat down; the Queen said nothing; the meeting broke up; Her Majesty was helped from her chair; and the Councillors departed.

On that same day Harley also submitted his resignation; and in tears, the Queen accepted it. She then sent for Marlborough to tell him that he was now free to resume his command.

Henry Boyle, Chancellor of the Exchequer, the second Earl of Cork's grandson, replaced Harley as Secretary of State. John Smith, the Whig Speaker of the House of Commons, became Chancellor; and Robert Walpole was appointed Secretary-at-War. Godolphin was reappointed Lord Treasurer.

Despite his dismissal 'Harley continued,' so Sarah said,

to have secret Correspondence with the Queen. And so that this might be the better managed she staid all the sultry Season, even when the [asthmatic Prince George] was panting for Breath in that small House [on Castle Hill at Windsor] she had formerly purchased which, though as hot as an Oven, was then said to be cool, because from the Park such Persons as Mrs Masham had a Mind to bring to her Majesty could be let in privately by the garden.

When the Prince died, the Duchess, according to her own account, 'knelt down by the Queen' and said all that she could imagine was appropriate 'from a faithful servant and one that she had professed so much kindness to', urging her to leave that 'dismal place', since 'nobody in the world ever continued in a place where a dead husband lay. But she seemed not to mind me but clapt her hands together, with other marks of passion.'

At length the Queen agreed to go to St James's and, handing the Duchess her watch and telling her at what time to return, she dismissed her with the words 'and send to Masham to come to me before I go'.

32

THE BATTLE OF OUDENARDE

'I have given such a blow to their foot that they will not be able to fight again this year.'

At half past six on the evening of 5 July 1708, the Dutch field deputy Sicco van Goslinga had arrived at Marlborough's headquarters at Anderlecht on the outskirts of Brussels. He had found him just about to mount his horse, having been in bed for most of the day and looking 'pale, worn out and disconsolate'.

The Duke had not been well for some time. There had been so much of late to worry and distress him, apart from the political upheavals in England. Earlier in the year, while he was still in England, there had been reports of a large Jacobite force gathering around Dunkirk with the apparent intention of invading England or Scotland to place James Stuart, now aged twenty, on the throne; and Marlborough had been kept occupied day and night in mobilizing troops and conferring with the Admiralty in attempts to raise a force strong enough to resist the Jacobite army at a time when so many troops were serving overseas. The would-be invaders, 6,000 in number, succeeded in evading the British battleships that had been sent under command of Sir George Byng to blockade Dunkirk; but, having entered the Firth of Forth, they would have been trapped there by Byng's flotilla had there not been a change of wind which allowed most of their ships to escape after thousands of James Stuart's men had perished as they waited in vain for orders to land, crowded together on the open decks and exposed to the most bitter February weather.

The sufferings of the British troops were hardly less severe and, to Marlborough's dismay, their losses were also heavy. 'We lay for further orders, laboring under many ilconveniences,' wrote one of them, Private Deane of the 1st Guards, 'haveing only ye bare deck to lye upon, wch hardship caused abundance of our men to bid adieu to the world.'

Scarcely had the Jacobite danger been averted than Marlborough was once more in Flanders, facing the far greater peril posed to his country by almost 110,000 troops under the nominal command of King Louis XIV's favourite grandson, the hot-tempered duc de Bourgogne, and the effective direction of the experienced and tough Marshal Vendôme, now fifty-four years old.

Marlborough assured Prince Eugène, whom he had met at The Hague on 12 April 1708, that he was, 'thank God', in as good health as one of his age, whose mind was 'not very much at ease' could expect to be. It was not only military problems that worried him: there had been rumours before he left England that he had been taking a less than passing interest in Hester Santlow, a beautiful and promiscuous dancer who had recently been making a name for herself on the London stage. It was, supposedly, because of this that, for the first time in their lives, the Duchess did not go down to the coast to wish him farewell.

General von Grumbkow, the Prussian commissary at the British headquarters, told King Frederick I that when news arrived that first Bruges then Ghent had surrendered after a remarkably swift march by the French, the Duke felt this misfortune so keenly that he believed he would succumb to it, being, indeed, 'so seized by it that he was afraid of being suffocated'. The blow which the enemy had dealt him 'was sufficient', Grumbkow thought, 'to do irreparable damage to the reputation and previous reputation of Mylord Duke'. General Natzmer, commander of the Prussian cavalry, was as concerned as Grumbkow by Marlborough's state of mind and excessive concern over the loss of Bruges and Ghent. 'Mylord Duke,' he wrote, 'was inconsolable over these sad happenings and discussed with me in touching confidence this sad turn in events.'

Prince Eugène was also alarmed by the effect which the loss of these two towns had upon the Duke's normal composure and equanimity, 'astounded' in fact to see such despondency in a general like Marlborough 'over a misfortune not relatively very important'.

'While Mylord Duke was writing to the Queen,' Grumbkow continued in his report to King Frederick,

Prince Eugène drew me aside and asked me what exactly all this meant. The Duke was incomprehensibly exhausted, and talked as though everything was lost . . . This morning Mylord Duke had a severe fever and was so ill that he had to be bled . . . I believe it would do him a great deal of good if your Majesty were to write him something consoling, and assure him of your continued good opinion of him, despite the misfortune he has suffered.

A day or so later Marlborough collapsed. His doctor suggested that he should be taken to Brussels, and orders to the army on 8 July 1708 were issued from Overkirk's tent. But that night, having been given some medicine to counteract what the chaplain-general termed a 'hot fever fit', he felt much better and by morning he seemed to be 'very well', greatly comforted to have received a letter from his wife, who wished to assure him that she no longer felt angry with him.

'I do not say this to flatter you,' he replied, 'nor am I at an age of making fond expressions, but upon my word, when you are out of humour, and are dissatisfied with me, I had rather dye than live.' Taking advantage of her contrite mood, he added that he hoped she would do all she could to restore her relationship with the Queen and not bother her with political argument and exhortations. Sarah paid some attention to this advice, but only for a time.

On the day before Marlborough's recovery from his fever, reports had reached the camp that the French were on the march towards Lessines on the Dendre, intending, so Marlborough rightly supposed, to seize the bridges there in order to cover a siege of Oudenarde, an important fortress on the Scheldt which, in enemy hands, would cut off the allies from the coast of Flanders.

Realizing that there was not a moment to lose, Marlborough issued orders for a forced march to Lessines, which, by covering thirty miles in thirty-six hours, they reached while the French were scarcely halfway there; and, at dawn on 11 July, William Cadogan was sent ahead towards the Scheldt at Oudenarde with sixteen

battalions, fifteen squadrons, a large number of pioneers with pontoons and over thirty guns Marlborough followed him with the rest
of the army at about seven o'clock, giving orders for the fastest
possible march, which became, in Goslinga's words, 'not so much a
march as a race'.

When Cadogan reached the high ground overlooking the Scheldt
below Oudenarde, he learned that the French, six miles or so away
to the north, had still not crossed to the west bank of the river.
Less than two hours later, Cadogan's pioneers began their work of
throwing seven pontoon bridges across the river on either side of
the existing two stone bridges in Oudenarde.

As soon as these pontoon bridges were ready, Cadogan crossed
the river with twelve of his infantry battalions and, on his left,
eight squadrons of Hanoverian cavalry, commanded by General von
Rantzau. Eleven battalions were left to guard the crossing.

So far these movements had escaped the notice of the French
army, the advanced guard of which − commanded by Lieutenant-
General de Biron − having now crossed the river, was on the march
towards Oudenarde. Astonished to see the allied army, in ever
growing numbers, approaching so unexpectedly, Biron sent a
number of messengers and aides-de-camp galloping back to his
headquarters with increasingly alarming news. They found Marshal
Vendôme eating his midday meal. He could not at first believe that
the reports were true: the allies' vanguard had been seen over fifteen
miles away the evening before; while the Duke of Marlborough's
headquarters were reported as having been almost fifty miles distant
two days ago. If the allies were, indeed, where they were now said
to be, Vendôme exclaimed that the devil must have carried them
there: such marching was 'impossible'. It was not impossible, though.
By the time the main body of infantry reached the pontoon bridges
over the Scheldt, the men had covered more than fifty miles in sixty
hours.

Ahead of them, at three o'clock, Cadogan, having called up the
four battalions he had left to protect the bridges, advanced to storm
the village of Eyne, while von Rantzau's Hanoverian cavalry
protected their left flank. With Brigadier Joseph Sabine's British
brigade in the centre of their line, the men advanced with measured

pace against the Swiss mercenaries in and around Eyne, holding their fire until they were within no more than twenty yards of the enemy. The musket fire, when at last it came, was devastating: three of the four Swiss battalions surrendered immediately; the fourth fell back towards the hamlet of Heurne and on to the swords of the Hanoverian cavalry, who slaughtered them out of hand before charging on to attack and scatter Biron's cavalry, sending them hurtling back towards the main body of the French army beyond the Norken river.

Serving with the Hanoverians was their Electoral Prince, who was one day to ascend the British throne as King George II, 'hacking and thrusting', in the words of his biographer, 'sweating and swearing like any trooper. His horse was shot dead, and the colonel who gave him his own was killed as he helped the Prince into the saddle.'

Outnumbered though they were, the Hanoverians galloped on, at von Rantzau's command, straight into the main body of cavalry of the French left wing, slashing with wild ferocity in the renewed mêlée until forced to withdraw, taking with them many prisoners and riderless horses as well as two kettledrums and ten standards.

Up till now, and for a further two hours or so, Marlborough and Prince Eugène acted together in the direction of the battle. But at about six o'clock, the Duke handed over command of the threatened allied right to the Prince and rode over to the left to oversee the fighting there. Count Grumbkow was much impressed by his energy and confidence: 'Mylord Duke shone in battle, giving his orders with the greatest sangfroid.'

He now supervised the entry into the field of Overkirk's Dutch troops, who were streaming across the Oudenarde bridges to support an attack being made upon the village of Diepenbeck by twenty battalions under the command of Count Lottum. With what has been described as his 'unerring eye for ground and tactical possibilities', Marlborough now successfully set in motion a most difficult manoeuvre, 'a movement at the height of the battle [which] needed a cool mind to conceive and great skill to execute'. After sending forward his Hanoverian troops as though to reinforce the attack upon Diepenbeck, he ordered Count Lottum to withdraw, re-form, and, with seventeen squadrons of British cavalry, to reinforce Prince Eugène on the right wing.

Confident of the Prince's ability to deal with the enemy forces which faced and outnumbered him, Marlborough could now concentrate on his own attack on the left: a powerful advance by the Hanoverians on Diepenbeck, combined with an extension of the line by the Dutch to outflank the French infantry, both movements being designed as a cover for his audacious final stroke. This was an approach, by way of a sunken road, of a strong contingent of Danish cavalry and Dutch foot, commanded by the nineteen-year-old Prince of Orange, which was to turn east abruptly when ordered to do so by Marlborough and launch an onslaught on the flank and rear of Vendôme's wing.

The Dutch and Danish forces galloped furiously forward at Marlborough's command, taking the enemy completely by surprise, scattering their astonished ranks by the rapidity of their charge, and so completely encircling the enemy that at one point near the mill at Royegem the Prince of Orange and General Cadogan actually fired at each other. By nine o'clock the French right wing had been thrown apart and the duc de Bourgogne, to the fury of Vendôme, who had not spoken to him for the past seven hours, ordered a general retreat on Ghent.

When the two French leaders met at Huysse beyond Royegem, on the far side of the Norken river, the Marshal, never the neatest of men at the best of times, was now as dishevelled and sweat-stained as any of the soldiers amid whom he had been fighting. He heatedly argued that the army must be re-formed and return to the fight; and, when the duc de Bourgogne attempted to speak, he burst out, 'Your Royal Highness must remember that you were appointed to this army only on condition that you obeyed my orders.'

The Marshal was, however, in a minority of one: it was generally conceded that the battle had been irreversibly lost. 'Very well, messieurs,' he said, before stomping away. 'I see you all think it best to retire. And you, Monseigneur,' he added with what Saint-Simon described as an 'énormité' of lèse majesté, 'have long had that wish.'

By now it was growing dark and a heavy rain had started to fall. 'We drove the enemy from ditch to ditch,' wrote Sergeant Millner of Hamilton's Regiment, 'from hedge to hedge and from out of one scrub into another in great hurry, confusion and disorder'; and, as Marlborough's trap began to close, with Overkirk driving in one flank while Prince Eugène drove in the other, there was such confused firing, as French soldiers strove to escape through the gaps in the allied lines, that orders for a general ceasefire were given. This did not prevent the capture of about 7,000 French troops, including over 700 officers, many of the soldiers being taken by Huguenot officers who went about calling out the names of French regiments to trick into captivity men who had been scattered in the rout: '*A moi, Picardie! Ici, Roussillon!*'

The allies lost some 825 men killed and 2,150 wounded; the French perhaps as many as 14,000 killed or wounded, taken prisoner or deserted. Certainly the battle had suddenly transformed the situation in Flanders and had enhanced the already outstanding reputation of Marlborough as a military commander. In the words of David Chandler, the military historian:

In this great military engagement we see Marlborough's talents fully displayed. He was able to snatch at a chance of giving battle under circumstances that few other commanders would have judged possible, let alone advisable. His eye for ground, his sense of timing, his ability to extemporise solutions with the aid of limited, though excellent resources, and his keen knowledge of his foes' characters, foibles and clashing personalities – all these attributes were amply demonstrated. Of course he was fortunate to have the experienced and gifted Prince Eugène at his side, and to be blessed with such capable subordinates as Cadogan, Lottum and Overkirk and such a loyal and reliable rank and file, but from first to last Oudenarde had been his personal achievement.

As Marlborough himself put it, referring to 'the terror that is in their army', 'I have given such a blow to their foot that they will not be able to fight again this year.'

33

FRANCE INVADED

*'. . . our parties have occasioned very
great terror in Picardy . . .'*

Soon after nine o'clock on the morning of 12 July 1708, to the cheers
of their soldiers, the Duke and Prince Eugène rode into the square
at Oudenarde, which was crowded with prisoners of war milling
about beneath the elaborately decorated façade and pinnacled roof
of the sixteenth-century town hall. The Duke was suffering from
one of his intermittent headaches, which became so painful that he
was obliged to cut short letters which he later wrote to Godolphin.
He went to lie down for a time and then, having discussed the next
move in the campaign with Prince Eugène, he attended a council of
war at which, with the Prince's approval, he proposed a westward
march across the Lys to threaten the French frontier. This move, he
hoped, would force King Louis to order Marshal Vendôme to
abandon Bruges and Ghent and return to protect their homeland.

The plan was accepted by most of the generals and Dutch deputies
with the predictable exception of the perverse Goslinga, who argued
that it would be far better to blockade Ghent and Bruges and starve
out the enemy there. None of the generals agreed with him, and
shortly before midnight the next day Count Lottum was ordered to
take thirty battalions and forty squadrons to occupy and pull down
the French defensive lines around the frontier fortresses of Warneton
and Comines.

Marching his troops as fast as he could take them, Lottum reached
the frontier in the middle of the next night and immediately began
the work of demolition. 'We slung our Firelocks,' Private Matthew
Bishop recorded, 'and every man had a Shovel in his hand; and when

we came to the place appointed, we ran upon their works. It was like running up the side of a house. When we got to the top we began to throw it down as fast as possible in order to make way for the army.'

The threat to France did not, however, have the desired effect, as Marlborough explained to Sarah in a letter written from his new headquarters at Werwicq on 16 July, a very hot day on which his headache was scarcely bearable:

I had good hopes that the diligence I have made in getting into the French country (for I am now behind their lines) would have obliged them to abandon Ghent; but as yet it has not had that effect but on the contrary M. de Vendôme declares he will sacrifice a strong garrison rather than abandon that town, which, if he keeps his word, will give me a great deal of trouble; for till we are masters of Ghent we have no cannon.

In a letter to Godolphin written later that same day, Marlborough emphasized the difficulties of acting more aggressively with a strong garrison at his rear in Ghent and expressed his continuing hope that, threatened by starvation, Vendôme would within 'four or five days' evacuate the town and come to the threatened frontier. 'In the meantime,' the Duke concluded his letter, 'I shall take what rest I can, in order to be the better able to serve, for this minute my head is so very hot that I am obliged to leave off writing.'

A week later Marshal Vendôme had still not moved from Ghent and, with that fortress blocking the movement of a siege train, Marlborough was using his 'utmost endeavours' to get some cannon and a 'battering train' from Holland, from Maastricht and from Antwerp. This, he told Godolphin, would necessitate the collection of no fewer than 16,000 horses to haul the hundred heavy guns with sufficient shot into position before Ghent. In the meantime, he added, he was sending raiding parties into France, which occasioned great fear.

As he had done in Bavaria in his campaign in 1704, he was now ravaging the countryside, villages and towns of France with 25,000 men, burning houses all over Artois and parts of Picardy, seizing stocks of food, plunder and hostages as well as horses and carts, and enforcing exactions of money. Yet, still Vendôme did not move.

'We have an account that our parties have occasioned very great terror in Picardy,' he wrote to Godolphin on 2 August, 'and that they exclaim very much against M. de Vendôme for staying where he is.'

Marlborough was becoming dismayed by the lack of progress. It was noticed how depressed he seemed at this time. His renowned frugality, what Lieutenant-General de Biron described as his 'shameful stinginess', precluded his giving the kind of dinner parties over which his senior officers presided; but, quiet and preoccupied, he was often to be seen at their tables, as he was in Prince Eugène's quarters, which were described by Biron, who was invited to dine there as a distinguished prisoner, as being of 'a quite royal magnificence'. Yet, wherever he was and however good the food, the Duke did not eat much.

Nor did he stay long, rising from the table as soon as he had finished his modest meal to return to his plans and correspondence. He was held in high esteem, but he would have been more popular with his officers had he been less parsimonious. Biron thought that they had 'a tacit preference' for Prince Eugène, 'without the Duke of Marlborough being jealous of it'.

The two commanders still got on as well with each other as they had always done in the past. But they did not see eye to eye over a plan for future operations which had long been developing in Marlborough's mind. This was for an invasion of France by a task force sailing across the English Channel under the command of Lieutenant-General Thomas Erle, an officer standing high in Marlborough's regard, who had been commander-in-chief in Ireland. The town of Abbeville, twelve miles from the mouth of the Somme, was to be taken and from here, as a port of supply, Marlborough and Prince Eugène were to march on Paris with 100,000 men. The Prince, however, did not think this risky plan practicable, even if the winds and waters of the English Channel allowed the necessary ships to cross; while the Dutch, as Marlborough put it, 'would not willingly give their consent for the marching of their army into France'. So it was decided that the important city of Lille, the greatest city in France after Paris, should be taken and occupied as a *place d'armes* before any further advance into France took place; and, for the siege of Lille, the huge artillery and siege train which had by now at last been assembled should be carried there in two convoys, each five miles long, and comprising in all over ninety heavy cannon, each drawn by twenty horses, as well as sixty mortars and 3,000 four-horse munition wagons.

If Lille were to be taken, such a powerful siege train would certainly be needed. The elaborate fortifications of the town had been designed by Vauban, who had created here one of his most masterly works of fortification. Protected by wide double moats, huge earthworks and outer defences, and by all the circumvallations, counterscarps, bastions, ravelins and ramparts which military engineers then demanded, the fortress was defended by some 15,000 troops, while within the defences stood a citadel which was considered virtually impregnable.

The besieging force of fifty battalions was commanded by Prince Eugène, who allowed numerous ladies to leave the city before the bombardment began, but who gave a noncommittal reply to a deputation of burghers who, 'with compliments and refreshments', came to his headquarters to express the hope that the population of the place would be spared too heavy a bombardment.

Marlborough commanded the field army, which stood, covering Prince Eugène's operations, between the town and the French field army commanded by the Jacobite Duke of Berwick.

On 27 August, a week after the lines of circumvallation had been completed, Prince Eugène's batteries opened up in a furious cannonade which, it was hoped, would bring the earthworks tumbling down into the moat and open up a breach. 'I begin to write to my dear soull early this morning believing I may be oblig'd to march, so that I shou'd not have time in this afternoon,' the Duke wrote to Sarah,

for if the intelligence I received an hour ago that the Duke of Vendomes Army as well as that of the Duke of Berwick were on their march to join be true, I must march. Our cannon began this morning to fyre at Lisle, so that in ten days we hope to have the town, and after that we must attack the citadel, which we think will give us full as much trouble. My hopes are that God will bless us in this undertaking which will very much forward my being quiet with You, especially if we have another success against the

Duke of Burgundy who has the King of ffrance's orders to ventur everything rather than suffer Lisle to be taken.

We have for these last ten days had extremely hott weather which I hope may give You good peaches at Woodstock, wher I shou'd be better pleas'd to eat even the worst that were ever tasted, than the good ons we have here, for every day of my life I grow more impatient for quiet . . . Having writ thus farr I have notice that Monsr de Vandome has begun his march. But I shall not march til to morrow, when I shall be more certainly inform'd of his intentions . . . By the slow motions of Monsr de Vandome it lookes as if he has resolv'd not to march to join the Duke of Berwick, but to make that Duke march his Army to Gramont where they will then join.

'This,' commented his biographer, Sir Winston Churchill, 'is exactly what they did . . . His power of putting himself in the enemy's shoes, and measuring truly what they ought to do, and what he himself would most dislike, was one of his greatest gifts.'

As Marlborough had forecast, the Dukes of Vendôme and Berwick met on 29 August at Grammont, where they had almost twice as many troops under their joint command as Marlborough had. Early in the morning of 5 September, however, Prince Eugène arrived to support him with a considerable force of infantry and cavalry withdrawn from the siege of Lille, while Baron Fagel, with seven Dutch battalions, also arrived soon after dawn. Even so, Marlborough was still greatly outnumbered and, for the first time in his life, he prepared to fight a major defensive battle.

Marshal Vendôme proposed an immediate attack, as a celebration of the King of France's birthday. The other French commanders, however, were less confident of success. The Duke of Berwick pointed out the difficulties of the marshy, wooded ground. The duc de Bourgogne was also hesitant. So, while the three marshals argued and reconnoitred, Marlborough ordered the entrenchment of his front to strengthen his position, which had now been weakened by the withdrawal of most of Prince Eugène's troops to Lille, where a strong sortie had been made on the temporarily weakened lines.

In their unresolved quandary the three French marshals spent all night discussing their problems in the duc de Bourgogne's tent,

Vendôme pressing for an attack and stressing the 'unsurpassable spirit' of the troops, Berwick and Bourgogne arguing that to attack might well invite not merely a rebuff but even 'a total overthrow'. In the end they decided to write to the King for a decision.

The King had no doubt as to what should be done: he had already urged an attack and an attack must accordingly be launched. He sent his minister of war to the French camp to ensure that his orders were carried out.

Chamillart, however, agreed with Bourgogne and Berwick: in the circumstances an attack would be too risky an undertaking, so the French army withdrew to Tournai; and by 17 September the duc de Bourgogne's headquarters were at Saulchoi.

On that day Marlborough wrote to Sarah of his concern that the siege of Lille went on 'so very slowly'. An assault had by then been made on the counterscarp, in the course of which four immense mines had been exploded by the French, killing numerous men of the storming party and all the engineers. The survivors endeavoured to scramble forward, but the enemy's fire drove them back and killed so many that the breach was piled high with their bodies.

Marlborough confessed to being 'in perpetual fear' that the siege would 'continue so long and consequently consume so much stores' that he would 'not have the wherewithal to finish, which would be very cruel'. Already the stocks of cannonballs had fallen so low that the shot which had been fired by the French at the allies' camp had all been gathered up to be used by Prince Eugène's guns. Moreover, the Duke's hopes of receiving a convoy of further ammunition were dashed when Marshal Vendôme and the duc de Bourgogne cut right across his line of communications with Brussels and Holland. Then came a further blow: during a determined sortie by the Lille garrison, in which the allies lost over 1,000 men, Prince Eugène was hit in the head by a musket ball which stunned him so severely that, although he endeavoured to remain on his feet, he was clearly incapable for the time being of taking any further part in the operations.

The next morning, when Marlborough went to see him, he found him protesting to his staff that he was perfectly capable of returning to the trenches; and was persuaded to return to his coach only when Marlborough undertook to take over the direction of the siege while still commanding the covering army. 'Upon the wounding of Prince Eugène,' he told Godolphin,

I thought it necessary to inform myself of everything of the siege; for, before I did not meddle in any thing but the covering of it. Upon examination I found they did not do well with the Prince, for when I told him there did not remain powder and ball for above four days, he was very much surprised. I own to you that I fear we have something more in our misfortunes than ignorance . . . I cannot prove what I am going to say . . . [But] I really believe that we have been from the very beginning of the siege betrayed . . . for great part of our stores have been embezzled.

The Duke's problems were exacerbated when a French officer with a large party of dragoons succeeded in replenishing the garrison's dwindling stocks of powder by carrying almost 60,000 pounds into Lille, having presented themselves at the lines of circumvallation as escorts of prisoners of war. Unless his own stocks of powder and shot were similarly replenished, the siege would have to be abandoned.

Unable to get supplies by land, Marlborough turned for help to Lieutenant-General Thomas Erle, who was still in England awaiting orders for the proposed expedition to the French coast. Admiral Byng was accordingly ordered to bring Erle's men and a convoy of ammunition to Ostend.

By the end of September this convoy was on its way south from Ostend. At Wynendael it was intercepted by a French force commanded by the comte de La Motte. Close by, however, was an allied force of about 4,000 foot and three squadrons of dragoons, which Marlborough had prudently dispatched under command of William Cadogan to cover the convoy on that stretch of road where it was most likely to be intercepted. In a brief and bloody engagement the allied troops, commanded by the High Tory, Major-General J. R. Webb, vigorously repulsed the French, and the convoy passed on to the allied camp with supplies of ammunition sufficient for another fortnight's bombardment.*

---

* In an account of this action sent to the *London Gazette* by Marlborough's secretary, Adam de Cardonnel, credit for its success was given to Cadogan rather than to Webb, whose resentment was bitter and long-lasting. Other malcontents in the army supported Webb, who 'was not averse from posing as the martyr of Whig

Marshal Vendôme now retaliated by breaking the dykes, opening the sluices and isolating Ostend by floods of water, which inundated the countryside for several miles on either side of the town, making it 'impracticable', as Marlborough put it, 'for our carts to pass'. So now, although the army was well supplied with ammunition, there was a serious shortage of bread; and Marlborough was obliged to spare men for the purpose of making up foraging parties to collect supplies from as far south as Armentières and the villages around Comines and La Bassée.

By then, the siege of Lille was reaching its climax, the besiegers

---

malevolence, and he became the hero of the hour'. 'Malignity went so far as to hint that the Duke of Marlborough was grievously chagrined by the repulse of the French at Wynendaele,' wrote Thomas Seccombe in his entry on Webb in the *Dictionary of National Biography*, 'inasmuch as he had entertained the offer of an enormous bribe payable upon the frustration of the siege operations which would have ensued upon the failure of the convoy' (*DNB*, xx, 1013).

In his novel, *The History of Henry Esmond, Esq., A Colonel in the Service of Her Majesty Queen Anne*, published in 1852, W. M. Thackeray headed one of his chapters 'General Webb wins the Battle of Wynendael'. In this chapter, as elsewhere in the book, Thackeray, while acknowledging Marlborough's great talents as a general, does not conceal his dislike of the man, his low opinion of his character, at once, as he took it to be, grasping, bland, parsimonious and deceitful. General Webb, to whom Thackeray was distantly related, is, however, treated with sympathy and admiration.

Thackeray depicts 'the brave warrior', gripped by righteous anger, protesting about the credit for the successful action at Wynendael being given to 'the Duke's favourite, Mr Cadogan', rather than to himself: 'He shook his fist in the air. "Oh, by the Lord!" says he. "I know what I had rather have than a peerage!" "And what is that, sir?" someone asked. "I had rather have a quarter of an hour with John Churchill, on a fair green field, and only a pair of rapiers between my shirt and his –" "Sir," interposes one. "Tell him so! ... I know every word goes to him that's dropped from every general officer's mouth. I don't say he's not brave. Curse him! He's brave enough."' When the report in the *London Gazette* reaches the army, Webb and Marlborough are attending a dinner given by Prince Eugène at Lille. Webb, having read the report, runs it through with the point of his sword and offers it to Marlborough. 'Permit me to hand it to your Grace,' he says. 'The Duke looked very black. "Take it," says he to his Master of the Horse, who was waiting behind him. General Webb persisted, to his dying day, in believing that the Duke intended he should be beat at Wynendael, and sent him purposely with a small force, hoping that he might be knocked on the head there' (*The History of Henry Esmond*, Book 2, ch. 15 and Book 3, ch. 1).

having braved the boiling pitch poured upon them to seize the counterscarp. On 19 October, the day after the death of 'poor M. Overkirk' (by whose demise, Marlborough noted characteristically, 'her Majesty will save the pension'), the Duke reported to Godolphin: 'We hope in four or five days to give a general storm, if they [refuse to surrender the city] which I fear they will. I wish I may be mistaken, since it will cost a great many lives. God continues to bless us with good weather.'

Marlborough's fears were groundless. Three days later his troops stood waiting for orders to make the final assault on Lille. But rather than expose it to the sack and pillage which defiance would, by the conventions of siege warfare, entail, the French commander, Marshal Boufflers, surrendered the city and withdrew into the citadel.

Two days later there was a serious setback: the garrison at Leffinghe, a key town on the Scheldt through which the convoy of artillery had been conveyed from Ostend to Lille, had been relieved by an allied force of British, Dutch and Spanish troops. Celebrating the fall of Lille, these troops, officers and men, had become incapably drunk and quite unable to resist the French assault, in which many of them were killed. The allies, consequently, could no longer make use of the road through Leffinghe to Ostend, so, cut off from the whole course of the Scheldt by a French army superior in numbers, they were also cut off from the sea.

In this situation Marlborough received a worried letter from Godolphin, who wanted to know how the Duke, with whom he could not communicate except by way of the 'precarious holland post', could now be sure of 'provisions & subsistence' for his army. 'How will you have money from Antwerp and Brussels?' he asked. 'Can you be sure the French will not destroy all Artois, & even Picardie, too, rather than that they shall furnish subsistence to your army? I could ask a great many more of these, wch perhaps you will call idle questions, but I should be glad to be sure they were so.'

Marshal Vendôme was now louder than ever in his demands that his army should attack the allies while they were thus placed; but the Duke of Berwick and the duc de Bourgogne again demurred, arguing against any such aggressive movement, proposing instead that, having left strong garrisons in Ghent and Bruges, the army should be disposed so as to protect the nearby French provinces.

In his anxiety, Marlborough fell ill again. Goslinga, who came to his tent one day in the early morning, found him sick and weary, as the Duke himself admitted, 'and sad and cast down to a far greater extent. He had just taken medicine.'

He was, even so, making detailed plans for a clever operation which was not explained to all his generals and certainly not to Goslinga. His aide-de-camp, Colonel Molesworth, later explained:

The point to be laboured was to deceive the enemy, and lead em into an opinion that we had . . . no design at that time to . . . make a movement towards the Schelde. And, to bring this about, orders were given for the carrying of all forage from the camp to Courtray and Mein [on the Lys] . . . as if to winter quarters. The Quarter-masters were sent to Courtray and ordered to take up convenient lodgings for my Ld Duke, his family [staff] and equipage; and to take out billets for all the Generalls . . . This farce was so well managed that . . . I'me confident all our Generalls, except those few whom it was necessary to admit into the bottom of the design, really thought it was intended (as was given out) to cantoone and refresh the army for a while.

Instead of going into winter quarters on the Lys, however, the allies turned east in four columns, the southernmost of these commanded by Prince Eugène, who left a small force behind at Lille to watch the citadel. Marching rapidly towards the Scheldt, the allies crossed the river and drove the French back towards Ghent and Tournai, while the Elector of Bavaria, who was laying siege to Brussels, suddenly abandoned it in disarray. Soon afterwards Boufflers surrendered the citadel of Lille; and on 29 December, the frost and ice of a bitter winter having given way to a thaw, followed by torrential rain, the comte de La Motte in Ghent also surrendered and was promptly court-martialled.

The surrender of Ghent was followed by that of Bruges, then by that of Leffinghe. Soon after this Marlborough learned, to his profound satisfaction, that Port Mahon, on the island of Minorca, had been taken from the French and, as he had long strongly advised, the British fleet had obtained a secure base for operations in the Mediterranean. He reported to Godolphin:

I was yesterday from ten in the morning till six at night seeing the garrison at Ghent and all that belonged to them march by me. It was astonishing to see so great a number of good men to look upon, suffer a place of this consequence to be taken at this season with so little loss. As soon as they knew I had possession of the gates of this town, they took the resolution of abandoning Brioges [Bruges]. This campaign is now ended to my own heart's desire, and as the hand of the Almighty is visible in this whole matter, I hope her Majesty will think it due to Him to return public thanks, and at the same time to implore His blessing on the next campaign. I can't express enough to you the importance of these towns.

'I think we may say without vanity,' he told Sarah, 'that France will with terror remember this campaign for a long time.'

34

CALLS FOR PEACE

*'You may be assured that I shall be wholeheartedly for peace,
not doubting that I shall find the goodwill which was promised
me two years ago by the Marquis d'Alègre.'*

Satisfied as he professed himself to be by the outcome of the campaign
of 1708, Marlborough had been much upset by worsening relations
between the Queen and his wife, who bombarded him with her
letters of complaint. Wearily he replied in one of his, 'I have neither
spirits nor time to answer your three last letters.'

It was the well-founded opinion of the Queen that the Duke had
a duty to make more of an effort than he did to control his obstreperous wife, to curb her indiscreet tongue and to press her to resume
her neglected duties. In February of that year the Queen had written
to him:

You know I have often had the misfortune of falling under the Duchess of
Marlborough's displeasure, and now, after several reconciliations she is
again relapsed into her cold, unkind way and I find she has taken a resolution
not to come to me when I am alone, and fancies nobody will take notice
of the change. She may impose upon some poor simple people, but how
can she imagine she can on any that have a grain of sense? Can she think
that the Duchess of Somerset and my Lady Fitzharding, who are two of the
most observing, prying ladies in England, won't find out that she never comes
near me as she used to do; that the tattling voice will not in a little time make
us the jest of the town? Some people will blame her, others me, and a great
many both. What a disagreeable noise she will be the occasion of making
in the world besides. God knows of what ill consequences it may be.

In his letter to Sarah giving her news of the victory at Oudenarde,
the Duke had added, 'I must, and you must, give thanks to God for his
goodness in protecting and making me the instrument of so much

happiness to the Queen and nation, if she will please to make use of it.'

The Duke had obviously not intended that this letter should be shown to the Queen, but Sarah did let her see it, having provoked an angry quarrel while driving with her in the state coach to a thanksgiving service for the victory at Oudenarde in St Paul's Cathedral. As Mistress of the Robes, she had set out the jewels she considered Her Majesty should wear for the service, even though, as she said, the Queen 'seldom woar Jewels'; and she noticed while rattling along in the coach that the Queen was not wearing any of them. Immediately blaming Abigail Masham, she chose to suppose that the discarding of the jewellery by the Queen was intended as an insult to the Duke and, by extension, to herself. Not only did she accuse the Queen of intending this deliberate insult, not only did she tell the Queen to be quiet on entering the cathedral, she sat down to put her grievances in writing upon their return to St James's Palace, enclosing the Duke's letter with her own:

I cannot help sending your Majesty this letter, to show how exactly Lord Marlborough agrees with me in my opinion . . . I think he will be surprised to hear that when I had taken so much Pains to put your Jewels in a Way I thought you would like, Mrs Masham could make you refuse to wear them in so unkind a Manner . . . Only I must needs observe that your Majesty chose a very wrong Day to mortify me, when you are just going to return Thanks for a Victory obtained by Lord Marlborough.

The Queen declined to answer this letter, but, having returned the Duke's to his wife, she wrote to him to ask what he meant by ending his letter about the victory at Oudenarde with the words 'if she will please to make use of it'.

The Duke replied that he had intended to suggest that she would be well advised to make use of the victory by following Godolphin's advice not to put her trust entirely in the Tories and, by implication, Robert Harley and Mrs Masham, but to become reconciled to the Whigs. He had already said as much in a letter giving her news of the battle of Oudenarde, to which the Queen's response had been, 'Oh, Lord, when will all this dreadful bloodshed cease':

The Circumstances in this last Battle I think shew the hand of God . . . a visible Mark of the Favours of Heaven to you and your Arms . . . Give me leave to say that I think you are obliged to Conscience & as a good Christian to forgive & to have no more Resentments to any particular Person or Party but to make use of such as will carry on this just War with Vigour.

The Queen, however, was strongly disinclined to become reconciled to the Whigs, despite the return of a decidedly Whiggish House of Commons in the general election of July 1708; and the more she resisted the Whigs' demands for more offices, the more Godolphin and Marlborough were attacked by them for not succeeding in persuading her to give way and by the Tories for endeavouring to do so. 'I find in all manner of ways I am to be found fault with,' the Duke complained, 'for when I am lucky, I am negligent and do not make use of the occasion; and if I should ever prove unfortunate, no doubt I should run the risk of being a fool or a traitor.'*

Like Godolphin, Marlborough again talked of resignation and retirement; but, well aware of how much she needed him, the Queen wrote to him, urging him not to abandon her:

I hope you will both consider better of it and not resort to an action that will bring me and our country to confusion . . . You may flatter yourselves that people will approve of your quitting, but if you should persist in these cruel and unjust resolutions, believe me, where one will say you are in the right, hundreds will blame you.

As soon as what he described as the 'very laborious campaign' of 1708 was over, Marlborough again started making plans and raising troops for the next, which he thought would be even 'more troublesome'. At the same time he was conducting negotiations for peace, travelling repeatedly from his headquarters at Brussels to The Hague,

---

* Marlborough's correspondence 'reeks of self-pity', Julian Hoppit has written. 'In many respects,' he added, Marlborough was a 'deeply unattractive character. His limitless ambition led him into disloyalty to both James II and, to a lesser degree, William III just as his beauty bred vanity and his success unbridled avidity . . . Yet a man who began life amidst the provincial gentry of Civil War England and ended it as a duke of the realm, living in a magnificent palace given to him for his great victory at Blenheim, must have had numerous abilities and virtues. He was charming, thorough, determined, tireless, patient, brave and, above all, imaginative' (*A Land of Liberty?*, 114).

where, to save the expense of taking a place of his own, he stayed in a house rented by General von Grumbkow, who told the King of Prussia:

My Lord Duke has obliged me to take a furnished house opposite the Orange palace and is living there himself. This costs me 20 louis d'or a month, and as I have very good Tokay, for which he has a passion, I gave his Highness a supper yesterday, which was attended by Prince Eugène, my Lord Albemarle, Cadogan, and Lieutenant-General Ros. They were all in the best spirits in the world.

During the course of the evening there was a discussion about the exchange of prisoners which resulted in the Duke exclaiming that he would stake his fortune on the matter being settled to Grumbkow's satisfaction. 'Good,' said Grumbkow, 'I will wager you ten pistoles.' 'Done,' replied the Duke, who then became agitated at the thought that he might lose them. 'Prince Eugène laughed loudly over the effect which a bet of ten pistoles had upon the spirits of my Lord Duke,' Grumbkow finished his account, 'and I cannot help assuring your Majesty that, if I had foreseen that my Lord Duke would take this matter so much to heart, I should have offered him fifty pistoles and gladly lost them.'

Although he was disturbed at the prospect of losing ten pistoles, the Duke's wealth was increasing month by month, not least by means of the 2.5 per cent commission upon the pay of foreign contingents to which he was entitled by the Queen's warrant. Part of the money due to him went upon the cost of his highly efficient and necessarily expensive intelligence network; but there remained huge sums available to swell his already immense fortune. He could also look forward to a large reward from the French when his efforts to bring peace to Europe proved successful. This reward was mentioned in a letter he wrote to the Jacobite Duke of Berwick on 30 October 1708: 'You may be assured that I shall be wholeheartedly for peace, not doubting that I shall find the goodwill which was promised me two years ago by the Marquis d'Alègre.' The marquis, King Louis's envoy, had at that time, Marlborough added, been instructed to offer him 'rewards worthy of a man of his standing', that was to say, in addition to 'whatever benefits he had already received from his own sovereign, two millions of French livres so as to raise him above the dangers to which eminence is always exposed in England, if not sustained by great wealth'.

'As I trust you without reserve,' Marlborough's letter to the Duke of Berwick continued, 'I conjure you never to part with this letter except to return it to me.'

The peace negotiations dragged on as both sides prepared for war, Marlborough raising over 150,000 men for his command in the Low Countries, the French – so his intelligence agents informed him, having intercepted a letter in January 1709 – being well on the way to raising the same number. But then France experienced more than three months of weather so cold that rivers were covered with thick ice from bank to bank, cattle, sheep and pigs froze to death and seeds were destroyed in the ground, while supplies of grain from Africa were intercepted by the English fleet in the Mediterranean. 'The cold is so grim that words fail me,' the duchesse d'Orléans wrote to her aunt, the Electress of Hanover. 'I am sitting in front of a roaring fire; there is a screen in front of the door, my neck is wrapped in sables and my feet are in a bearskin sack but, all the same, I am trembling with cold . . . As soon as you leave the house, you are followed by the poor, black with hunger.'

Men and women died of starvation; dogs ate corpses in the streets; hungry and desperate gangs attacked markets and chateaux; there were reports of cannibalism. When Marshal Villars inspected the French army in March, he found the troops in a 'deplorable condition, without clothes, without arms and without bread'. On every side came calls for peace.

The French foreign minister, the marquis de Torcy, was sent to Holland to do his utmost to bring it about. Taking a leading Rotterdam banker with him, he went immediately to see Heinsius, who told him that he could do nothing without the authority of the States-General and the States-General could do nothing until 'they knew the sentiments of the Queen of Great Britain by the return of the Duke of Marlborough', who was then on a short visit to England.

Torcy believed, as he put it, that 'at the present conjuncture Marlborough holds the key and there are means of making him choose peace'. He was authorized by King Louis to inform the Duke that His Majesty would be glad for him to receive the reward which had been promised him by the marquis d'Alègre and that, if various matters could be settled, a total of four million livres would be available.

According to Torcy, when this enormous *douceur* was offered him, Marlborough 'reddened and appeared to wish to turn the conversation'. The money did not then change hands; but after prolonged and tedious negotiations it seemed that both sides were satisfied and peace was assured. Writing from The Hague, Marlborough reported to Sarah:

Everything goes so well here that there is no doubt of its ending in a good peace . . . You must have in readiness the sideboard of plate, and you must let the Lord Treasurer know that since the Queen came to the crown I have not had either a canopy or chair of state, which now of necessity I must have, so the wardrobe should have immediate orders.

'I beg,' he added with his usual regard for economy, 'you will take care so that it may serve for part of a bed, when I have done with it here, which I hope will be by the end of the summer.'

Marlborough's hope for a 'good peace' was not to be realized: the terms which Torcy took back to Versailles after days of argument, concession, rewording, flaring tempers, pacification, compromise and intransigence, were not after all acceptable; and, on 7 June 1709, Marlborough wrote to Godolphin:

The Marishall de Villars has given his advice to the King for the venturing a Battel . . . but if that should happen, and God Almighty as hetherto bless with Success the Armes of the Allyes, I think the Queen shou'd then have the honour of insisting upon putting the ffrench Government upon their being againe govern'd by the three Estates.

By then, however, the French army, strengthened by peasants driven into the ranks by hunger, had recovered from its lamentable state in March, whereas Marlborough was worried by his own. Having but recently suffered from one of his frequent prolonged and 'extreame headeakes', he was beset by the problems presented by the now rain-soaked ground and half-empty magazines. 'The account we have concerning forage is so terrible,' he told Godolphin on 9 June, 'that I fear *that* much more than the Marshal de Villars's gasconading.' As for the local inhabitants, it 'grieved [his] heart to see the sad condition all the poor country people are in for want of bread . . . They had not the same countenance they had in other years . . . One must be a brute not to pity them.'

Three days later he and Prince Eugène set out with an escort of 200 horse to reconnoitre the ground over which the forthcoming battle was likely to be fought; and, having presided over several councils of war, he rejected proposals for a frontal attack and proposed instead an advance along the coast by way of Boulogne and Abbeville, then up the Somme on the road to Paris. Prince Eugène, however, was of a different mind. Making light of the advantages the allies would have in being able to use their control of the sea to supply the army in this proposed invasion of France, he suggested instead a siege of the fortress of Tournai; and in this he was supported by most of the other generals as well as by the Dutch deputies, one of whom, Goslinga – characteristically insinuating later that the Duke had favoured a sea route in order to put the harbours along the coast into the hands of the English – recorded that Marlborough gave way 'without hesitation to the views of the Prince' and of the other generals. So, indeed, he might well have been expected to do, since the British troops in the international army he commanded represented scarcely a seventh of its total strength.

For the moment, though, Marlborough could not move in any direction since, as he explained to Heinsius, they needed three or four days of continuous sunshine to dry out the ground, which was at present so wet that to march over it might 'ruin the foot, for, there being no straw in the country, if they [were] obliged to lye on the wet ground, the greatest part of them [would] fall sick'.

By the last week in June, however, the weather had cleared and Marlborough set in motion one of those diversionary marches which he executed with such skill. Marching towards La Bassée, with carts loaded with six days' rations and ammunition, he misled Villars into supposing that he intended to attack his left. The Marshal accordingly withdrew a large part of the garrison from Tournai to reinforce what seemed to be the threatened flank. Then, in the middle of the night, the allied soldiers, having no idea where they were going, were suddenly ordered to march in the opposite direction and, when darkness fell again on 27 June, Tournai's garrison, reduced to a bare 5,000 men, half the number required to defend it, found themselves surrounded by a massive enemy force.

The siege, directed by Marlborough while Prince Eugène commanded the covering army, was a dreadful experience for the allied troops. It was not to be imagined how bad the weather had become again, Marlborough told Sarah. 'The poor soldiers in the trenches are up to their knees in dirt, which gives me the spleen to such a degree that makes me very uneasy, and consequently makes me long for retirement . . . In all likelihood we shall not find forage to enable us to make a long campaign, and that is what I fear the French know as well as we.'

It was essential, therefore, that an assault on Tournai was made as soon as possible, and very soon it was: three attacks were launched on separate gates, one by Prussian troops, one by Saxon and the third by the Dutch. Before there could be a general assault, the town surrendered, the allies having lost over 3,000 men.

The citadel remained in French hands, however; and since the defences which could be seen above ground were so formidable, rendering the fortress, so it was said, 'one of the best fortified places in the world', the besieging force had to approach it underground. And in the dark tunnels, in the mines and countermines, French and allied soldiers, edging forward with picks and shovels, would suddenly come upon each other as the walls of earth between them fell away; and then they would jump and rush upon their enemies, wielding their tools and smashing each other to the ground. From time to time mines would explode, throwing up cascades of earth, burying up to forty bodies at a time, and once killing almost 400 in one deafening explosion. A soldier on the allied side, Private Bishop, reported:

We were prodigious hard at work in sapping the Enemy who sapped under us, and sprung several mines, which stifled great Numbers of our Men. Then those that were above would work with all their Might, in order to give them below Air. By that means we did save some lives . . . [But once] there was almost a whole Regiment of Scotch Hollanders [Scottish troops in the Dutch service] blown up. There was a report spread through all our Army that it was their intention to blow us all up.

And Marlborough wrote to Godolphin:

By the enemy's daily springing of new Mynes our Ingeniers advance so very slowly that the Pr. of Savoye and myself thought it for the Service to Come hether in order to push on the attacks, but as this is the first Siege where we have met with Myns, we find our soldiers apprehend them more than they ought, so that we must have patience for some little time that thay may be used to them.

Another fortnight, therefore, passed by with the soldiers taking 'every Step with Apprehension of being blown up with Mines below them or crushed by the Fall of Earth above them', before, on 31 August, the garrison commander, his supplies almost exhausted, hoisted a flag of surrender.*

A few weeks before, on 27 June, near the Russian town of Poltava, the army of Peter the Great decisively defeated Charles XII, King of Sweden, who, the French King had still hoped, might be persuaded to enter the war on his side. 'Constant success for ten years!' Marlborough commented on the King of Sweden's misfortune. 'Two hours' mismanagement!'

---

* A huge marble bust of King Louis XIV, weighing thirty tons, stood on the citadel. Marlborough thought it would do very well for Blenheim. It was, accordingly, transported to the coast and across the Channel to England. It now stands above the south portico of the palace. 'By a stroke of Providence, the *busto*, complete with luxurious wig and the breath of a moustache, was on just the right scale' (Green, *Blenheim Palace*, 108).

35

THE DUCHESS AND
THE BEDCHAMBER WOMAN

*'. . . a strange competition between one that has gained you
so many battles, and one that is but just worthy to brush
your combs.'*

No sooner had Marlborough accepted the surrender of Tournai than
he marched his army away in the pouring rain to lay siege to Mons.
The French army, commanded by Marshal Villars, also marched
towards Mons, but then turned sharply south to take up a position
near the village of Malplaquet, a position which he himself described
as being 'narrow enough to give the enemy a formidable task in
forcing it, yet well protected by woods on the flanks to prevent our
being overlapped on the flank by superior numbers'.

When Marlborough and Eugène rode out together to reconnoitre
the ground on the misty morning of 9 September 1709, they saw
how well chosen the French position was; and, although the enemy
were energetically making it stronger by throwing up ramparts,
digging trenches, sharpening wooden stakes and chaining together
the trunks of trees, they decided not to attack until they were joined
by a further nineteen battalions still on the march under the command
of General Henry Withers.

Their plan of attack was a simple, not to say unimaginative, one:
the whole French position could not be outflanked, so the allies had
to attack the heavily fortified front, initially on the enemy flanks,
then, once Villars had brought men from his centre to deal with
these attacks on his right and left, massively on the centre.

The onslaught began in the early morning of 11 September as the
allied army marched forward across the sodden landscape. Repulsed,
the men came on again and again, tramping through the mud and
over the bodies of the dead, the Duke of Argyll leading the Buffs

and pulling open his coat to show them that he wore no breastplate. 'In all my life,' wrote Colonel Blackadder of the Cameronians, 'I have not seen dead bodies lie so thick as they were in some places about the retrenchments.' Nor had General Orkney witnessed such slaughter: 'I really think I never saw the like . . . In many places [the dead lay] as ever did a flock of sheep . . . I hope in God it may be the last battle I may ever see . . . None alive ever saw such a battle. God send us a good peace.'

'It was certainly,' said Marlborough, 'a very bloody battle.' 'In so great an action,' he told Godolphin,

it is impossible to get the advantage but by exposing men's lives; but the lamentable sights and thought of it have given me so much disquietude that I believe it is the chief cause [of my subsequent headaches and fever]; for it is melancholy to see so many brave men killed with whom I have lived these eight years.

And Captain Parker wrote:

It was, indeed, the most obstinate and bloody battle that had been fought in the memory of any then living; and our generals were greatly condemned for throwing away so many brave men, when there was not any necessity of coming to a battle . . . It gave a handle to his Grace's enemies at home to exclaim loudly against him.

As many as 24,000 allied troops were thought to have been killed or wounded, a very high proportion of them Dutch, rather less than 2,000 of them British. The French were reported to have lost between 12,000 and 15,000 officers and men, certainly far less than the allies.

The Dutch general Count Oxenstiern fell dead at the side of the Prince of Orange, whose horse collapsed, leaving him to advance on foot. Colonel Cranstoun, hit by a round shot which struck him in the chest and came out at his back, fell from his horse without a word.

The French general Chemerault was killed. His colleague, the chevalier d'Albegotti, was wounded. So was Marshal Villars, who, carried to a nearby cottage, endeavoured to conduct the battle, until he fainted; and, almost as a matter of course, Prince Eugène was also wounded, hit by a bullet behind the ear. Characteristically he refused to withdraw, saying, 'If we are to die here, [the wound] is not worth dressing. If we win, there'll be time to-night.'

In his tent near the mill of Sart, Marlborough sat down to finish a letter to Sarah, which he had begun two days before. Despite the ferocity of the battle, the 'very murdering battle', as he called it in a letter to Godolphin, which had left such heaps of dead – many stripped of their uniforms – upon the churned-up ground, his hand-writing gave no indication of either stress or exhaustion. 'God Almighty be praised,' he wrote to Sarah, 'it is now in our power to have what peace wee please, and I may be pretty well assured of never being in another battel, but that nor nothing in the world can make mee happy if you are not kind.'

It was, as he supposed, his last battle; but it did not give the allies power to have the peace they sought. On the contrary, the French, having inflicted far more casualties on their enemies than they had themselves suffered, could represent the battle as a victory and Marshal Boufflers, who had brought their army off the field in good order, as a hero worthy of comparison with the badly wounded Marshal Villars.

During the days that followed the battle, Marlborough did what he could for the thousands of wounded men, mostly from the allied contingents, Prussian and Dutch, with whom the medical services of the various nationalities had not the capacity to deal. 'I have hardly had time to sleep,' he said, 'being tormented by the several nations for care to be taken of their wounded.' And he sent a message to Marshals Villars and Boufflers asking them to send wagons to take away all the wounded French officers and men – many of whom had 'crept into the neighbouring houses and woods, wounded and in a miserable condition for want of assistance' – asking only for an undertaking from them that they would not serve against the allies again. To Villars he wrote to say how sorry he was to hear of his wound and expressed the wish that he would soon be quite well again.*

*

* Thackeray, who always took the trouble to ensure that his descriptions of military episodes were accurate, provided a convincing account of the gloom that settled over the army in the aftermath of the battle of Malplaquet: 'We dared not speak to each other, even at table, of Malplaquet, so frightful were the gaps left in our army by the cannon of that bloody action. 'Twas heart-rending, for an officer who had a

Before the month of September was over, Marlborough was again conducting the army's operations in laying siege to Mons, during which, to his deep concern, 'poor Cadogan was wound'd in the neck'. 'I hope he will do well,' he told Sarah,

but til he recovers it will oblige me to do many things, by which I shall have but little rest. I was with him this morning when they drest his wound. As he is very fatt there greatest apprehension is [his] growing feaverish. We must have patience for two or three dressings before the surjeans can give their judgement. I hope in God he will do well, for I can intierly depend upon him.

Four days after this letter was written, Mons surrendered; and Marlborough was able to give his full attention to the French request for a general armistice. In order to strengthen his position he had already asked to be appointed Captain-General for life, and he had sent his agent, James Craggs, to London to search for precedents for such an appointment. It was an overly ambitious request, which, once it became known, was the talk of coffee houses in which the pretensions of the man were indignantly discussed: he would not be content with being Captain-General for life; he would soon want to be crowned King John II. Robert Harley had no hesitation in advising the Queen to refuse the Duke's request. Nor did the Queen hesitate to refuse it, having followed Harley's advice and consulted various men likely to urge her to turn down the Duke's application. One of these was the Duke of Argyll, who had recently returned home and was improbably said to have told the Queen, 'Your Majesty need not be in pain, for I would undertake whenever you

---

heart, to look down his line on a parade-day afterwards and miss hundreds of faces of comrades – humble or of high rank – that had gathered but yesterday full of courage and cheerfulness round the torn and blackened flags. Where were our friends? As the great Duke reviewed us, riding along our lines with his fine suite of prancing aides-de-camp and generals, stopping here and there to thank an officer with those eager smiles and bows of which his Grace was always lavish, scarce a huzza could be got for him, though Cadogan, with an oath, up and cried – "D—n you, why don't you cheer?" But the men had no heart for that, not one of them but was thinking, "Where's my comrade . . . that fought by me?" 'Twas the most gloomy pageant . . . and the Te Deum sung by our chaplains, the most woeful and dreary satire' (*The History of Henry Esmond, Esq.*, Book 3, ch. 1).

command to seize the Duke at the head of his troops and bring him away dead or alive.'

Relations between the Marlboroughs and the Queen had for some time been growing increasingly worse, as the tone of her letter of refusal of the Duke's request to be appointed Captain-General for life, coupled with the intimation of his wish to resign his active command at the end of the war, made quite clear:

I saw very plainly your uneasiness at my refusing the mark of favour you desired, and believed from another letter I had from you on that subject you fancied the advice came from Masham; but, I do assure you, you wrong her most extremely, for upon my word she knows nothing of it . . .

You seem to be dissatisfied with my behaviour to the Duchess of Marlborough. I do not love complaining, but it is impossible to help saying on this occasion I believe nobody was ever used by a friend as I have been by her . . . I desire nothing but that she should leave off teasing and tormenting me, and behave herself with the decency she ought . . . and this I hope you will make her do.

Marlborough and Godolphin were tiresome enough in the Queen's eyes, if not quite as tiresome as the extreme Whigs; but the Duchess was intolerable, all the more so because the Queen could scarcely dismiss her from her offices without creating deeper troubles for herself.

Increasingly, almost pathologically, jealous of the influence of Mrs Masham,⋆ the Duchess plagued the Queen with her grievances, writing tart and grumpy letters, asking for favours which she knew could not be granted, insinuating that she harboured an unnatural desire for her indulged companion, and deriving perverse pleasure in having further grievances to complain of, bothering the Duke with letters requiring him to share her sense of injury, and complaining of his lack of support and understanding when he told her that it had

---

⋆ One day in 1710 the Duchess said to Bubb Dodington, the rich diarist, 'Young man, you come from Italy; they tell me of a new invention there called caricature drawing. Can you find someone that will make me a caricature of [Mrs] Masham describing her covered with running sores and ulcers that I may send to the Queen to give her a slight idea of her favourite?' (George, *English Political Caricature to 1792*, 12).

always been his 'Observation in Disputes' that 'all Reproaches, though ever so just, serve to no End but making the Breach wider'. He advised her to withdraw to a more retired life and not bother the Queen by petty and impossible requests.

One such request was for some recently vacated rooms at St James's Palace which would make it easier for the Duchess to obtain access to her own apartments. She maintained these rooms had been promised to her as soon as they became empty. The Queen, who had promised them to Mrs Masham, said she did not recall that the Duchess had ever spoken to her about them.

'But suppose I am mistaken, surely my request cannot be deemed unreasonable,' Sarah protested, according to her own account of the interview.

'I have a great many servants of my own,' the Queen told her, 'and some of them I must find room for.'

'Your Majesty then does not reckon Lord Marlborough or me among your servants? . . . It would be thought still more strange were I to repeat this conversation and inform the world that, after all Lord Marlborough's services, Your Majesty refuses to give him a miserable hole to make a clear entry to his lodgings. I beg, therefore, to know whether I am at liberty to repeat this to any of my friends.'

After a lengthy pause the Queen said she might repeat it if she wished.

'I hope Your Majesty will reflect upon all that has passed,' the Duchess said impertinently before leaving the room.

Not content to leave the matter there, she sat down to write one of her long, reproachful and insolent letters, setting down the services she had rendered the Queen in the past, reminding her of her sinfulness in taking the Sacrament when harbouring feelings of enmity and demanding to know the cause of Her Majesty's displeasure.

'It is impossible for you to recover my former kindness,' the Queen replied. 'But I shall behave myself to you as the Duke of Marlborough's wife and as my Groom of the Stole.'

Exploiting the Queen's growing antipathy were Abigail Masham and Mrs Masham's kinsman, Robert Harley, who was now master of the Tory party and at pains to do all he could to persuade his colleagues that the Whigs were bent upon leading the country to perdition and that the ambitions not only of the Duchess of Marlborough but those of the Duke also must be thwarted. The notoriously avaricious Duke, Harley hinted, was in favour of prolonging the war to line his own pockets, which were already bulging with the profits he had made out of it. Nor was it only money he was after: he actually had it in mind to usurp the authority of the Queen, who had raised him to his ill-deserved eminence and who was being treated with such disgraceful disrespect by his wife. Admittedly, his army had won some notable victories. But at what appalling cost! He had sent tens of thousands of men to their deaths; their corpses lay thick upon the battlefields of Europe and he had taken good care to ensure that he had not shared their fate.

The increasingly discordant relations between the court and the Marlboroughs were now greatly exacerbated by what seemed at first a quite trivial matter. On 10 January 1710 Lieutenant-General the Earl of Essex, Constable of the Tower of London and Colonel of the 4th Regiment of Dragoons, died; and candidates had to be found worthy of succeeding him in these appointments. It was the custom in such circumstances for the Captain-General to be consulted for his advice as to suitable candidates. Marlborough intended recommending the Duke of Northumberland as Constable of the Tower; but when he submitted Northumberland's name to the Queen, she told him, 'Your Grace has come too late.' On the advice of Harley, she had already appointed one of his supporters, the handsome and dissolute Lord Rivers. For the command of the Dragoons, Marlborough suggested the Duke of Somerset's son, Lord Hertford, only to be similarly rebuffed: he received a letter from the Queen informing him that she had already made the appointment to that post also. To his astonishment and dismay, the Duke read that Her Majesty's candidate, chosen over the heads of numerous other, more worthy candidates, was Colonel John Hill, Mrs Masham's ill-qualified brother.

Well aware that the rejection of his advice in favour of such an unsuitable choice was most likely to be interpreted in the army as an indication that the Queen had lost faith in her Captain-General and would encourage his critics in their murmurs against him, Marlborough decided that he could not accept this rebuff and, having ensured that he would have the support of his friends, he sought another audience of the Queen to point out the inadvisability of Colonel Hill's appointment and the disaffection it was likely to arouse in the army as a whole as well as in the 4th Dragoons in particular.

The Queen, however, cold and distant, stood her ground: she had decided that Colonel Hill was a suitable candidate for the colonelcy and the colonelcy he must have. According to Sarah, the Duke 'could not draw one kind expression from her', while he, for his part, was clearly and unaccustomedly angry. 'It is, Madam,' he said, referring to Hill's appointment, 'to set up a standard of disaffection to rally all the malcontent officers in the Army.'

Soon after this audience, without taking their leave of the Queen, the Duke and Duchess left London for the Ranger's Lodge at Windsor; and, at a subsequent meeting of the Cabinet, Marlborough's chair was unoccupied. The ministers, unwilling to support him in his proposed demand that the Queen must choose between Mrs Masham and himself, made no reference to his absence. Nor did the Queen, from whose presence the Duke had departed in so harassed an emotional state that, when he returned to his wife, there were, she said, 'tears in his Eyes which was a very unusuall thing in him'.

At the Ranger's Lodge, the Duke and Duchess settled down to compose a letter to the Queen, placing his demand on record. When they had finished the draft, it was sent to Godolphin for his comment. Godolphin, hoping to bring about some sort of compromise in the painful and dangerous situation, was afraid that the letter might well make it more intractable than it already seemed to be. So did those Whigs with whom he discussed the matter. Lord Somers, a former Lord Chancellor and leading member of the Whig Junto, was asked to approach the Queen on the Duke's behalf.

'May I,' he said to her, 'take the liberty to observe that the Duke of Marlborough is not to be considered merely as a private subject, because all the eyes of Europe are fixed upon him, and business is transacted with him under the notion of one who is honoured with your Majesty's entire trust and favour . . . The Army also unanimously obeys him.'

The Queen listened without paying marked attention to what was said, made some brief allusion to the Duke's services, then allowed Somers to depart without entering any further upon the reason for his asking to see her.

'If this business can be well ended, which I must doubt,' the Duchess told a friend, 'there must always be an entire union, as I have ever wished, between Lord Marlborough and the Whigs. But he will not say so much as he thinks upon that subject at this time because I believe he imagines it would have an ill air, and look like making a bargain for help.'

With the Whig Junto wavering in his support and with Godolphin advising caution, Marlborough, reluctant to stand alone – as he usually was in such circumstances – decided to modify the draft of the letter he proposed writing to the Queen and to omit from it a specific threat that he would resign if Mrs Masham were not dismissed. His letter now ran:

By what I hear from London, I find your Majesty is pleased to think you are of the opinion that you are in the right in giving Mr Hill the Earl of Essex's regiment. I beg your Majesty will be so just to me as not to think that I can be so unreasonable as to be mortified to the degree that I am, if it did proceed only from this one thing. It must be a prejudice to your service, while I have the honour to command the army, to have men preferred by my professed enemies to the prejudice of general officers of great merit and long service . . . Let me beg your Majesty to reflect what [those] who have been witnesses of the love and zeal and duty with which I have served you . . . must think when they see, after all I have done, it is not able to protect me against the malice of a bedchamber woman.

On receipt of this letter the Queen – who had by then decided 'not to insist on the appointment of Colonel Hill to the regiment' – sent for Godolphin and showed him the letter. It was, he thought, 'a very good letter'.

'Do you think,' the Queen asked him, 'the conclusion of it is good?'

Godolphin contented himself with observing that it showed how mortified the Duke was. The Queen said she would reply to it. But she did not do so. Her ministers were now inclined to the view that Her Majesty, by not insisting on Hill's appointment, had gone far enough to satisfy the Duke, who was persuaded to return to London.

Marlborough himself still wished to demand Mrs Masham's resignation as his price for remaining at the head of the army; but both Godolphin and the Junto pressed him not to go so far, and, the Duke, still unwilling to proceed alone, gave way to their advice.

So the Queen, content in the knowledge that he would not now insist on the removal of 'the bedchamber woman', welcomed him with some show of her former regard. And it was, so she replied to an address from the Commons, 'with a just sense of the Duke of Marlborough's eminent services' that she agreed to his being sent back to the Continent as 'general and plenipotentiary', the man 'most capable of discharging two such important trusts'. The Duchess's comment on the whole affair was characteristic: it had been, she told the Queen, 'a strange competition between one that has gained you so many battles, and one that is but just worthy to brush your combs'.

25. Marlborough pointing at a plan of Bouchain held by his chief engineer, John Armstrong. Of this portrait by an unknown artist, probably Enoch Seeman, the Duchess told one of her grandchildren, 'I really think that picture of your grandfather with Mr Armstrong as like him as ever I saw ... and [the artist] was so humble as to ask me 77 guineas for both figures.'

26. Tapestry depicting the battle of Blenheim, woven by Judocus de Vos after Lambert de Hondt. In the foreground a grenadier furls a captured standard.

27. Eugène, Prince of Savoy, in the war against the Turks, c. 1700. A painting of the contemporary Dutch school.

28. Marshal the duc de Villars, painted in 1714 after Hyacinthe Rigaud.

29. Sébastien Le Prestre de Vauban, the great military engineer: a portrait attributed to Charles Le Brun.

30. A detail of the tapestry at Blenheim Palace depicting the siege of Bouchain, woven by Judocus de Vos after Lambert de Hondt.

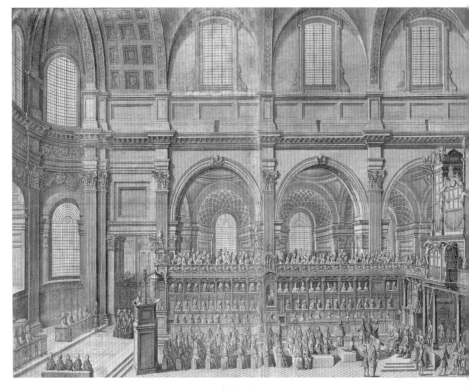

31. The thanksgiving service in St Paul's Cathedral for the victory at Ramillies, in 1706, attended by Queen Anne and members of both Houses of Parliament: an engraving by Robert Trevitt.

32. Sir Godfrey Kneller's portrait of Marlborough in 1712, after his dismissal.

33. Hester Santlow, the dancer with whom Marlborough was rumoured to be having an affair, portrayed as a harlequin woman by John Ellys.

34. Lady Mary Churchill, Marlborough's daughter, with her husband John, second Duke of Montagu, and their daughter Lady Mary Montagu, c. 1730, by Gawen Hamilton.

35. An engraving of a view by C.V. Fielding, 1796. Blenheim Palace is seen in the distance across the park. Vanbrugh's bridge is behind the trees on the right.

36

THE QUEEN AND THE DUCHESS

'As soon as she had done raving, she flounced out of the room,
and said she did not care if she never saw her more . . .'

The Duchess continued to plague the Queen with her complaints and demands. Before he left the country, Sarah had persuaded her husband to ask the Queen to grant her permission to spend most of her time away from court, even though her duties as Groom of the Stole required her presence in London. She also asked that, when the war was over, she might be allowed to resign the office in favour of her daughters Henrietta and Anne.

The Queen was only too ready to give permission for her obstreperous Groom of the Stole to remain in the country for as long as she liked; but that her daughters should succeed her was more than she was prepared to grant. When the Duchess protested that Her Majesty had already consented to this, the Queen replied, 'I do not remember that I was ever spoke to about it.' And when the Duchess persisted in her claim, Her Majesty told her crossly, 'I desire that I may never be troubled any more on the subject.'

Thereafter Sarah rarely spoke of the Queen without making some contentious or insulting remark, which was as likely as not to be repeated and to find its way to Mrs Masham and thence to the Queen.

The Queen was a ready target for such calumnies. She was only forty-five but frequent pregnancies and illnesses had aged her prematurely. The year before she had struck Sir John Clerk, one of the commissioners for the union with Scotland, which had taken place in 1707, as being the most dispicable mortal [I] had ever seen in any station. The poor lady as I saw her twice before, was again under a severe fit of gout, and in extreme pain and agony, ill-dressed, bloated in her countenance, and surrounded with plaisters, cataplaisma [poultices] and dirty-like rags . . . Her face, which was red and spotted, was rendered something frightful by her negligent dress.

She found difficulty in walking up the stairs and frequently had to be carried up in a chair, eventually being lowered through a trapdoor into the room below and hauled up again by means of ropes and pulleys as Henry VIII had been. Too fat to ride, she still drove after the hounds in Windsor Forest at a furious place, 'like Jehu', so Jonathan Swift told Esther Johnson, the 'Stella' of his *Journal*. She drove herself in a narrow, one-horsed calash with extraordinarily high wheels which carried her rattling through cornfields and across the most formidable obstacles.

She had hoped that the waters which were brought up every day from a well on the far side of Eton would cure her dropsical complaint, but they proved useless. So did the medicines, restoratives and drugs which her doctors prescribed, the oil of millipedes, the spa water, the hiera picra, the quinine, the laudanum, 'Sir Walter Raleigh's Cordial', the bleeding and the cupping, the aperients and emmenagogues, the aloes and canella. She spent long hours looking out across the fields and woods at Windsor, sitting in the large and heavy chair in which Colonel Parke had found her when bringing news of Marlborough's great victory at Blenheim years before. Her once beautiful hands were red and swollen and it was only with difficulty that she could sign her name. She was really in no fit state to deal with the lectures and harangues to which she was subjected by her Groom of the Stole.

Lord Dartmouth, a future Secretary of State for the Southern Department, was given an account, by one of the Queen's ladies, of a characteristic harangue:

Mrs Danvers who was then in waiting told me that the duchess reproached her for above an hour with her own and her family's services, in so loud and shrill a voice, that the footmen at the bottom of the back-stairs could hear her: and all this storm was raised for the queen's having ordered a bottle of wine a day to be allowed for her laundress, without her acquainting her grace with it. The queen, seeing her so outrageous, got up, to have gone out of the room: the duchess clapped her back against the door, and told her that she should hear her out, for that was the least favour she could do her, in return for having set and kept the crown upon her head. As soon as she had done raging, she flounced out of the room, and said she did not care if she never saw her more: to which the queen replied very calmly, that she thought the seldomer the better.

When the Duchess learned that stories about her reckless indiscretions and impertinent comments about the Queen, much exaggerated in the telling, had reached Windsor Castle, she demanded an audience so that she could contradict them. The Queen did all she could to avoid so painful an experience, making excuses on three separate occasions when it was suggested that the Duchess might come and, on a fourth, cancelling the appointment and setting out for Kensington.

The importunate Duchess, refusing to be put off in this way, followed the Queen to Kensington, where, so she said herself, having told a page of the backstairs to inform the Queen that she was waiting to see her, she sat down in an antechamber 'like a Scotch lady with a petition, instead of a trusted and lifelong confidante'.

Eventually she was admitted to the Queen's room, where Her Majesty interrupted the flow of her denials and protests by observing, 'Whatever you have to say, you may put it in writing.' She repeated these words four or five times as the Duchess persisted in her indignant claim that she merely wished to make it plain that she had not made the insulting remarks of which she stood accused. The Queen turned her face away, but still the Duchess continued to state her case: there were 'those about the Queen' who made her believe stories which were totally false; she was no more capable of saying such things as she was of killing her children; she 'seldom spoke of Her Majesty in company and never without respect'. To this the Queen replied equivocally, 'Without doubt there are many lies told.' She then reminded the Duchess that in her letter asking for an audience she had written that Her Majesty would not be obliged to answer what she would have to say in her own defence, 'You desired no answer and shall have none.' The Queen repeated the words several times before rising with great difficulty from her chair and limping to the door.

'When she came to the door,' so the Duchess continued her account, 'I fell down in great disorder. Streams of tears flowed down against my will and prevented me speaking for some time.' Witnessing this display, the Queen evidently took pity on the woman, and allowed her to continue with her protests, which were from time to time interrupted by the refrain, 'You desired no answer, and you shall have none.'

Defeated at last, the Duchess withdrew with the parting shot, 'I am confident your Majesty will suffer in this world or the next for such an instance of inhumanity.' She then swept from the room and, having sat down for a moment in the Gallery to wipe her eyes before she 'came within sight of anybody', she left Kensington Palace in what the Abbé Gaultier, a French envoy in London, described as 'a fury'.

When she gave her husband an account of this episode, he sensibly advised her not to 'expose [herself] any more in speaking to her masjesty'. In fact, she had no opportunity of doing so, for neither at Windsor nor at St James's or Kensington did the Duchess ever see the Queen alone again.

She was, however, not prepared to stop writing to her, 'whatever resolution Lord Marl. might make'. Although she solemnly protested that she would 'not have more to doe with her than other ladys for all the treasure on earth', she was determined to go on writing and to 'vex her soe much as to convince even her own stupid understanding that she has used me ill & then lett her shutt herself up with Mrs Masham'.

Although she was to see the Queen only once again, she received comforting reports about her and Mrs Masham from Arthur Maynwaring, the witty satirist, devoted lover of the actress Mrs Oldfield, member of the Kit-Cat Club and Whig Member of Parliament for West Looe, whom the Duchess described as her 'secretary' and others as her 'spy'.

'In all the days of my life,' he reported in one satisfying letter, having seen Mrs Masham one day at court, 'I never saw so odious a creature, and she was so extream hot that her Fan work'd like a windmill . . . I do really believe the creature is rotten & shou'd be removed as Card[inal] Wolsey was design'd to be for his stinking breath [lest] sacred majesty shou'd be infected.'

At The Hague the Duke and Prince Eugène were considering what form the campaign of 1710 should take. There were two alternatives: the allies, having taken Tournai, could either march to the coast and, relying on the British navy for support, make for Abbeville and Paris. Or they could invade France by the most direct route, attacking the enemy centre and advancing on Douai and Arras.

Having agreed with Prince Eugène that they should make this frontal attack, and having marched forty miles in three days without meeting any opposition, Marlborough was able to write to Sarah from Lens, north of Vimy Ridge, on 22 April 1710:

In my last I had but just time to tell you that we had passed the lines [from which the French had retreated]. I hope this happy beginning will produce such success this campaign as must put an end to the war. I bless God for putting it into their heads not to defend their lines . . . God be praised, we have come here without the loss of any men. The excuse the French make is, that we came four days before they expected us.

A week later the lines of circumvallation were completed around Douai. But it was more than another week before the siege train of 200 guns arrived; and not until 11 May that these guns opened fire on the fortress; and by that time Marshal Villars, although still suffering from the wound in his leg, was on the march towards the allied army and, by the end of the month, both Marlborough and Prince Eugène thought that a battle might well be imminent. The Duke reported to Godolphin:

Marshal Villars' army increases every day . . . He gives out that his army will be 160,000 strong . . . But I believe, by the sickness they have at this time in their foot, we have as many men as they . . . I am this day [sixty years old]; but, I thank God, I find myself in so good health that I hope to end this campaign without being sensible of the inconveniences of old age.

Although his physical health was good, however, the Duke was in increasingly low spirits. There had been days that spring when, so he confessed to Sarah, he felt 'so weary' that he was 'very indifferent' as to how anything went and longed only for a 'quiet life'. To add to his troubles, the engineers were incompetent, and Douai did not surrender until the end of June, when the commander of its garrison, chevalier d'Albegotti, marched out to be invited to dinner by the Duke and Prince Eugène. By then the allies had lost 8,000 men in the capture of the fortress and the campaign, begun well enough, had come almost to a standstill.

As he repeated in a letter to Godolphin, Marlborough now longed more than ever for an end to the war. He confessed he did not have 'the same sanguine, prophetic spirit' he used to have. He was deeply upset by the carping remarks which he knew were being made about him by disgruntled officers under his command, among others by the Earl of Orrery, who attributed his disappointment in not being promoted to the rank of major-general to the 'exorbitant power' exercised in the army by 'His Highness', who, so Orrery complained to Harley, 'plainly disposes of preferments here with no other view but to create a faction sufficient to support him against the Queen and her friends in case every other prop should fail'.

The Duke of Argyll, jealous of the Duke's high reputation and success, was equally critical of the conduct of 'the mighty Prince of Blenheim', as Marlborough well knew. 'The discourse of the Duke of Argyll,' he told Godolphin, 'is that when I please there will then be a peace; I suppose his friends speak the same language in England, so that I must every summer venture my life in a battle, and be found fault with in the winter for not bringing home a peace, though I wish for it with all my heart and soul.'

Marlborough's depression was exacerbated by the misery to be encountered on all sides amid the country people. 'At least one half of the people of the villages' were dead, and the rest looked as though they had just come out of their graves. It was so 'mortifying that no

Christian [could] see it without wishing with all his heart for a speedy peace'.

There was much sickness also among his own men. His steward died of typhus; so did his 'poor coachman', who had been with him so long. His 'favourite cook', Daniel, seemed likely to follow them; his beloved dog, 'poor Tulliar', was also dead.

At the beginning of July, he and Prince Eugène hoped still to take Arras, but when they came up against the newly constructed French lines outside the fortress they deemed the position too strong to attack. So they turned their attention north to Béthune, which surrendered, after the loss of a further 3,500 men, on 29 August, the day upon which the Duke of Argyll wrote to Harley:

The town of Béthune has deigned to capitulate . . . What our mighty Prince of Blenheim will think of doing afterwards I know not; but if we [are] to take any more towns, our infantry will be quite destroyed and our horse so much out of order that we shall be obliged to stay as long in garrison next spring as the enemy, and I don't know but his Grace may think it his interest to have it so.

From Béthune the army moved north to take Saint-Venant, which did not fall until the end of the following month; and it was not until 9 November that the fortress of Aire, a few miles to the east of Saint-Venant, also surrendered after the allies had suffered heavy losses of 7,000 men, excluding the sick, many of whom, 'poor men', as Marlborough said, had been 'up to their knees in water' in the appalling winter weather.

Depressed as he was by the very heavy losses which he had suffered in this his ninth campaign, Marlborough was also saddened and frustrated by what was simultaneously happening in England, where events made him 'every minute wish to be a hermit', and where his recent unremarkable achievements were contrasted with the triumphs of earlier years, much as he had endeavoured to do to magnify their importance in the letters and dispatches he sent home.

His base at home was being undermined by those whom he described in a letter to Sarah dated 19 May as 'tigers and wolves'.

I hear of so many disagreeable things that make it very reasonable both for myself and you to take no steps but what may lead to a quiet life. This being the case, am I not to be pitied, that am every day in danger for exposing my life for the good of those who are seeking my ruin?

He had a 'heavy heart', he told her in another letter. 'The present humours in England give me a good deal of trouble; for I cannot see how it is possible they should mend till everything is yet worse.'

Already in April the Queen, advised by Robert Harley, so Marlborough supposed, had dismissed the Whig Lord Chamberlain, the Marquess of Kent, and, without consulting either Marlborough or Godolphin, had appointed the Duke of Shrewsbury in his place. Then, as a threat to Marlborough's authority in the army, Colonel Samuel Masham, Abigail's husband, and Colonel John Hill, her brother, were both raised to the rank of brigadier, although neither was high enough on the colonels' list, as submitted by the Duke, to qualify for such promotion. Marlborough had wanted to protest, but the Whigs once again would not support him. Nor would they do so when the next blow fell, the removal from office as Secretary of State of his son-in-law Charles, Earl of Sunderland.

The Duke had long feared that he would be dismissed and that thereafter 'everything [would be] in confusion'. 'I am sorry Lord Sunderland is not agreeable to the Queen,' he had written on 9 June to Godolphin in a letter intended for Her Majesty's eyes.

But his being, at this time, singled out, has no other reason but that of being my son-in-law. When this appears in its true light, I am very confident every man in England will be sensible that my enemies have prevailed to have this done, in order to make it impossible for me, with honour, to continue at the head of this glorious army, that has, through the whole course of this war, been blessed by God with surprising successes.

Sunderland accepted his dismissal with dignified equanimity and when the Queen, conscious of the fact that she had no reason for dismissing him other than a personal distaste for him, offered him a generous pension of £3,000 a year, Sunderland refused it with the words, 'If I cannot have the honour of serving my country, I will not plunder it.' 'It is true indeed,' the Queen had written sharply to Godolphin the day before,

that the turning a son-in-law out of his office may be a mortification to the Duke of Marlborough; but must the fate of Europe depend on that, and must he be gratified in all his desires, and I not in so reasonable a thing as parting with a man whom I took into my service with all the uneasiness imaginable, and whose behaviour to me has been so ever since, and who, I must add, is obnoxious to all people except a few [?] . . . I have no thoughts of taking the Duke of Marlborough from the head of the army [she added the next day when there was widespread talk that both Godolphin and Marlborough were about to hand in their resignations] . . . and if he and you should do so wrong a thing at any time, especially at this critical juncture, as to desert my service, what confusion would happen would be at your door, and you alone would be answerable and nobody else, but I hope you will both consider better of it.

This letter was followed by another, to Marlborough, more tact-fully phrased and signed by thirteen of the Queen's ministers, includ-ing the Duke of Newcastle, Lord Privy Seal, Lord Somers, President of the Council, and Lord Cowper, now Lord Chancellor, who expressed themselves as being 'fully convinced that it [was] impossible for your Grace to quit the service at this time without the utmost hazard to the whole Alliance'. 'We must therefore conjure you,' these ministers continued,

by the glory you have already obtained, by the many services you have done your Queen and country, by the expectation you have justly raised in all Europe, and by all that is dear and tender to you at home, whose chief dependance is upon your success, that you should not leave this great work unfinished, but continue at the head of the Army.

To this plea the Austrian Emperor, addressing him as 'Illustrious Cousin and most dear Prince', added his voice. So did Heinsius, who begged him not to 'give way to vexation, but on the contrary, to prove by the continuation of [his] service that [he] took the common cause more to heart than the resentment he felt'.

Lord Ailesbury, living in Brussels, where Marlborough went to visit him after the campaign of 1710 was over, did his best to comfort and reassure him. He felt the man needed all the solace he could find, particularly so as, thinking his morning levees would be 'as crowded as heretofore', the Duke had been disillusioned by being visited by no more than 'two or three insignificant persons', 'a true emblem', Ailesbury commented, 'of this selfish and flattering world'.

'My Lord, you seem melancholy,' Ailesbury said to him by way of greeting. 'I thought you understood an English court better than to be surprised at changes . . . One is as sure of keeping an employment at Constantinople as in London . . . You have a fine family and a great and noble seat. Go down thither, live quietly and retired, and you may laugh at your enemies.'

Marlborough could not, however, bring himself to live quietly yet; and he was as much concerned as anyone else to discover what Count von Gallas, the Imperial ambassador, described as the question uppermost in everyone's mind in London: whether or not the Queen would confine her important changes to Sunderland.

A deputation of Directors of the Bank of England asked for an audience of the Queen, at which they put to her this very question, since the rumours of a change of government were undermining all credit. She told them that she did not intend to make any more changes for the moment. But ministers themselves believed that the position of Lord Godolphin as Lord Treasurer was now far from secure.

The Queen still saw him from time to time, but his advice was rarely followed and on occasions ostentatiously ignored. He had not been informed when Robert Harley's friend, the Duke of Shrewsbury, was appointed Lord Chamberlain; and when he nominated men for appointments in his own department his suggestions were overlooked.

Yet for Marlborough's sake and for the good of the allied cause, he clung to the office of Lord Treasurer, which enabled him to ensure that the army received its supplies and pay. He could not suppose, however, that he would be able to retain his office much longer. 'It will be no great surprise to you,' he warned Marlborough, 'to hear in some very short time that I am no longer in a capacity for doing you any further service.'

It was, indeed, not long before the axe fell. On 8 August Godolphin received a letter from the Queen:

The uneasiness which you have showed for some time has given me very much trouble . . . And the very unkind returns I have received . . . makes it impossible for me to continue you any longer in my service; but I will give you a pension of four thousand a year and I desire that, instead of bringing the staff to me, you will break it, which I believe will be easier for us both.

In obedience to these instructions, Godolphin broke the white staff of the office of Lord Treasurer which he had held for so many years and threw the pieces into an empty grate. His dismissal, which gave Marlborough 'very melancholy thoughts', was followed by that of his son from the office of Cofferer to the Royal Household and by the appointment of Mrs Masham's kinsman, Robert Harley, Marlborough's *bête noire*, as Chancellor of the Exchequer and, in effect if not in name, the Queen's First Minister. Harley formed an entirely Tory ministry; and in the general election in October 1710 the Tories triumphed at the polls with a majority of 170 over the Whigs.

Believing that the dismissal of his faithful friend might induce Marlborough to resign his command, Godolphin wrote to him, urging him 'by no means to think of leaving' his post and assuring him that nothing could ever make him neglect doing all that he could for the Duke's 'honour and safety'.

The Duke, in return, did what he could to make Godolphin's enforced retirement less unpleasant. A widower with little money, his innate honesty having prevented his enriching himself as others in his position might well have done, Godolphin had no need of financial help – which, it was alleged, it would have greatly pained Marlborough to give him – since his elder brother died that month, leaving him £4,000 a year, a most welcome sum, all the more so because the pension the Queen had offered him did not materialize. The Duke and Duchess pressed Godolphin to stay with them whenever he cared to do so; and, grateful for this offer, he spent much of the rest of his life at Holywell.

37

THE DUCHESS DISMISSED

'The Duke had a very cold reception.'

Within hours of Godolphin's dismissal, the Queen assured Marlborough that she would take care that the army would 'want for nothing'. But the Duke's remaining in command of that army, now power in London had so completely changed hands, was more than ever in doubt; and, at the beginning of September, Marlborough told Sarah that the Amsterdam *Gazette* had announced that a British envoy, Lord Rivers, had been sent from London to Hanover to offer the command to the Elector. Marlborough told his wife that he wished the Elector would accept the offer, since it might free him from all the 'incumbrances [he] now lay under'; but that he doubted that either the Dutch or Prince Eugène would agree to it.

As it happened, however, the Elector did not approve of it either, writing to Marlborough to tell him that he hoped that nothing would induce the Queen to take the command of the army from a general who had 'acquitted himself with so much glory and so much success'.

Yet, while his enemies in the new administration were disappointed in their endeavours to arrange his enforced supersession in command of the army, they now did all they could to engineer his resignation. Among these new antagonistic ministers was Henry St John, Secretary of State for the Northern Department.

Able and ambitious, the Old Etonian grandson of the second Earl of Warwick, St John was thirty-two years old at the time of his appointment. In his earlier youth he had been wild and irresponsible. A heavy drinker, living with a woman described as the 'most expensive demirep of the kingdom', he had, it was said, once 'run naked through the park in a fit of intoxication'. Marriage to an heiress 'did not improve his morals', but, having been elected to the House of Commons as Member for the family borough of Wootton-Bassett in Wiltshire, he became less irresponsible, though no less unscrupulous, and was soon recognized as a talented speaker, a highly promising supporter of Robert Harley.

Although he had, as recently as 1708, as Secretary-at-War, been on terms of the closest friendship with Marlborough who, both liking and trusting him, had arranged for his allowance to be raised and even, it was believed, helped him to pay off his debts, St John, the 'ungrateful rogue' as Sarah referred to him, was now as resolute as any of his fellow ministers in their attacks on Marlborough. He wrote of him scornfully in his letters and joined with his colleagues in doing all they could to demonstrate that he no longer enjoyed any political influence. Denying promotion to his known supporters, they favoured and encouraged his critics, and used all manner of means to provoke his departure.

Exasperated and wounded though he was, the Duke did not give way, encouraged by the support given him by the Elector of Hanover, who threatened to withdraw his troops from the alliance if Marlborough felt obliged to resign, by the King of Prussia, who made a similar threat, and by Prince Eugène, who let it be known that he would not serve in Flanders if the Duke did not serve with him.

Meanwhile the provocation continued, and the Queen added her share. Prompted by Lord Orrery, one of his most persistent critics, who suggested in a letter to Harley that she should grant leave for him and the Duke of Argyll to return to England without the customary courtesy of their asking permission of the Captain-General, the Queen obediently gave her consent.

'This is so very extraordinary a step,' Marlborough commented in a letter to Godolphin, 'that even the Duke of Argyll came to me yesterday to assure me that he had made no application [directly to the Queen] and that, when he should desire to go for England, he should apply to me for my leave. The folly and ingratitude of the Queen make me sick and weary of everything.'

As though to give Marlborough further anguish, the Duke of Argyll – of whom the Duke said, 'I cannot have a worse opinion of anybody than of the Duke of Argyll' – was now promoted general of infantry. 'After everything that has taken place between him and Marlborough during the last two campaigns, the appointment will cause Marlborough vexation,' reported Johann von Hoffman, the Imperial envoy in London. 'This is, however, what it is meant to do. He will be insulted until he resigns voluntarily.'

Certainly, the insults continued. Three generals who were all his friends, Meredith, Honeywood and George Macartney, were reported to have drunk to the health of the Duke in camp and had joined their toast with another to the damnation of his enemies in the new administration, naming in particular Robert Harley. Although they were all capable officers, if not, in Macartney's case, much respected for character, they were immediately cashiered without further enquiry.

'All officers speak on behalf of the three,' wrote Hoffman in another of his reports. 'If generals are to be cashiered on information supplied by an informer, even the most guiltless are no longer secure. Macartney [a Member of Parliament as well as a general] admits freely that he had drunk to the confusion of Marlborough's opponents. But having punished these three officers, they really ought to punish the whole army.'

To add to Marlborough's resentment, the Earl of Orrery, an outspokenly dissident officer, who had long hankered after the rank, was promoted major-general to fill one of the vacancies created by the cashiering of Macartney, Meredith and Honeywood; while the Earl of Orkney, another dissident, husband of William III's mistress, Elizabeth Villiers, was appointed Colonel of the Fusiliers.

Then there was an unfortunate episode in the House of Lords, when Lord Scarborough, an elderly, indecisive man who had been an intimate friend of Charles II, unwisely proposed that the Duke of Marlborough should be officially thanked for the great military successes of the past year. This gave the Duke of Argyll the opportunity to rise and ask indignantly, 'What reason can there be for such a message of thanks, unless custom is to be made the reason? Four strongholds have no doubt been captured; but only one of them, Douai, is of importance. The other three have cost the best blood of the army.'

Argyll was warmly supported by two other generals, Lords North and Grey; and, in the face of such opposition, Lord Scarborough tamely withdrew his proposal. 'One would imagine,' St John commented with satisfaction in a letter to one of his correspondents, John Drummond, a Scottish merchant in Amsterdam who acted as the new administration's chief intelligence and political agent in Holland, 'that Lord Scarborough was hired by somebody who wished the Duke of Marlborough ill to take so ill-concerted and ridiculous a measure.'

The Duke himself feared that such crass attempts to praise him, as well as the attacks upon him by Argyll and Orrery and their friends, would undermine his authority and reduce his popularity in the army. But far from this being the case, his reputation with both officers and men – whose pay and food he had always taken such care to see supplied – remained as high as ever. So did his reputation among the allied leaders, as John Drummond was at pains to point out to St John and Harley:

It is not for his person, but for the public good that I argue or presume to meddle in so important an affair, for well do I know all his vices as well as his virtues, and I know as well that though his covetousness has gained much reproach and ill-will . . . yet his success in the field, his capacity or rather dexterity in council . . . and his personal acquaintance with the heads of the Alliance and the faith they have in him, make him still the great man with them, and on whom they depend . . .

There is no Englishman who they have any opinion of for the command of an army but himself . . . and his agreeing so well with Prince Eugen is one of their greatest contentments . . .

Pensionary Buys came to me two days after Lord Rivers left this place [Amsterdam], with tears in his eyes, saying 'Lord! What shall become of us. Lord Rivers would give me no satisfaction that the Duke shall return. For God's sake write to all your friends, let him but return for one more campaign till the French [make new proposals for peace]. Then let the Queen afterwards do with him what she pleases, but must the safety of us all be put in the balance with personal pique?'

I hope the Queen will forbear her further resentments till a better occasion . . . Baron Gersdorff was here: He is envoy at the Hague for the Elector of Saxony . . . He assured people in a general assembly of society that his master would recall his troops if the Duke was not to command.

★

Trusted and well-liked as he was by the heads of the alliance and in the army, the Duke of Marlborough was also much admired by the people of England. This was well attested when he arrived home at the beginning of 1711. Crowds gathered round his coach in such numbers in the City that, rather than give his critics an excuse to condemn him for exciting the mob, he drove quickly to Montagu House in Bloomsbury, where his daughter Mary lived with her husband, the second Duke of Montagu, instead of going to St James's as expected.

Having remained at Montagu House until the crowds dispersed, the Duke then drove in a hired carriage to St James's, where, according to Hoffman, he 'remained with Her Majesty only a quarter of an hour'. 'People think him very much thinner and greatly altered,' Hoffman added, 'to which his fatiguing journey, when he had no sleep for five nights, may also have contributed'. He 'no longer looked like himself'.

The next day the Duke had another and longer audience of the Queen, who said to him formally, 'I am desirous you should continue to serve me, and will answer for the conduct of all my Ministers towards you . . . [But] I must request you should not suffer any vote of thanks to you to be moved in Parliament this year, because my Ministers will certainly oppose it.'

'I shall always be ready to serve your Majesty,' Marlborough replied, 'if what has recently passed should not incapacitate me.'

'The Duke had a very cold reception,' Harley reported to the Lord Privy Seal, the Duke of Newcastle. 'He made great confessions of compliance . . . How long he will keep his temper I cannot tell.'

He did keep his temper; but he declined to say whether or not he would accept the command of the army in the next campaign, hoping that his hesitation might dissuade the Queen from insisting upon the fulfilment of her intention, recently expressed, of dismissing his wife from her offices at court.

It was not merely his affection for Sarah that prompted him to try to protect her from dismissal: the loss of her offices would be a severe blow to his own prestige which his enemies would be quick to seize upon.

Well aware of this, Sarah steeled herself to write a contrite letter to the Queen, begging for her forgiveness and undertaking not to bother her in the future with any more political harangues. The Duke took the letter to the Queen, who, having read it, said that she could not alter her resolution: the Duchess must leave her service. Marlborough went so far as to kneel before Her Majesty in supplication. The Queen was unmoved: the Duchess must go; within three days the gold key, the symbol of her office, must be given up. The Duke asked for ten days to arrange this. The Queen, reducing the time limit to two days, said, 'I will talk of no other business till I have the key.'

Marlborough went home to tell Sarah that he had failed in his mission. Upon which, so the story went about the drawing rooms of London, the Duchess in a fury hurled the key into the middle of the room at her husband's feet, telling him he 'could carry it to whom he pleased'.* He picked it up and, told by his wife to change back into the court dress which he had just discarded, obediently returned it to the Palace, where the Queen 'mumbled something which hee could not understand nor make anything of', 'an easy way,' the Duchess commented, 'that I have often known her practise with great success upon many occasions when she has not known what to say which is to move only her lips & make as if she had said something when in truth no words were uttered.'

The office of Groom of the Stole was now bestowed upon the Duchess of Somerset, the Duke of Northumberland's daughter and sole heiress, whose husband was in Marlborough's justified opinion

---

* Soon after the Duchess's dismissal, Lord Cowper called upon the Marlboroughs and found Marlborough, tired out, in bed, with his wife sitting beside him and 'railing in a most extravagant manner against the Queen'. Marlborough told Cowper not to mind what the Duchess said: 'She was used to talk at that rate when she was in a passion, which was a thing she was very apt to fall into, and there was no way to help it' (Burnet, *History of My Own Time*, 1833, vi, 34).

A visitor to Holywell once also noticed how difficult the Duke found it to persuade his wife to do anything she felt disinclined to do. Noticing her sitting at family prayers, he indicated that he would like her to kneel 'but she obeyed not' (Lady Verney (ed.), *Verney Letters of the Eighteenth Century*, 1930, i, 338, quoted in Harris, *A Passion for Government*, 189).

a 'witless' fellow fitted well enough to be Master of the Horse but nothing more. The Duchess of Marlborough's other office, that of Keeper of the Privy Purse, was bestowed upon Abigail Masham, whose two-year-old daughter, for good measure, was appointed Ranger of St James's Park. As a recompense the Duchess claimed, with arrears, the annuity of £2,000 offered her by the Queen nine years before, a sum she calculated as being now worth £18,000. 'I did not much like doing this,' she confessed, 'but I was advised to do it and I did do it.' The Queen 'blushed and appeared to be very uneasy . . . as if she had much rather not have allowed it'. As the price of getting rid of the Duchess, however, she did allow it. But the Duchess was not satisfied there: she helped herself also to the locks of the apartments she had occupied, these, so she claimed, having been installed by herself. It was said that she had taken away the marble chimney pieces also, but this she strongly denied. In any event, the Queen was so cross that she threatened to put a stop to all further supplies of money for Blenheim. She 'would build no house for *her*', she said, since 'she had pulled [the Queen's own house] to pieces'.

In summarizing the latest developments for the benefit of the Emperor, after a conversation with Marlborough, Count von Gallas, Hoffman's colleague as Austrian envoy in London, wrote:

It is becoming daily more apparent that the reflex of the Queen's animosity falls back so heavily upon [the Duchess of Marlborough's] husband that if he is left in command it will be merely out of fear of public opinion which demands his retention . . . I think he will be kept in command but in such a way that he will be hardly anything more than a mere name. He will be surrounded by enemies, and a beginning has already been made by sending Lord Orrery to replace his friend and supporter, Cadogan . . . Attempts will be made to maltreat him so that he may be brought to resign or else die of anger and disappointment. Very good progress has been made towards this last object, for Marlborough has suffered so much that he looks like a different man.

Even so, the Duke did accept the command and, with Harley, St John and other ministers, he attended regular meetings to discuss the forthcoming campaign. He regarded it with foreboding; but when he left for the Continent again in the spring of 1711 he was at least reassured to know that Parliament had voted more than £6 million for its conduct.

38

THE LAST CAMPAIGN

'He completely disarmed me in an instant.'

The Duke, so he complained to Sarah, was conscious of a general and very fast 'dekay', suffering from headaches and earaches, giddiness, 'swimmings' in his head and 'often sickness' in his stomach. Yet he was tireless in his application to the work of accommodating difficult allies, smoothing ruffled feathers and corresponding regularly with St John and with Harley, who, having survived an attempt at assassination by a former priest and adventurer calling himself the marquis de Guiscard, had been created Earl of Oxford. Both men, responding to his diplomatic manner, assured him of their warm support and took pains to ensure that those officers, such as Lord Orrery, who had spoken so slightingly of him in the past, were given employment elsewhere.

The Duke's responsibilities and difficulties, however, as well as his poor health, weighed heavily upon him, as did the loss of much of his prestige consequent upon his having forfeited the confidence of his Queen. 'The dayly Vexations I meet with,' he lamented, 'dose not only break my sperit but also my Constitution.'

Five of his best British regiments were withdrawn from his command to take part in a disastrous expedition to Canada; the Emperor Joseph had died of smallpox; and Marlborough's army had been further weakened when Prince Eugène, to whom he had written '*au nomme de Dieu*' to come to join him, had been called away to Vienna with all the troops of the new Emperor, Charles VI, to face a French threat on the Rhine, leaving the Duke with no more than 90,000 men to face Marshal Villars's 120,000.

Moreover, the King of Prussia was proving difficult again; the brave young Prince of Orange had been drowned when his boat had capsized on crossing the Rhine on his way back to The Hague; and the Duke was plagued by the Dutch deputy, Sicco van Goslinga, who had, mercifully, not been with the army to exasperate him the previous year, but who had now returned, more of an interfering nuisance than ever, taking no care to disguise his belief that the absence of Prince Eugène was greatly to be deplored since his 'genius for war' was, as he often insisted, 'far superior to that of the Duke'.

Yet Marlborough remained as apparently unruffled, composed and conciliatory as usual. The Prince of Anhalt-Dessau conceived the notion that the Duke had in some way offended him and he went to see him, determined to air his grievance. But his anger was immediately dissipated by the welcome accorded him and the compliments bestowed upon him and the men he commanded. 'There are no troops I depend on like those under your command,' the Duke told the Prince ingratiatingly, 'nor any general in the army but yourself whose head and heart I can trust so.' 'I was unable to utter an angry word,' the Prince told his friends after the interview. 'He completely disarmed me in an instant . . . The ascendancy of the man is inconceivable.'

The Duke was to need far more than tact and affability, however, if he was to force the long defensive line of flooded ground and well-defended fortifications which had been constructed after the siege of Douai the summer before and which now extended all the way from west of Montreuil through Arras and Valenciennes to beyond Maubeuge. The name adopted by Marshal Villars for these fortifications was *ne plus ultra*, a phrase said to have been used by the Duke of Marlborough's tailor in describing the perfection of a new red coat which he had made for him.

At the beginning of May 1711, the Duke set his army in motion against these strong defensive works as a preliminary to the capture of Bouchain, a fortress guarding the junction of the rivers Sensée and Scheldt; and on 6 July, in a night attack, a force of 700 men captured Fort Arleux on the river Sensée. A fortnight later the rest of the army was transferred to the western sector of the lines beyond Arras, while Villars, as the Duke had hoped he would, retook Arleux. He then sent his baggage and cannon under escort towards Douai. Led to believe that the allies would now attack him within two or three days, Villars gave orders for the already strong fortifications west of Arras to be hastily extended and strengthened.

Marlborough, pretending to have been made 'very peevish' by the loss of Arleux, seemed, indeed, to be preparing his troops for an attack in this area west of Arras. As so often in the past, his real intentions in this cunning manoeuvre were known to only a few, and those who were not told of them were alarmed. One of these was the Earl of Albemarle, who told John Drummond on 1 August:

God give us good success in case we undertake this great affair [an attack on the lines west of Arras]. Marlborough tells me he is resolved to do it, but I declare that I doubt the result. The enterprise appears to me to be very dangerous. The enemy, in spite of detachments, is yet much superior to us; and it is true that the [desertions in] our army have been terrible this campaign and still continue.

Three days after Albemarle's letter was written, Marlborough, attended by an unusually large staff, set out to reconnoitre the French fortifications west of Arras. Captain Parker, who had received permission to accompany the party, was concerned to see how strong the lines appeared to be, how well they were defended and how thoroughly the approach to them had been

cleared of everything that might be any kind of shelter to those that approached them. Notwithstanding all this, the Duke's countenance was now cleared up, and with an air of assurance, and as if he was confident of success, he pointed out to the General Officers, the manner in which the army was to be drawn up, the places that were to be attacked . . . In short, he talked more than his friends about him thought was discreet, considering that Villars had spies at his very elbow. And indeed some began to suspect that the ill-treatment he had met with at home, might have turned his brain, and made him desperate.

The apprehensive army awaited orders which would send them into an assault so perilous that some officers believed, as Parker said, that the Captain-General had, indeed, gone out of his mind, while Marshal Villars felt confident of imminent victory.

On 4 August Marlborough told his officers that their men must be prepared for an attack in the morning. Soon after darkness fell, however, the troops were aroused from their slumber, told to strike tents and turn out on parade; and within half an hour the whole army was marching quickly in the moonlight to the east back towards Arleux. The rate of the march was so fast that many men fainted, collapsing to the ground, and others died where they fell. The survivors, scarcely more than half the number of those who had set out, covered thirty-six miles in sixteen hours, while the enemy, abruptly woken from their sleep two or three hours after the allies' departure had been confirmed, were also marching fast, parallel to the allied columns on the other bank of the river. 'It was a perfect race between the two armies,' Captain Parker said, 'but we, having the start of them by some hours, constantly kept ahead.' Staff officers rode along beside the grimly treading ranks, to tell them where they were going and why, and urging upon them the essential need for marching as fast as they could.

By the morning of 5 August, those who had kept up with the march had crossed the Sensée and were within the enemy lines. Cadogan, who had received orders to take command of the artillery sent to Douai and to seize the river crossings at Arleux, climbed towards the top of the church tower in the village of Framegies, accompanied by Goslinga, and clearly saw the French approaching. Returning to the ground, they both attended a council of war convened by Marlborough, who, having crossed the *ne plus ultra* lines at Arleux, asked the generals, one by one, what they thought should now be done. If the ground was favourable, should they stand here and fight? Opinions were divided. Marlborough then said that an offensive battle here would be fought at grave disadvantage. The men were tired; they had been obliged to march across country while the enemy had the benefit of roads; and they had had to cover ten more miles than the French. As matters stood, Marlborough decided, the army must cross the Scheldt and lay siege to Bouchain.

As in the past, Goslinga blamed Marlborough for what he called his 'damnable politics which, by avoiding battle, only sought to prolong the war' for his personal financial advantage. The Grand Pensionary also, as John Drummond said, was much concerned 'at the allies not fighting'. 'The States Deputies called out to attack,' Drummond told Robert Harley, the Earl of Oxford.

The Duke called a council of war . . . and his Grace, contrary to his practice throughout all this war, voted not to attack . . . The Duke may have good reason for what he has done, besides a great majority on his side of old generals . . . However, Count Sinzendorf [the Imperial ambassador at The Hague] added as his opinion, that if he were a Prince who had a General who had gained twenty battles, and had been guilty of this one neglect, he would hang him for it.

While Marlborough's army encircled Bouchain, Marshal Villars, outnumbering his opponent by several thousand men, occupied a position some two miles distant to the south and sent the chevalier d'Albegotti with a strong detachment to take the high ground across the Sensée river in his front.

The Duke decided that before the siege operations could begin it would be as well to drive Albegotti from this position, and as large a force as could be mustered was assembled for this purpose. Before launching the attack, however, the Duke rode forward to make sure that the task was not too difficult. Captain Parker, who 'did not like the aspect of the thing', was greatly relieved when he saw the Duke, 'quite unattended and alone, ever watchful and ever right', examining the enemy's fortifications, in the course of one of those personal reconnaissances by which he set such store. He wrote:

It is quite impossible for me to express the joy which the sight of this man gave me at this very critical moment. I was now well satisfied that he would not push the thing, unless he saw a strong probability of success. Nor was this my notion alone: it was the sense of the whole army, both officer and soldier, British and foreigner. And indeed we had all the reason in the world for it; for he never led us on to any one action that we did not succeed in. He stayed only three or four minutes, and then rode back; we were in pain for him while he stayed, lest the enemy might have discovered him, and fired at him; in which case they could not well have missed him. He had not been longer from us than he stayed, when orders came to us to retire. We were not long about it, and as the corn we stood in was high, we slipped off undiscovered, and were a good way down the hill, before [the French] perceived that we were retiring; and then they let fly all their great and small shot after us.

Sending to The Hague for no fewer than 6,000 pioneers and 700 wagons, the Duke now oversaw the construction of lines of circumvallation around the fortress of Bouchain and the digging of approach trenches. His siege train arrived from Tournai on 21 August and the bombardment began on the 30th. A fortnight later, a white flag was raised and the governor undertook to surrender, provided he was granted the right to march out with the honours of war. This was refused: the Duke insisted that the garrison must consider themselves prisoners of war and the bombardment was resumed. The governor then said he would agree to his men being recognized as prisoners of war if they were allowed to remain on parole in France: the Dutch, he complained, fed their prisoners such dreadful food. The bombardment began again, and at last the governor agreed to an unconditional surrender.

The Duke's campaign, his tenth, came to a close with the capture of this minor fortress. His men marched off to winter quarters and he was never to fight again. His last campaign had been an anticlimax; as Professor J. R. Jones has written:

After Malplaquet, Marlborough's strategy had lost its validity. He could never expect to extort total capitulation, which was what the allies were now demanding from Louis, by virtuoso manoeuvres and sieges. From 1709 the war was becoming a war of attrition as the chances of ending it by one great victory steadily receded.

It seemed that, at the age of sixty-one and with 'frequent and sensible remembrances of growing old', Marlborough's long-expressed desire for a quiet life was at last to be fulfilled. 'As I am now convinced that peace will be conclud'd this Winter, I shall take my measures for living a retier'd life,' he wrote. 'If it be in England I shall be glad of it, if not my business shall be to seek a good climate, for my Constitution is extreamly spoilt.'

Going home by way of The Hague, Marlborough landed at Greenwich on 17 November 1711. He took this letter with him:

DEAR GRANDPAPA

I did not write to you before because I could not congratulate you for any victory but now I heartily do upon that glorious success of passing the Lines performed by her Majestys Arms under your command in the low countries. I hope you will go on in winning of Battles, taking of towns & beating & routing the French in all manner of ways, and then come home with a good peace & look back upon those glorious toils of the battles . . . I am now at the Lodge in the little Park & like it very well the Birds are very pretty. I wish you all happiness & good success in all your undertakings. I hope you will think nothing of all this flattery, for it is my thoughts. On thursday 2 of August I presented the Banner to the Queen & was received but coldly. You see I write on tho I have no answer. Your dutifull Grandson, W[illiam] Godolphin.

The day that Marlborough stepped ashore at Greenwich was the anniversary of the succession to the throne of Queen Elizabeth. It had been traditional on that day for a procession of staunch Protestants, patriots and Whigs to parade through London bearing effigies of their bugbears, including the Pope, the Pretender and leading Tories.

On this occasion, however, the authorities, having put it about that troublemakers would take advantage of the celebrations to organize attacks on the houses of the Queen's ministers, even to depose the Queen herself, banned the parade. Hearing about this, Marlborough thought it as well not to go on to London immediately but to stay that night and the next at Greenwich Hospital and to seek an audience of the Queen on the 19th.

'The Duke of Marlborough came to me yesterday as soon as I had dined,' Her Majesty reported to St John after this audience. 'He made a great many usiall proffessions of duty and affection to me. He seemed dejected and very uneasy . . . stayed heare an hour and saw nobody heare but my self.'

It was only to be expected that the Duke should be dejected, for, while he was at The Hague, he had learned that accusations of financial irregularity by Lord Godolphin when Treasurer and the extraordinary claim that no less than £35,000,000 were unaccounted for were to be examined by a House of Commons Commission of Public Accounts. The obviously moderate means of Godolphin in and out of office made it extremely unlikely that he had been dishonest; but no such defence could be raised in the case of the Duke of Marlborough, who was well known to be extremely, not to say inordinately, rich, having for so long been receiving such generous salaries, annuities, commissions and percentages. It seemed that, following secret negotiations conducted by Oxford and St John, 'both time and place', in the Queen's words, 'having been appointed for opening the treaty of a general peace', the Duke of Marlborough was no longer required as Captain-General and could accordingly be destroyed.

Evidence was given to the Commission by the government contractor, Sir Solomon Medina, about yet further payments made to the Duke by way of commission on supplies of bread and other commodities. In a letter to the Commissioners, the Duke explained:

Having been informed on my arrival here that Sir Solomon de Medina has acquainted you with my having received several sums of money from him . . . I would lose no time in letting you know that this is no more than what has been allowed as a perquisite to the . . . Commander-in-Chief in the Low Counties even before the Revolution . . . And I do assure you that whatever sums I have received on that account have been constantly employed for the service of the public in keeping secret correspondence and getting intelligence of the enemy's motions and designs . . . I hope you will allow I have served my Queen and country with that faithfulness and zeal which become an honest man . . .

In the debate in the House of Lords, following a cruel reference in the Queen's speech to the arts of those 'who delight in war', Lord Anglesey repeated Goslinga's persistent accusation that peace with France might have been secured long since had it not been 'put off by some persons, whose interest it was to prolong the war'.

The Duke then rose to speak in his own defence.

I think myself happy in having an opportunity of vindicating myself before a person [here he bowed to the Queen] who, knowing the integrity of my heart, and the uprightness of my conduct, will not fail to do me justice . . . I can declare with a safe conscience, in the presence of Her Majesty, of this illustrious assembly, and of that Supreme Being . . . before Whom I must soon appear to give an account of my actions, that I was ever desirous of a safe, honourable and lasting peace; and that I always have been very far from any designs of prolonging the war for my own private advantage as my enemies have most falsely insinuated. My advanced age [he was sixty-one] and the many fatigues I have undergone, make me earnestly wish for retirement and repose, to think of eternity during the remainder of my days . . . I have not the least motive to desire the continuance of the war . . .

Whether or not the Lords were to be persuaded that Marlborough had, indeed, no desire to see the war continued, the Earl of Oxford and St John were both determined to ensure that the charge of embezzlement was satisfactorily made out. The report of the Commissioners of Public Accounts was circulated to Members of the Commons on 21 December on the condition that its contents remained secret. The House was then adjourned for the Christmas recess until 14 January 1712. Oxford and St John hoped that in these three weeks the talk of the town would centre upon the supposed contents of the report, while speculation about the seriousness of the charge in it would spread far and wide.

In the meantime they worked upon the Queen to persuade her that Marlborough must be dismissed before he and those Whigs who supported him usurped her very throne, and that to ensure his downfall, having got rid of the Whig Duke of Somerset, she must create twelve additional Tory peers – among them Mrs Masham's brother, Colonel Hill – so as to have a majority against him in the Upper House and ensure that a vote was not carried against the peace. Upon the appearance of these new peers in the House, Lord Wharton enquired sardonically whether they would give their vote individually or collectively by their foreman.

When the Duke appeared at court on 30 December it was clear that his days of power and influence were coming to an end. He was shunned on all sides. 'Nobody hardly took notice of him,' Swift told Esther Johnson.

The next day the Cabinet recorded their decision: 'Being informed that an information against the Duke of Marlborough was laid before the House of Commons by the Commissioners of the Public Accounts, Her Majesty thought fit to dismiss him from all his employments, that the matter might undergo an impartial investigation.' On hearing the news of his dismissal, Louis XIV commented, 'The affair of displacing the Duke of Marlborough, will do for us all we desire.'

On New Year's Day the names of those who were to succeed

Marlborough were published in the *Gazette*. The Duke of Ormonde, the future ineffective Jacobite leader, a man later described by Lady Mary Wortley Montagu as 'quite insignificant', was to be Captain-General and Colonel of the 1st Guards. Lord Rivers, 'an arrant knave' in Swift's opinion, was to be Master-General of the Ordnance.

Marlborough threw the Queen's peremptory letter informing him of his dismissal into the fire.

While ministers were still elaborating their case against the Duke of Marlborough, they were also considering proceedings against Robert Walpole, the Leader of the Opposition, and the most effective Whig debater in the Commons, whose pamphlet in defence of Whig financial administration, *The £35,000,000 Accounted For*, had satisfactorily answered the Tory charges. Unfortunately Walpole, while not himself considered guilty of corruption, had become involved in a highly questionable transaction while he was Secretary-at-War by authorizing the payment of £1,000 to a friend of his in a contract for forage.

The Speaker of the House of Commons was asked to convene a meeting, at which he declared that the expulsion of Walpole from the House was now an essential procedure. On 17 January 1712 it was accordingly moved that Walpole was 'guilty of a high breach of trust and notorious corruption'. A subsequent motion that he be expelled from the House was carried by a slender majority. He was then arrested and sent to the Tower, where, despite his re-election by his faithful constituents, he remained for almost five months during which he had many visitors, including the Duke of Marlborough.

The Duke was the Tory ministers' next victim. Oxford and St John well recognized that great care and skill would be required to proceed against a man so admired by the people at large, a man whose continuing popularity was demonstrated at this time when he and Prince Eugène, who was on a visit to London – and being praised by ministers so as to minimize Marborough's contribution to allied success – were both loudly cheered upon their appearance at the opera and again upon their departure from the theatre. Care and skill would also be required in dealing with the House of Commons, in which the Duke was so regularly praised for his great military achievements, and in which James Brydges, the future of Duke of Chandos, the Paymaster and Accountant-General, gave notice that he would speak up on Marlborough's behalf. So, to make Marlborough less popular and a peace with France more so, the talents of Jonathan Swift were called upon.

39

THE DUKE ON TRIAL

'. . . as covetous as Hell, and ambitious
as the Prince of Darkness . . .'

Jonathan Swift, the most gifted satirist of his generation, had been born of Protestant parents in Dublin in 1667. His father, who died shortly before Jonathan's birth, was the son of an English clergyman. His mother's father was also an English parson from Leicestershire. Educated in Ireland at Kilkenny School and Trinity College, Dublin, Swift left for England, like many other Protestants, when it was feared that a Jacobite victory might make life insupportable for them in the country of their birth. In England he found employment as secretary to Sir William Temple of Moor Park, Surrey, where he began to make a name for himself as a writer and met Esther Johnson, the eight-year-old daughter of Temple's housekeeper, who was to become the most important woman in his life and the recipient of the letters published in his *Journal to Stella*.

Introduced to politics by Temple, at first he supported the Whigs, but his interest in the Anglican Church drew him towards the Tories, to Robert Harley and Henry St John, and to those who sought the end of the war with France. His polemical and devastatingly effective pamphlet *On the Conduct of the Allies* appeared in 1711.

The Duke of Marlborough, the husband of a rabid Whig, the director and promoter of the costly war, a man clinging to power for the sake of the public funding of that outrageously costly palace at Woodstock, a man who owed his early rise to his ingratiating manners as a court favourite and to his success with women, was the prime target of Swift's attack, a victim who had to be destroyed in the interests of peace.

On the Conduct of the Allies, as its author told 'Stella', was designed to 'open the eyes of the nation who are half bewitched against a peace . . . Few of this generation can remember anything but war and taxes.' The war had been a conspiracy to bring about 'the ruin of the public interest and the Advancement of a Private increase in the Wealth [estimated earlier by Swift at £540,000] and Grandeur of a particular Family'. Questioning Marlborough's skill and motives, his honour and the conduct of his allies, the pamphlet was so widely read that it had to be reprinted six times. Swift prided himself on the fact that, in speaking in favour of peace and against the conduct of the allies, Members of the Commons 'drew all their arguments from my book, and their votes confirmed all I writ'.

To keep himself well informed as to what was going on at court, Swift frequently dined with Abigail Masham, a person whom he depicted in a far more favourable light than Lord Dartmouth had done. She was, in his stated opinion, 'of a plain, sound understanding, of great truth and sincerity, without the least mixture of falsehood or disguise . . . and full of love, duty and veneration for the Queen'.

Swift was annoyed, however, by Abigail's frequent pregnancies, which prevented her from keeping the Queen as steadily fixed as he would have liked in her opposition to the Whigs and the pretensions of the Marlboroughs. Indeed, on one occasion when Abigail stayed at home to nurse a sick child, he declared that she 'should never leave the Queen, but stick to what is so much the interest of the public as well as her own. This I tell her but talk to the winds.'

Swift's attitude to the Duke of Marlborough was more equivocal than his published writings about the man led his readers to expect. He was certainly 'as covetous as Hell, and ambitious as the Prince of Darkness', yet it had to be admitted that 'he had been a successful general'; and Swift told 'Stella' that he hoped he would be allowed to retain his command. After all, it was doubtful that 'any wise state ever laid aside a general who had been successful nine years together'. 'I think our friends press a little too hard on the Duke of Marlborough,' he added; and certainly he sometimes ameliorated the attacks upon the Duke which were suggested by the Tory government in the proposals for articles and pamphlets sent to him. Sharing St John's regard for Marlborough's military talents, he 'really' thought that ministers did 'not do well in mortifying the man, though indeed it [was] his own fault'.

Swift wrote to the Duke himself to assure him that he was not the author of the 'hardest things' against him which had been printed, and that he personally 'desired everything should be left him, except power'.*

In their proceedings against the Duke of Marlborough, Oxford and St John faced a problem: the House of Commons could not commit a peer to prison, so the Government would have to impeach him, a highly contentious, uncertain and lengthy undertaking. To avoid proceeding to these lengths, it was proposed to Marlborough's supporters in the House that he should accept the findings of the Commission, in return for which acceptance he would be censured in the most gentle manner. As Swift explained to 'Stella':

The Ministers' design is that the Duke of Marlborough shall be censured as gently as possible, provided his friends will not make head to defend him, but if they do, it may end in some severer votes. A gentleman, who was just now with him, tells me he is much cast down, and fallen away; but he is positive, if he has but ten friends in the House, that they shall defend him to the utmost, and endeavour to prevent the least censure upon him, which I think cannot be, since the bribery is manifest. Sir Solomon Medina paid him six thousand pounds a year to have the employment of providing bread for the army, and the Duke owns it in his letter to the Commissioners of Accounts.

Much as Marlborough was inclined to defend himself before the bar of the Commons, however, Godolphin and his friends urged him not to do so. There was too much at stake, they told him; the fate of the Government might well depend upon their victory over him; the greatest efforts would be made to ensure that this was brought about. It would be far better, they advised,

---

* Always extremely sensitive to criticism, the Duke was deeply upset by Swift's attacks. Most other men in public life learned to ignore the aspersions cast upon them by political opponents or personal enemies; but Marlborough, concealing an emotional, susceptible and secretive nature behind that veneer of accommodating urbanity, was never able to bring himself to do so.

to prepare a statement refuting all the charges in the Commissioners' report. This Marlborough did, repeating his claim that the contractors for bread and bread-wagons had always paid a yearly sum as a perquisite to the commander-in-chief in the Low Countries; that the money he had received as commission on the employment of foreign troops was used for 'carrying on the Secret Service without any expense to the public, or grievance to the troops'; that this inevitably most expensive intelligence service was conducted with the greatest efficiency and success, and that 'all other parts of the service' had been 'carried on with all the good husbandry that was possible'.*

The debate in a crowded House was long and heated, 435 Members, a majority of them Tories, taking part in the division, many of them prepared to vote purely on party lines without examining at all closely the charges involved. Able speeches were made in the Duke's defence by Sir John Germain, who, having served in the Low Countries under Prince Waldeck, declared that that commander had received the same allowances and perquisites as Marlborough had; by Sir Charles Hedges, a former Tory Secretary of State; and by James Brydges, who declared that the proceedings were 'a scandal to the British people'. But when the vote was taken it was carried, by a majority of 270 against 165, that 'the taking of several sums of money annually by the Duke of Marlborough from the contractor for foraging the bread and bread-wagons in the Low Countries was unwarrantable and illegal' and that 'the deduction of 2½ per cent from the pay of the foreign troops in Her Majesty's service is public

---

* 'Marlborough employed an extensive network of spies, informers and reporters who supplied him with intelligence . . . He received a regular stream of letters reporting on troop movements in the French army, and naval activity at Brest, Dunkirk and elsewhere. The most extraordinary letters were those sent from Paris, from an unknown correspondent, who provided amazingly accurate information about the court of Louis XIV and meetings of the King's councils . . . [John de] Robethon, the private secretary of the Elector of Hanover, presided over an impressive intelligence network of his own and kept Marlborough regularly supplied with information gleaned from intercepted French correspondence. Some of the material was sent at the direction of the Elector, but it appears that Marlborough also bought some of the information directly from Robethon' (Snyder (ed.), *The Marlborough–Godolphin Correspondence*, i, xxx).

money, and ought to be accounted for'. The sums involved were calculated to amount to £420,000.

For accepting a customary perquisite of 500 ducats on the sealing of each bread contract, Adam de Cardonnel, the Member for Southampton, was expelled from the House, while the Paymaster of the Forces, Benjamin Sweet, who had accepted what was also a customary fee, was ordered to be prosecuted. Yet the Duke of Ormonde, the new commander-in-chief, was authorized to take the same commission on the bread contract and the same 2.5 per cent commission on the pay of foreign troops, a commission which had been approved in Marlborough's case by the Elector of Hanover and the other rulers of the states involved.

The commissions which he received from Medina and the percentages from the pay of foreign troops were not the only payments which the Duke stood accused of receiving dishonestly. The Tory *Examiner*, for which the poet Matthew Prior and Jonathan Swift both wrote, not content with implying that the Duchess of Marlborough was Lord Godolphin's mistress, suggested that the Duke had diverted money intended for the medical services of the army into his own pocket.

What a deplorable Sight it was to see Men with their Limbs shot off lying upon the Field in such an abandoned, wretched Condition that Ravens and Crows have fallen upon them for Carrion, wanting proper Persons to dress their Limbs, their wounds petrified to such a degree that Dogs knawed their Flesh while they were yet alive. Amidst this Torture thousands expired that might have been preserved if the General had not sunk the Money designed for Medicines and Surgeons. No Age, no Country, how barbarous so ever, hath given us such an Instance of Cruelty and Avarice.

A fortnight or so after the publication of this libel, during a debate in the House of Lords, Earl Poulett, an ill-favoured, prevaricating busybody known as 'Swallow', who rarely spoke in the House, stood up to voice a calumny which the Duke's enemies had hinted at before. Referring to the conduct of the Duke of Ormonde as commander-in-chief in Flanders, Poulett said, 'Nobody could doubt the Duke of Ormonde's courage and bravery . . . He was not like a certain

General, who led troops to the slaughter to cause a great number of officers to be knocked on the head in a battle, or against stone walls, in order to fill his pockets by disposing of their commissions.'

This outrageous slander was not to be tolerated. Marlborough approached Lord Mohun, a rakish fellow member of the Kit-Cat Club, who agreed to act as his second and to go to Poulett to demand satisfaction or, as challenges to duels were then known, 'to take the air in the country'. 'I shall accompany the Duke of Marlborough,' Mohun said, 'and your Lordship will do well to provide a second.'

Poulett, greatly alarmed and ignoring conventional behaviour in such circumstances, told his wife what had happened, though without telling her who his challenger was. Lady Poulett, the mother of his eight children, wrote to Lord Dartmouth, Secretary of State, begging him to 'order the guards to be ready upon two noblemen's falling out'. She said she would 'listen when Lord Mohun comes, and will send a more speedy and exact account'. After Mohun's call at her house she wrote again: 'I listend and itt is my Lord Mallbouro that has challings my Lord by Lord Mohun. Pray lett him be secured immediately.' This letter was followed by three more.

Lord Dartmouth lost no time in going to Marlborough to ask him not to leave the house. At the same time he had two guards placed outside the Pouletts' house. Then he wrote to the Queen, who, in turn, wrote to Marlborough ordering him to 'go no further' and to let her have his undertaking that he would not do so. The contretemps ended with Poulett's guarded apology.*

Soldiers serving in the army in Flanders read of the manner in which Marlborough was being treated in England and of the scurrilous stories being spread about him with disgust. 'In one of their celebrated papers the *Examiner*,' wrote Captain Robert Parker,

I remember to have read a passage wherein the author asserts, 'That the Duke of Marlborough was naturally a very great coward: that all the

---

* Soon afterwards Mohun was killed in a notorious duel with the Duke of Hamilton, who was also slashed to death. Mohun's second was Marlborough's friend, General George Macartney, who went into hiding and then fled abroad (Stater, *High Life, Low Morals*).

victories and successes that attended him were owing to mere chance, and to those about him; for whenever he came to be engaged in action, he was always in a great hurry, and very much confounded upon every little emergency that happened, and would cry in great confusion to those about him, "What shall we do now?"' Had I not read these very words, I should never have believed that any man could have the face to publish so notorious a falsehood . . .

It may be thought perhaps that I am prejudiced against the men that were then at the helm, and that I am too sanguine in favour of the Duke of Marlborough, and that my attachment to him may be occasioned by favours received from him. But for my part, I never lay under any private or personal obligations to his Grace; on the contrary he once did me injustice by putting a captain over my head. This however I knew he could not well avoid doing sometimes, for men in power are not to be disobliged. My zeal for the man is founded on his merit and his service, and I do him no more than bare justice.

Parker's men, now under the command of the Duke of Ormonde, much regretted the Duke's departure and were loud in their complaints about their irregular supplies and the intolerably poor quality of the bread, the 'extreme badness' of which actually provoked a mutiny at Ghent. Discipline was, in fact, close to breaking down altogether and, on one occasion, it did so when a party of British soldiers, about 600 in number, advanced upon a village with the intention of plundering it. The inhabitants armed themselves and barricaded the approaches. Shots were exchanged; some soldiers were hit; the rest burst into the village, driving the people into the church, which they burned to the ground with all the 400 men, woman and children inside.

Within sight of the rich French landscape, the soldiers, so Parker said, were 'greatly disappointed at not being led into this "promised land" as they called it, which they reckoned they had dearly earned the plunder of . . . Here they often lamented the loss of the "old Corporal" which was a favourite name they had given the Duke of Marlborough.'

Matthew Bishop was one of those many soldiers who bitterly regretted the departure of the Duke, whose 'attention and care was over us all'. At the time of the 'great Disturbance at Ghent', which ended with ten of the ringleaders being executed, he said to an officer, 'Sir, with submission, what can the Meaning be that all our Garrisons are disturbed in this Manner? It is an instance that never happened during the Time of the Duke of Marlborough' and went on: 'O, the Duke of Marlborough that gained the Love of all his men [who] were obsequious [obedient]. Now they become refractory, and neglect their Duty.'

The lull in the fighting had been brought about by the negotiations for peace which had been in train for months past and culminated in a proposed treaty with France which had been drawn up between that country and England without the concurrence of the other allies. In the House of Lords on 6 June 1712, the Duke spoke out against this underhand dealing, declaring that the 'measures pursued in England for a year past were directly contrary to Her Majesty's engagements with the Allies, sullied the triumphs and glories of her reign, and would render the English name odious to all other nations'. This view had been endorsed by Baron von Bothmar, the Hanoverian minister, who had protested against peace terms which, he said, were 'glorious' to the French King, 'ruinous to the victorious Allies and destructive to the liberties of all Europe'. Yet the treaty terms were approved by a wide margin, only Godolphin, Devonshire, Somerset, Mohun, Nottingham, Cowper, Marlborough and twenty-nine others voting against them in the House of Lords.

The Duke was never to speak in the House again during the Queen's reign, and, having made his protest, he left Marlborough House for St Albans, where on Blenheim Day, 13 August, he gave a garden party, receiving his guests on the bowling green, standing in the tent which had been a familiar sight in his campaigning days and which was now pitched there for the benefit of a curious public, who were admitted inside to inspect it for an entrance charge of sixpence a head.

40

EXILE

'The Honours they have don me in all Places
upon the Duke of Marlborough's Account is
not to be imagined.'

Marlborough had not been at Holywell long, however, before he decided to leave England. It was rumoured that the Earl of Oxford, anxious to get him out of the country, had obliged him to go by threatening to disclose letters supplied by the French government which revealed both his contacts with the Jacobites and his correspondence in 1708 about a possible reward for negotiating a peace settlement. It was certain at least that there was little now to keep him in England apart from his friends and family, and Sarah would follow him, as eager, she confessed, 'to bee out of this horrid countrey' as once she was 'to come into it'. Besides, to remain would mean that the Duke would have to endure the insults of cantankerous Tories in a new session of Parliament as well as to face the prospect of having to find the money for the fines which had been imposed upon him, in addition to £30,000 which was claimed from him for work authorized at Woodstock and for the wages of the labourers and craftsmen at work on the palace there.*

* Marlborough was also concerned that the negotiations which were to result in the Peace of Rastadt between the French and Austrians might involve the loss of his principality of Mindelsheim, as, indeed, they did. However, he retained the title, which he was able to pass on to future Dukes of Marlborough (Hatton, *George I: Elector and King*, 107). Another reason for his going was to persuade the Elector of Hanover and the other allies to send an invading force to England to overthrow the government and prevent a Jacobite invasion, which the Whigs supposed might well be the outcome of the peace. A conversation with the Elector, however, was soon to disabuse Marlborough of any idea that such an invasion might be mounted: the

On the Continent, Marlborough hoped, attitudes towards him would be quite different from those displayed in government circles in London. He was respected beyond the Channel, not only as a general who had won great victories but as a Prince of the Holy Roman Empire.

After what St John described as 'a good deal of contest', permission to leave the country was granted him, and a pass was accordingly issued.

Taking this with him, he drove down to Dover on 24 November 1712, accompanied by one or two servants, leaving Sarah to follow him later. For a week the winds were unfavourable; but on 1 December he set sail in the public packet-boat for Ostend, having had to pay two months' wages by way of compensation to a laundrymaid who declined to leave the country.

He was greeted on the boat's arrival by a salute of cannon on the sea front and the ramparts, by large crowds at the landing place and by William Cadogan, who was then serving on the Continent as envoy extraordinary and minister plenipotentiary to the Dutch States-General. Marlborough asked Cadogan if he would consider resigning that appointment to accompany him on his travels. Cadogan accordingly wrote to Lord Oxford:

The Duke of Marlborough's ill-health, the inconvenience a winter's journey exposes him to, and his being without any one friend to accompany him, make the requesting leave to wait on him an indispensable duty to me, who so many years have been honoured with his confidence and friendship and [owe] all I have in the world to his favour.

Quite content to have Marlborough out of the country as long as possible, Oxford approached the Queen, who readily gave her consent to Cadogan's being relieved of his duties in Holland. So, leaving his friend to accompany him when he could get away, the Duke set out for Antwerp, the roar of the cannon on the ramparts and of the guns of the English ships in the harbour bidding him farewell.

As at Ostend, cheering crowds greeted him at Antwerp, where

Elector refused to consider any open interference in English politics while Queen Anne was still alive (Gregg, 'Marlborough in Exile, 1712–1714').

they were, indeed, so vociferous in their welcome that he thought it as well to avoid such demonstrations in future lest reports of them caused offence in London. So he decided to travel by a roundabout route on his onward journey towards Maastricht. Crossing into Dutch territory, accompanied now by Cadogan and his old comrade-in-arms the Dutch general Dopff, he was received by soldiers drawn up as a guard of honour and by what appeared to be the entire population of the surrounding countryside. The reception he had wished to avoid by taking narrow byroads from Ostend was inescapable as he drove on to Aachen, troops of cavalry riding up from the nearby camps and garrisons to escort him on his way. At Aachen, on 21 January 1713, he wrote to Sarah to warn her that, after 'a thorough thaw', she would find the 'ways extremely bad' and, since Aachen was 'extreamly durty', he had resolved not to linger there but to go on to Maastricht at 'the beginning of the week'. He looked forward to welcoming her there. 'I send this letter to Ostend,' he added, 'in hopes it may meet You there . . . I wish you in safety with all my heart, so that I may have the happyness of having Your Company.' A fortnight later, he wrote to her again, from Maastricht:

If you have observed by my letters that I thought you would have left England sooner than you have been able to do, I hope you will be so kind and just to me, to impute it to the great desire I had of having the satisfaction of your company. For I am extremely sensible of the obligation I have to you, for the resolution you have taken of leaving your friends and country for my sake. I am sure, if there be anything in my power that may make it easy to you, I should do it with all imaginable pleasure. In this place you will have little conveniences; so that we must get to Frankfort as soon as we can . . . I fear you will not be easy till we get to some place where we may settle for some time; so that we may be in a method and orderly way of living; and if you are then contented, I shall have nothing to trouble me.

In England the Duchess was having trouble in deciding what to take with her. Among many other things, in the end she settled upon forty cloaks and petticoats, a tea-kettle holding five pints, a chocolate pot, a powder puff, quantities of linen and seven leopard-skin muffs.

In the course of packing all these items into 120 large packages, she came across what Swift maintained was a small Picture, enamelld work & sett in gold, worth about 20ls, a Picture I mean of the Queen which she gave to Dutchess Marlborough sett in Diamonds. When the duchess was leaving England she took off all the Diamonds & gave the Picture to one Mrs Higgins (an old intriguing . . . insignificant woman) . . . bidding her make the best of it she could . . . Was ever such an ungrateful Beast as that Dutchess? or did you ever hear such a Story . . . Is she not a detestable Slut?

The Duchess – accompanied by several servants and a decidedly Protestant chaplain with the unsuitable name of Whadcock Priest – met the Duke at Maastricht in February and soon afterwards she wrote to a cousin to give him her impressions of 'all the Places one pass's thro in these Parts' on the road to Antwerp by way of Aachen and Frankfurt. They were not very favourable impressions, the towns and countryside having 'an Air very different from London' and 'all the French women', so she had already decided, being 'cheats'. 'The most considerable people' she had seen had 'but just enough to live on, and the ordinary People . . . [were] half-starved'. She went on, 'The Honours they have don me in all Places upon the Duke of Marlborough's Account is not to be imagined.'

Although it was, indeed, as he had said, 'extreamly durty', Marlborough returned to Aachen in March for 'the advantage of one month of the hot baths there', while Sarah passed her time 'visiting Nunnerys and Churches', where she heard of 'such Marvels' and saw 'such ridiculous Things' as would appear to her correspondent 'incredible'. It was, indeed, 'beyond all [she] ever saw or heard of in England', whose 'wise Cittysons', so she wished, 'could travell & see with their own Eyes the sad effects of Popary and arbitrary Power'. She was, however, warmly welcomed by the nuns, writing home to a friend:

If our Ennimies do prevail to our utter ruin, I think I had best go into a monastery. There are several in this Town [Aachen], and tis all the entertainment I have to visit [them]. I supp'd with about twenty [nuns] t' other night but twas a very slight [meal] nothing but brown bread and butter . . . They were as fond of me as if I had not been a Heritick . . .

The priests have three Parts in four of all the land in the Country, yet they are not contented but squeeze the poor deluded People to get more, who are really half starved by the vast number of Holydays in which they can't work, and the Mony they must pay when they have it, for the Forgiveness of their Sins . . . In one Church where I was lately, there were 27 jolly-face Priests that had Nothing in the World to doe but to say Mass for the living, and to take the dead Souls the sooner out of Purgatory by their Prayers.

At Frankfurt, where they arrived in the middle of May – and where, from her window, Sarah saw 'a great many Troops passed that were under the command of P. Eugene' – the 'D. of Marl. was paid all the Respects as if hee had been in his old Post'.

To see so many brave Men marching by was a very fine Sight. It gave me a melancholly Reflections, and made me weep; but at the same Time I was so much animated that I wishd I had been a Man that I might have ventured my Life a thousand Times in the glorious Cause of Liberty . . .*

When I had written so far I was called to receive the Honour of a Visit from the Elector of Mianze [Mainz]. I fancy hee came to this Place chiefly to see the D. of Marl. His shap is, like my own, a little of the fatest, but in my Life I never saw a Face that expressed so much Opennesse, Honesty, and good Nature . . . I can't help repeating Part of his Compliment to the Duke of Marl., that he wished any Prince of the Empire might be severely punished if ever they forgot his Merit. It would fill a Book to give you an Account of all the Honours done the D. of Marl. in all the towns . . . as if he had been King of them.

The Duchess was homesick, though; and she dreaded the prospect of having to spend the rest of her life in 'these durty Countrys'. 'Tis much better to be dead,' she thought, 'than to live out of England.' She confessed that she 'wished earnestly' to see her friends in England again and 'to be in a clean, Sweet House and Garden, tho' ever so small'. There was 'nothing of that kind' in Frankfurt; 'and in the Gardens there the Sand that goes over one's Shoes [was] so disagreeable' that she preferred by far 'to walk in the Roads and Fields', as,

---

* This was by no means the only occasion upon which she expressed the wish to be a man: 'I am confydent,' she once declared, 'I should have been the greatest Hero that ever was known in the Parliament Hous if I had been so happy as to have been a Man' (*Letters of Sarah . . . at Madresfield Court*, 37).

indeed, she did 'every Day in the Afternoon' with her husband. ' 'Tother Day,' she wrote,

we were walking together upon the Road, and a Gentleman and his Lady went by us in their Chariot who wee had never seen before, and after passing us with the usual Civillitys, in half a quarter of an Hour or less, they bethought themselves and turned back . . . and desired that wee would go into their Garden . . . desiring us to accept of a Key. This is only a little Tast of the Civillity of People abroad, and I could not help thinking that wee might have walk'd in England as far as our Feet would have carryd us before Anybody that we had never seen before would have lighted out of their Coach to have entertained us.

For his part, Marlborough endured his exile more easily than his wife. The summer days passed idly into autumn, the autumn into winter; and Sarah, who had gone about 'on errands of mercy', carrying money and other gifts with her own hands to anyone whom she discovered in desperate straits, criticized her husband for being so 'intolerably lazy'. He seemed, in her eyes, to grow older by the month. He could not even bring himself to write to his daughters; and when he learned of the death from smallpox of his beloved child, his third daughter, Elizabeth, Countess of Bridgwater, his head dropped with such force on to the marble mantelpiece against which he was learning that he fell, so it was reported, unconscious to the floor.

41

THE DUKE'S RETURN

*'My Lord Duke, I hope your troubles
are now all over.'*

The Queen also was nearing the end of her life, suffering from recurrent attacks of gout, fevers and painful abscesses on her legs. In December 1713 it was feared for a time that she was on the point of death. She recovered from that illness, and was well enough to open Parliament in the middle of the following February. But the next month she fell ill again and, once more, her life was reported to be in danger. Anxious to ensure that, whatever happened upon her death, he would be able to preserve his fortune and estates and return with due respect to England, to Marlborough House and Blenheim Palace, the Duke, in his devious way, continued to keep in touch both with Hanover and, like several leading Tories, with the court of the Stuart Pretender, whom Oxford and St John, now Lord Bolingbroke, vainly pressed to change his religion.

Marlborough, in communication with the Duke of Berwick, assured the Pretender of his goodwill, going so far as to ask for a pardon for having deserted him. At the same time, anxious not to find himself on the losing side, he maintained a close contact with the Electress Sophia, her son the Elector and their ministers.

The Electress still held Marlborough in high regard. Her son's relationship with him, however, was not so harmonious, though he was always ready to accept the Duke's offers of help and advice. When asked by the Elector's confidential secretary and his colleagues how their master should act on the Queen's death, Cadogan replied on Marlborough's behalf:

It was the Duke's opinion that the Elector should go to England immediately with full powers from the Electress as her lieutenant-general. The Kings of England frequently invested lieutenants to govern the kingdom in their absence, with all the authority and power they possessed themselves.

Marlborough further suggested that, once confident of the loyalty to the Protestant succession of the allied army on the Continent, he himself would follow the Elector to England, leaving General Cadogan and the Elector's son, the Electoral Prince, who had fought so bravely at Oudenarde, in command. In anticipation of being called upon to act in this way, Marlborough left Frankfurt for Antwerp to be closer to the scene of action; and at Antwerp he accepted the Elector's commission for him to act as commander-in-chief when the time came.

While staying in Antwerp the Marlboroughs kept open house for young Englishmen on their way to and from Italy on the Grand Tour. One of these, a particularly handsome and attractive man, fell ill with smallpox and was nursed with the utmost care by the Duchess, who, with her habitual contempt for the medical profession, turned out the doctor. 'Without laughing,' she told a friend, 'I do believe I am better than any Physician even in England, because I have been very well instructed, and leave out all the knavish part of the profession.' In her care the boy fully recovered.

The Marlboroughs were still in Antwerp when the details of the last Treaties of Utrecht were being negotiated to bring to an end the long War of the Spanish Succession, the Tory administration having already been for some time now in separate discussions with the French and, to the disgust of their allies in arms, having withdrawn their army from the Continent.

In accordance with the Utrecht treaties, France and Spain were to remain separated and the Spanish Netherlands were to be given to Austria. France recognized the Hanoverian succession and ceded to Britain Hudson Bay and Newfoundland. Britain also gained Gibraltar and Minorca in the partition of the Spanish Empire; and, by what was known as the *Asiento*, she won the right to supply African slaves to South America and the West Indies.

★

'Pray be pleased to take an opportunity of acquainting his Electoral Highness,' Marlborough wrote to the Elector's secretary on 18 June 1714, 'that my best friends think my being in England may be of much more use to the service than my continuing abroad, upon which I design to return as soon as the Parliament is up.'

Sarah was delighted by the prospect of getting away. She had had quite enough of the Continent and of the 'very inconvenient' house in which they were living at Antwerp. She told Mrs Clayton, the wife of the Duke's agent at Woodstock:

We shall be three days going to Ostend, and stay there rather than come without a very good [wind] because it is intolerable to goe to bed in those boats; but if we can have a [fair] wind, and in the daytime, wee may hope to get to Dover without going to bed, and it will be easy enough to sit upon the deck.

A fortnight later, having been wished well on their way by all the officers of the Royal Irish and Webb's Regiment, later the 8th Foot, drawn up in two lines to demonstrate 'the respect [they] still retained for his Grace', the Duke and Duchess were still at Ostend in what Sarah described as 'a very clean house with everything good but weather'. At the beginning of August 1714 the wind stood fair, however, and they set sail for England.

They landed on the second of the month at Dover, where they heard that the Queen had died the day before. They left immediately for London by way of Rochester and Chatham, where, in the words of the *Flying Post*, 'they were received with great expressions of joy from the people, especially those at Chatham, who strewed their way with flowers as they adorned their houses with green boughs, and welcomed them with repeated shouts and acclamations'. In London 'they were received and escorted by the civic authorities, a train of coaches and a troop of militia with drums and trumpets'.

By contrast, Marlborough's rivals and enemies had been awaiting his return to London with apprehension, even dread. 'We are all frightened out of our wits,' Matthew Prior told St John, now Lord Bolingbroke, who was dismissed from office and later, under the pretence of seeking advice, came to Marlborough to enlist his help, only to be warned that his life was in danger and advised to fly abroad immediately. Bolingbroke, having borrowed £20,000 from the rich James Brydges, left for Dover that night and made his way to the court of the Pretender, where he was appointed Secretary of State.

Lord Oxford, who, like Bolingbroke, 'had played the double game of intrigue with the courts of Saint-Germain and Hanover less expertly than the Duke of Marlborough', was committed to the Tower. The Duke of Ormonde was dismissed. Abigail Masham – having, so it was said, left the dying Queen 'for three hours to go and ransack for things at St James's' – retreated with her husband to the country, where she disappeared into obscurity and died after a long illness in 1734. The Duke of Marlborough, however, was received by the Elector of Hanover, now King George I, with the welcoming words, 'My Lord Duke, I hope your troubles are now all over.' He was reappointed Master-General of the Ordnance as well as Captain-General and Colonel of the 1st Guards. When Dr Samuel Garth, the King's physician and Marlborough's admirer, received the first knighthood of the new reign and asked to have the honour bestowed upon him with the Duke of Marlborough's sword, His Majesty was quite ready to oblige him.

All these appointments were made and these honours bestowed rather as acts of policy than evidence of affection or personal regard; but when the King was entertained at a banquet at Marlborough House, he did seem – while by no means relishing the role of King of England he was now called upon to play – perfectly at home in the Duke's gracious, polished, deferential presence.

Marlborough's friends, supporters and relations were also given, or confirmed in, positions of influence or profit. Lord Townshend, his amiable colleague in his negotiations for peace, became Secretary of State for the Northern Department and was later offered an earldom; Lord Stanhope, who had served under the Duke as colonel of what became the 11th Foot, was appointed Secretary of State for the Southern Department; Townshend's fellow Old Etonian, Sir Robert Walpole, released from the Tower in July 1712, was given the lucrative post of Paymaster of the Forces. Cadogan was appointed Master of the King's Robes and Colonel of the Coldstream Guards. Marlborough's four sons-in-law were all found appointments: Lord

Sunderland became Lord-Lieutenant of Ireland, Lord Godolphin Cofferer of the Household, the Earl of Bridgwater Lord Chamberlain to the Prince of Wales's Household, the Duke of Montagu the commander of a regiment, while Marlborough's daughter Mary, the Duchess of Montagu, was appointed Lady-in-Waiting to the Princess of Wales.

Marlborough himself became once more a personage much respected and of great influence at court, where his levees were attended by numerous sycophants, place-seekers, officers in pursuit of promotion and politicians in search of office. He himself, so Lady Mary Wortley Montagu said, made 'the same figure at Court that he did when he first came into it'.

Marlborough was also highly influential in government. Indeed, the Prussian envoy in London reported that the Duke, together with the Hanoverian minister Count Bernsdorf, the Hanoverian diplomatist Baron von Bothmar and Lord Townshend, 'settled everything'. But Marlborough's health was failing fast, and he did not long remain a considerable figure in this quadrumvirate, his place at the heart of government being increasingly taken over by Walpole and Stanhope. During the abortive Jacobite rising of 1715, he was only nominally in command, and it was left to these younger men to deal decisively with the crisis, he himself having taken care to ingratiate himself with the Pretender, in case his invasion was successful, by offering to provide him with money.

42

A PARALYTIC STROKE

'There was once a man.'

On 28 May the following year, 1716, shortly after the death of his beloved, gifted and pretty daughter, Anne, Countess of Sunderland, at the age of thirty-two, the Duke, who had for weeks been suffering from the headaches, exacerbated by giddiness, which had troubled him intermittently for so many years, suffered a paralytic stroke at Holywell – the result, it was alleged, of his wife's wild tirades against the doctors who had ineffectually treated their daughter, accusing one of them of having murdered her as certainly as if he had shot her through the head.

Dr Garth, called down from London to treat the young woman's father, cupped and bled his patient, who, having been unconscious for three days, gradually recovered his power of speech and clearness of mind, and was then taken to Bath for a course of the waters from the town's mineral springs.

Sarah was in dutiful attendance. But she had little faith in the efficacy of the spa's waters, while the town was 'the most disagreeable . . . of all the places on earth'. Also she did not altogether trust Dr Garth, by now Sir Samuel. Admittedly he was a good-natured man, 'most honest and compassionate', a Whig and a member of the Kit-Cat Club; but he wrote poetry and was fond of dancing, and the Duchess thought it as well to consult other physicians in London.

So this she did and at great length, writing of her husband's inability to climb the stairs 'without uneasiness', his limbs being weaker than they had been at St Albans. He was 'pritty chairfull' on occasions and able to enjoy a game of ombre, but on others depressed and concerned about his condition, declining to drink the ass's milk which was prescribed for him, 'fancying it did not agree with him'. 'And some times,' the Duchess reported,

hee has something that I don't know very well how to express & bemoaning of him self that looks like sickness or want of spirits, but when I ask him if he is sick hee says no, but hee is uneasy & won't or can't describe what it is. Hee says his belly is harder than it used to bee & tis certain that his cote does not button easy that was too big when wee came here [to Bath].

The Duchess was told that 'vipors boyl'd in the Duke of Marlborough's broath' would be 'an admirable thing', that they would 'mend his blood & take off the lownesse of his spirits'. But, Sarah wrote, 'the Duches of Shrewsbury says there is non good in England & that I must send into France & they have the best in the world that comes from Mumpillio [Montpellier]. She talks of having them come alive in boxes with holes fill'd with bran.' By the time she had ordered some from France, however, she had been advised that 'the loathing of the vipers' would make 'other food less useful to him & that jelly of hartshorn & calves feet was much better'.

In November 1716 the Duke suffered a second stroke at a house on the Blenheim estate, and again for a time he could not speak. On this occasion also, he soon recovered his senses and was able before long to play at ninepins and to go to take the waters at Tunbridge Wells, where, although people whom he knew said that when he saw them at the spa, he did not recognize them, he seemed physically much improved by the cure, and cheered by the company of Richard Steele, the Irish essayist and dramatist, whose 'The Englishman's thanks to the Duke of Marlborough' had appeared in 1712, just after the Duke had been dismissed from all his offices, and whose hope it was to be asked to write the Duke's official biography.

'Hee is always the better for travelling,' the Duchess reported from Blenheim on their return. 'After being at the building in the morning, he went to see the old manor house where he went up a vast number of steps while I was glad to take my ease in a chair at the bottom of it.'

He was also well enough to ride out to watch the builders at work; and was often to be seen by Vanbrugh's bridge complacently surveying the progress of the monumental house and its landscaped grounds which meant so much to him. But, while his mind remained clear, he was never again to talk with his erstwhile clarity, certain words quite defeating him; and so embarrassed was he by this that he was reluctant to talk to people he did not know well; and even with his own family he would often sit in gloomy silence, 'a melancholy memento', as the younger Craggs called him, bent in a chair, in a 'dark corner of the roome by the Chimney', speaking not a word, 'nor taking any notice of what was doing'. Yet, after his death, many of their friends remarked to his widow that they remembered 'with pleasure the things they heard him say, and the just observations he made upon what others had said to him, and he gave many instances of remembering in conversation what others had forgot'.

Unlike Wellington and Napoleon, he rarely, it seems, if ever, spoke of his campaigns or of the great events of the past in which he had played so prominent a part. It was as though his palace, which Vanbrugh was decorating with so many military emblems, would itself tell his story for his own and future generations. One day, in the state rooms at Blenheim, he was observed gazing upon his portrait by Sir Godfrey Kneller, murmuring as he turned away, 'There was once a man.'

Yet, for the next five years, he continued to make appearances in the House of Lords; and, when he offered to resign as Captain-General, the King, reluctant to risk receiving a request from his much disliked son, the Prince of Wales, to succeed to the command, pressed the Duke to retain it.

So Marlborough lived on in office, receiving chosen visitors at Holywell and the Lodge in Windsor Park, in London at Marlborough House, and making regular visits to Woodstock, to the slowly developing palace.

43

THE MATCHMAKER AND
HIS 'PILE OF STONES'

'I will never trouble you more Unless the Duke of Marlborough
recovers so far to shelter me from such intolerable Treatment.'

Work at Blenheim progressed most erratically, having been stopped altogether on the Duchess's orders in 1710, when over £130,000 had already been spent, when more than £10,000 was still owed to the masons, the Edward Strongs, father and son, and when several workmen, who had received no wages for months, had been paid on his own authority by Samuel Travers, Marlborough's agent at Woodstock, who had written to the Duke on 8 October that year:

The people who had been turned off without their wages were full of complaints and tears and then threats and violence . . . To prevent therefore any tumult that might be set on foot . . . and in compassion to so many poor starving people . . . I borrowed £300 here on my own credit . . . to pay off the poor labourers . . .

A few months later, the Earl of Oxford had authorized a grant of £10,000 so that work could be resumed before the abandoned fabric was damaged by neglect. For this the Duke had been duly thankful and, overcoming his dislike of the man, had written to him to say that, if he had the good fortune to spend any part of his life at Blenheim, he would always have 'a remembrance of the obligations' he owed to him on this account.

But the work had again been stopped in June 1712 before the Marlboroughs went to live on the Continent, leaving what the Duchess called the 'pile of stones' in the care of Henry Joynes, Vanbrugh's former clerk of the works, and committing the grounds into the hands of a gardener, Tileman Bobart, who, like Joynes, had little or nothing to do, and occupied his time by showing visitors round the place and fishing for trout and chub in the lake.

Construction on the house had once more been resumed in 1716, but, by this time, several of those craftsmen and workmen still alive refused to return to a building on which work was likely to be interrupted yet again. Among these were Grinling Gibbons, who had been responsible for much of Blenheim's fine statuary, and Henry Joynes, soon to be appointed clerk of the works at Kensington Palace. Henry Wise, the head gardener, also left and not long afterwards retired to an estate he had bought near Warwick, where he died in 1738, 'being then worth £200,000'.

The Duchess reckoned that the work at Blenheim had now cost over £250,000 and she thought it was high time that a stop was put 'to such a rediculous maddnesse'.

Although Bartholomew Peisley, a highly experienced mason from Oxford, and his son, together with a large team of assistants, were working on Vanbrugh's 'bridge in the air' – which had as yet almost no water beneath it nor any proper approaches – there were no rooms in the great house fit to live in. The Duchess 'did not wish to vex the Duke when his health [was] so bad', but, she wrote,

At the same time, I think I owe it to him & to my family to prevent if I can having a great estate thrown away in levilling of hills, filling up pricipices & making bridges in the air for no reason that I or anybody else can see but to have it said hereafter that Sr John Vanbrugh did that thing which was never don before.★

The relationship between the Duchess and Vanbrugh was by now approaching its crisis. The trouble arose over the projected marriage of the Duchess's rather plain and diffident but amiable granddaughter, Lady Harriet Godolphin, to one of the architect's closest friends, a fellow member of the Kit-Cat Club, the young Duke of Newcastle,

★ Contemptuous as the Duchess was of the bridge, Bartholomew Peisley, the master mason who had worked on it under Vanbrugh's direction, was highly satisfied with it. 'The Great Arch of the Bridge is Keyed,' Marlborough was informed by the Treasury when that work had been completed, 'and it has succeeded to admiration, which Peisley the Builder is very proud and overjoyed at, it being a great and nice piece of work' (Edward Hibbert, *Vanbrugh House, Oxford*, 5).

who, in the Duchess's opinion, was 'very silly and good-natured and easily persuaded to anything'.

She asked Vanbrugh to approach Newcastle so as to discover what terms might be arranged. When Vanbrugh spoke to Newcastle about the proposed match, he found that his young friend had decided views upon the kind of wife he wanted. He had, indeed,

made more observations on the bad Education and wrong manners of the Ladys of the Court and Towne than one wou'd have expected; And own'd he shou'd think of Marriage with much more Pleasure than he did, if he could find a Woman (fit for him to marry) that had such a turn of Understanding, Temper and Behaviour As might make her a useful Friend, as well as an Agreeable Companion, but of Such a One he seem'd almost to despair. [However, the possibility of] having a Posterity descend from the Duke of Marlborough had an extraordinary weight with him.

Before the matter could proceed any further, though, it was considered necessary that Vanbrugh should consult the Whig leadership in the shape of Sir Robert Walpole. So Vanbrugh was sent to see Walpole, returning with the unwelcome proposal that Newcastle, having regard to the girl's plain features and his own encumbered estates, would expect a dowry of £40,000, a figure which provoked the indignant Duchess of Marlborough to protest that she had 'never heard of such a Fortune' being required in such circumstances. Her husband, who was eventually persuaded, most reluctantly, to part with £20,000, commented that he had never before paid more than £10,000. There for the moment the matter rested, while, following the Duke of Marlborough's first stroke, relations between Vanbrugh and the Duchess went from bad to worse; for now Vanbrugh had to deal with the Duchess without being able to appeal to the good sense of the far more amenable Duke. He did his best to awaken an enthusiasm for Blenheim which she had never shown. 'The beauty of this place at this time is hardly to be conceived,' he told her in one characteristic letter; and in another: 'Mr Thornhill [James Thornhill, who was painting the Hall ceiling] goes on a pace in the Hall, and has begun with a better Spirit in his paintings than anything I have seen of his doing before.'

But the Duchess was not to be persuaded that the vast expense of

Blenheim was justified. Much annoyed by Vanbrugh's having moved into the ancient, partially reconstructed manor house, she upbraided him for the 'rediculous' bridge which he had built across the trickle of a stream. She had, she said sarcastically, counted thirty-three rooms in it and a house in each corner. 'But that which makes it so much prettier than London Bridge,' she added, 'is that you may sit in six rooms and look out at a window into the high arch, while the coaches are driven over your head.'

What was worse in her opinion was that she now discovered that a sum of no less than £900 a year was being spent, entirely without her knowledge, on two elaborate causeways on either side of the bridge. Vanbrugh strongly denied that this work was being carried on without being authorized: the Duke of Marlborough and Lord Godolphin, the Duke of Shrewsbury, the late Duke of Montagu and Sir Christopher Wren had all been consulted. Admittedly no fixed sum had been allocated to the work; but the Duke had 'agreed to employ a moderate number of men' on the causeway and he had not done so 'after a short word or two but a great deal of plain intelligible talk' with Vanbrugh himself and with Henry Wise, the gardener. 'So I shall be much disappointed,' Vanbrugh concluded, 'if when I wait upon you at Blenheim, I do not find you very well satisfied with my defence about the Causeway.'

The Duchess was not at all satisfied.

She and the Duke arrived at Blenheim on 16 October 1716 from Bath in the company of their granddaughter, Lady Harriet. Vanbrugh was also there with Hawksmoor; but the Duchess said nothing to him about the proposed marriage to the Duke of Newcastle, negotiations for which she had by now placed in the hands of a professional matchmaker.*

Annoyed to find that the Duchess had dispensed with his own services in this capacity without a word to him on the subject,

---

* Having originally stood out for a £40,000 dowry, Newcastle agreed to accept £20,000. He married Lady Harriet on 2 April 1717. But the posterity for which he had hoped did not appear. He died in November 1768, when his dukedom devolved upon his nephew, the ninth Earl of Lincoln. His widow died in 1776.

Vanbrugh was even more put out to discover that she had decided also to dismiss him as the architect of Blenheim.

During her visit there on 16 October she had marched about the place, evidently displeased with what she shortsightedly saw, though superficially quite polite to him and even bringing herself to speak well of him to Hawksmoor. Soon afterwards, however, Brigadier-General Michael Richards, the engineer supervising the waterworks at Blenheim, showed him some enormously long documents which he had received from the Duchess and in which she accused Vanbrugh of having 'brought the Duke of Marlb: into [his present difficulties over the building of the palace] Either to leave the thing Unfinished, and by Consequence useless to him and his Posterity, or by finishing it, to distress his Fortune, And deprive his Grandchildren of the Provision he inclin'd to make for them'.

This was too much for Vanbrugh to bear. On 8 November he wrote the 'Abominable Woman', 'that wicked woman of Marlborough', a pained and angry letter:

Madam,

When I writ to your Grace on Tuesday last I was much at a loss, what cou'd be the ground of your having drop't me in the service I had been endeavouring to do you and your family with the Duke of Newcastle . . . But having since been shown by Mr Richards a large packet of building papers sent him by your Grace, I find the reason was, That you had resolv'd to use me so ill in respect of Blenheim, as must make it impracticable to employ me in any other Branch of your Service. These Papers Madam are so full of Far-fetched Labour'd Accusations, Mistaken Facts, Wrong Inferences, Groundless Jealousies and strain'd Constructions: That I shou'd put a very great affront upon your understanding if I suppos'd it possible you cou'd mean anything in earnest by them . . . I will never trouble you more Unless the Duke of Marlborough recovers so far to shelter me from such intolerable Treatment. I shall in the mean time . . . ever retain the greatest Veneration [for him] . . .

I am,

Your Graces most obedient Ser[t]

J. Vanbrugh

Upon reading this letter, the Duchess predictably flew into a temper; and the Duke suffered his second stroke the next day.

After his recovery, although he would have liked to do so, Marlborough never saw Vanbrugh again. 'I thought after this [final quarrel with the Duchess] I could not wait upon the Duke when she was present,' Vanbrugh regretfully explained. 'And that if I endeavoured to do it, at any other time, she wou'd not like it.'

So long as the Duke lived, Vanbrugh did not lose his high regard for the man who 'never once found fault' with him and who was largely responsible for obtaining for him one of the first knighthoods of the new reign.*

Delighted as he was to receive his money 'in Spight of the Huzzys teeth', Vanbrugh was greatly annoyed to be foiled in his attempt to see the palace when it was almost completely built.

An opportunity to do so occurred in the summer of 1725 when Vanbrugh's client, the Earl of Carlisle, decided to make 'a good agreeable Expedition' on his way back with his daughter from London to Yorkshire. He invited Vanbrugh and Vanbrugh's young wife, Henrietta, to accompany them. 'We Stay'd two nights in Woodstock, My Lord and the Ladys having a mind to View Blenheim in every part with leisure,' Vanbrugh told his friend Jacob Tonson.

But there was an order to the Servants, under her Graces own hand, not to let me enter any where. And lest that shou'd not mortify me enough, She having somehow learn'd that my wife was of the Company, sent an Express the Night before we came there with orders, if she came with the

---

* After the Duke's death, however, Vanbrugh was indignant to discover that, although he left so huge a fortune, 'this Man [who] wou'd neither pay his workmen their bills nor his Architect his Salary', had made no provision to settle Vanbrugh's account. But he had 'given his Widow (may a Scotch Ensign get her) £10,000 a Year to Spoil Blenheim her own way, and £12,000 a Year to keep her Self clean and go to Law' (quoted in Green, *Sarah, Duchess of Marlborough*, 228–9). In the end, with the help of Sir Robert Walpole, Vanbrugh contrived to get the money owing to him by having it deducted from a sum due to the Marlborough estate before 'that B.B.B.B. old B. the Dutchess of Marlbh' could get her own hands on it (Whistler, *Sir John Vanbrugh*, 286).

Castle Howard Ladys, the Servants shou'd not suffer her to see either House, Gardens, or even enter the Park, which was obey'd accordingly, and She was forc'd to Sit all day and keep me Company at the Inn.

The Duchess did not relent; but she did bring herself to dictate to her secretary an explanation to Lord Carlisle:

My Lord,

I shall allways take it for a Great honour when ever your Lordship will give yourself the trouble to see anything that belongs to me, but it is a great while since I have given directions to all my servants never to suffer Sr John Vanbrugh to come into my house or park . . . His behaviour was so saucy to me both in his letters and everything that he said to me and of me that one should wonder at any other person after such proceedings should desire to come within my walls; I am sure your Lord'p would not suffer such a one to come within yours if there were any person capable of such behaviour as Sir John had had to me.

44

RAGING QUARRELS

*'They did not come to comfort
me but like enemies . . .'*

The Duke and Duchess moved into rooms in the east wing of
Blenheim Palace in the summer of 1719, the Duchess having made
detailed inventories of their possessions to be moved there, gold
dishes and silver plate, lamps and candlesticks, kettles and chamber
pots, furniture and furnishings, tapestries from Brussels, brass figures
from Florence, silks from Genoa, marble from Alicante, sculpture,
statues, busts and pictures, Titians and Raphaels, portraits by Van
Dyck, Kneller and Closterman, and historical paintings by Rubens.*

The packing took weeks; the inventories covered page after page;
the valuations amounted to enormous sums, for, however parsimonious he had been throughout his life, the Duke had never begrudged
money spent on his palace.

He seemed happy to be in residence at last.† He could be heard
laughing at the drolleries and anecdotes of his chaplain, the jovial

---

* 'The old Duchess of Marlborough was fond of the historical pieces by Rubens,'
wrote William Hazlitt. 'She had during her husband's wars and negotiations in
Flanders, a fine opportunity of culling them "as one picks pears", saying "This I like,
that I like still better," and from the selection she has made it appears that she
understood the master's genius well' (*Criticisms on Art*, 1843, 211).

† It was generally doubted that anyone could actually be comfortable there. Alexander Pope expressed a common opinion: 'The chimneys are so well designed, /
They never smoke in any wind. / The gallery's contrived for walking, / The
windows to retire and talk in; / The council chamber for debate, / And all the rest
are rooms of state, / Thanks, sir, cried I, 'tis very fine, / But where d'ye sleep, or
where d'ye dine? / I find, by all you have been telling, / That 'tis a house, but not a
dwelling.'

and boisterous Dean Barzillai Jones, as they played whist together. He could be seen with his Duchess and grandchildren, driving about the park, where the keepers herded the deer together for them to observe: 'a very pretty sight,' said the Duchess who, nevertheless, had them all 'put at liberty' because she thought that they 'apprehended' the humans had come to 'destroy them'. And, on occasions, the Duke could be seen in his wife's Bow Window Room, enjoying plays performed for him by his grandchildren and their friends. Once, in this room, they performed John Dryden's drama in blank verse, *All For Love*, a version of the story of Antony and Cleopatra as censored and bowdlerized by the Duchess, with the cast gorgeously dressed in the rolls of material soon to be cut for curtains and covers. The Duke was so taken by the piece that, having seen it twice, he asked for it to be repeated a third time.

Although he generally seemed content enough, he was never at ease, so Sarah said, when she was not within call; and could not but be distressed when he learned of some new quarrel or feud in which his tempestuous wife had embroiled herself.

Ready as she was to give and take offence, to express her dislikes and prejudices, to give unsolicited and unwanted advice, to express opinions as indisputable facts, to charm with her vivaciousness, to delight with her wit, to antagonize with her outspoken censure, and to insist upon having her say upon every possible occasion, she quarrelled with Lord Townshend and the Duke's chaplain, that 'very great hypocrite', the 'disagreeable' Dean Jones. She renewed her quarrel with her son-in-law, Lord Sunderland, who, after Anne's death, married, as his third wife, Judith Tichborne, a young woman of Irish descent and large fortune whom the Duchess considered to be not only socially beneath him but also far too young at 'about fifteen' to become the wife of a man of forty-two. It was 'marrying a kitten', the Duchess protested. It was 'really very odd' for a man of his age 'to come out of his library to play with puss'. It might be true that the girl's character was unblemished for the time being; but God knew what it might become, 'even as to that', when she was 'put upon a foot so different from anything she [had] been used to'.

Sunderland then caused additional offence by making financial arrangements which she thought unfair to her grandchildren, who would now have to put up with 'another brood of children – beggars with the titles of lords and ladies – that can have nothing but what he almost robs his former children of'.*

Sunderland had offended the Duchess most particularly at the time of the financial scandal known as the South Sea Bubble, from which, displaying her exceptional acumen in money matters, she had emerged, together with her husband, with an astonishing £100,000 profit, having insisted that the Duke sell his shares in the scheme before the collapse which she foretold took place. Like many others in the Government and in London society generally, Sunderland had been involved in the chicanery which the Duchess determined to expose. In the ensuing arguments, insults, countercharges and accusations, tempers had been lost and Sunderland, in the Duchess's words, had been

put into such a violent passion that he sent immediately to speak with the Duke of Marlborough and said all that [could be] imagined ill of me to him, and amongst the rest he assured the Duke that I was in a plot to bring in the Pretender . . . This conversation harassed the poor Duke of Marlborough so much that he came home half dead . . . I revived him with a great glass of strong wine and toast . . . But he was so ill when he went to bed that I sat up with him two or three hours and recovered him with a double dose of Sir Walter Rawleigh's cordial [a restorative containing, among many other ingredients, ground ambergris].

As well as with Sunderland, the Duchess quarrelled bitterly with Cadogan, a man whose 'passion for money' was 'beyond anything'. She accused him of misapplying the sum of £50,000, which the Duke had entrusted to him at the time of his exile and Cadogan had invested – for his own benefit, she said – in Austrian securities which showed a higher return than the Dutch funds which the Duke had

---

* In fact, all Sunderland's three children by Judith Tichborne predeceased him in infancy. Sunderland himself died in April 1722. The Duchess lost no time in crossing out the few favourable comments she had formerly made about him in her papers, describing him instead as a 'furious madman without any principle'. There was 'nothing base or foolish that hee ded not do' (quoted in Green, *Sarah, Duchess of Marlborough*, 209).

specified. The Austrian securities had since greatly depreciated, and the Duchess insisted, and successfully so, that the money thus lost must be repaid to her husband.

She quarrelled also with James Craggs, a future Secretary of State, the son of the James Craggs who had served in the Duke of Marlborough's household and had been sent by him to find precedents for his appointment as Captain-General for life. This James Craggs senior had so impressed the Duchess by his financial acumen and administrative ability that she had asked him to help her manage her business affairs; but she had eventually decided that he was 'wicked enough to do anything'. As for the younger Craggs – with whom she was not on speaking terms for nine years – he had offended the Duchess not only by trying to rape one of her servants at Holywell but also by a most impertinent comment which he made to her, having accepted an invitation to call upon her and the Duke on his way to a masquerade. Appearing in the guise of a friar, he told her that he was surprised that she would give a general invitation to masqueraders since her enemies might come as well as her friends. 'I said who are my Enemies?' the Duchess recorded. 'Then he answer'd, "The Duchess of Montagu or my Lady Godolphin may come and, not [recognizing] them, you may give them a cup of Tea or a Dish of Coffee." '*

The impertinence was all the more unforgivable since, to the

---

* The younger James Craggs, the handsome and amusing Member of Parliament for Tregony, who was to die of smallpox at the age of thirty-four, was notorious for his cheek and bravado. One day at court he came across Lady Mary Wortley Montagu at the foot of the main staircase in St James's Palace. She boasted to him that the King had 'pressed her to stay longer'. Immediately he snatched her up in his arms 'as a nurse carries a child – hoop, petticoats, train, fan and all – ran full speed with her up-stairs, deposited her within the ante-chamber, kissed her hands respectfully, (still not saying a word) and vanished. At once the page flung wide the doors to the inner chamber and before she had recovered her breath, she found herself again in the King's presence.' Lady Mary supposed that Craggs owed the indulgence he enjoyed at court, as the Duke of Marlborough had once done, to his sexual charms (Grundy, *Lady Mary Wortley Montagu*, 84).

His behaviour would never have been tolerated in the days of Queen Anne, whose knowledge of court procedure and protocol was profound and whose court was accordingly at once extremely ceremonious and peculiarly dull.

36. Gerbrand van den Eeckhout's portrait of Anthonie Heinsius, the Grand Pensionary of Holland, engraved by L.A. Claessens.

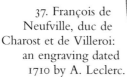

37. François de Neufville, duc de Charost et de Villeroi: an engraving dated 1710 by A. Leclerc.

38. Surgery on the battlefield during the War of the Spanish Succession: an engraving by Christian Johann Rugendas, 1707, after a painting by Georg Philip Rugendas.

39. Sir William Cadogan, later first Earl Cadogan, Marlborough's quartermaster-general and principal staff officer: a portrait attributed to Louis Laguerre, 1716.

40. A market tent in a soldiers' camp, 1707, by Marcellus Laroon II.

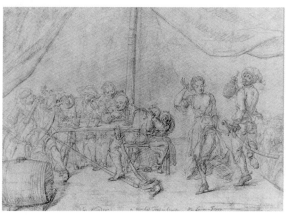

41. Ramillies flags taken in procession to Guildhall: an engraving by Anthony Walker.

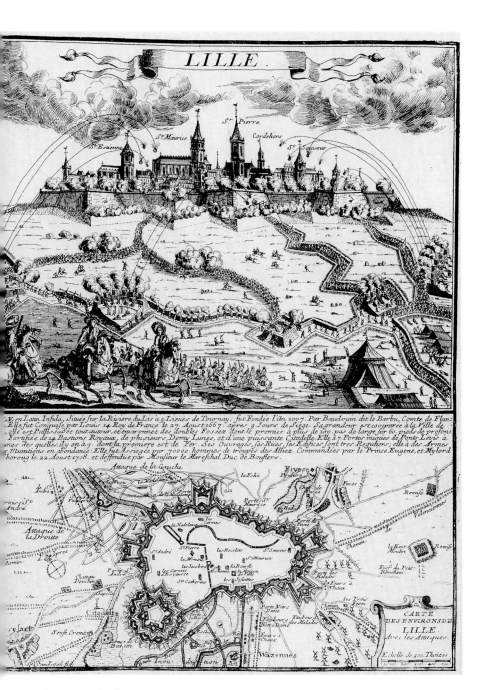

42. The siege of Lille, 1708.

43. Sir Godfrey Kneller's drawing of Marlborough, in black chalk heightened with white.

44. Sir Godfrey Kneller's painting of Sarah Marlborough after she had cut off her long hair during a quarrel with the Duke.

45 High Lodge, Blenheim Park, where the Marlboroughs stayed from time to time while the palace was being built, 1752.

46. John Vanbrugh: a portrait by Sir Godfrey Kneller, c. 1704–10.

47. Grinling Gibbons: a red-chalk portrait by Sir John Medina. Fine examples of Gibbons's work can be seen at Blenheim Palace.

48. *A North View of Blenheim House and Park in the County of Oxford*, 1752, by J. Boydell, with the fluted Doric Column of Victory in the foreground.

49. Lady Henrietta Churchill, later second Duchess of Marlborough, c. 1709, by Sir Godfrey Kneller.

50. Lady Anne Spencer, later Viscountess Bateman: a portrait by Enoch Seeman.

51. Bernard Lens's 1720 portrait of three children of Charles, third Earl of Sunderland, and Anne Churchill, Countess of Sunderland. Left to right: Charles Spencer, later third Duke of Marlborough; the Honourable John Spencer; and Diana Spencer, later Duchess of Bedford.

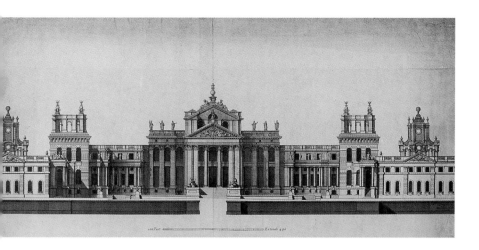

52. 'The Generall Front of Blenheim Castle ... designed by Sir John Vanbrugh K.T.'

53. The Honourable John Spencer, grandson of the first Duke and Duchess of Marlborough, with his son, John, and his black servant, Caesar Shaw: a portrait attributed to George Knapton.

54. 'Death and funeral of the invincible Malborough [*sic*]' – taken from a
French broadsheet, 1722.

Duke's great distress, their mother was, indeed, on the worst possible terms with these two surviving daughters, who, loving their father, much resented the manner in which she, in her possessive, haughty way, attempted to keep him to herself. In the end, when the daughters came to visit their father, they would ostentatiously ignore their mother.

'What I had hid so long They made publick,' the Duchess complained. 'For they never came to see their Father in a morning, but att the hours when Company was there, going up towards him without taking any notice of me, as if they had a pleasure in shewing everybody that they insulted me.'

'I have seen such behaviour from them to her that young as I was it has shock'd me,' commented Lady Cairns. 'The Dutchess used to say she had made them such fine ladies that it had turned their heads.'

Rather than go to see her father and perforce also her grumpy mother, the Duchess of Montagu asked him to visit her:

If You could have the least pleasure in the Variety of coming here, any afternoon, it would be a great one to Me, and to anybody, I am sure, that You would let meet You. My Lord Sunderland is a very good Whisk [whist] player, and my Sister Godolphin can play and would be pleas'd with it (I know), in Your Company. I hope You will come, and be so good as to let me know when, that I may send to them, or anybody You like. I know my Dear Father can never be with anybody that don't love him, but I am sure that there is no body that does it more than

Your most Dutifull
M. Montagu

The Duke thanked his 'Dear Child' for her letter, but was saddened that she did not extend the invitation to her mother. 'You can't imagine,' he wrote, 'that any Company can be agreeable to me, who have not a right behaviour to Her.' He was, he added in another letter, 'not only concerned but surprised' at her 'manner of expressing' herself about her mother. Mary's own 'expressions of duty and tenderness' to him would give him 'the greatest satisfaction if they were joined to that duty and kindness which [she] really owed to so good a mother'.

'I am not well enough to write so long a letter with my own

hand,' yet another sad and gentle reprimand concluded, 'and I believe
I am the worse to see my children live so ill with a Mother for whom
I must have the greatest tenderness and regard.'

In June 1722, not long after his seventy-second birthday, the Duke
suffered a recurrence of the paroxysms which had presaged a stroke
in the past. His mind remained clear, but his body was now growing
weaker by the month. On 15 June his two daughters called to see
him. Her sister being ill, Henrietta had previously called on her own
as soon as she had heard of their father's stroke. 'She took no more
notice of me,' her mother had written, 'than if I had been the nurse
to snuff the candles.' For the Duke's sake, however, she pretended
to be on good terms with Henrietta and 'the morning she took her
leave,' the Duchess continued,

I went thro the rooms with my arm in hers to hide this matter even from
the servants; and when she came into her own chamber, as I was talking to
her without disguise, she seem'd mighty easy & indifferent & looked in the
glass, upon which I said, 'You're extream pretty' . . . When we returned
to London we went on in the usual manner – dogged rudeness, and I trying
to hide it.

When Henrietta and her sister subsequently came together to see
their dying father, their mother was, she said, 'mightily surprised and
troubled' by their unexpected visit. 'I am sure it is impossible for my
tongue to express what I felt at that time; but I believe any body that
ever lov'd another so tenderly as I did the Duke of Marlborough
may have some feeling of what it was to have one's children come
in, in these last hours.' She knew her husband was dying and was
equally convinced that, as she put it, her daughters

did not come to comfort me but like enemies that would report to others
whatever I did in a wrong way . . . Yet I could not refuse them to come in
. . . So I desir'd Mrs Kingdom [Jane Kingdom, her friend and Windsor
neighbour] to go to them to tell them that I did not know what disorder
it might give their father to go to him now, but I desir'd they would judge
themselves and do as they liked, but I begged of them that they would not
stay long in the room because I could not come in while they were there,
being in so much affliction. Mrs Kingdom deliver'd this message and she

told me that the Duchess of Montagu answer'd that she did not understand her but that if she meant that they were not to see their mother they were very well used to that.

They staid a great while (as I thought) and, not being able to be out of the room longer from Him, I went in though they were [still] there & kneel'd down by Him: They rose up when I came in & made Curtsys but did not speak to me and after some time I called for prayers. When [these prayers] were over I ask'd the Duke of Marlb: if he heard them well and he answer'd Yes & He had join'd in them.

His daughters were still in the crowded room when their mother sent Jane Kingdom across to them with a message asking them to leave. They did not do so. Their mother repeated the request twice before they went. When it was almost dark, the Duchess asked her husband if he would feel easier now in bed, 'the couch being too narrow'. He said, 'Yes.' So his couch was carried into his own room, where he lay in a coma throughout the rest of the night. He died next morning as the sun rose. His widow, so she said, felt the soul 'tearing' from her body.

45

SUITORS

'Give mee but your most charming Person, I neither covet nor
desire Greater Riches . . .'

The Duke's widow insisted upon paying the cost of the funeral
herself, determined to avoid the criticism that might be made of
her for 'laying the expense upon the publick to save money to a
family that [had] so much'. But when the bills came in she was
horrified: the total sum came to over £5,000. She cast her eye with
characteristic care over the figures, noticing that the plumes for the
horses had been invoiced twice and that she had been charged for
no less than forty-eight yards of black cloth for the mourning coach,
enough, she said, to cover her garden. Also, she had been charged
for seven trumpeters and two chaplains, who, she discovered, had
not, in fact, been present. And she had to pay Giovanni Bononcini,
composer for the Royal Academy of Music, £100 for his music
because the Duchess of Buckingham had paid this sum for a similar
family engagement and Francis Godolphin thought that his mother-
in-law ought to match it, though 'had there not been that precedent
for it, perhaps half the sum would have been very thankfully
accepted'.

The funeral chariot was another expensive item, though the
Duchess of Buckingham pretended not to believe so. She asked the
widow if she might borrow it for her son's funeral. The Duchess of
Marlborough haughtily replied, 'It carried my Lord Marlborough
and shall never be profaned by any other corpse.'

'The undertakers tell me,' retorted the Duchess of Buckingham,
'that I may have a finer chariot for twenty pounds.'

Whatever its cost, the chariot, covered with a velvet pall and drawn by eight horses, presented a moving sight in the funeral procession to Westminster Abbey from Marlborough House, where the Duke's embalmed body had lain in state under a black cloth, on which was placed a suit of armour together with the insignia of a Knight of the Garter, a ducal coronet and the cap of a Prince of the Holy Roman Empire.

In procession with the Guards, their colours furled and drums muffled, were eight dukes in their coaches, including the Duke of Montagu as chief mourner in Sarah's own black coach, and nine generals including Cadogan, now Earl Cadogan, commander-in-chief and Master-General of the Ordnance. Then came seventy-three Chelsea Pensioners and all the Heralds of England, with the one notable exception of Sir John Vanbrugh.

From the Bell Tavern in King Street to the Abbey they walked on a carpet of black cloth. Black cloth also hung from the windows overlooking the route behind which, in rooms as crowded as the streets below, meals were being served 'with wine and chocolate' as the funeral chariot rolled by bearing the remains of 'The most noble Prince John, Duke of Marlborough, Marquis of Blandford, Baron Churchill of Sandridge, Baron of Aymouth in Scotland, Prince of the Holy Roman Empire, Knight of the most noble Order of the Garter'.

'Nothing could be finer nor better executed . . . than the Melancholy Ceremony that was performed yesterday,' the Duchess was told. 'No disorder whatsoever, nor one Stop from the beginning to the End; and Everybody agreed that the Musick that Bononcini made was the finest & the most proper for the occasion that could be imagined. A more General Concern was never seen. Even the Mobb were touch'd for the loss of the Glorious Assertor of their Liberties.'

Within a few months of her husband's death, Lord Coningsby visited the Duchess at Blenheim. He was a kindly if occasionally grumpy man of sixty-six, four years older than the Duchess, who remained a most attractive woman, though she still considered herself too fat. She had 'the most expressive eyes', Lady Mary Wortley Montagu commented, 'and the finest hair imaginable, the colour of which she said she had preserved by the constant use of honey-water'.*

Lord Coningsby had been employed in various minor posts in Whig administrations and, having divorced his first wife, by whom he had seven children, he had married a daughter of the Earl of Ranelagh, who had died not long afterwards. His greatest desire now, so he wrote to her, was to make the Duchess – his 'dearest, dearest, Lady Marlborough' – 'ye happyest of all Wemen' as she was already 'the wisest and ye Best'. But, content enough to have Coningsby, who had much admired her husband, as a friend, the Duchess could not contemplate the idea of marrying him; and when he subsequently called upon her in London at Marlborough House, she declined to see him.

Nor could she contemplate the subsequent overtures of the Duke of Somerset, the man of whose capacities the Duke of Marlborough had entertained so low an opinion and whom the Duchess dismissed in her memoirs as 'a man of very mean abilities, but of an inflexible pride and resentment never to be conquered'. His first wife was the daughter and sole heiress of the last Earl of Northumberland and he had become master not only of Alnwick Castle in Northumberland and of Northumberland House in the Strand, but also of Syon House and Petworth. A handsome man of quite extraordinary pretension, an art collector and Chancellor of Cambridge University, he was known as the 'Proud Duke': he was said to communicate with his servants by signs and to have roads scoured by outriders so that he should not be looked upon by the vulgar. It was also said that he had deducted £20,000 from his daughter's inheritance because she had sat down without permission in his presence, and that when his second Duchess, a daughter of the Earl of Nottingham, had the impertinence to tap him with her fan, he reprimanded her with the words, 'Madam, my first Duchess was a Percy and *she* never took such a liberty.'

In the summer of 1723 Somerset wrote to the Duchess of Marl-

---

* She told Lady Mary that once, in a fury with her husband, she had cut off locks of her hair and that, while at the time he had affected indifference, she had discovered, after his death, the shorn hair carefully kept in a drawer, and she had burst into uncontrollable tears.

SUITORS

borough to protest that his 'Heart and Soul' had for many years 'been struggling under a most unfeigned and most unalterable Love and Admiration for [her] Grace, tho [he had] not dared to declare it till now.' He continued,

Madam, there is no person on Earth I do love and desire more than you, for no other person on Earth can make me so perfectly happy . . . Your Grace shall command & make your Tearmes and Conditions . . . Give mee but your most charming Person, I neither covet nor desire Greater Riches for that is the onely and most valuable Treasure to mee . . . Apoynt mee an hour when I may lay myself at your ffeet 'till my Fortune is sealed.★

The Duchess replied firmly and politely in her scrawling hand:

I am confydent that there is very few wemen (if any) that would not be extreamly pleased with what your grace proposes to me; but I am resolved never to change my condition and if I know anything of myself, I would not marry the Emperor of the world tho I were but thirty years old. I hope your grace will not dislike my truth in this declaration, and that you will reward it by giveing me the honour of your friendship [which] I will endeavour upon all occasions to deserve as much as I can by shewing that I am, with all respect imaginable, your Grace's most faithfull and most humble servant, S. Marlborough.

The next week the Duke was invited to dinner by the Duchess and, while 'every moment kindled new fires within [his] breast', he was disconcerted that the meal was not tête-à-tête but that a third party was there in the person of a clergyman, one of Queen Anne's former chaplains, whose presence provoked Somerset to observe to his hostess that his 'heart and Soul would truely [have enjoyed] far

★ One of Somerset's letters, dated 17 July 1723, ends on a characteristically beseeching note and with such scant regard for the conventions of grammar and orthography as would no doubt have distressed his former tutors at Trinity College, Cambridge: 'I have more to say on this Subject, but durst not at present, untill you are graciously pleased to Grant mee soe Happy an oportunity to ashure your Grace that untill my Life shall be at its End my Heart and Soul will love & admire you for I am with the utmost sincerely [sic] and Respect Determined to bee eternelly, Madame, your Grace's most Dutyfull & most obedient Humble Servant' (Seymour of Berry Pomeroy Papers, 1392 M/L 18, Devon Record Office).

greater raptures of happiness' had Dr Clarke been invited on another occasion.

He persisted for some time in his pursuit of the unwilling Duchess, who, for a while, allowed him to do so, receiving letters which assured her that the Duke loved and adored her 'with an inviolable passion'. 'Madam,' he wrote, 'my life, my heart & my soul now are & must bee forever with you, they are no more mine.'

At last the Duchess, so it is traditionally said, silenced him with the often quoted although apocryphal words: 'If I were young and handsome as I was, instead of old and faded as I am, and you could lay the empire of the World at my feet, you should never share the heart and hand that once belonged to John, Duke of Marlborough.'

Even after she had recommended him to Lady Charlotte Finch, who was to become his second wife, Somerset continued to address her in the same manner, protesting that 'noe change in the way of life or of ffortune' would ever affect his feelings for her: 'You are the woman, the only woman I doe love, I doe value, I doe adore the most . . . my most Dear Dear Dear charming Souveraine.'

Gratified by his attentions, and having discovered a sense of humour lurking behind his pride and pomposity of manner, the Duchess changed her earlier opinion of Somerset and crossed out various passages in which she considered that she had been too severe on him in her writings, where he had been referred to as a 'mean and ungrateful man', 'full of compliments & prodigious professions but of no real worth'.

46

DAUGHTERS

'. . . famlys seldom agree to live easyly together.'

Shortly after the death of the Duke, his grieving widow received a cold, curt note forwarding a misdirected letter. It came from their eldest daughter, Henrietta, who, since there was no male heir to the title, was now the second Duchess of Marlborough: 'Madam, I am very sorry for the accident of this letter coming to me, but indeed I took it for myself, as indeed your Grace may be sure. And I am, Madam, your Grace's most obedient servant, Marlborough.'

The icy relationship between mother and daughter, so bitterly represented in this formal communication, was much exacerbated the following year when the forty-one-year-old Henrietta, whose last child had been born almost twenty years before, gave birth to another baby after returning home from Bath, where she had frequently been seen in the company of her lover, the good-natured, gregarious and witty dramatist William Congreve, who limped and stumbled about, suffering from both gout and cataract.

This was a disgrace to the family which her mother found it as impossible to forgive as the intimacy that existed between Henrietta and the late Duke of Marlborough's sister, Arabella, the former mistress of King James II and mother of a 'train' of his bastards. It was of little consequence that Arabella, of whom her brother had been fond, was now contentedly married to a perfectly respectable army officer, Colonel Charles Godfrey, by whom she had two daughters to add to the five children, including the two sons with Jacobite titles, the Dukes of Albemarle and Berwick, whom she had had by her royal lover. Duchess Sarah had never liked her and had not been pleased when, through her husband's influence, Colonel Godfrey had been appointed to two profitable offices, Clerk Controller of the Green Cloth and Master of the Jewel Office.

When Congreve died in January 1729 after a carriage accident at Bath, it was reported that Henrietta's mind had become unhinged to such an extent that she commissioned an ivory or wax figurine of him which she had placed on her dining-room table, 'addressed as if alive, served with food and treated for an imaginary sore on his leg'. She was in no sense comforted by Congreve's having left her £10,000, most of his fortune, to her a mere trifle, which, so a friend of hers commented, would have been much better bequeathed to his former mistress, the actress Anne Bracegirdle, who nearly always played the part of his heroines and was bequeathed a legacy of a mere £200.*

The story of the figurine of Congreve did not greatly surprise those who knew Henrietta well. She had always been slightly odd. Her mother remembered and recorded a dispute there had been when Henrietta's children had come to tea with their grandmother in 1712, when the Duchess was 'melting in tears' at the thought of going into exile in Flanders. She had offered them a second cup of tea, which they refused, as 'Mama had said they should drink but one cup'. So their grandmother 'made the second half milk and said they might drink it' for she would take the responsibility of assuring them 'it should do them no hurt'. The next day she received a long letter from Henrietta protesting at what had been done, reminding her that she herself had been brought up to regard all that her mother said to her children as law and that this indulgence about the tea would 'sertinly' encourage her own children to do other things that were forbidden.

When Henrietta died in 1733, her mother confessed to feeling much more than she 'imagined formerly [she] could ever do'. 'I can

---

* By her will, Henrietta, Duchess of Marlborough, left 'all Mr Congreves Personal Estate' and 'all [her] own money' to her daughter Mary, wife of the Duke of Leeds. 'It is my desire & express will,' she added, 'that my body be not at any time hereafter or on any pretence whatsoever carried to Blenheim' (BL Add. MS 2807, fos. 34–9, quoted in Green, *Sarah, Duchess of Marlborough*, 256). She was, in fact, buried in Westminster Abbey.

say with Job,' she told one of her granddaughters, 'my eyes are dim with sorrow.'

'She had many good things in her, with some oddnesses'; she had 'a good nature and was the modestest young creature that ever [was seen], till she was flattered and practised upon by the most vile people on earth', 'wretched' friends like John Gay and other 'low poets', and men such as Congreve. 'Tis certain it was the company she had long kept, both men and women, which corrupted all her morals,' the Duchess told one of her granddaughters, '& she shewd, at last, that she had no principle of any sort, was vastly ill-natur'd to everybody . . . But famlys seldom agree to live easyly together.'

Not content with taking Congreve as a lover, Henrietta actually commissioned a monument for him in Westminster Abbey with an inscription written by herself: 'Set up by Henrietta, Duchess of Marlborough, as a mark of how dearly she remembered the happiness and honour she enjoyed in the friendship of so worthy and honest a man, whose virtue, candour and wit gained him the love and esteem of the present age and whose writings will be the admiration of the future.'

Of Henrietta's sister Mary, Duchess of Montagu, who died in 1751, her mother could find no good to report. Indeed, she wrote to tell a friend that she would never have any more to say to her on any subject, and she trusted that the friend would never again mention her name. Mary's letters to her mother were returned to her unopened. In a letter to her favourite granddaughter, Diana Spencer, daughter of Anne Churchill and Charles, Earl of Sunderland, she described Mary as 'an ill wife, a cruel daughter and mother, and a very harsh mistress' with a 'very bad heart'. As for Mary's husband, the dilettante Duke of Montagu, 'all his talents [lay] in things only natural in boys of fifteen years old' – though he was over fifty – such things as 'to get people into his garden and wet them with squirts, and to invite people to his country house, and put things into their bed to make them itch, and twenty such pretty fancies like these'.

Montesquieu, author of *L'Esprit des lois*, who came to England at the suggestion of Lord Chesterfield in 1729, heard that the Duke of Montagu 'did write to [the Duchess of Marlborough] upon her daughter's F[ucking] with M. Craggs'. The Duchess answered in a brief note: 'Milord, I have received your gracious letter. I am sorry you are a cuckold, my daughter a whore . . . and my niece such a bawd: I am your Grace's etc.'

The Duchess of Montagu's daughter, Isabelle, quarrelled with her mother and was consequently a favourite of her grandmother, like her cousin Diana Spencer. But Duchess Sarah's grandsons did not so much endear themselves to her.

47

GRANDSONS

*'. . . you will have a better estate
than most people have in England.'*

Henrietta's son William, or 'Willigo', the Marquess of Blandford, the heir to the dukedom, was an unsatisfactory spendthrift, 'very odd', in his grandmother's opinion, 'if not a very weak man'. She believed that neither Blenheim nor Marlborough House would be 'of any use to him'; and, in an early draft of one of the numerous wills which she made, she left Marlborough House to another of her grandsons, her daughter Anne's eldest son, 'poor, dear' Robert, fourth Earl of Sunderland, a far more promising young 'man of sense', who, while travelling on the Continent, succumbed to the 'Ignorance of the Physicians in France', a country which, his grandmother said, could not claim to have a single proficient doctor.★

Robert never married, while Willigo, to his grandmother's additional annoyance, found what she believed to be a most unsuitable wife in a Dutch woman considerably older than himself, Maria de Jonge, daughter of a burgomaster in Utrecht, who provided her with a dowry of £30,000. His grandmother, who had hoped that he would marry a daughter of the Duke of Bedford, did all she could to prevent such a misalliance, so 'impudent a match', which the young man had arranged without consulting her. Writing to 'Lord Worthless', as he was generally known, she said:

★ The Duchess was required to settle an enormous bill of £8,430, including £1,379 for the apothecary, £200 for a coffin, £650 for embalming the body and £600 for bringing it home (quoted in Green, *Sarah, Duchess of Marlborough*, 277).

I do profess I was never so much affected at any thing that has ever happened to me . . . except the death of the Dear Duke of Marlborough and my only son. I have had no sort of pleasure but in doing everything in my power to perpetuate the glorious actions of the first & before his death I took more pains than you can easyly believe . . . to establish you in the place of a son and when I am dead, which I believe is not far off, you will have a better estate than most people have in England . . . I hope you will not return this by breaking my heart, which it will certainly do to see the Duke of Marlborough's heir marry to a burger master's daughter. As to what you say that she is as good a Gentlewoman as any in Holland, I think [that] is not saying much.

It was all very well for Willigo to say that the woman's sister had married the Earl of Denbigh, she herself remained 'a woman unknown to all the world but low people . . . a very low and odd woman'. It was absurd also to claim that she was beautiful. The Duchess had 'heard several say that she was neither handsome nor so much as agreeable'. She herself felt obliged to observe 'that in all the time she had been in Holland' she saw 'only one woman that looked like a human creature', though she had to admit when she met Maria de Jonge that she was perfectly agreeable, if quite unsuitable as a wife for her grandson. 'If any body saw her by Chance,' she declared, 'they would be ready to ask her to shew them what Lace she had to sell.'

Fortunately there were no surviving children of the marriage, which, despite the Duchess's furious protests, took place on 25 April 1729; and, while Willigo's grandmother, on learning of his premature death after an over-convivial dinner at Balliol College, Oxford, two years later, could bring herself to declare that she would have given half her estate to save him, and hoped that the Devil would pick the bones of the man who had taught him to drink, there was a general sense of relief that the dukedom would now pass to the Spencer line of the family, in effect to Charles Spencer, fifth Earl of Sunderland, the twenty-four-year-old son of Sarah's daughter Anne.

The Duchess did not share this relief, such as it was. The year after Willigo's death, she described Charles Spencer as being 'extremely like his father, violent and ill-natured. But his understanding is infinitely worse'. 'He seems to be very fond of his person, though not a very pleasing one,' she added, 'and to bestow a good deal of time upon dress.' It was a prejudiced and unjust description, though Charles Spencer was certainly dull, heavy in body and spirit, notably sententious and, to his grandmother's irritation, extravagant and financially incompetent.* Travelling on the Continent had done little to improve him. As his governor had observed, 'Mr Charles has very little curiosity & looks upon all travelling as a very insipid entertainment & thinks of Italy with great dread.' On his return his grandmother was disappointed to find no improvement in him and complained to his governor:

He speaks without opening his mouth, thro his teeth, & it is difficult to know even whether he says yes or no, without great attention, which few things are worth . . . There are several wemen in this country who don't articulate & who think it pritty to make a noise like a bird . . . I am very anxious to know whether Johnny [Charles's younger brother] has got into the same manner of speaking. If he has, I think it is very indifferent what language he talks in.

Charles further annoyed and distressed his grandmother by marrying a woman of whom she deeply disapproved, Elizabeth Trevor, the very plain daughter of the second Lord Trevor, the son of a man who had earned Duchess Sarah's enmity by helping to pass what was in her view the most unsatisfactory Peace of Utrecht. It was, she said, an absurd marriage, one which allied the dukedom of Marlborough to 'a disagreeable Family . . . of Beggars and odd people' represented by an insignificant bride who did not know how to behave, had 'a very indifferent Person and very bad Teeth'. Quite as bad as all this, the marriage was accompanied by a financial settlement arranged behind her back. Charles could have married anyone, yet he chose to connect himself with a family all of whom were 'so mean & rediculous that no man of sense but must be ashamed to have any of them seen in the house'. She had already heard tell that the girl's grandfather 'was not a Gentleman'.

The Duchess, that 'Fury of a Grandmother', wrote an angry letter

---

* When he died, Lady Mary Wortley Montagu commented that the only people to regret him were the 'tradespeople and usurers' who would never now be paid (Grundy, *Lady Mary Wortley Montagu*, 582).

to her grandson, who expressed his intention to 'kick her Arse & bid her kiss [his] own', and replied in a letter described by its recipient as 'Foolish, Brutal and Ungrateful':

I receiv'd Your Grace's extraordinary Letter last Night, & I own my Discerning won't let me see any Reason in what your Grace is pleas'd to say against my Marrying; unless Invectives are to be look'd on as Arguments. As for your putting me out of your Will, it is some Time since I either expected or desir'd to be in it. I have nothing more to add but to assure Your Grace, that this is the last time I shall ever Trouble you by Letter or Conversation. I am your Grace's Grandson, Sunderland.

To this the Duchess replied, 'You end that you are my Grandson: Which is indeed a very Melancholy Truth; but very lucky for You. For all the World except yourself is Sensible, that, had you not been my Grandson, You would have been in as bad a Condition as you deserve to be.'

She never fully forgave Charles's brother Johnny for going to the wedding, nor for taking his brother's side in the court case which their grandmother initiated over Charles's marriage settlement. But she had been fond of Johnny – who was more sensitive than his brother, and a lover of music – ever since she had taken care of him as a boy of nine when his mother died, and had nursed him and Charles when they contracted smallpox, having them to sleep in her bed. For all their occasional disagreements, she remained as close to Johnny as she did to any other male member of the family, excusing faults in him which she strongly condemned in his brother. Yet the young man's sexual escapades, from which he contracted syphilis, were a source of constant concern to her, as was his wild extravagance. This fault caused particular disquiet to a woman as careful with money as herself and one whose husband had been so parsimonious that it was said he would still walk home in his old age to save the sixpence he would have to pay for a sedan chair, while these two grandsons, Charles and Johnny, both of whom lost extremely large sums gambling, were reported to pay chairmen in guineas, ostentatiously declining to touch silver.

48

GRANDDAUGHTERS AND
THEIR HUSBANDS

*'It would be too much to repeat the monstrous usage
which I received.'*

The Duchess's relationships with some of her granddaughters were quite as strained as they were with her two surviving daughters. She remained, however, on the friendliest terms with Charles and Johnny's sister, dear 'little Dye' Spencer, whom her grandmother called Cordelia. 'That is the name I intend to call you for the future, which is the name of King Lear's good child,' she explained, 'and therefore a proper title for you, who have always been good to me . . . You are charming in all your thoughts and actions'. Evidently she considered that Diana would make an excellent bride for King George II's son Frederick, Prince of Wales, with a dowry of £100,000. But Sir Robert Walpole vetoed this idea, and Diana herself refused the hand of Lord Chesterfield and, more predictably, that of William Conolly, the Irish Lord Justice, the son of a publican or a blacksmith whose single recommendation seems to have been that he had inherited from an uncle an enormous sum of money which was to enable him to leave a fortune of £27,000 a year.

In 1731 Diana Spencer married Lord John Russell, who, the next year, succeeded his brother as Duke of Bedford. Less than four years later, however, she died of consumption. Her grandmother, who had gone to see her 'dearest Dye' at Bedford House in Bloomsbury Square, wrote a cross letter to the widower, whom she blamed for not being allowed into Di's room when she lay dying, just as she had been denied entrance to the bedroom of another of her granddaughters, Harriet, Duchess of Newcastle, when she was so ill that her husband, 'weeping very much', feared she would not recover, and Sarah, 'forgetting all the ill-usage' she had met from him, 'sat down and wept with him'.

'Your Grace knew very well,' the Duchess told Bedford, 'that I [have had] more experience than any body about her. It would be too much to repeat the monstrous usage which I received . . . But I sat silently in outward rooms, bathed in tears', for her heart, as she had once told Di, had 'allways been [hers] and [would be so till she died] and after for all eternity, if that can be'.

She upbraided the Duke violently, accusing him of murdering his wife by denying her proper care; and she condemned him for his heartlessness when he was married for the second time, less than two years later, to the eldest daughter of the first Earl Gower, lambasting him for not having had the courtesy to return to her the great Duke's campaign tent, which she had sent to Woburn so that 'dearest Dye' could rest, while enjoying the benefit of the early autumn air, in her 'dear Grandfather's tent where he did such wonderful things to secure the nation from being enslaved by the French King'.

For her other granddaughter, Anne, a managing woman, the wife of the first Viscount Bateman, the rich son of a director of the South Sea Company, Sarah had no such fondness as she had for 'dearest Dye'. She rarely spoke of her – the 'worst Woman', the 'vilest Woman', she had ever known in her life – without strong disparagement. Indeed, Horace Walpole heard that she once blacked over a portrait of her, writing beneath it, 'She is more black within.' She warned Diana that Anne Bateman was 'a Disgrace to anybody's sister' and she ought to have nothing to do with her. 'I don't mean,' she added, 'that you should not see your brothers . . . they can't help their weakness. But for Lady Bateman I must declare that I can never have any satisfaction in the conversation of any body that has any commerce with her . . . You must be very plain with Lady Bateman in letting her know that you can have no commerce with her.' In vain did Francis Hare bring himself to tell her, as tactfully as he could, that in dealing with the female members of her family she sometimes 'carried things to too great an extremity'. 'One must wink hard and contrive at many faults to preserve peace & love in familys.'

★

The Duchess's animosities and feuds in her widowhood were by no means limited to her family, although family rows tended to be the most bitter. As Lady Mary Wortley Montagu observed, 'The most vindictive Highland chief never had so many feuds, but her deadliest were in the bosom of her own clan.' She was liable to erupt with fury and with anyone at a moment's provocation. The Earl of Bristol's son, John, Lord Hervey, called her 'Mount Aetna' after the Sicilian volcano. She quarrelled with lawyers and architects and doctors, one of whom, foolhardly enough to suggest that she would die if she were not blistered, was vehemently contradicted with the words, 'I won't be blistered and I won't die.'

She had a furious altercation with the Duke of Bridgwater over the ownership of two marble statues of Fame and Glory which graced Bridgwater's house. She quarrelled with her friends Lady Lechmere, daughter of the Earl of Carlisle, and Mrs William Clayton, wife of her late husband's agent. She quarrelled with both her chief stewards, Charles Hodges, 'a very bad man', and Thomas Norgate, 'a very great rogue'. She quarrelled with Christopher Lofts, the Under-Ranger of Windsor Park; with Henry Joynes, clerk of the works at Blenheim, whom she took to court; with John Hughes, the gardener; with the author Nathaniel Hooke, who had the impertinence to try to convert her to popery; with Sir James Thornhill over his charges for painting the Hall ceiling at Blenheim; with the Duke of St Albans, whom she endeavoured to prevent driving through Windsor Park; with Roger Morris, the architect, who had led her grandson Charles into permitting such wild extravagance at Althorp as a replica of an Inigo Jones church for his stables; and with Sir Robert Walpole, King George II's chief minister, over his administration of the loans she made to them, the interest which she received for these being, in her opinion, far too low. Then Walpole gave additional offence by withdrawing permission for her to drive through St James's Park on her way to Marlborough House, a right she had enjoyed without question in the time of Queen Anne. Walpole complained that she 'refused to submit to the usual forms of doing business', making demands 'where she should have asked favours or submitted formal petitions, and [taking] offence if they were not immediately complied with'.

She also fell out with the King, to whom she was rude at court, giving him to understand he was 'too much of a German', and with his wife, Queen Caroline, over a disputed road across land which she had bought at Wimbledon. The Queen, a woman more politically astute and better educated than herself, retaliated by asking Sir Robert Walpole to stop paying the £500 a year which the Duchess still received as Ranger of Windsor Park.

The Duchess, jealous of the Queen, wrote about her with caustic and derisive humour, recalling her expression of inane happiness at her coronation and her hair 'clotted all over with powder'. In a characteristically scornful and amusing passage, she recounted:

Two or three days ago Her Sacred Majesty was in great danger of being ravished. She was walking from Kensington to London early in the morning and, having a vast desire to appear more able in everything than other people, she walked so fast as to get before my Lord Chamberlain and the two princesses, quite out of sight . . . Lord Grantham meeting a country clown asked him if he had met any person and how far they were off? To which he answered he had met a jolly crummy woman with whom he had been fighting some time to kiss her. (I am surprised at the man's fancy!) And my Lord Grantham was so frightened that he screamed out and said it was the Queen. Upon which the country fellow was out of his wits, fell upon his knees, cried and earnestly begged of my Lord Grantham to speak for him, for he was sure he should be hanged for what he had done. But he did not explain further what it was. And Her Majesty does not own more than that he struggled with her, but that she got the better of him.

When Queen Caroline died the Duchess readily admitted that she was glad.

49

THE DUCHESS AT HER WRITING
TABLE AND AT BLENHEIM

*'Upon the whole I beleive everybody will allow that there is a
great deal very fine in this house . . .'*

Until gout in her fingers forced her to turn to amanuenses, the
Duchess filled sheet after sheet of paper in her scrawling spiky hand
– which she herself described as 'very rediculous'. Her 'oridgenal
speeling' was quite as idiosyncratic as her husband's, though she was
always ready to criticize what she considered to be faulty orthography
in others. She kept inventories of furniture, plate and books, wrote
entries in her commonplace books, 'vindications' of her past conduct,
memoirs, a history of England, beginning with the reign of Charles
II and not progressing much further, calculations of her assets and
the lists of the generous sums which she gave to various charities,
which amounted in all, so it has been estimated, to 'upwards of a
quarter of a million of money'.

There were numerous witnesses to her charity. Henry Fielding,
who thought her a 'glorious woman', believed there was not a man
or a woman who equalled her 'in acts of private munificence'. Those
in receipt of this munificence ranged from the poet John Gay, author
of *The Beggar's Opera*, who had fallen on hard times, to the 'forty
miserable old creatures' whom she provided with almshouses at
St Albans at a cost of £50,000, and a number of Swiss peasants who
were given the means of emigrating to America.

The Duchess was clever with money, as she had demonstrated at
the time of the wild speculation in the shares of the South Sea
Company; and she had a great deal of it to be clever about, having
not only received a fortune on her husband's death but made the most

of the opportunities offered her when her influence was supreme at court. She was widely rumoured, for example, to have received no less than £10,000 from the Duke of Kent when he was appointed Lord Chamberlain in 1704.

So good a head for business did she have, in fact, that Arthur Maynwaring said that she was more capable of business than any man he had ever known. As the law then stood, she could not hold stocks or property in her own name while her husband was alive; but after his death she began to speculate with great perspicacity, buying no fewer than twenty-seven estates in twelve counties within thirty-odd years, including one at Wimbledon, which cost no less than £25,000, the property of Sir Theodore Janssen, a bankrupt director of the South Sea Company, and another, Holdenby House, three miles from Althorp, built at vast expense by Sir Christopher Hatton, who had waited vainly for ten years for Queen Elizabeth I to come to visit him there.★

The Duchess wrote careful notes on all these estates, maintaining a sharp look-out for evidence of dishonesty in her agents and keeping detailed accounts of rents and expenditure with the efficiency of a trained accountant rather than the uncertainty of an elderly woman whose sketchy education had come to a halt when she went to live at court as a girl.

The Countess of Bute told her daughter, Lady Louise Stuart, that she had often watched the Duchess

in the curious process of casting up her accounts. Curious because Her Grace, well versed as she was in all matters relating to money, such as getting it, hoarding it, and turning it to the best advantage, knew nothing of common arithmetic. But her sound, clear head could devise an arithmetic of its own; to lookers-on it appeared as if a child had scrabbled over the

---

★ There was a half-finished house on the Wimbledon estate which she ordered to be demolished and replaced. Although he was, in her opinion, 'often mad and always very odd', she employed Lord Herbert as architect but soon dismissed him. The house which he designed 'looked as if it was making a Curtsie'. Nor did she like Wimbledon itself: 'Though it is high, it is upon clay, an ill sod, very damp and I believe an unhealthy place, which I shall very seldom live in; and consequently I have thrown away a vast sum of money upon it to little purpose' (quoted in Rowse, *The Early Churchills*, 394). The house was burned to the ground in 1785.

paper, setting down figures here and there at random; and yet every sum came right to a fraction, in defiance of [Edward] Cocker [the seventeenth-century mathematician].

To no accounts did the Duchess devote closer attention than those connected with the completion and embellishment of Blenheim Palace and its grounds. She had never grown to care for the place, that 'fierce unmerciful Hous', that great 'heap of stones', that 'unnecessary and rediculous thing', 'so vast a place that it [tried] one almost to death to look after it and keep it in order'.*

She far preferred both the Windsor Lodge and the Spencers' house, Althorp, 'the most agreeable place in the world'. She liked it 'ten thousand times better than Blenheim'. 'I mortally hate all grandeur,' she told her grandson, Johnny Spencer. Her taste was 'always to have things plain and clean, from a piece of wainscot to a lady's face'. Yet, her husband had envisaged Blenheim as a memorial to his victories and his soldiers and as a grand setting for his descendants and, now that she had lost him, she was anxious to ensure that his wishes were carried out.

When he had been serving abroad, his letters had been full of pleas that she should go over to Blenheim to ensure that the work was progressing satisfactorily:

Pray press on my house and gardens . . . I beg you to do all you can that the house at Woodstock may be carried up as much as possible, that I may have a prospect of living in it . . . Woodstock is extremely at my heart . . . I find your heart is not set on that place as I could wish . . . You know my heart is sett upon the house of Woodstock and you say nothing to me how it goes on . . . As this is the third year of the trees at Woodstock, if possible, I should wish that you might, or somebody that you can rely on, taste the

---

* 'The Duchess of Marlborough used to ridicule the vanity . . . of beginning an edifice which one could never inhabit or probably see finished,' Lady Mary Wortley Montagu told her daughter. 'Building is the general weakness of old people. I have had a twitch of it myself, though certainly it is the highest absurdity, and as sure a proof of dotage as pink-coloured ribands, or even matrimony . . . [The Duchess said] one might always live upon other people's follies, yet you see she built the most ridiculous house I ever saw, since it is really not habitable from the excessive damps' (Lady Mary Wortley Montagu to Lady Bute, 23 May 1759).

fruit of every tree, so that what is not good might be changed. On this matter you must advise with Mr Wise as to what plan may be proper for the ice-house; for that should be built this summer so that it meight have time to dry . . . You say nothing of going to Blenheim, but the weather is so fine I could wish you there, by which the finishing within doors, I believe, would go on faster . . . As to the design for the Orange-houses, that must, in its due time go on . . . I am advised by every body to have the Portico, so that I have writt to have itt; and which I hope you will like for I shou'd be glad we were allways of one mind, which shall allways be endeavour'd for I am never so happy as when I think you are kind.

Sarah had not been as attentive to these requests as she might have been; and, as though concerned to make amends for her past carelessness and neglect, she determined to involve herself earnestly in the completion of the building, which was eventually accomplished – after prolonged lawsuits and actions against over 400 named persons to expose the 'fowle practices of builders' – at a cost of some £300,000, about £60,000 of which came from the Marlborough estate.

For some time after her husband's death, however, she was unable to bring herself to deal with the problems of the palace, being, as she said, 'more melancholy than anyone else when I reflect where hee is now for whom it was built'.

But, resilient as always, she overcame her depression before long and began again to march about her property, once more, as Godolphin had said, 'being extremely prying into'. Having dispensed with the services of Vanbrugh, and not often consulting Hawksmoor – after all, so-called architects were, with very few exceptions, either 'mad or rediculous' and their 'very high flights' had to be 'kept down' – she took it upon herself to communicate directly with her clerk of the works, Henry Joynes's successor, John Desborough, and with the craftsmen and others at work on the site, with the gardeners, Charles Bridgman and John Hughes, and with the masons, Bartholomew Peisley the younger and William Townesend, who was, like Peisley, a member of a family of Oxford masons responsible for the embellishment of many buildings in the University and responsible also, under Hawksmoor's direction and with Peisley's help, for the decoration of Blenheim's magnificent Long Library.*

The Duchess on her rounds was forced to be, as she put it, 'perpetually on the watch'. But she relied much on the advice of James Moore, a skilled cabinetmaker, whose consoles and pierglasses can be seen in the Bow Window Room. She referred to him as her 'oracle' and greatly admired his richly carved and gilt gesso pieces. He had his own room at Blenheim, and this, inevitably, led to his falling out with the Duchess in the end.

Bossy, demanding and tiresome as she was, the Duchess did eventually contrive to ensure that, without undue extravagance, the palace turned out to be a fitting memorial to the Duke and his achievements, completed at less cost than the £10,000 a year which,

---

* As Vanbrugh worked from east to west, the Long Library (180 feet in length) was one of the last rooms to be decorated. Hawksmoor was anxious that it should be completed as he had designed, and in 1728 he wrote to the Duchess: 'Ther's none can judg so well of the designs as the person who composed it, therefore I should beg leave to take a Convenient time to Slip downe.' That year the stucco decoration of the ceiling, with its two false domes, was completed to the designs of Isaac Mansfield. The plain blue panels would, no doubt, have been painted with allegorical scenes by Sir James Thornhill had not the Duchess insisted on lower rates than those charged by Thornhill for the ceilings elsewhere.

Van Dyck's equestrian portrait of Charles I, now in the National Gallery, used to hang at the northern end of the Library where the Willis organ, installed by the eighth Duke, stands today (Green, *Blenheim Palace*, 37).

Opposite it, at the southern end, is Rysbrack's statue of Queen Anne, commissioned by the Duchess and bearing the inscription 'To the memory of Queen Ann under whose auspices John Duke of Marlborough conquered and to whose munificence he and his posterity with gratitude owe the possession of Blenheim'.

In telling her granddaughter, Diana Spencer, of her decision to commission this sculpture in 1735, Sarah wrote, 'I am going to Rysbrack to make a bargain with him for a fine statue of Queen Anne which I will put in the Bow Window room with a proper inscription. It will be a very fine thing and though but one figure it will cost me £300. I have a satisfaction in showing this respect to her, because her kindness to me was real. And what happened afterwards was compassed by the contrivance of such as are in power now' (Thomson, *Letters of a Grandmother*, 152).

The bookcases in the Long Library once contained the Sunderland Library, which was assembled between 1710 and 1728 by the first Duke's son-in-law, Charles, Earl of Sunderland, and which eventually found its way into the possession of the Churchills in acknowledgement, so it is believed, of a financial loan. The Library remained at Blenheim until it was sold by auction in 1872 by the sixth Duke. It fetched £30,000 (Reid, *John and Sarah, Duke and Duchess of Marlborough*, 119).

as Vanbrugh had pettishly said, the Duke had left his widow in order that she might 'Spoil [it] her own way'.

With an eye to economy and simplicity, she not only curtailed the activities of Sir James Thornhill and Louis Laguerre, she was also pleased to report that the Chapel was finished 'very plain', and added, 'Considering how many Wonderful Figures and Whirligigs I have seen Architects finish a Chappel withal that are of no Manner of Use but to laugh at, I must confess I cannot help thinking that what I have designed for this Chappel may as reasonably be call'd finishing of it, as the Pews and Pulpit.'*

What was not so plain, however, was the tomb in the chapel designed by William Kent and executed by Michael Rysbrack for £2,200. This was a dramatic memorial to the Duke and Duchess, whose figures are flanked by those of their son, John, who died at Cambridge in 1703, and of another son, who died in infancy, none of their four daughters being found a place. Their father's body was brought to Blenheim from Westminster Abbey when his Duchess died in 1744 and was buried beside her.†

Equally dramatic on its massive pedestal is the finely fluted Doric Column of Victory, for which Hawksmoor had prepared various designs but which was eventually entrusted to Henry Herbert, ninth Earl of Pembroke, and Roger Morris, favoured architect of the Earl, for whom he designed the beautiful Palladian bridge at Wilton.

Over 130 feet high, it is surmounted by a larger than life-size lead statue of the Duke by Robert Pit, a craftsman otherwise unknown. Begun in 1727 and finished three years later, the column stands at

* She did not, however, hesitate to spend money when she deemed it necessary to make the furnishings of the palace as fine as her husband would have wanted. For example, the Duke of Manchester, when ambassador in Venice, was commissioned to purchase for her no fewer than 3,500 yards of damask and velvet in yellow, blue, scarlet, green and crimson (Blenheim Papers, quoted in Reid, *John and Sarah, Duke and Duchess of Marlborough*, 445).
† Sir John Vanbrugh had tried to persuade the Duchess to build a mausoleum in the park, 'a plain but magnificent durable monument' which would have been a 'noble' show to 'many future ages', and he had criticized the Duchess for spending so much instead on her husband's funeral, an 'idle show' which would be 'forgot in two days' (Williams, 'A Factor in His Success: The Missing Years', 13–14).

the entrance to the Grand Avenue. For an inscription both Alexander Pope and Francis Hare were approached without success, and the wording was eventually entrusted to Lord Bolingbroke, who, having been granted a pardon by King George I for having deserted him for the Pretender, had returned to England. The Duchess said of him that he had 'forfeited all pretensions to any one single vertue'; yet she had 'grown to bee wonderful fond of useful knaves', and Bolingbroke had, after all, greatly admired the Duke and now additionally recommended himself to Sarah because of his opposition to Walpole. She did what she could to ensure that the name of the author of the inscription was not generally known; but the drama of the words much moved her: 'The Battle was Bloody: the Event decisive. The Woods were pierced: the Fortifications trampled down. The Enemy fled. The Town was taken . . .'

'When I read it,' the Duchess wrote, 'I thought it the finest thing that was possible for any man to write, and as often as I have read it I still wet the paper.'

There is another, simpler and less grammatically correct inscription on Hawksmoor's triumphal arch, that 'spacious portal of Corinthian order', which leads into the grounds of the palace from Woodstock:

This Gate was built the year after the death of the most illustrious John, Duke of Marlborough, by order of Sarah, his most beloved wife, to whom he left the sole direction of the many things that remained unfinished of this fabric. The services of this great man to his country the Pillar will tell which the Duchess has erected for a lasting monument of his glory and her affection for him.

It was through this arch that King George III was to approach the palace on a visit with his friends, the Earl and Countess Harcourt. Emerging from it and coming suddenly upon the view of the lake and the Grand Bridge, the hanging beechwoods and the palace, the King exclaimed in admiration, 'We have nothing to equal this!' James Boswell was also to be deeply impressed when he drove through the park with Samuel Johnson in March 1776:

It was a delightful day. When I looked at the magnificent bridge built by John Duke of Marlborough, over a small rivulet, and recollected the Epigram made upon it,

'The lofty arch his high ambition Shows
The stream, an emblem of his bounty flows'

and saw that now by the genius of Brown★ a magnificent body of water
was collected, I said, 'They have *drowned* the Epigram.' I observed to
[Johnson], while in the midst of the noble scene around us, 'You and I,
Sir, have, I think, seen together the extremes of what can be seen in Britain:
– the wild rough island of Mull, and Blenheim Park.'

The Duchess had turned her attention to the setting of the palace
with more enthusiasm than she had been able to muster when
considering the work on the palace itself. In a letter to the Duke of
Somerset describing the waterworks designed by the engineer
Colonel John Armstrong, she told him:

I believe it will be very beautiful. The Canal & Bason (which is already
don) look very fine. There is to be a lake & a cascade . . . which I think
will bee a great addition to the place. Sir John [Vanbrugh] never thought
of this cascade which will bee the finest & largest that ever was made . . .
The fine green meadow between the hous & the wood is to remain as it
is, & I beleive Your Grace will think in that nature cannot be mended,
tho' Sir John formerly sett his heart upon turning that into a lake as I
will do it on the other side & I will have swans & all such sort of things
in it.

She added:

I have reduced the stables to one third of what was intended by Sir John
and yet I have room for about fourty fine horses . . . But what I value
myself most upon is the fourniture which I have don at home & have made
very little use of upholsterers, which has made it cost less by a vast sum &
it is ten times more agreeable & handsome than if it had been done by
them . . . Upon the whole I beleive everybody will allow that there is a
great deal very fine in this house, as well as many great faults which I can
bee very well contented with since they were not by my derection . . .

★ Lancelot 'Capability' Brown was employed at Blenheim after the Duchess's death.
He built a dam and cascade near Bladon and sent water pouring through Vanbrugh's
bridge, flooding the ground floor and creating the lakes on either side of it. 'The
lake at Blenheim,' Sir Sacheverell Sitwell considered, 'is the one great argument of
the landscape gardener. There is nothing finer in Europe. In its way this is one of
the wonders of the eighteenth century' (Sitwell, *Sacheverell Sitwell's England*, 79).

It will certainly bee a wonderfull fine Place ... and I am glad it will bee so, because it was the dear Duke of Marlborough's Passion to have it don.

In her later years the Duchess spent an increasingly large part of her time at her writing table. She told Lady Mary Wortley Montagu that she enjoyed the solitude and the opportunity to indulge what she called her 'contemplative way of living', the hours spent in 'reflexion' as well as 'improvement of the mind'. She was a vivid writer; and in her 'Account of the Cruell Usage of my Children', which she sent to various friends for their comments and approval, she brought scene after scene from the past to memorable life, as, for instance, when recounting a drive to Hyde Park in the company of her daughter Henrietta, with whom she was at that time on unusually good terms: 'She did not call for me till it was almost dark and I remember we met the company coming out of the Ring. However, I never reproached her, loving her, and seeing her of a careless temper, and we sang all the way.'

Her description of the Duke of Bridgwater's attempt to force his daughter Anne to go to live with him and his new wife at Ashridge is also characteristic. The girl had been living in the tender care of her grandmother, the Duchess of Marlborough, since the death of her mother, and her father now had a mind to take her away so that he could increase his family's fortune by a future marriage of the child to the third Duke of Bedford. The Duchess of Marlborough was determined that Anne should not be taken from her and, at her grandmother's dictation, the girl wrote to her father: 'My Grandmama hopes you will excuse her for not sending me now, I have had so great a cold and pain in my ear that my head is now wrapt up in Flanel.' 'My Lady Dutches,' she added, 'is in a melancholy condition which makes her unwilling to part with me.'

On receipt of this letter, Bridgwater stormed into the forecourt of Marlborough House at eleven o'clock at night 'with a candle and lanthorn before him, and the air of being quite mad ... The first person that saw him was Lady Anne's woman who made as much haste as she could to come & tell the Dutchess of Marl. . . .' Sarah's account continued:

My Lord ran after her & bid her say to the Dutchess that he desir'd she would not make his child undutiful to him. The Dutchess of Marl: was apprehensive that he would have come in to her which would have been extream disagreeable . . . [But the angry Duke] made the servant come into the Dutchess of Marl: who was in bed, to tell her that if Lady Anne was sick it was she that had made her so. He would not go into any room . . . but walk'd about the Hall like a madman with the most ill natur'd Countenance that ever was seen in any humane Creature. As soon as Lady Anne was dress'd she came down, but being half dead with grief, the servants gave her some water & drops, & after that the Duke took her away [in hysterics] in his coach.*

In composing her *Account of the Conduct of the Dowager Duchess of Marlborough from her First Coming to Court to the Year 1710*, she had had the help of Pope's friend, the author of a four-volume history of Rome, Nathaniel Hooke, before he annoyed her by his ill-advised attempts to convert her to Roman Catholicism. He was paid £5,000 for his assistance and considered the large fee very well justified: on his arrival, for the first time he found her in bed, from where she dictated to him without much pause for six hours.

Having provided materials for both Richard Steele and Lord Molesworth, neither of whom produced anything from them – Steele having pawned the papers she handed over to him – the Duchess approached the poets David Mallet and Richard Glover for a biography of the Duke. But, like Steele and Molesworth before them, neither wrote a single line, no doubt annoyed by the Duchess's insistence that Lord Chesterfield should supervise their labours and intimidated by the precise instructions as to the content and style of the work, including her injunction that it would need 'no Flourishes to set it off, but short plain facts'. Glover is believed to have returned his fee, and Mallet, so Samuel Johnson said, 'groped for materials; and thought of it till he had exhausted his mind', having for years given himself 'an air of consequence' because of his commission. Bishop William Warburton thought that, had he not exhausted it, he would not have done much to satisfy the Duchess anyway: in his

---

* Lady Anne was married to the third Duke of Bedford in April 1725. The Duke died in 1732, and seven months later his widow married the third Earl of Jersey.

life of Bacon he 'had forgotten that he was a philosopher and if he should write the Life of the Duke of Marlborough he would probably forget that he was a General'.

LAST DAYS

'It is impossible for your Grace to converse without warmth &
force as it is for you to be dull or ugly . . .'

Although writing so much, the Duchess found more time for reading than she had done in the recent past; certainly more time than her husband, who, so Lord Chesterfield said, 'was exceedingly ignorant of books', while 'extremely knowing in men'.

As a young woman, her small library at St Albans had included the plays of Shakespeare and Dryden and volumes of poetry by Suckling, Waller and her 'beloved' Abraham Cowley, and from these she often quoted in her conversation and letters.

Now she read works by Swift's patron, Sir William Temple, and quoted a passage which had struck her fancy for the benefit of her granddaughter Diana Spencer: 'The greatest pleasure of life is love, the greatest treasure contentment, the greatest possession health, the greatest ease is sleep, the greatest medicine is a good friend.' As for Swift himself, she was enthralled by *Gulliver's Travels*, 'quite in raptures by it', the author was told. 'She says she can dream of nothing else since she read it . . . She had not been as pleased with anything she had read for a long time.' For this one book she could easily forgive Swift 'all the slaps' he had given her and the Duke of Marlborough in the past.

She was almost equally enthusiastic about *Don Quixote*. But she seems not to have read much other fiction, and evidently preferred to look into books on medicine and architecture, history and biography. She once recommended to Diana Spencer a biography of James I, 'a great deal' of which was 'tedious', but the King's love letters to the Duke of Buckingham were 'incomparable', and it would make

Di laugh 'to read what his Sacred Majesty did and said'. She also recommended a translation of Socrates and the works of John Locke, under the influence of whose *Thoughts Concerning Education* she had one of her grandsons removed from Eton to be educated by a private tutor.

But she could not abide poetry in general. Indeed, when it came to commissioning a life of the great Duke, she made it a stipulation that it should not contain a single piece of verse.

Predisposed to dislike most poets, she was also disappointed in Voltaire, who called upon her in the autumn of 1727 at Blenheim. Finding 'infinite pleasure in the agreeable vivacity of his conversation', she had it in mind to ask him to help her with the papers she was assembling; but, well aware of how many enemies such an association with the Duchess was likely to make for him, he declined the request, to her annoyance; and when he offered some criticism of what she had written, she snatched the papers from his hand. 'I thought the man had sense,' she complained, 'but I find him at bottom either a fool or a philosopher.' He found her useful, however. She gave him an account of her husband's dealings with King Charles XII, which he incorporated in his biography of that monarch.

As well as supervising accounts of her husband's career and compiling narratives of her own, the Duchess, by far the richest woman in her own right in England, spent hours writing and rewriting the numerous drafts of her will, 'contriving schemes of plaguing some, and extracting praise from others, to no purpose,' Lady Mary Wortley Montagu told her daughter, 'eternally disappointed and eternally fretting'.*

Her 'chief Design', so she told Lord Pengelly, Lord Chief Baron of the Exchequer, to whom she turned for advice, was 'to take care of those who happen to be the most valuable part of the dear Duke of Marlborough's family, to whom he gave very little considering his great estate. And he knew that he might depend on

---

* The Duke had spent almost as much time dealing with his will. The final document extends to thirty-two long and closely written pages (National Army Museum Archives, 6510-146(2)-57).

me for giving what was in my power to those that deserved it best, or where it would be most useful.'

She left some £1 million and an income of £27,000 a year to her grandson Johnny, on condition that neither he nor his son ever accepted a government post, bequeathing as little as she could of what was not already entailed to his brother Charles, the third Duke, who was already in debt to the tune of £500,000.

Despite the bitter quarrels they had endured, she mentioned her only surviving child, the Duchess of Montagu, without rancour and bequeathed her a gold snuffbox and a set of miniatures of various members of her family. Her man of business, James Stephens, and her servants, her porter, her chairmen and the indoor servants were all mentioned, Grace Ridley, an Oxfordshire clergyman's daughter, her faithful maid of many years' service, being left £16,000 as well as a miniature of the Duke of Marlborough and a picture of the Duchess by Sir Godfrey Kneller. In all, over twenty people were given annuities, while £300 were to be distributed among the poor of Woodstock. More surprisingly, her best diamond ring, as well as £20,000, were left to Lord Chesterfield, and £10,000, together with landed property in Buckinghamshire, Northamptonshire and Suffolk, to William Pitt 'upon Account of his Merit in the noble Defence he has made for the support of the laws of England and to prevent the Ruin of his Country'.★

When she wrote the twenty-sixth and final draft of her will, the Duchess of Marlborough was well over eighty years old. She had long been accepted as a kind of national institution, a *monstre sacré* who fully deserved the welcome accorded to her at King George II's coronation, when she marched past in procession to Westminster Abbey in her duchess's robes, the train of her cloak five feet in length and her cape bordered with six bands of ermine. Exhausted by the effort, she 'took a drum from a drummer and seated herself on it', recorded a French observer of the scene. 'The crowd laughed and shouted at seeing the wife of the great and celebrated General Duke

★ Like Chesterfield, Pitt was treated so generously partly because of his opposition to Sir Robert Walpole, a man she detested.

of Marlborough seated on a drum in her robes of state and in such a solemn procession.'

Tempestuously throwing herself through life, highly emotional, exasperating, meddlesome, demanding and argumentative, she was at the same time capable of arousing great affection and of acts of generosity and kindness. Once, for example, taking pity on a chimney sweep's climbing boy, 'a most miserable creature without shoes, stockings, breeches or shirt', she arranged for him to be sent to Windsor with a servant, who was instructed to 'equip the poor creature with what he wanted'. When staying at Bath for a course of the waters, she was once seen driving down from her lodgings to the spring carrying a big bag of silver coins for distribution to the poor.

She relished disputation and consequently enjoyed the company of Alexander Pope and seems not to have taken it amiss when he fell asleep when she was talking to him at excessive length or when he started insinuating that a mention of him in her will would be more than welcome. More surprisingly, she also enjoyed the company of the devout Methodist the Countess of Huntingdon, to whom she wrote to thank her for being so 'very good' to her and for all her 'kindness and attention'. She assured her that, having 'no comfort in [her] own family', she must look for that 'pleasure & gratification that others can impart'. In one letter she confided:

In truth I always feel more happy & more contented after an hour's conversation with you than I do after a whole week's round of amusement. When alone my reflections and recollections almost kill me & I am forced to fly to the society of those I detest & abhor. Now there is Lady Frances Saunderson's great rout tomorrow night – all the world will be there & I must go. I do hate that woman as I hate a physician, but I must go if for no other purpose than to mortify and spite her. This is very wicked I know, but I confess all my little peccadillos to you for I know your fondness will lead you to be mild and forgiving. Perhaps my wicked heart will get some good from you in the end.

And on another occasion she wrote:

My dear Lady Huntingdon is always so very good to me, I really do feel so very sensibly all your kindness and attention ... Your concern for my improvement in religious knowledge is very obliging & I do hope I shall be the better for all your excellent advice . . . You are all goodness and kindness & I often wish I had a portion of it. Women of wit, beauty & quality cannot bear too much humiliating truths – they shock our pride. But we must die – we must converse with earth and worms.*

She was not afraid of death. 'If I could have walked out of this world, I would have departed long ago,' she declared, 'if only to get rid of so many tiresome people.' One evening, in the twilight, a friend entered a room where she normally sat. 'In the growing darkness', he stumbled over something on the floor and, to his consternation, found it was the Duchess. He asked if she were ill, and she replied, 'No, I am only praying. I am so wicked a woman that I lie on the floor rather than kneel.'

A friend less demanding than Lady Huntingdon in the last years of the Duchess's life was Lady Mary Wortley Montagu, who had 'more wit than anybody [she] ever knew' and 'talked mighty prettily'. Sarah enjoyed Lady Mary's company so much, indeed, that she gave her an open invitation to come to stay with her for a month each summer.

The Duchess herself talked prettily too and often very amusingly, even though, as Francis Hare was once brave enough to tell her, she sometimes talked too much. 'Where Lord Godolphin said ten words at table before servants or in mixt company,' Hare wrote, 'your Grace will give me leave to believe you say 10,000.'

But then, he conceded, Godolphin's silence

perhaps would not become your Grace; it would take too much off from ye life of conversation & destroy the pleasure you give your friends by saying perpetually things which are extremely diverting & agreeable . . . It is impossible for your Grace to converse without warmth & force as it is for you to be dull or ugly, to whom God has given so fine an understanding & so much beauty.

The beauty, faded though it was, remained with her to the end, despite her sufferings, the gout in her hands and knees – for the

* Doubt has been thrown on the degree of her intimacy with the Countess of Huntingdon, and the authenticity of their correspondence. However, the self-possessed and sardonic tone of some of her comments rings true (see Harris, *A Passion for Government*).

'Violent fits' of which she took a medicine composed of an ounce and a half of opium 'put into a pint of the best Brandy' – the rheumatism in her legs, the desperately irritating eczema, the scurvy and erysipelas, the exasperating weakness of her legs, her eyes which were dim and her missing teeth which might have been preserved, she thought, had she chewed tobacco, a practice which 'most people' now observed 'in this country' and one which she urged upon her grandchildren. 'I can't get out of my chair without two people to help me,' she complained, '& when I am got out I can't stand nor go one step without two chair men to hold me up . . . I am generally wrapped up in Flannell, and wheel'd up and down my Rooms in a Chair.' She compared her sufferings to Job's.

It is dismal to be always alone, and the generality of company one meets with is yet worse. Most people are disagreable for one thing and another, and I think if I could walk out of life without the pain one suffers in dying I would do it tomorrow . . .

Whoever has been once so happy as I have been & have nothing left but money, which from my humour I don't want much of, deserves to be pittyd.

She was quite resigned to her death. 'It is impossible that one of my age and infirmities can live long,' she wrote; 'and one great happiness there is in death, that one shall never hear any more of anything they do in this world . . . I have always thought that the greatest happiness of life was to love and value somebody extremely that returned it, and to see them often.'

She still enjoyed listening to music. When at Marlborough House, she was carried to the opera, and when in the country, she listened with pleasure to a chamber organ which, bought for £1,000, played the 'finest piece of music that ever was heard'. For companionship, when there were no visitors, she relied upon her dogs. Not long before her death she wrote:

I am very fond of my three dogs. They have all of them Gratitude, Wit and good Sense – Things very rare to be found in this country. They are fond of going out with me, but when I reason with them and tell them it is not proper, they submit, and watch for my coming home, and meet me with as much joy as if I had never given them the good advice.

On her good days she was still capable of enjoying herself, despite her protestation of manifold infirmities. She played ombre with her friends, paying not too close attention to her cards in her eagerness to talk; held parties which went on until the early hours of the morning; went to listen to the music and eat cheesecake in the rather disreputable Marylebone Gardens; helped the Duchess of Manchester furnish her London house in Dover Street; and had her great-grandchildren, John and Diana Spencer, to tea, commenting:

They are both of them charming, and they talk enough. And I find they are mighty fond of coming to me. For I play darts with 'em and they both beat me shame-fully . . . I heard they have been told I intended to give them a Present. Upon which they press'd Grace [Ridley] mightily to know what it was. And after she acquainted me with this curiosity I ask'd them if they would have a Kiss or Gold and they both cry'd out very eagerly Mony.

In the summer of 1744 she told her son-in-law Francis Godolphin that she was 'packing up to be gone'; and two months later, at Marlborough House, she did go. She was 'in the 85th year of her age,' Tobias Smollett recorded, 'immensely rich and very little regretted either by her own family or by the world in general'. 'Four score years of arrogance,' commented Horace Walpole, qualifying his unkind summation by adding, 'so fantastic an understanding'.

She had outlived all but one of her children, and for over twenty years she had been a widow. Yet thoughts of her husband were never far from her mind. He had loved her devotedly and she had loved him.

'Wherever you are,' she had assured him years before, 'whilst I have life, my soul shall follow you, my ever dear Lord Marlborough, and wherever I am I should only kill the time wishing for night that I may sleep and hope the next day to hear from you.'

NOTES ON SOURCES

The first biography of the Duke of Marlborough appeared in three volumes in 1705, seventeen years before his death, under the title of *The Life and Glorious History of John, Duke and Earl of Marlborough . . . containing a Relation of the Most Important Battles*. This was by Dr Francis Hare, who had been tutor to the Duke's son John, Marquess of Blandford, and who later became chaplain-general to the army in Flanders and Bishop of Chichester; see 'Marlborough's First Biographer' by Robert D. Horn in the *Huntingdon Library Quarterly*, 20, 1957.

Hare's biography was followed in 1711 by *A Short Narrative of the Life of His Grace, John, Duke of Marlborough, from the Beginnings of the Revolution to this Present Time, with Some Remarks on His Conduct*. The author was described as 'an Old Officer of the Army'. The work has been attributed to Daniel Defoe, but it is more likely that it was written by an army chaplain or surgeon. It was followed, two years later, by *The Lives of Two Illustrious Generals, John, Duke of Marlborough, and Francis Eugene, Prince of Savoy*. The author's name does not appear on the title page, but he has been identified as Ralph Montagu and, more recently, as Arthur Maynwaring. These three books all defend the Duke against the various charges made against him.

The first comprehensive posthumous biography was published in three volumes in 1736 under the title *The Life of John, Duke of Marlborough, with Original Letters and Papers*. This was by Thomas Lediard, who, when an attaché at the embassy in Hamburg, was seconded to Marlborough's staff as a secretary and accompanied the Duke on his mission to Charles XII of Sweden in 1707. This work did not meet with the Duchess's approval. 'This History takes a great deal of Pains to make the Duke of Marlborough's Extraction very ancient. This may be true for aught I know,' she wrote. 'But it is no matter whether it be true or not in my opinion. For I value nobody for another's merit.' On another occasion she took exception to Lediard's comment that the Duke had 'made a Considerable Figure among the Beau Mond'. 'That,' she said, 'I interpret to be a fop. He was naturally genteel without the least affectation, and handsome as an angel tho' ever so carelessly dress'd.'

After Lediard's work came a far less useful work in 1741: John Banks's

History of John, Duke of Marlborough . . . Including a More Exact, Impartial and Methodical Narrative on the Late War . . . Then, in three volumes in 1818–19, appeared the first biography to be based upon the Marlborough Papers. This was by William Coxe, Archdeacon of Wiltshire, who had been tutor to the fourth Duke of Marlborough's son. Coxe's valuable work was published in a second edition in six volumes in 1820 and, revised by John Wade, reprinted in 1847–8.

The year 1848 also saw the publication in Edinburgh of Sir Archibald Alison's *Life of John, Duke of Marlborough with Some Account of His Contemporaries and the War of the Spanish Succession*. This book, issued in an enlarged edition in two volumes in 1852, offers little material not to be found in the earlier works. By then, Marlborough's character and political activities had come under unfavourable scrutiny by both the Tory historian David Hume, in his *History of Great Britain* (two vols., 1754–7), and by the Whig Lord Macaulay, in his *History of England from the Accession of James II* (six vols., 1849–61).

In 1894 a more laudatory work in two volumes by General Viscount Wolseley was published by Richard Bentley and Son. This, however, covered only the years up to the accession of Queen Anne and was not altogether reliable about these.

Several more books about Marlborough appeared in the first half of the last century, among them C. T. Atkinson's *Marlborough and the Rise of the British Army* (1921), Sir John Fortescue's *Marlborough* (1932) and Hilaire Belloc's *The Strategy and Tactics of the Great Duke of Marlborough* (1933). The first volume of Sir John Fortescue's classic *History of the British Army* (1899; 2nd edn, 1910) provides a good account of Marlborough's campaigns. So does Winston S. Churchill's essential *Marlborough: His Life and Times*, published in four volumes in 1933–8 and reissued in two volumes in 1947. In 1939 one of Churchill's research assistants, Maurice Ashley, published his *Marlborough*, which, he said, 'differs from Churchill's apologia in some respects'.

In the second half of the twentieth century several more studies appeared. Among those which concentrate upon Marlborough's life as a soldier and upon military affairs generally are R. E. Scouller's *The Armies of Queen Anne* (1966); Ivor F. Burton's *The Captain-General: The Career of John Churchill, Duke of Marlborough, from 1702 to 1711* (1968); David Chandler's excellent *Marlborough as Military Commander* (1973) and his *Art of Warfare in the Age of Marlborough* (1976); and four books by John Childs published by Manchester University Press: *The Army of Charles II* (1976), *The Army, James II and the Glorious Revolution* (1980), *The British Army of William III, 1698–1702* (1987) and *The Nine Years War and the British Army* (1991).

Collections of Marlborough's correspondence and dispatches can be found in Sir George Murray's *The Letters and Despatches of John Churchill, the First Duke of Marlborough, from 1702 to 1712* (5 vols., 1845); Henry L. Snyder's edition of *The Marlborough–Godolphin Correspondence* (3 vols., 1975); *The Correspondence, 1701–11, of John Churchill, First Duke of Marlborough, and Anthonie Heinsius, Grand Pensionary of Holland,* edited by B. van 't Hoff (1951). Excellent introductions to the historical background of Marlborough's life are the three volumes of G. M. Trevelyan's *England under Queen Anne* (1930–34), Peter Earle's *The World of Defoe* (1976), J. B. Hattendorf's *England in the War of the Spanish Succession* (1987), *Stuart England* (ed. Blair Worden, 1986), and Sir George Clark's *The Later Stuarts, 1660–1714* (2nd edn, 1955); while the most illuminating of recent studies are *Marlborough* by J. R. Jones (1993) and the handsomely illustrated and well-written *Marlborough* by Correlli Barnett (1974). Other biographies published in recent years include Bryan Bevan's *Marlborough: The Man: A Biography of John Churchill, First Duke of Marlborough* (1975) and George Malcolm Thomson's *The First Churchill: The Life of John, First Duke of Marlborough* (1979). *The Early Churchills: An English Family* by A. L. Rowse (1956) provides a lively sketch of the Duke as well as of other members of his family.

His Duchess, Sarah, overshadows her husband in Stuart Reid's *John and Sarah, Duke and Duchess of Marlborough, 1650–1744,* which, based on the unpublished letters and documents at Blenheim Palace, was published in 1915. More recent studies are Virginia Cowles's *The Great Marlborough and His Duchess* (1983); Iris Butler's *Rule of Three: Sarah, Duchess of Marlborough and Her Companions in Power* (1967); David Green's *Sarah, Duchess of Marlborough* (1967); and Frances Harris's scholarly *A Passion for Government: The Life of Sarah, Duchess of Marlborough* (1991). There are good biographies of Queen Anne by David Green (1970) and Edward Gregg (1980). Lord Godolphin's biography has been written by Sir Tresham Lever (1952), Robert Harley's by B. W. Hill (1988), and Sir John Vanbrugh's by Laurence Whistler (1938) and Kerry Downes (1987). The history of Vanbrugh's masterpiece, Blenheim Palace, has been written by David Green (1951).

Lastly there are two bibliographical works of importance: William T. Morgan's *A Bibliography of British History 1700–1715, with Special Reference to the Reign of Queen Anne* (5 vols., 1939–42; reprinted 1972) and Robert D. Horn, *Marlborough: Survey: Panegyrics, Satires and Biographical Writings, 1688–1788* (1975).

ABBREVIATIONS:

BL: British Library

HMC: Historical Manuscripts Commission

MGC: *The Marlborough–Godolphin Correspondence* (ed. Henry L. Snyder)

W.S.C.: Winston S. Churchill, *Marlborough: His Life and Times*

Brown: B. Curtis Brown (ed.), *The Letters and Diplomatic Instructions of Queen Anne*

Coxe: William Coxe, *Memoirs of John, Duke of Marlborough, with His Original Correspondence*

Hoff: B. van 't Hoff (ed.), *The Correspondence, 1710–11, of John Churchill, First Duke of Marlborough, and Anthonie Heinsius, Grand Pensionary of Holland*

References to Coxe are to the six-volume edition of 1820, and to Churchill to the two-volume edition of 1947.

Full bibliographical details are given on pages 374–83.

CHAPTER 1 Wolseley's description of Ashe comes from his *Life of John Churchill*, i, 13; Winston Churchill's comments on the effects which his ancestor's boyhood had upon his subsequent career from W.S.C., i, 31–2; the instruction of the 'sequestred Clergyman' from [Montagu], *The Lives of the Two Illustrious Generals*, 5. Both the accounts of Marlborough's studying Flavius Vegetius Renatus and of his being 'whipt at St Paul's School' are quoted in W.S.C., i, 46 and 48. The description of James II as 'a remorseless masochist' is by Maurice Ashley in *History Today*, May 1963. Arabella Churchill is the subject of ch. 5 of Rowse's *The Early Churchills*, 117–38.

CHAPTER 2 The account of Barbara Villiers is in Burnet, *History of My Own Time*, i, 94. Pepys's delight in her petticoats is in Latham and Matthews's edition of the *Diary*, iii, 87; Charles II's admonition in W.S.C., i, 60; Charles II's indulgence, Churchill's rewards and Barbara Villiers's extravagance and generosity in Fraser, *King Charles II*, 208–9 and 286–7; W.S.C., i, 60–61; Trevelyan, *England under Queen Anne*, i, 179; and Rowse, *The Early Churchills*, 141–5. Monmouth's comment on Churchill's bravery is in W.S.C., i, 92; Churchill at Enzheim in Atkinson, *Marlborough and the Rise of the British Army*, 55–9; Turenne's 'handsome Englishman' in Barnett's *Marlborough*, 41; the account of Churchill's looks and accomplishments in Chesterfield's *Letters to His Son*, 221.

CHAPTER 3 Sarah Jennings's pride in her hair is quoted in Harris, *A Passion for Government*, 14; the quarrel between mother and daughter in HMC, Rutland Papers, XII, ii, 32–4; Sarah on her mother's provocation in BL Add. MS 61453, fo. 14, and Harris, 15. The letters that passed between Sarah and Churchill are in BL Add. MS 61427, fos. 12, 21, 22, 27, 30 and 59; and variously quoted in W.S.C., i, 107–13 and 121–8, in Harris, in Green, *Sarah, Duchess of Marlborough*, ch. 1, and Barnett, *Marlborough*, ch. 5. Catherine Sedley's comment is in Harris, 21; and Barbara Villiers's departure for France in Harris, 19. Courtin's report is in *Correspondance politique en Angleterre*, 7 Dec. 1676, quoted in W.S.C., i, 118, and Sarah's comments on court life in the *Diary of Mary, Countess Cowper*, 196–7.

CHAPTER 4 Courtin's observation on Churchill and the 'sister of Madame Hamilton' is quoted in W.S.C., i, 114; Churchill's letter to Sarah about being called to London is quoted in Wolseley, *Life of John Churchill*, i, 202–3; Sarah on mothers-in-law in Green, *Sarah, Duchess of Marlborough*, 39, and Bishop Burnet's on Prince William in *Supplement to Burnet's History of My Own Time*, 192, see also Jesse, *Continuation of Memoirs*, i, 192. The duchesse d'Orléans's shock is recorded in Dutton, *English Court Life*, 168. Charles II's welcome of his brother is in the Carte MS 232, fo. 5, quoted in W.S.C., i, 141. For Churchill's letter of concern to Sarah see W.S.C., i, 145–6; for his diplomatic skills see Goslinga, *Mémoires relatives à la Guerre de Succession*, 42–4; for James II's unwillingness to part with Churchill see the Clarendon and Rochester correspondence quoted in Rowse, *The Early Churchills*, 165, and in Wolseley, i, 231; for Churchill's charm and artfulness, Dobrée's edition of Chesterfield's *Letters*, iii, 261. The *Gloucester* affair is described in Thomson, *The First Churchill*, 36–7, Turner, *James II* and W.S.C., i, 157–8, quoting the Spencer MS.

CHAPTER 5 For 'Let's cut our meat with spoons' see W.S.C., i, 164; for Princess Anne see the biographies of Gregg and Green; for the Jermyn Street household, Harris, *A Passion for Government*, 24; for Sarah's money see Ailesbury, *Memoirs*, ii, 245; for Celia Fiennes's description of St Albans, Morris (ed.), *The Journeys of Celia Fiennes*; and for Sarah's professed enjoyment of a quiet life, BL Add. MSS 61453, fo. 24 and 61454, fo. 111, and Harris, 69. Churchill's letter about presents is in the *Calendar of Treasury Books*, 1892, quoted in Rowse, *The Early Churchills*, 175; his letter about his daughters in Rowse, 76; and his plea for tolerance of his daughters' errors in Green, *Sarah, Duchess of Marlborough*, 111. His daughters' letters to their mother are in Green, 230–31. For Charles II on Prince George see Fraser, *King Charles II*, and Jesse, *Continuation of Memoirs*, i, 336. Sarah's account of Queen Anne is in her manuscript 'Faithful Account of Many Things', quoted in W.S.C., i, 167 and 170; and Lord Dartmouth's description of Anne is in Gregg, *Queen Anne*, 12. Charles II's death is described in Fraser, 455–7.

CHAPTER 6 The account of James II is based on the biographies of Turner, Clarke and Miller, and that of Prince William of Orange and Princess Mary in ch. 6 of Kenyon's *The Stuarts*, Baxter's *William III* and the Van der Zees' *William and Mary*. Churchill's mission to Paris is in W.S.C., i, 183; his comment about 'trouble' and 'honor' comes from Clarendon, *Correspondence and Diary*, i, 141; and his assurance that his men were 'in good heart' from HMC, Northumberland Papers, iii, 198. Churchill's letter to Lord Clarendon is quoted in Rowse, *The Early Churchills*, 180. Charles II's comment on Judge Jeffreys comes from Clarendon, i, 82–3; Defoe's presence at Sedgemoor from Earle, *The World of Defoe*, 6; Churchill's alleged observation on James II's cold heart Fraser, *The Weaker Vessel*, 363. Churchill's declaration of Lord Delamere's innocence is in Burnet, *History of My Own Time*, i, 688. The Monmouth Rebellion is well described in Earle's *Monmouth's Rebels*, Clifton's *The Last Popular Rebellion* and Chandler's *Sedgemoor 1685*.

CHAPTER 7 Burnet's comment on James II is in Burnet, *History of My Own Time*, i, 168; the Duke of Somerset's altercation with the King in W.S.C., i, 216; Churchill's conversation with the King from [Montagu], *The Lives of the Two Illustrious Generals*, 19–21; Burnet's observations on Churchill's relationship with James in *Supplement to Burnet's History of My Own Time*, 293. Churchill's letter to Prince William is in Coxe, i, 26–7. Barillon's report is in *Correspondance politique en Angleterre*, quoted in W.S.C., i, 210. Princess Anne's letter to her sister is in the Spencer Papers, quoted in W.S.C., i, 210–12, and Churchill's letter to Prince William in W.S.C., i, 240. The desertion of Lord Cornbury is in Gregg, *Queen Anne*, 63, and Princess Anne's letter to Prince William in Brown, 43–4. Winston Churchill's defence of his ancestor is quoted from W.S.C., i, 261; and Godolphin and Churchill skipping down the castle gallery is from Clarke's *Life of James II*, ii, 218. Churchill's excuses for his desertion are quoted in Clarendon, *Correspondence and Diary*, ii, 214; and Churchill's explanation to the King in Coxe, i, 30–31.

CHAPTER 8 For Princess Anne's flight see Gregg, *Queen Anne*, 65–6; Rowse, *The Early Churchills*, 196–7; and Green, *Sarah, Duchess of Marlborough*, 53; for the Princess's remark that she would jump out of the window rather than face her father see BL Add. MS 61421, fos. 5–6; for Sarah at Nottingham, Cibber, *An Apology for the Life of Colley Cibber*, 40–41; for the King's despair, Gregg, 66; and for King James at Sheerness, W.S.C., i, 272–3. Princess Anne's merry mood and dressing herself in orange is in Gregg, 68. William's refusal to be governed by the Churchills is from Foxcroft (ed.), *The Life and Letters of Sir George Savile*, ii, 203; and Schomberg's comment on Churchill's desertion in Clarke's *Life of James II*, ii, 220. For Churchill's behaviour generally see Ashley's *Glorious Revolution of 1688* and Childs's *Army, James II and the Glorious Revolution*.

CHAPTER 9 Waldeck's reports are in the *London Gazette*, 428, quoted in W.S.C., i, 281; King William's praise of Marlborough in W.S.C., i, 294;

the example of William's greed in Sarah's *Account of the Conduct*, 129; and Keppel on his taciturnity in Macpherson, *Original Papers*, i, 284. Ailesbury's comments on Marlborough's opportunities to increase his fortune are in his *Memoirs*, i, 244–5; see also Childs's *British Army of William III*, 25. Daniel Defoe's 'way of making war' is extracted from his *Essay upon Projects* (1697) quoted in Earle, *The World of Defoe*, 98. The account of contemporary weaponry is based on Earle, *Monmouth's Rebels*, 98, and Barnett's *Britain and Her Army*, 126–62.

CHAPTER 10 Marlborough's road accident is from W.S.C., i, 335; his dislike of foreign generals being placed in command of British troops from Childs's *British Army of William III*, 74; William III's remark about a duel with Marlborough from Ranke, *History of England*, vi, 177 and W.S.C., i, 341; and Sarah's refusal to persuade Prince George about his going to sea in her *Account of the Conduct*, 38–41. Harley's comment on the quarrel between the Cockpit and Kensington is taken from HMC, Portland Papers, iii, 16 February 1691; Sarah's anger at having to repay £800 from Thomson, *Memoirs of Sarah*, 70; Princess Anne's and Queen Mary's quarrel from Sarah's *Conduct*, 172. Nottingham's instructions to dismiss Marlborough are in Jones, *Marlborough*, 48; and Marlborough's questioning by the King about the divulgence of military intelligence in Wolseley's *Life of John Churchill*, ii, 265. The Austrian envoy's report to Vienna about Marlborough is printed in Klopp, *Der Fall des Hauses Stuart*, vi, 375, as quoted in W.S.C., i, 344. Evelyn's diary entry is under the date 24 January 1692; and Queen Mary's letter to her sister about her bringing Lady Marlborough to court is in W.S.C., i, 346–7. Princess Anne's reply is in Brown, 53. The Lord Mayor of Bath's instructions not to accompany Princess Anne to church are quoted in Sarah's *Conduct*; and Princess Anne's letter begging Sarah not to leave her in Brown, 56–7.

CHAPTER 11 Sarah's being jeered by the mob is in BL Add. MS 61421, fos. 26–7, quoted in Harris, *A Passion for Government*, 67; the affectionate letters to her from the Queen in Brown, 55–62. Bishop Sprat's account of the inquisition is quoted in W.S.C., i, 358–9; the Earl of Danby's observations in W.S.C., i, 361; and Sarah on her anxiety at the number of generals being killed in HMC, Portland Papers, quoted in Harris, 74. The Brest expedition fiasco is described in Childs's *British Army of William III*, 222–36, and Jones, *Marlborough*, 50–52. The extract from Macaulay's *History* is in iv, 514; and Shrewsbury's letter about the King receiving Marlborough back into favour and King William's reply in his *Private and Original Correspondence*, 44–7. Queen Mary's comment on Marlborough is quoted in Harris, 57; Bishop Burnet's on Queen Mary's death in Jesse, *Continuation of Memoirs*, i, 160, 222–4. Fenwick's accusation about Marlborough's involvement is in HMC, Buccleuch Papers, ii, 393–6; George Churchill's condemnation of Fenwick in Ailesbury, *Memoirs*, 412; Macaulay's account of Marlborough's 'slightly contemptuous' behaviour in his *History*, iv, 723–4; Burnet's of Fenwick's composure in his *History of My Own Time*, 637; Smalridge's comment on Fenwick's punishment in Nichols, *Illustrations of Literature*, iii, 253–5.

CHAPTER 12 Chesterfield's comments on Marlborough's diplomacy are in his *Letters*, iv, 221–2; Evelyn's on his ambition and charm in his diary entry for 30 December 1702; Goslinga's on his qualities and failings in *Mémoires relatives à la Guerre de Succession*, 42–4; Prince Eugène's on his parsimony in Burnet's *History of My Own Time*, iii, 267; Pulteney's anecdote in Seward, *Anecdotes of Some Distinguished Persons*, 237; the story of the lantern in W.S.C., i, 412; that of the gaiters in Trevelyan, *England under Queen Anne*, ii, 7; Lord Ailesbury's on Marlborough's treatment of his servants in *Memoirs*, 121; the story of the cloak in Seward, 249, and of the cheating Lovegrove in W.S.C., i, 417; Sarah's comment on her husband's appearance and dress is in W.S.C., i, 411, and her insistence on his honesty and compassion in W.S.C., i, 416. Cadogan's account of his presiding over a feast for his officers is in Seward, 257.

CHAPTER 13 The Duke of Gloucester's attendant's account of his games with Marlborough's son is in W.S.C., i, 445; Marlborough's appointment by the King is described in [Montagu], *The Lives of the Two Illustrious Generals*, 127. The Queen's warning to Sarah about Abigail Hill is in Rowse, *The Early Churchills*, 282, and Reid, *John and Sarah, Duke and Duchess of Marlborough*, 146. Swift's account of Godolphin is in his *Prose Works*, x, 26. Sarah's opinion of Lord Spencer is quoted in Harris, *A Passion for Government*, 82; and her weeping at weddings in BL Add. MS 61415, fo. 46. The sketch of Godolphin is based on Lever's biography. James Vernon's conversation with Shrewsbury about Marlborough's suggested change of appointment is in Wolseley, *The Life of John Churchill*, ii, 328. The King's attitude towards the 'obnoxious' Irish Bill is described by Coxe, i, 102. Marlborough's confession that he did not know how to behave towards the King is in HMC, Buccleuch Papers, ii, 647. Marlborough 'a glorious living portrait of a Milord' is from Trevelyan, *England under Queen Anne*, i, 144. Marlborough's exclamation against the plans of the Dukes of Bolton and Newcastle is in Burnet's *History of My Own Time*, v, 540n.

CHAPTER 14 The account of Anne's early days as Queen is based on the biographies of Gregg (151–81) and Green (90–112); accounts of Sarah's appointments and of her handsome page in Harris, *A Passion for Government*, 87; the Queen's letter to Sarah on 19 May 1702 is in Green, *Queen Anne*,

100. Marlborough's letter written after parting from Sarah at Margate is in Coxe, i, 83–4. Hoffman's dispatch about the Queen's popularity is quoted in W.S.C., i, 531; and Count Wratislaw's about the leaking of secret intelligence in W.S.C., i, 533, Shrewsbury's comment about his distaste for 'business of state' in Lecky's *History of England*, i, 58.

CHAPTER 15 The account of the British army at this time is based largely upon the works of Fortescue, *History of the British Army*, i; Childs, *The British Army of William III*; Chandler, *The Art of Warfare*; Atkinson, *Marlborough and the Rise of the British Army*; Scouller, *The Armies of Queen Anne*; Walton, *History of the British Standing Army, 1660–1700*; and Barnett's *Britain and Her Army*, ch. 6.

CHAPTER 16 Marlborough's comment on his divided command is in W.S.C., i, 579; his pleasure, with reservations, at receiving Sarah's letters in Harris, *A Passion for Government*, 89, 95 and 97, and Reid, *John and Sarah, Duke and Duchess of Marlborough*, 110. The Duke of Berwick's comment on the allies' failure to attack is in his *Memoirs*, i, 170. Marlborough's regret that Boufflers 'will be gone' in Millner, *Journal (1701–12)*, 26; his report to Godolphin in Coxe, i, 180–81; and his explanation to the enemy as to why he does not attack in W.S.C., i, 591. Marlborough on the danger of losing 'all the frute' of the campaign is taken from Hoff, 46; Cohorn giving him 'the spleen' from Hoff, 47; his complaint 'If this be zele' from Hoff, 51; and that of 'the backwardness' of the 'pepell' quoted in Barnett, *Marlborough*, 52. Swift on Cutts is in Henry Manners Chichester's entry on Cutts, in *DNB*, v. Parker describes his men rushing forward in Chandler (ed.), *Robert Parker and Comte de Mérode-Westerloo*, 22–3; Richard Kane takes up Parker's story in his *Campaigns of King William and the Duke of Marlborough*, 189. Parker's accounts of the assault and of Marlborough's first campaign are in Chandler (ed.), 25. Marlborough's party's interception is described in W.S.C., i, 606–9; Thomson, *The First Churchill*, 104–5; and Barnett, 54. His welcome in The Hague is based on a description in a letter in Coxe, i, 194.

CHAPTER 17 The Queen's offer of a dukedom was made on 22 October 1702 and is in Brown, 97. Marlborough's letters to Sarah on this offer are in Coxe, i, 204; the Queen's to Sarah offering £2,000 a year in Brown, 103. John Evelyn's comment on the 'excess of honors' is under the date 30 December 1702 in his diary; the description of Francis Hare in Gordon Goodwin's entry in the *DNB*, viii. Godolphin's letters about Blandford are quoted in Barnett, *Marlborough*, 64; the Queen's to Sarah in Coxe, i, 218. Marlborough's to Sarah both in Coxe, i, 220. The letters exchanged about the death of their son and the distress of his parents are in Rowse, *The Early Churchills*, 238; W.S.C., i, 631; Harris, *A Passion for Government*,

99; and Barnett, 70. Marlborough's letter about Bonn to Sarah is in W.S.C., i, 656; his low opinion of Opdam in Coxe, i, 123; and his having 'spleen to a very great degree' in Hoff, 133.

CHAPTER 18 Swift on ladies' quarrels is quoted in Thomson, *Memoirs of Sarah*, 111; the Duke on the 'very little noise' made by the siege of Huy in Coxe, i, 128; the Dutch medal for Huy and Limbourg in W.S.C., i, 692. Marlborough's claim that he would 'rather dye' than 'doe nothing' which did not have the '*unanimous consent* of the Generals' is in Hoff, 142, as in his comment on the 'bravarie of the troupes'. The army being able to do no more than 'eat forage' is in W.S.C., i, 682; Queen Anne's letter begging 'the Freemans' not to desert her is in Brown, 125. Marlborough's regret that he allowed his daughter to marry Sunderland is quoted in W.S.C., i, 724; his letter of concern about Sarah's health in Harris, *A Passion for Government*, 103. His further letters of worried concern about her health are taken from Coxe, i, 320; his anguished letter of April 1704 about Sarah's suspicion 'as to this woman' is in W.S.C., i, 723–4. His protestation that he 'never sent to her' in his life and his letter to Godolphin about saving the Empire are quoted in Barnett, *Marlborough*, 77 and 78. His letter beginning 'You are so good to take notice' is in W.S.C., i, 734; and his gratitude for the comfort of Sarah's letters in Harris, 108. The letter telling her he is going 'higher up into Germany' is in W.S.C., i, 734–5.

CHAPTER 19 Marlborough's letter to Sarah from Kühlseggen is in W.S.C., i, 753. The march to the Danube is described in Barnett, *Marlborough*, 82–96; Thomson, *The First Churchill*, 119–26; Verney, *The Battle of Blenheim*, 42–58; Millner, *Journal (1701–12)*, 7–16; Trevelyan, *England under Queen Anne*, i, 348–55; Chandler, *Marlborough as Military Commander*, 126–31; Chandler (ed.), *Robert Parker and Comte de Mérode-Westerloo*, 29–36; Atkinson, *Marlborough and the Rise of the British Army*, 186–212; and W.S.C., i, 740–69. Marlborough's letter to Sarah written from a house of the Elector Palatine, discouraging her from joining him, is in Coxe, i, 333.

CHAPTER 20 The account of Prince Eugène of Savoy is based largely upon Henderson's biography. See also Macmunn, *Prince Eugène: Twin Marshal with Marlborough* and Malleson, *Prince Eugène of Savoy*.

CHAPTER 21 Marlborough comparing Prince Eugène to Shrewsbury is in Coxe, i, 341; Prince Eugène's comments about Marlborough are in Henderson, *Prince Eugen of Savoy*, 101. Marlborough later estimate of the Prince is in *Feldzüge*, vi, supp. 131, quoted in Barnett, *Marlborough*, 97. Their mutual compliments are recorded in Francis Hare's journal, BM Add. MS 9114. The unnamed Englishman's forecast that Marlborough will either gain 'a great reputation' or be ruined is in W.S.C., i, 783. The 'common ingredient' in Marlborough's tactics is identified in Jones, *Marlborough*, 232. La Colonie's account of the storming of the Schellenberg is from his *Chronicles of an Old Campaigner*, 185. The official German report is in *Feldzüge*, vi, 837, quoted in W.S.C., i, 804. La Colonie's continued account is in his *Chronicles*, 191. The Electress Sophie's letter to Leibniz is in Leibniz's *Werke* (1873), ix, 91, quoted in W.S.C., i, 807.

CHAPTER 22 Adam de Cardonnel's letter to Prior, in HMC, Bath Papers, iii (Prior Papers), 433, is quoted by Trevelyan in *England under Queen Anne*, i, 371; the Margrave's letter about the devastation of Bavaria in W.S.C., i, 821; and Marlborough's letters to Sarah and Godolphin in W.S.C., i, 817. Prince Eugène's criticisms of 'this slowness on our side' comes from *Feldzüge*, vi, supp. 131, quoted in Barnett, *Marlborough*, 101, and in W.S.C., i, 821; and his urging of speed upon Marlborough in a translation from the French in W.S.C., i, 837.

CHAPTER 23 The battle fought on 13 August 1704 is described in Verney, *The Battle of Blenheim*, 105–67; Chandler, *Marlborough as Military Commander*, 141–50; Chandler (ed.), *Robert Parker and Comte de Mérode-Westerloo*, 37–46 and 166–75; Falls (ed.), *Great Military Battles*, 30–42; W.S.C., i, 845–68; Lediard, *Life of John, Duke of Marlborough*, i, 429; Hare's Journal, BL Add. MS 9114; Barnett, *Marlborough*, 104–21; Trevelyan, *England under Queen Anne*, i, 378–412; Henderson, *Prince Eugen of Savoy*, 91–114; Thomson, *The First Churchill*, 140–53; Atkinson, *Marlborough and the Rise of the British Army*, 213–47; Deane, *A Journal of Marlborough's Campaigns*, 10–12; and [Montagu], *The Lives of the Two Illustrious Generals*, 70–84. The comte de Mérode-Westerloo's comments are in Chandler (ed.), 207 and 214; Marlborough's letters to Sarah in W.S.C., i, 863 and 877; and the chaplain-general's remarks in W.S.C., i, 871. The exchange between the Duke and Marshal Tallard is in [Montagu], 73; Marlborough's letter to Godolphin after the battle is from Barnett, 124–5; and the Electress's appraisal of Marlborough in W.S.C., i, 909.

CHAPTER 24 For Queen Anne's conversation with Parke see Gregg, *Queen Anne*, 187; for the letter to Sarah see Coxe, i, 231; and for the Queen's letter to Marlborough, Brown, 149–150. For the joyful celebrations in London see Trevelyan, *England under Queen Anne*, i, 396–7; and for Henry Davenant's letter, Trevelyan, i, 395. Marlborough to Sarah about his reluctance to become involved in her political imbroglios is in BL Add. MS 61466, fo. 118; Harris, *A Passion for Government*, 112; his subsequent letter to Godolphin lamenting the necessity of visiting continental courts in Coxe, ii, 59. Marlborough's letter to Sarah of 2 December is in Coxe, ii, 63; Lord Cowper's address and Marlborough's reply are in W.S.C., i, 914–15, and in Lediard, *The Life of John, Duke of Marlborough*, i, 470. Marlborough's civility to John Evelyn is recorded in Evelyn's diary under the date 9 February 1705. Godolphin's opinion of the proposal for a statue is in HMC, Bath Papers, i, 63.

CHAPTER 25 The account of Vanbrugh's career is largely based on Downes's and Whistler's biographies. His time in India was revealed by Robert Williams in an article in *The Times Literary Supplement*, 3 September 1999, 13–14. The College of Arms historian's comments on his being appointed Clarenceux King-of-Arms is in Whistler, 96–8; the Duke being 'desirous of living at Woodstock' in W.S.C., ii, 340; and Lord Ailesbury's observation regarding the Duke choosing Vanbrugh in Whistler, 117. The financial arrangements for Marlborough House and the dismissal of Wren are described in Gregg, *Queen Anne*, 202, and Harris, *A Passion for Government*, 155. For the building of Blenheim Palace see Green, *Blenheim Palace*. Vanbrugh's conception of the 'national monument' as 'emphatic as an oath' and his comments on the pleasure of building a palace for another 'when one should find very little in living in it oneself' are quoted in Thomson, *The First Churchill*, 163, and Downes, 383. The extract from William Upcott's diary is taken from Whistler, 121. For Wren's estimate see Green, 43; for Marlborough's instruction to 'press ahead' and for Sarah's apprehension see Harris, 120, and MGC, 495; and for Wise's trees and plants, Green, 57 and 70–71.

CHAPTER 26 Marlborough's letter on his rough crossing, 11 April 1705, is quoted in Barnett, *Marlborough*, 140. 'You see what a miserable thing a German army is' comes from Coxe, ii, 97; Marlborough's longing to be with his 'dearest soul' in W.S.C., i, 927; his letter to Godolphin of 2 June in W.S.C., i, 933; and his complaint that he is 'weary of life' from Coxe, i, 281–2. The account of the forcing of the Lines of Brabant is based on W.S.C., i, 943–66; Barnett, *Marlborough*, 149–51; Thomson, *The First Churchill*, 170–71; Chandler, *Marlborough as Military Commander*, 118–20; and Atkinson, *Marlborough and the Rise of the British Army*, 201–6. Orkney's account is in 'Letters of the First Lord Orkney', 313. Marlborough's letters to his wife recounting his success and the good behaviour of his troops are in Coxe, ii, 143 and 146; and his letter reassuring her that he does not expose himself unnecessarily in Coxe, ii, 147. Cranstoun's strictures are in HMC, Portland Papers, iv, 253; and Marlborough's suggestion about the award for Colonel Durel in Coxe, ii, 144; Harley's letter of congratulation is also in Coxe, ii, 148–9. Marlborough's letter to Heinsius about the need for a unified command is in Hoff, 318; and his flattery of Slangenberg quoted in Barnett, 154.

CHAPTER 27 Marlborough's address to his officers is in Hare's letter of 20 August 1705, quoted in W.S.C., i, 974–5; his letter to Sarah on the necessity for withdrawal is in Coxe, ii, 170; his letter to Godolphin in Coxe, ii, 176; his letter to Heinsius in Hoff, 124; Prince Eugène's letter of sympathy to him in Coxe, ii, 190, and the Queen's in Coxe, ii, 189. The dinner at Oxenstiern's is recounted in Ailesbury's *Memoirs*, ii, 585–7; the award of the princedom of Mindelheim in W.S.C., ii, 48–9. The letter from the Electress is in W.S.C., ii, 53; and that to Sarah ending with a request for news of Blenheim Palace in W.S.C., ii, 85. Marlborough's 'heavy heart' on his return to the Continent is also in W.S.C., ii, 87–9; his letter to Robert Harley on the eve of the Ramillies battle in W.S.C., ii, 93.

CHAPTER 28 This account of the battle of Ramillies is largely based on Atkinson, *Marlborough and the Rise of the British Army*, 288–97; Chandler, *Marlborough as Military Commander*, 172–8; W.S.C., ii, 95–118; Barnett, *Marlborough*, 161–9; Trevelyan, *England under Queen Anne*, ii, 103–13; and Thomson, *The First Churchill*, 180–86. Colonel de La Colonie's account is in his *Chronicles of an Old Campaigner*, 309; that of Colonel Cranstoun is quoted in W.S.C., ii, 109–10. Marlborough's congratulating himself in a letter to Godolphin is in Coxe, ii, 365; the following letter to Sarah in Coxe, ii, 354.

CHAPTER 29 Marlborough's letters to Sarah after the battle are quoted in Coxe, ii, 366–8; and in Barnett, *Marlborough*, 170–71; the Queen on his 'Glorious Success' is in W.S.C., ii, 128; and his letter to Heinsius about his proposed appointment as viceroy in Hoff, 401. Vendôme's letter to Chamillart is in Vault and Pelet, *Mémoires militaires relatifs à la Succession d'Espagne sous Louis XIV*, vi, 94; Marlborough's letter to Sarah about Cadogan is in Coxe, iii, 104–6; the one written after Prince Eugène's victory in Coxe, i, 460. Marlborough to Heinsius about the French's misfortunes in Italy is in Hoff, 452. Marlborough urging Godolphin not to resign is in Coxe, iii, 104–6; the Queen's letter with the same intent in Brown, 196–7.

CHAPTER 30 Marlborough's embassy to the King of Sweden is based on Stamp, 'Marlborough and Charles XII'; W.S.C., ii, 215–28; Lediard, *The Life of John, Duke of Marlborough*, ii, 166–8; and Trevelyan, *England under Queen Anne*, ii, 291–2; see also Hatton, *Charles XII of Sweden*. Marlborough's letter to Sarah of October 1706 is in Coxe, iii, 116–17; his observation regarding Charles's interest in Russia is in Voltaire's *Histoire de Charles XII*, quoted in W.S.C., ii, 226; his letter to Godolphin in W.S.C., ii, 223; and his comments on the 'ill success in Spain' in Coxe, iii, 207. John Chetwynd's letters are quoted in W.S.C., ii, 253. The account of the Toulon fiasco is based on Trevelyan, ii, 293–4; Henderson, *Prince Eugen of*

Savoy, 139–46; W.S.C., ii, 244–58; and Atkinson, *Marlborough and the Rise of the British Army*, 316–22.

CHAPTER 31 Marlborough's letters to Sarah about Blenheim Palace are in Coxe, iii, 231 and 262–3. The Queen's loving letters to Sarah are quoted in Green, *Sarah, Duchess of Marlborough*, 101. Swift's description of a drawing room is from *Journal to Stella*, 328; the Queen's remark on Bolingbroke's wig from Jesse, *Memoirs of the Court of England*, vii, 303; Sarah's comments on her conversation from Sarah's *Account of the Conduct*, 172; her description of Abigail Hill tripping across the Queen's room also from *Conduct*, 169, as is her description of Samuel Masham, 185–6. The Queen's insistence that she asked Abigail 'a hundred times' to reveal her marriage is in BL Add. MS 61422, fo. 6, and in Harris, *A Passion for Government*, 137. Abigail's condescending answer to Sarah's accusation of 'secret management' is in BL Add. MS 61417, fo. 94. Lord Haversham on George Churchill is quoted in John Knox Laughton's entry in the *DNB*, iv, 314. Marlborough's letter to the Queen about the appointment of Whigs is quoted in Barnett, *Marlborough*, 191, and Lever, *Godolphin*, 164. Sarah's opinion of Harley is quoted in Green, 117; Marlborough's threat of resignation is in Coxe, iv, 24. Sarah's account of Harley's continuing to see the Queen is in Green, 135; and her conversations with the Queen after Prince George's death in *Conduct*, 44, and Green, 136.

CHAPTER 32 Grumbkow's report to King Frederick is taken from W.S.C., ii, 350; Marlborough's response to Sarah's contrite letter in MGC, 991 and 1014. The account of the battle of Oudenarde is based largely on Barnett, *Marlborough*, 206–12; W.S.C., ii, 356–80; Henderson, *Prince Eugen of Savoy*, 156–63; Thomson, *The First Churchill*, 211–16; Atkinson, *Marlborough and the Rise of the British Army*, 338–44; Chandler, *Marlborough as Military Commander*, 213–23; and Trevelyan, *England under Queen Anne*, ii, 354–66. The description of the future George II 'hacking and thrusting' is in Trench, *George II*, 18.

CHAPTER 33 Private Bishop's description of the demolition of the French lines is in his *Life and Adventures*, 162; Marlborough's letter on the difficulties facing him at Ghent is in Coxe, iv, 156–7; his letter to Godolphin of 2 August in Coxe, iv, 172; and that to Sarah about the siege of Lille in W.S.C., ii, 429–30. Sir Winston Churchill on Marlborough's 'power of putting himself in the enemy's shoes' in W.S.C., ii, 430. Prince Eugène's activities at Lille are in Henderson's biography, 163–70. Marlborough's letter to Godolphin about the shortage of powder and ball is in Coxe, quoted in Barnett, *Marlborough*, 221; his letter to Godolphin about the prospect of a general storm is in Coxe, iv, 261. Godolphin's letter to

Marlborough about 'provisions & subsistence' is in W.S.C., ii, 457–8. Colonel Molesworth's letter is also in W.S.C., ii, 460. Marlborough's letter to Godolphin about the evacuation of Ghent is in Coxe, iv, 298; and his letter to Sarah in W.S.C., ii, 471.

CHAPTER 34 The Queen's letter about Sarah is in Brown, 244–5. Marlborough's letters to Sarah and the Queen about the victory at Oudenarde are in Green, *Sarah, Duchess of Marlborough*, 132–3. The affair of the jewels is described in Green, 134. Sarah's letter to the Queen written on her return from St Paul's is in Green, 135. The Queen's letter hoping that Marlborough and Godolphin will think better of leaving her service is in Brown, 256–7. Grumbkow on Marlborough at his house in The Hague is related in W.S.C., ii, 519–20. Marlborough's letter about the reward offered him by d'Alègre is in W.S.C., ii, 499, and Trevelyan, *England under Queen Anne*, ii, 397–8. The duchesse d'Orléans's account of the intense cold in France is quoted in Thomson, *The First Churchill*, 233; the report of Torcy's conversation is taken from W.S.C., ii, 500–501, 533 and 540; Legrelle, *La diplomatic française et la succession d'Espagne*, iv, 385–7; and Torcy, *Mémoires*, 606. Marlborough's request for a canopy is in Coxe, iv, 390. His letter to Godolphin of 7 June 1709 is in Sarah's *Private Correspondence*, ii, 324; his letter of 9 June in W.S.C., ii, 563; and his concern about the soldiers' health in W.S.C., ii, 564. For the siege of Tournai see Barnett, *Marlborough*, 233–5; W.S.C., ii, 573–87; Trevelyan, iii, 7; and Atkinson, *Marlborough and the Rise of the British Army*, 385–8. Bishop's account is in his *Life and Adventures*, 127; and Marlborough's report of the siege to Godolphin in W.S.C., ii, 581.

CHAPTER 35 The account of the battle of Malplaquet is based largely upon Atkinson, *Marlborough and the Rise of the British Army*, 393–409; W.S.C., ii, 601–27; Trevelyan, *England under Queen Anne*, iii, 13–20; Barnett, *Marlborough*, 236–40; Henderson, *Prince Eugen of Savoy*, 172–80; Thomson, *The First Churchill*, 239–44; and Chandler (ed.), *Robert Parker and Comte de Mérode-Westerloo*, 86–90. Marlborough's letters conveying the news of it to Sarah and Godolphin are in Coxe, v, 70, and MGC, 1359. Prince Eugène's refusal to withdraw from battle is quoted in W.S.C., ii, 613; Marlborough's report on the French wounded is in Murray (ed.), *Letters and Despatches*, iv, 599; his commiseration with Villars in Barnett, 240; his concern about Cadogan in W.S.C., ii, 636. The Queen's refusal of his request to be appointed Captain-General for life is in Brown, 285–6. Marlborough's letter warning Sarah against 'making the Breach wider' is in her *Account of the Conduct*, quoted in Green, *Sarah, Duchess of Marlborough*, 144; see also MGC, 1136 and 1345. The Queen's quarrel with Sarah is fully recounted in Harris, *A Passion for Government*; Green; Butler, *Rule of*

Three; and W.S.C., ii, 649–51. For the promotion of Hill see W.S.C., ii, 662–3. Sarah notices tears in Marlborough's eyes in BL Add. MS 61418, fo. 135. The affair of Marlborough versus Abigail is recounted in W.S.C., ii, 664–9; *Conduct*, 274–6; Coxe, v, 143; Green, ch. 7; and Harris.

CHAPTER 36 Sir John Clerk's description of the Queen is from his *Memoirs*, 71–2; the inefficacy of the waters from the well near Eton from Hill, *Windsor and Eton*, 102; the variety of the Queen's medicines from Green, *Queen Anne*, Appendix 1; Mrs Danvers's account of Sarah's haranguing the Queen in Burnet, *History of My Own Time*, v, 454. For Sarah's last meeting with the Queen see Green, *Sarah, Duchess of Marlborough*, ch. 7; and for Maynwaring's letter about Mrs Masham, Green, *Sarah*, 161. Marlborough's letter to Sarah from Lens is in W.S.C., ii, 689; his report to Godolphin on his sixtieth birthday in Coxe, v, 194; his longing for 'a quiet life' is quoted in Barnett, *Marlborough*, 246; his complaint about Argyll in Coxe, v, 197. Orrery's letter to Harley is in HMC, Portland Papers, iv, 544, and Argyll's letter to Harley in HMC, Portland Papers, iv, 569. Marlborough's dispirited letters to Sarah are quoted in Barnett, 246. Marlborough's letter about Sunderland is in Coxe, v, 259–60; the Queen's letter on the same subject in Brown, 303–4. The letter from the Queen's ministers pleading with Marlborough not to resign is in Sarah's *Account of the Conduct*, 301. Ailesbury's attempts to comfort Marlborough are in his *Memoirs*, ii, 62–5. The Queen's letter dismissing Godolphin is in Coxe, v, 322; so is Godolphin's letter urging Marlborough to stay on.

CHAPTER 37 The letters from Marlborough and the Elector of Hanover about the command of the army are in W.S.C., ii, 749–51. For the career of Henry St John (Viscount Bolingbroke) see Hart's biography. Marlborough's letter to Godolphin about Argyll is in Coxe, v, 360; Hoffman's dispatches are in W.S.C., ii, 772 and 773. The Duke of Argyll is quoted in W.S.C., ii, 772; St John's comment about Scarborough is in Bolingbroke, *Letters and Correspondence*, i, 24. John Drummond's letters are in HMC, Portland Papers, iv, 620–21. Harley's account of Marlborough's 'very cold reception' is in HMC, Portland Papers, ii, 224. Sarah's dismissal is recounted in W.S.C., ii, 796–7, as well as in Harris's *A Passion for Government*; Green's *Sarah, Duchess of Marlborough*; Butler's *Rule of Three*; and Burnet, *History of My Own Time*, vi, 33–4. Count von Gallas's report is in Klopp's *Der Fall des Hauses Stuart*, quoted in W.S.C., ii, 797–8.

CHAPTER 38 Marlborough's 'dayly Vexations' are quoted in Harris, *A Passion for Government*, 182. Goslinga on Prince Eugène is quoted in his *Mémoires relatives à la Guerre de Succession*, 116, and Henderson, *Prince Eugen of Savoy*, 184; the Prince of Anhalt-Dessau is in W.S.C., ii, 832–3. Robert Parker's description of Marlborough's survey of the *ne plus ultra* lines is in Chandler (ed.), *Robert Parker and Comte de Mérode-Westerloo*, 100–101. For the forcing of the lines see Atkinson, *Marlborough and the Rise of the British Army*, 436–53; W.S.C., ii, 842–57; Barnett, *Marlborough*, 258–61; Thomson, *The First Churchill*, 263–4; and Trevelyan, *England under Queen Anne*, iii, 130–33. Drummond on Marlborough's decision not to attack comes from HMC, Portland Papers, v, 68; and Parker's relief from Chandler (ed.), 108–9. Professor Jones's comments on this last campaign come from his *Marlborough*, 233. Marlborough's complaint that his constitution is 'extreamely spoilt' is in W.S.C., ii, 870, and his grandson's letter is in ii, 872. The Queen's letter to St John about Marlborough's audience is in HMC, Bath Papers, i, 217, and Brown, 358. Marlborough's letter of explanation to the Commissioners is in Coxe, vi, 124–5. His speech in his defence appears in *Parliamentary History*, vi, 1037–8, and is quoted in W.S.C., ii, 906; and the Cabinet's decision is recorded in Coxe, vi, 152. Louis XIV's comment on Marlborough's dismissal is quoted in Rowse, *The Early Churchills*, 279. For Walpole's expulsion see Plumb's biography. For Prince Eugène's visit to England see Henderson, 192–7, and W.S.C., ii, 914–23.

CHAPTER 39 The sketch of Swift is based largely upon Glendinning's biography and Foot's *The Pen and the Sword*. Swift's opinion of Abigail Masham is in his *Works*, vi, 33; his wish that she should 'never leave the Queen' in iii, 204; his belief that ministers did not do well to mortify Marlborough in Glendinning, 113; and his wish that everything should be left to the Duke except power in Glendinning, 114. His explanation to 'Stella' of the ministers' design is in *Journal to Stella*, 23 January 1712. Marlborough's defence against the charge of peculation is in *Parliamentary History*, vi, 1088, quoted in W.S.C., ii, 931–4, and the debate in ii, 934–5. The *Examiner's* report on the wounded at Malplaquet is in Laprade's *Public Opinion and Politics in Eighteenth-Century England*, 120. The Earl Poulett affair is recounted in W.S.C., ii, 951–2; Trevelyan, *England under Queen Anne*, iii, 208; HMC, Dartmouth Papers (1887), iii, 309–10; and Stater, *High Life, Low Morals*, 208. Parker's condemnation of the *Examiner* is in Chandler (ed.), *Robert Parker and Comte de Mérode-Westerloo*, 114–15. Corporal Bishop's defence of Marlborough is in his *Life and Adventures*, 264–5. Bothmar's condemnation of the treaty terms is quoted in Thomson, *The First Churchill*, 269.

CHAPTER 40 Sarah's wish to be out of this 'horrid countrey' is in Harris (191), whose book *A Passion for Government* gives a careful account of the Marlboroughs' life in exile. Other accounts will be found in Green, *Sarah,*

Duchess of Marlborough, 183–95; Rowse, *The Early Churchills*, 316–19; Thomson, *The First Churchill*, 281–92; Butler, *Rule of Three*, 268–77; and W.S.C., ii, 967–90. William Cadogan's letter to Lord Oxford is in HMC, Portland Papers, v, 257. Marlborough's letter to Sarah from Aachen is from W.S.C., ii, 978; and that from Maastricht from W.S.C., ii, 978–9. Sarah as a 'detestable Slut' comes from *Journal to Stella*, 11 April 1713. Sarah's accounts of her visits to the nuns and of the '27 jolly-face Priests' are in Harris, 193; Sarah's wish that 'wise Cittysons' should see 'the sad effects of Popary' in Green, 189; and her description of the Elector of Mainz in *Letters . . . at Madresfield Court*, 32–3. The hospitality offered to her by the 'Gentleman and his Lady' on the road is in HMC, Bath Papers, i, 37–8; and her errands of mercy are recounted in Reid, *John and Sarah, Duke and Duchess of Marlborough*, 476.

CHAPTER 41 Cadogan's letter about the Elector's return is quoted in Macpherson, *Original Papers*, ii, 478. Sarah's nursing and her contempt for physicians are in Harris, *A Passion for Government*, 196; her letter to Mrs Clayton about going to Ostend in BL Add. MS 61463, fo. 137. The extract from the *Flying Post*, 5 August 1714, is quoted in W.S.C., ii, 1016. Bolingbroke and Oxford playing 'the double game of intrigue' is from Foot, *The Pen and the Sword*, 361. Lady Masham leaving the Queen to 'ransack for things' is quoted in Rowse, *The Early Churchills*, 324, from Cartwright (ed.), *Wentworth Papers*. Lady Mary Wortley Montagu on Marlborough's appearance at court is quoted in Michael, *England under George I*, 95. Marlborough's contacts with the Pretender are described by Hatton in *George I*, 176.

CHAPTER 42 Sarah, the physicians and her caring for her husband are described in Green, *Sarah, Duchess of Marlborough*, 200–202, and her husband's improved health on 210. For his silences see Harris, *A Passion for Government*, 226; for his still keen memory, see Coxe quoted in Barnett, *Marlborough*, 270; and for his comment on Kneller's portrait, Reid, *John and Sarah, Duke and Duchess of Marlborough*, 413.

CHAPTER 43 Samuel Travers's letter is in the footnote to W.S.C., ii, 763; and Marlborough's letter of thanks to Oxford in Green, *Sarah, Duchess of Marlborough*, 173. The account of the works at Blenheim is based largely on Green's *Blenheim Palace*. Sarah's complaint about Vanbrugh's 'filling up pricipices & making bridges in the air' is from Harris, *A Passion for Government*, 213. The negotiations for the marriage of Lady Harriet Godolphin to the Duke of Newcastle are recounted in Whistler, *Sir John Vanbrugh*, 208–16; Vanbrugh's cross letter to 'that wicked woman of Marlborough' is in Whistler, 217–18, and Downes, *Sir John Vanbrugh*, 369–70. For the

Duchess's refusal to allow Vanbrugh to enter the palace, see Whistler, 283.

CHAPTER 44 The description of the Duke driving about the park and the keepers herding the deer is in Harris, *A Passion for Government*, 214; his wishing always to have his wife within call is in Coxe quoted in Barnett, *Marlborough*, 270. Sarah's anger at Sunderland's third marriage is in Harris, 219. For her speculation in the South Sea Company see Reid, *John and Sarah, Duke and Duchess of Marlborough*, 413; Thomson, *The First Churchill*, 296; Green, *Sarah*, 217; Rowse, *The Early Churchills*, 377–8; and W.S.C., ii, 1032–3. Cadogan's 'passion for money' is mentioned in Thomson, 296; the Duchess's complaint that having made her daughters 'such fine ladies' had 'turned their heads' in Harris, 226. The Duchess of Montagu's letter to her father is in W.S.C., ii, 1034–5; and her father's replies in W.S.C., ii, 1035. Sarah's relationship with Henrietta and her daughter's 'dogged rudeness' are in BL Add. MS 61463; in Green, 207; and in Harris, 215; and Sarah's account of her daughters' behaviour during their father's last hours in her 'Green Book'.

CHAPTER 45 Sarah's insistence on paying for the funeral to avoid accusation of 'laying the expense upon the publick' is in BL Add. MS 61436, fos. 10–12; and Bononcini's payment in Green, *Sarah, Duchess of Marlborough*, 230. The argument with the Duchess of Buckingham is in Sutherland, *Background to Queen Anne*, 'Funeral of the Duke of Marlborough'. The report of the 'Melancholy Ceremony' of the funeral is in Green, 229. The Lord Coningsby and Duke of Somerset overtures are also in Green, ch. 12. Somerset's final letters declaring his constant love for her are in BL Add. MS 61457, fos. 97 and 103.

CHAPTER 46 Henrietta's letter to her mother is quoted in Reid, *John and Sarah, Duke and Duchess of Marlborough*, 420; the story of her wax effigy of Congreve in Leslie Stephen's entry on Congreve in the *DNB*, iv. For Sarah's eyes 'dim with sorrow' at Henrietta's death see Thomson (ed.), *Letters of a Grandmother*, 96; for Sarah's wish that her daughter Mary's name should never be mentioned again see Reid, 429. The Duchess of Montagu 'F[ucking] with M. Cragg' is in Montesquieu, *Oeuvres Complètes* (ed. Roger Callois, Paris, 1951, 1579), quoted in Butler, *Rule of Three*, 325.

CHAPTER 47 Sarah's castigation of French physicians is in Green, *Sarah, Duchess of Marlborough*, 276; her letter of protest about 'Willigo's' marriage in BL Add. MS 61440, fos. 112–15; her comparison of the bride to a lace-seller in BL Add. MS 61440, fo. 168; her complaints about Charles Spencer's person and dress are in Thomson (ed.), *Letters of a Grandmother*,

44 and 51; her further complaints about her grandson's manner of speaking in Green, 284; and her comments on Elizabeth Trevor and her family in Green, 287. Charles's 'Foolish, Brutal and Ungrateful' letter to his grandmother is in BL Add. MS 61446, fo. 21, as is the Duchess's reply, fo. 23.

CHAPTER 48 For Lady Diana Spencer's relationship with her grandmother see Massey, *The First Lady Diana*; for her grandmother's explanation of the name of Cordelia for Diana see Thomson (ed.), *Letters of a Grandmother*, 153–7. The possibility of Diana marrying the Prince of Wales is in Rowse, *The Early Churchills*, 387; Sarah's weeping with the Duke of Newcastle in Green, *Sarah, Duchess of Marlborough*, 215; her letter to Bedford is in Thomson (ed.), 96; and 'dearest Dye' in her 'dear Grandfather's tent' comes from Harris, *A Passion for Government*, 311. The story of Sarah blocking over Lady Bateman's portrait is in Walpole, *Reminiscences*, 90; Francis Hare's advice about preserving peace in families in Green, 254. Robert Walpole's complaint about the Duchess's refusal to submit to the usual forms of doing business is quoted in Harris, 266; the Duchess's account of Queen Caroline and the 'country clown' in Thomson (ed.), 74; and her admission that she was glad when Queen Caroline died is in her *Memoirs*, 279, quoted by Rowse, 387.

CHAPTER 49 Henry Fielding's eulogy is in his *Full Vindication*; and Sarah's receipt of £10,000 from the Duke of Kent is in Hatton's *George I*, 155; the twenty-seven estates are listed in an appendix to Harris, *A Passion for Government*. The Countess of Bute's description of the Duchess's idiosyncratic arithmetic is in *The Letters and Works of Lady Mary Wortley Montagu*, ii, 114. The account of the Duchess's involvement with the building and decoration of Blenheim Palace is almost entirely based upon the biographies of Vanbrugh by Whistler and Downes and on Green's and Harris's biographies of the Duchess, and Green's *Blenheim Palace*. The Duchess's belief that architects should be 'kept down' is in Downes, 199; James Boswell's comments to Johnson are in *Life of Johnson* under the date 21 March 1776; Sarah's letter to the Duke of Somerset about the 'Canal & Bason' is in Green, *Sarah, Duchess of Marlborough*, 246; she and Henrietta 'singing all the way' in Green, 234–5; the account of her dispute with the Duke of Bridgwater over his daughter Anne also in Green, 239, and her enjoyment of 'a contemplative way of living' in Grundy, *Lady Mary Wortley Montagu*, 294. Mallet's 'exhausted mind' is in *Life of Johnson* under the date 24 April 1779; and Warburton's comment on the likelihood of his forgetting that Marlborough was a general under the date 22 September 1777.

CHAPTER 50 For Sarah's library at St Albans see Harris, *A Passion for Government*, 58; and for Voltaire's visit, Mason, *Voltaire*, 17, quoting A.-M.

Rousseau, *L'Angleterre et Voltaire*. Lady Mary Wortley Montagu's comment about Sarah's fiddling with her will is contained in a letter to Lady Bute of 30 September 1757. For the final will see Harris, 326–7, and Sarah's *True Copy of the Last Will*. Sarah's behaviour at George II's coronation is described by Saussure in *A Foreign View of England*, 249–50. The letters to the Countess of Huntingdon are from [Seymour], *The Life and Times of Selina, Countess of Huntingdon*, i, 25–6. Sarah's letter declaring her willingness to die 'if only to get rid of so many tiresome people' is in Reid, *John and Sarah, Duke and Duchess of Marlborough*, 482; the story of her praying in a darkened room in Reid, 474. Sarah's open invitation to Lady Mary Wortley Montagu is in Grundy's *biography*, 190; Francis Hare's criticism of the Duchess's verbosity is quoted in Green, *Sarah*, 253; Sarah's cure for gout in Green, *Blenheim Palace*, 180; her 'greatest happiness in life' to love someone who returned love in Sarah's *Memoirs*, 302–3; her organ in Green, *Blenheim Palace*, 180; her love of dogs in *Opinions of Sarah, Dowager Duchess of Marlborough*, 129, and Reid, 473. The account of her games with her great-grandchildren is in Butler, *Rule of Three*, 336. Smollett on her death is in Sarah's *Letters . . . at Madresfield Court*, xviii; Horace Walpole's verdict in his *Catalogue of the Royal and Noble Authors of England* (1758), quoted in Grundy, 559; and Sarah's declaration of love for the Duke in W.S.C., i, 130.

BIBLIOGRAPHY

MANUSCRIPTS

The Marlborough Papers are now in the British Library: see Add. MSS 61101–413; Add. MSS 70938–46; Add. MSS 33273, 36795, 38498–9; Add. MSS 33273, 36795, 38498–9; Add. MSS 69379 (letters to Lord Cutts); Add. MSS 5130, 9094–113; Add. MSS 71135–43 (letters to Anthonie Heinsius); Add. MS 70290 (letters from the Earl of Oxford); Add. MS 41178 (letters to Lord Townshend), Stowe MSS 222–46 and Stowe MS 751 (letters to James Craggs). There are also relevant manuscripts in the Public Record Office: WO 55/343f and SP 87/6 (correspondence with Frederick I of Prussia); the National Library of Scotland: MSS 2879–80; the National Archives of Scotland: GD 1/1158; the Bodleian Library: North MSS; the Hertfordshire Archives and Local Studies: D/EPF63 (letters to Lord Cowper); the Churchill Archives Centre, Churchill College, Cambridge (correspondence with Thomas Erle); the National Library of Ireland (correspondence with the Duke of Ormonde); and the National Army Museum, Acc. Nos. 7405–25, 6309/9/3 and 6510–146(2)57.

The Papers of Sarah, Duchess of Marlborough, are also in the British Library: see Add. MSS 61414–80; Add. MS 35853; Add. MS 51386; Add. MSS 62569–70; Add. MSS 61456, 63640S; Add. MS 38056; D/ED/C38 and Stowe MS 751 (letters to James Craggs). For her life I have also consulted the Berkshire Record Office: D/ESV (B) F92/2, D/ESV (B) F30/1–10, Q/SR 19/5, D/EHY F34–35 (Duchess of Marlborough correspondence); the Hertfordshire Archives and Local Studies: D/EP F63, D/EP F79, D/EP F206–7, D/EP F228 (Duchess of Marlborough correspondence).

Other manuscripts I have consulted or referred to are in the University of Nottingham, Hallward Library (Portland Collection); the Devon Record Office, Exeter (Seymour of Berry Pomeroy Papers); the Northamptonshire Record Office (Shrewsbury correspondence); the Hove Reference Library (Wolseley Collection); in Leicestershire, the Leicester and Rutland Record Office (Finch MSS); and in Maidstone, the Centre for Kentish Studies (Alexander Stanhope and General James Stanhope correspondence).

BOOKS AND ARTICLES

The place of publication is London unless otherwise stated.

Ailesbury, Thomas Bruce, 2nd Earl of, *Memoirs*, ed. W. E. Buckley (2 vols., 1890)

Alison, Sir Archibald, *The Life of John, Duke of Marlborough with Some Account of His Contemporaries and the War of the Spanish Succession* (Edinburgh, 1848; 2nd enlarged edn, 2 vols., 1852)

Anne, Queen *see* Brown

Ashley, Maurice, *Marlborough* (1939)

—— *The Glorious Revolution of 1688* (1966)

Atkinson, C. T., *Marlborough and the Rise of the British Army* (1921)

—— 'Marlborough's Sieges', *Journal of the Society for Army Historical Research*, Winter, 1934

Banks, John, *History of John, Duke of Marlborough . . . Including a More Exact, Impartial and Methodical Narrative on the Late War* (1741)

Barnett, Correlli, *Britain and Her Army, 1509–1970: A Military and Social Survey* (1970)

—— *Marlborough* (1974)

Baxter, S., *William III* (1966)

Beattie, J. M., *The English Court in the Reign of George I* (Cambridge, 1967)

Belloc, Hilaire, *The Strategy and Tactics of the Great Duke of Marlborough* (1933)

Berwick, James Fitzjames, Duke of, *Memoirs of the Marshal Duke of Berwick* (2 vols., 1779)

Bevan, Bryan, *Marlborough: The Man: A Biography of John Churchill, First Duke of Marlborough* (1975)

Bishop, Matthew, *Life and Adventures* (1744)

Black, Jeremy, *European Warfare, 1660–1815* (Cambridge, 1994)

—— *Warfare: Renaissance to Revolution* (Cambridge, 1996)

Blackadder, Lt-Col. John, *Diary (1700–1728)*, ed. Andrew Crichton (Edinburgh, 1824)

Blouche, François, *Louis XIV* (Paris, 1986)

Bolingbroke, Henry St John, Viscount, *Letters and Correspondence*, ed. G. Parke (4 vols., 1798)

Boswell, James, *Life of Johnson*, ed. R. W. Chapman (Oxford, 1976; 3rd edn, ed. J. D. Freeman, 1983)

Boyer, Abel, *The History of the Reign of Queen Anne, Digested into Annals* (1703)

Bradlaugh, Charles, *John Churchill, Duke of Marlborough* (1884)

Brown, B. Curtis (ed.), *The Letters and Diplomatic Instructions of Queen Anne* (1935)

Bryant, Arthur, *Charles II* (1931)

Burnet, Bishop, *Burnet's History of My Own Time*, ed. M. J. Routh (6 vols., Oxford, 1833)

—— *Supplement to Burnet's History of My Own Time*, ed. H. C. Foxcroft (Oxford, 1902)

Burton, Ivor F., *The Captain-General: The Career of John Churchill, Duke of Marlborough, from 1702 to 1711* (1968)

Butler, Iris, *Rule of Three: Sarah, Duchess of Marlborough and Her Companions in Power* (1967)

Cannon, John and Ralph Griffiths, *The Oxford Illustrated History of the British Monarchy* (Oxford, 1988)

Carswell, John, *The South Sea Bubble* (1960)

Cartwright, J. J. (ed.), *The Wentworth Papers* (1883)

Chandler, David, *Marlborough as Military Commander* (1973)

—— *The Art of Warfare in the Age of Marlborough* (Tunbridge Wells, 1976)

—— *Sedgemoor 1685* (1985)

—— (ed.), *Robert Parker and Comte de Mérode-Westerloo: The Marlborough Wars* (1968)

—— and Ian Beckett, *The Oxford Illustrated History of the British Army* (Oxford, 1992)

—— *Blenheim Preparation* (2001)

Chesterfield, Earl of, *Letters to His Son*, ed. Lord Mahon (1845–53)

—— *Letters*, ed. Bonamy Dobrée (5 vols., 1932)

Chidsey, Donald Barr, *Marlborough: Portrait of a Conqueror* (1930)

Childs, John, *The Army of Charles II* (Manchester, 1976)

—— *The Army, James II and the Glorious Revolution* (Manchester, 1980)

—— *The British Army of William III, 1698–1702* (Manchester, 1987)

—— *The Nine Years War and the British Army* (Manchester, 1991)

Churchill, Winston S., *Marlborough: His Life and Times* (4 vols., 1933–8; new edn, 2 vols., 1947)

Cibber, Colley, *An Apology for the Life of Mr Colley Cibber* (2nd edn, 1740)

Clarendon, Edward Hyde, Earl of, *Correspondence and Diary* (2 vols., 1828)

Clark, Sir George, *The Later Stuarts, 1660–1714* (2nd edn, Oxford, 1955)

Clarke, J. S., *The Life of James II* (2 vols., 1816)

Clifton, Robert, *The Last Popular Rebellion* (1984)

Colley, Linda, *In Defence of Oligarchy: The Tory Party 1714–1760* (Cambridge, 1982)

Coombs, D., *The Conduct of the Dutch: British Opinion and the Dutch Alliance during the War of the Spanish Succession* (The Hague, 1958)

Cowles, Virginia, *The Great Marlborough and His Duchess* (1983)

Cowper, Spencer (ed.), *Diary of Mary, Countess Cowper* (1865)

Cowper, William, 1st Earl, *The Private Diary*, ed. E. C. Hawtrey (1833)

Coxe, William, *Memoirs of John, Duke of Marlborough, with His Original*

Correspondence (3 vols., 1818–19; 6 vols., 1820, rev. J. Wade 1847–8)

Creighton, Louise, *Life of John Churchill, Duke of Marlborough* (1904)

Davies, Godfrey, 'The Seamy Side of Marlborough's War', *Huntingdon Library Quarterly*, San Merino, November 1956

Deane, John Marshall, *A Journal of Marlborough's Campaigns during the War of the Spanish Succession, 1704–1711*, ed. with an introduction by D. G. Chandler (1984)

[Defoe, Daniel], *A Short Narrative of the Life of His Grace, John, Duke of Marlborough, from the Beginnings of the Revolution to This Present Time, with Some Remarks on His Conduct by an Old Officer of the Army* (1711)

Delany, Mary, *The Autobiography and Correspondence of Mary Granville, Mrs Delany* (6 vols., 1861–2)

Dickenson, H. T., *Bolingbroke* (1970)

Dobrée, Bonamy, *Sarah Churchill* (1927)

Downes, Kerry, *Hawksmoor* (1969)

——*Sir John Vanbrugh: A Biography* (1987)

Downie, J. A., *Robert Harley and the Press* (Cambridge, 1979)

Drake, Captain Peter, *Memoirs* (Dublin, 1755)

Dutton, Ralph, *English Court Life* (1963)

Earle, Peter, *The World of Defoe* (1976)

——*Monmouth's Rebels* (1977)

Edwards, Henry John and Ethel Ashton, *A Short Life of Marlborough* (1926)

Evelyn, John, *The Diary of John Evelyn*, ed. E. S. de Beer (6 vols., Oxford, 1955)

Emerson, V. I. R., *Monmouth's Rebellion* (New Haven, 1951)

Examiner, The, 1710–12

Falls, Cyril (ed.), *Great Military Battles* (1964)

[Fielding, Henry], *A Full Vindication of the Duchess of Marlborough* (1742)

Fiennes, *see* Morris

Fitzmaurice, Lord, *The Life of William, Earl of Shelburne* (2 vols., 1912)

Foot, Michael, *The Pen and the Sword* (1958)

Fortescue, The Hon. Sir John, *History of the British Army* (vol. i, 1899; 2nd edn, 1910)

——*Six British Soldiers* (1928)

——*Marlborough* (1932)

Foxcroft, H. C. (ed.), *The Life and Letters of Sir George Savile, First Marquis of Halifax* (2 vols., 1898)

Fraser, Antonia, *King Charles II* (1979)

——*The Weaker Vessel: Women's Lot in Seventeenth-Century England* (1984)

Fuller, Major-General J. F. C., *The Decisive Battles of the Western World* (vol. i, 1955)

Geikie, Roderick and Isabel A. Montgomery, *The Dutch Barrier* (Cambridge, 1930)

George, M. D., *English Political Caricature to 1792* (Oxford, 1959)

Glendinning, Victoria, *Jonathan Swift* (1998)

Goslinga, Sicco van, *Mémoires relatives à la Guerre de Succession de 1706–1709 et 1711* (Leeuwarden, 1857)

Green, David, *Blenheim Palace* (1951)

—— *Sarah, Duchess of Marlborough* (1967)

—— *Queen Anne* (1970)

—— *Blenheim Palace, Woodstock, Oxfordshire* (Norwich, 1999)

Gregg, Edward, 'Marlborough in Exile, 1712–1714', *Historical Journal*, 15 (1972), 593–618

—— *Queen Anne* (1980)

Grundy, Isobel, *Lady Mary Wortley Montagu: Comet of the Enlightenment* (Oxford, 1999)

Guy, Alan J. and Jenny Spencer-Smith, *1688: Glorious Revolution: The Fall and Rise of the British Army, 1660–1704* (2001)

Halsband, Robert, *The Life of Lady Mary Wortley Montagu* (Oxford, 1956)

—— *Lord Hervey* (Oxford, 1973)

Hamilton, David, *The Diary of Sir David Hamilton, 1710–1714*, ed. P. Roberts (Oxford, 1875)

[Hare, Francis], *The Life and Glorious History of John, Duke and Earl of Marlborough . . . Containing a Relation of the Most Important Battles* (1705)

—— *The Conduct of the Duke of Marlborough during the Present War* (1712)

—— Journal (BL Add. MS 9114)

Harris, Frances, *A Passion for Government: The Life of Sarah, Duchess of Marlborough* (Oxford, 1991)

Hart, Jeffrey, *Bolingbroke: Tory Humanist* (1965)

Hastings, Max (ed.), *The Oxford Book of Military Anecdotes* (Oxford, 1985)

Hattendorf, J. B., *England in the War of the Spanish Succession* (New York, 1987)

Hatton, Ragnhild, *Charles XII of Sweden* (1969)

—— *George I: Elector and King* (Cambridge, Mass., 1978)

Henderson, Nicholas, *Prince Eugen of Savoy: A Biography* (1964)

Hervey, John, Lord, *Some Materials towards Memoirs of the Reign of George II*, ed. Romney Sedgwick (1931)

Hibbert, Edward, *Vanbrugh House, Oxford* (Oxford, 1982)

Hill, B. J., *The Growth of Parliamentary Parties, 1689–1742* (1976)

—— *Robert Harley: Speaker, Secretary of State and Prime Minister* (New Haven, 1988)

Hill, Christopher, *The Century of Revolution, 1603–1714* (Edinburgh, 1961)

Historical Manuscripts Commission Reports:

Buccleuch Papers (ii)

Cowper Papers (iii)

Dartmouth Papers (iii)

Downshire Papers
Earl of Denbigh's Papers (7th Report)
Finch Papers (iv)
Hare Papers (14th Report)
Mar Papers
Marlborough Papers (8th Report)
Northumberland Papers
Ormonde Papers (iv and v)
Portland Papers
Rutland Papers (ii)
Seafield Papers
Townshend Papers
Verney Papers

Hoff, B. van 't (ed.), *The Correspondence, 1710–11, of John Churchill, First Duke of Marlborough, and Anthonie Heinsius, Grand Pensionary of Holland* (The Hague, 1951)

Holmes, Geoffrey, *British Politics in the Age of Anne* (1967)

—— 'Revolution, War and Politics 1689–1714' and 'The Augustan Age 1689–1714' in Blair Worden (ed.), *Stuart England* (1986)

[Hooke, Nathaniel], *An Account of the Conduct of the Dowager Duchess of Marlborough from Her First Coming to Court in the Year 1710* (1742)

Hoppit, Julian, *A Land of Liberty?: England, 1689–1727* (Oxford, 2000)

Horn, Robert D., *Marlborough: A Survey: Panegyrics, Satires and Biographical Writings, 1688–1788* (Folkestone, 1975)

—— 'Marlborough's First Biographer: Dr Francis Hare', *Huntingdon Library Quarterly*, 20, 1957

Hudson, H., *Cumberland Lodge* (Chichester, 1989)

Hume, David, *The History of Great Britain* (2 vols., Edinburgh, 1754–7)

Huntingdon, *see* Seymour

Ilchester, Lord (ed.), *Lord Hervey and His Friends* (1950)

Jesse, J. H., *Memoirs of the Court of England during the Reign of the Stuarts* (7 vols., 1840)

—— *Continuation of Memoirs of the Court of England from the Revolution in 1688 to the Death of George II* (3 vols., 1843)

Johnston, S. H. F. (ed.), 'Letters of Samuel Noyce, Chaplain of the Royal Scots, 1703–4', *Journal of the Society for Army Historical Research* (1959)

Jones, D. W., *War and Economy in the Age of William III and Marlborough* (Oxford, 1988)

Jones, J. R., *The Revolution of 1688 in England* (1972)

—— *Marlborough* (Cambridge, 1993)]

Kane, Brigadier-General Richard, *Campaigns of King William and the Duke of Marlborough* (1735)

Kearsey, A. H. C., *Marlborough and His Campaigns* (1931)

Kenyon, J. P., *Robert Spencer, Earl of Sunderland* (1958)
—— *The Stuarts* (1958; 2nd edn, 1970)
Klopp, Onno, *Der Fall des Hauses Stuart* (14 vols., Vienna, 1880–1905)
La Colonie, Jean Martin de, *The Chronicles of an Old Campaigner*, trans.
 W. C. Horsley (1904)
Laprade, W. T., *Public Opinion and Politics in Eighteenth-Century England*
 (1936)
Lecky, William, *History of England in the Eighteenth Century* (8 vols., 1878–
 90)
Lediard, Thomas, *The Life of John, Duke of Marlborough, with Original Letters
 and Papers* (3 vols., 1736; 2nd edn, 1743)
Legrelle, A., *La diplomatic française et la succession d'Espagne* (vol. iv, Paris,
 1892)
Lees-Milne, James, *The Last Stuarts* (1983)
Lever, Sir Tresham, *Godolphin: His Life and Times* (1952)
Lloyd, E. M., 'Marlborough and the Brest Expedition', *English Historical
 Review*, 9 (1894), 130–32
Longford, Elizabeth (ed.), *The Oxford Book of Royal Anecdotes* (Oxford,
 1989)
Luttrell, Narcissus, *A Brief Historical Relation of State Affairs* (6 vols., Oxford
 1857)
Macaulay, T. B., *The History of England from the Accession of James II* (6 vols.,
 1849–61)
McGuffie, T. H. (ed.), *Rank and File: The Common Soldier at Peace and War*
 (1964)
McInnes, Angus, *Robert Harley, Puritan Politician* (1970)
Mack, M., *Alexander Pope* (New Haven, 1985)
Macmunn, G. F., *Prince Eugène: Twin Marshal with Marlborough* (1934)
Macpherson, James, *Original Papers containing the Secret History of Great Briton*
 (2 vols., 1875)
Malleson, G. B., *Prince Eugène of Savoy* (1888)
Marchmont, *see* Rose
Marlborough, John Churchill, First Duke of, *see* Hoff, Murray and Snyder
 (correspondence)
Marlborough, Sarah Churchill, Duchess of, *A True Copy of the Last Will
 . . . of . . . Sarah, late Duchess Dowager of Marlborough* (1744)
—— *Opinions of Sarah, Dowager Duchess of Marlborough* (1788)
—— *Private Correspondence of Sarah, Duchess of Marlborough . . . with Sketches
 and Opinions of Her Contemporaries* (2 vols., 1838)
—— *Letters of Sarah, Duchess of Marlborough . . . at Madresfield Court* (1875)
—— *An Account of the Conduct, see* Hooke
Mason, Haydn, *Voltaire* (1991)
Massey, Victoria, *The First Lady Diana: Lady Diana Spencer, 1710–35* (1999)

Mérode-Westerloo, *see* Chandler

Michael, Wolfgang, *England under George I: The Beginnings of the Hanoverian Dynasty* (1936)

Miller, J., *James II* (1989)

Miller, O. B., *Robert Harley* (1925)

Millner, Sergeant John, *Journal (1701–12)* (1733)

Mingay, G. E., *English Landed Society in the Eighteenth Century* (1963)

Montagu, Lady Mary Wortley, *Journal* (1733)

—— *The Letters and Works of Lady Mary Wortley Montagu*, ed. Lord Wharncliffe (2nd edn, 3 vols., 1837)

—— *Complete Letters*, ed. Robert Halsband (3 vols., Oxford, 1965–7)

[Montagu, Ralph], *The Lives of the Two Illustrious Generals, John, Duke of Marlborough, and Francis Eugene, Prince of Savoy* (1713)

Morgan, William T., *A Bibliography of British History 1700–1715, with Special Reference to the Reign of Queen Anne* (5 vols., Bloomington, Indiana, 1939–42; reprinted 1972)

Morris, Christopher (ed.), *The Journeys of Celia Fiennes* (1949)

Murray, Sir George (ed.), *The Letters and Despatches of John Churchill, the First Duke of Marlborough, from 1702 to 1712* (5 vols., 1845)

Nada, John, *Carlos the Bewitched* (1962)

Nichols, John, *Illustrations of Literature* (vol. iii, 1817)

Nicholson, T. C. and A. S. Turberville, *Charles Talbot, Duke of Shrewsbury* (1930)

Ogg, David, *England in the Reigns of James II and William III* (Oxford, 1955)

O[ldmixon], J[ohn], *The Life . . . of Arthur Maynwaring* (1715)

Orkney, George Hamilton, Earl of, 'Letters of the First Lord Orkney during Marlborough's Campaigns', ed. H. H. E. Cra'ster, *English Historical Review*, April 1904

Parker, *see* Chandler

Parnell, Arthur, *The War of the Succession, 1702–1711* (1888)

Pelet, *see* Vault

Pennington, D. H., *Seventeenth-Century Europe* (1970)

Pepys, Samuel, *The Diary of Samuel Pepys*, ed. Robert Latham and William Matthews (11 vols., 1970–83)

Petrie, Sir Charles, *Bolingbroke* (1937)

—— *The Marshal Duke of Berwick* (1953)

Plumb, J. H., *Sir Robert Walpole: The Making of a Statesman* (1956)

—— *The Growth of Political Stability in England, 1675–1725* (1967)

Pope, Alexander, *Works*, ed. W. Elwin and W. J. Courthope (10 vols., 1871–89)

—— *Correspondence*, ed. G. Sherburn (5 vols., Oxford, 1956)

Ranke, Leopold von, *History of England Principally in the Seventeenth Century* (Oxford, 1875)

Reid, Stuart, *John and Sarah, Duke and Duchess of Marlborough, 1650–1744* (1915)

Rogers, H. C. B., *The British Army of the Eighteenth Century* (1977)

Rogers, Pat, *Grub Street: Studies in a Sub-Culture* (1972)

Roscoe, E. S., *Robert Harley* (1902)

Rose, G. H. (ed.), *A Selection from the Papers of the Earls of Marchmont* (3 vols., 1831)

Routh, E. M. G., *Tangier: England's Last Atlantic Outpost* (1912)

Rowse, A. L., *The Early Churchills: An English Family* (1956)

Saint-Simon, *Mémoires du duc de Saint-Simon* (vols. iii–iv, Paris, 1878–86); trans. and ed. Lucy Norton, *Memoirs of the Duc de Saint-Simon* (12 vols., 1999)

Saussure, César de, *A Foreign View of England in the Reigns of George I and George II*, ed. Mme van Muyden (1902)

Savile, *see* Foxcroft

Scouller, R. E., *The Armies of Queen Anne* (1966)

Seward, William, *Anecdotes of Some Distinguished Persons* (1798)

[Seymour, A. C. H.], *The Life and Times of Selina, Countess of Huntingdon* (2 vols., 1839)

Shrewsbury, Charles Talbot, Duke of, *Private and Original Correspondence*, ed. William Coxe (1821)

Sichel, Walter, *Bolingbroke and His Times* (1901)

Singer, S. W., *The Correspondence of Henry Hyde, Earl of Clarendon* (2 vols., 1828)

Sitwell, Sacheverell, *Sacheverell Sitwell's England*, ed. Michael Raeburn (1986)

Snyder, Henry L., 'The Duke of Marlborough's Request of His Captain-Generalcy for Life', *Journal of the Society of Army Historical Research*, 45 (1967), 67–85

——(ed.), *The Marlborough–Godolphin Correspondence* (3 vols., Oxford, 1975)

Somerville, D. H., *The King of Hearts: Charles Talbot, Duke of Shrewsbury* (1962)

Spectator, The, Everyman edition (4 vols., 1907)

Spencer, Charles, *The Spencer Family* (1999)

Sprat, Thomas, *A Relation of the Late Wicked Contrivance of . . . Robert Young* (2 parts, 1692–3)

Stacke, H. Fitzmaurice, 'Cavalry in Marlborough's Day', *Cavalry Journal*, October 1934

Stamp, A. E., 'Marlborough and Charles XII', *Transactions of the Royal Historical Society*, vol. xii

Stater, Victor, *High Life, Low Morals: The Duel That Shook Stuart Society* (1999)

Strickland, Agnes, *Lives of the Queens of England* (vol. viii, 1852)

Sturgill, C. C., *Marshal Villars and the War of the Spanish Succession* (1965)

Sutherland, John, *Background to Queen Anne* (1939)

Swift, Jonathan, *Works*, ed. Sir W. Scott (19 vols., 1883)

—— *The Prose Works of Jonathan Swift*, ed. H. Davis (13 vols., 1939–59)

—— *Correspondence*, ed. Harold Williams (5 vols., Oxford, 1963)

—— *Journal to Stella*, ed. Harold Williams (Oxford, 1974)

Taylor, Frank, *The Wars of Marlborough* (2 vols., Oxford, 1921)

Thomson, George Malcolm, *The First Churchill: The Life of John, First Duke of Marlborough* (1979)

Thomson, G. Scott, *Letters of a Grandmother, 1732–35* (1943)

Thomson, K., *Memoirs of Sarah, Duchess of Marlborough* (2 vols., 1839)

Torcy, Jean-Baptiste Colbert, *Mémoires*, ed. Michaud and Poujoulet (Paris, 1850)

Trench, Charles Chenevix, *George II* (1973)

Trevelyan, G. M., *England under Queen Anne*: vol. i, *Blenheim* (1930); vol. ii, *Ramillies and the Union with Scotland* (1932); vol. iii, *The Peace and the Protestant Succession* (1934)

Turner, F. C., *James II* (1948)

Vanbrugh, John, *Complete Works*, ed. Bonamy Dobrée and G. Webb (4 vols., 1928)

Vault, F. E. de and J. J. G. Pelet, *Mémoires militaires relatifs à la Succession d'Espagne sous Louis XIV* (11 vols., Paris, 1835–62)

Verney, Lady, *Memoirs of the Verney Family during the Seventeenth Century* (1925)

Verney, Peter, *The Battle of Blenheim* (1976)

Villars, Claude Louis Hector, *Mémoires* (Paris, 1887)

Wace, Alan, *The Marlborough Tapestries at Blenheim Palace* (1968)

Walpole, Horace, *Letters*, ed. Mrs Paget Toynbee (19 vols., 1918–25)

—— *Reminiscences*, ed. Mrs Paget Toynbee (Oxford, 1924)

Walton, Clifford, *History of the British Standing Army, 1660–1700* (1984)

Whistler, Laurence, *Sir John Vanbrugh: Architect and Dramatist, 1664–1726* (1938)

—— *The Imagination of Vanbrugh and His Fellow Artists* (1954)

Whittle, John, *An Exact Diary of the Late Expedition* (1689)

Wilkinson, Spencer, *From Cromwell to Wellington: Twelve Soldiers* (1899)

Williams, Robert, 'A Factor in His Success: The Missing Years. Did Vanbrugh learn from Mughal mausolea?', *The Times Literary Supplement*, 3 September 1999

Wilson, C. T., *James II and the Duke of Berwick* (1876)

Wolseley, General Viscount, *The Life of John Churchill, Duke of Marlborough, to the Accession of Queen Anne* (2 vols., 1894)

Worden, Blair (ed.), *Stuart England* (Oxford, 1986)

BIBLIOGRAPHY

Yorke, P. C., *The Life and Correspondence of Philip Yorke, Earl of Hardwicke* (3 vols., Cambridge, 1913)

Zee, Henri and Barbara van der, *William and Mary* (1973)

INDEX

The Duke of Marlborough's name is abbreviated to M, the Duchess's to Sarah, and Queen Anne's to QA

their children, 26; on her strictness with their children, 27; upon parting, 92; he misses her, 104; on dukedom, 111; Blandford's illness, 114; on her health, 121–2; of comfort, 122; her suspicion of his adultery, 122–3; his happiness at their reconciliation, 125; discourages her from joining him, 129–30; his headaches, 143n.; longs to be with her, 158, 173; Marlborough House, 166–7; sea-sickness, 172; references to Blenheim Palace, 185, 337; in low spirits, 197, 198, 258; after her displeasure, 216; hoping she will soon join him, 292

money: early circumstances, 3; prudence, 8; presents from Duchess of Cleveland, 8, 11n., 15; his father appeals for help, 15; improved finances, 24; Sarah on his thrift, 77; salary as governor to Duke of Gloucester, 80; salary as lieutenant-general, 81n.; joint income with his wife, 91; rewards Gell, 109n.; avoids signing bills, 170; Durel's reward, 177; viceroyship of Belgic provinces, 194, 195; increasing wealth, 235; Louis XIV offers him a bribe, 235–6, 237; inheritance from his brother, 261; accused of financial irregularity, 277–8, 285–6; Swift's estimate of his wealth, 283; charge for entrance to campaign tent, 289; fines, 290; for work at Woodstock, 290; compensation to laundrymaid, 291; granddaughter's dowry, 306; Vanbrugh's salary unpaid, 309n.; expenditure on Blenheim Palace, 311

personal: appearance, 6, 10, 74–5, 77, 267; Holywell House, 25; his children, 26; staunch Protestant, 36–7, 38, 40, 43; criticisms of, 47;

daughters' marriages, 83; Blandford, 114, 115; thinks of retirement, 120; Sunderland, 121; denies charge of adultery, 121; misery, 123; excellent Moselle, 127; Eugène of Savoy, 135–6; physical and emotional exhaustion, 157–8, 159; home after eight months' absence, 160; Kit-Cat Club, 165 *and* n.; vexations, 172; dislikes Harley, 178; enjoys praise, 178; unease about fate of Cadogan, 196; in low spirits, 197, 198, 256–8; his mind 'not very much at ease', 215; modest eater, 223; Thackeray's opinion of, 228n.; Godolphin's dismissal, 261–2; and St John, 264; on Argyll, 265; letter from grandson, 276–7; in dejection, 277; popularity with the people, 280; Vanbrugh's regard for, 309; happy to be in residence, 311–12; relations between Sarah and their daughters, 315; and daughter Mary, 315–16; his will, 347n.

personality: frugality, 3, 223, 237; diplomacy, 22, 271, 296; 'deep dissimulation', 22; discretion, 56; charm, 56, 79, 183, 208; in Floyd's eyes, 68; over Fenwick affair, 72; parsimony, 74–8, 182, 223, 311; unfathomable, 79; Trevelyan on, 86; in negotiations, 87; petty saving, 116; urbanity, 119; politeness, 119; treatment of prisoners of war, 155, 193; Electress Sophia on, 160, 183; Evelyn struck by, 161; courtesy, 193; tolerance, 193; composure, 208, 272; Hoppit on, 234n.; compassion, 238, 242, 257; sensitivity to criticism, 284n.; deviousness, 296; Chesterfield on, 346

politics: Lord Justice, 84; forfeited Irish estates, 84–5; ambassador

and Marlborough: M in love with, 13;
unconvinced of his love, 13–14;
married, 15; dwellings, 17–18, 24;
he reassures her, 20; mutual love,
22; M's staunch Protestantism, 43n.;
his dismissal, 59; his arrest, 63; on his
thrift and generosity, 77; in The
Hague, 88; parting, 92; dukedom,
110; first serious quarrel 121, 122;
her miserable behaviour to him,
123; reconciliation, 124–5;
limitations of her influence, 170n.;
Hester Santlow, 215; and her
relationship with QA, 245–6, 268;
his illness, 301–2; his death, 317; her
devoted love, 352
money: income, 24; disagreement with
Queen Mary over, 58; her
daughters' dowries, 83, 306;
emoluments under QA, 91;
Marlborough House, 167; Blenheim
Palace, 170, 305, 307; pension for
Bedingfield's widow, 189n.; claims
pension, 269; financial acumen, 313,
335–6; M's funeral expenses, 318;
death of grandson, 327n.; anxiety
about grandson's extravagance, 330;
contributions to charity, 335; keeps
accounts, 336–7; and Thornhill,
339; statue of QA, 339n.; riches,
347
personal: personality, 12, 14, 95, 207,
312, 333, 339, 349; appearance, 13,
319–20, 350; thankful to leave
court, 15–16; at Holywell House,
25; apothecary, 25; phantom
pregnancy, 115; weary of court
ceremony, 206; and Abigail
Masham, 207–8, 213, 233, 245 *and*
n.; dislikes Harley, 211; wishes she
had been a man, 294 *and* n.;
homesick, 294; nursing care, 297;
and Vanbrugh, 305–10 *passim*; on
Newcastle, 306; letter to Carlisle,

310; Rubens's paintings, 311n.;
quarrels, 312–14, 333; Cadogan,
313–14; Craggs, 314; suitors,
319–22; on Somerset, 320; on
Queen Caroline, 334; her taste, 337;
resilience, 338; writings, 343–4;
reading, 346; her will, 347–8; and
Lady Huntingdon, 349–50, 350n.;
and Lady Mary Montagu, 350;
talkative, 350, 352; physical
sufferings, 350–51; resigned to
death, 351; enjoyments, 351–2;
death, 352
and Queen Anne:
as Princess: intimate friendship, 28;
flight during Glorious Revolution,
44; Princess's love for, 57; Queen
Mary orders her dismissal from
Princess's service, 58, 61; and
Abigail Hill, 81

as Queen, appointments, 91; QA
writes to her, 110; deteriorating
relations, 205–7, 210, 232; death of
Prince George, 213; quarrel, 233;
QA complains to M of her
behaviour, 245; affair of Hill's
appointment, 248, 250; plagues her
with complaints and demands, 251;
importunes her, 253–4; writes to
vex her, 255; QA dismisses her, 268;
'railing' against her, 268n.;
commissions statue of, 339n.
Marlborough House: Wren, 166;
Sarah's London residence, 166; cost,
167; later architects and occupants,
167n.; M at, 303; M lies in state,
319; Coningsby calls, 320; Sarah's
route to, 333; opera-going from,
351; Sarah's death, 352
Mary of Modena, Queen
(1658–1718), 36, 82
Marsin, Ferdinand, 143–4, 148, 150,
152, 174
Martinet, Jean, 99